TECHNIQUES OF FINANCIAL ANALYSIS

TECHNIQUES OF FINANCIAL ANALYSIS

Erich A. Helfert, D.B.A.

Sixth Edition

1987

Homewood, Illinois 60430

© RICHARD D. IRWIN, INC., 1963, 1967, 1972, 1977, 1982, and 1987

ISBN 0-256-03625-X

Library of Congress Catalog Card No. 86–82589

Printed in the United States of America

5 6 7 8 9 0 MP 4 3 2 1 0 9 8 7

To Anne

PREFACE

This book gives the student, analyst, or business executive a concise, practical, usable, and up-to-date overview of the key financial analysis tools needed to understand financial reports, develop basic financial projections, evaluate capital investment decisions, assess the implications of financing choices, and derive the value of a business or a security. The techniques and measures are clearly described and demonstrated in the context of the underlying financial concepts, yet *without* delving into theoretical abstraction. Self-study exercises and problems are provided after each chapter so the reader can practice applying the analytical tools. The materials are discussed from a *decision-making* point of view which takes into account that in a going business, *investment*, *operational*, and *financing* decisions are linked and interrelated. The presentation also takes into account the *viewpoints* of the major parties interested in the performance of a business: *managers*, *owners*, and *creditors*. Practicality is paramount, however, and issues and concepts beyond the essentials are left to the more specialized texts and articles identified in the references.

Originally published almost 25 years ago, the book has maintained a unique appeal for both students and practitioners because of its clarity and common sense presentation. An outgrowth of the compact technical briefing materials used in the MBA program at the Harvard Business School, which supplement practical case study discussion with essential background, the book has been regularly updated every five years. The sixth edition reflects not only the latest practice in the use of the various financial techniques, but also the experience gained over five editions through the widespread use the book continues to enjoy in both university courses, graduate and undergraduate, and in hundreds of executive development seminars and in-company programs in the United States, Canada, and overseas. Translated into five foreign languages over the years, the book has transcended the confines of American business practice on which it is built, because the way the analytical methods are described makes them almost universally applicable.

This sixth edition has been completely rewritten to further improve the integration of all the materials. The first four chapters form a unified section that covers basic financial statement analysis, funds flow patterns and their impact on liquidity, basic financial projection techniques, and culminates in an integrated model of business, e.g., a dynamic system affected by operating and financial leverage and by management's business strategies and financial policies.

Chapters 5 through 8 cover the more specialized topics of capital investment analysis, cost of capital and return standards, the choice among long-term financing alternatives, and valuation of a business and its securities, including basic concepts of merger and acquisition values. The chapters on cost of capital and valuation are new additions, necessary to reflect recent developments in corporate financial theory and practice. Three appendixes have also been added: a brief overview of inflation concepts, a description of basic financial information sources and financial quotations (formerly the final chapter), and solutions to more than two thirds of the self-study exercises and problems accompanying every chapter. This last feature now makes the book truly self-contained for the student or practitioner wishing to test his or her understanding of the materials.

The complete revision of the book has left intact, however, the book's primary focus on the doable and practical—an "executive briefing" concept—and on building the reader's basic ability to grasp financial relationships and issues. As before, the book only presupposes that the reader has some familiarity with fundamental accounting concepts.

I would again like to express my appreciation to my former colleagues at the Harvard Business School for the opportunity to develop the original concept of the book. My thanks also go to my business associates and to my colleagues at universities and in executive development programs here and abroad, too numerous to mention individually, for their continued extensive use of the book and for the many expressions of interest and constructive suggestions that have supported the book's evolution. Finally, I continue to be most gratified by the positive responses from so many users at all levels of experience who have found the book truly helpful.

Erich A. Helfert

CONTENTS

Weighting. Market versus Book Values. Calculation of Weighted Cost of Capital. Cost of Capital and Return Standards: *Cost of Capital as a Cutoff Rate. Risk Categories. Cost of Capital in Multibusiness Companies. Multiple Rate Analysis.* Key Issues.

INTRODUCTION

When a student, analyst, or business executive has to solve a financial problem related to business investment, operations, or financing, analytical techniques—and sometimes rules of thumb—are needed to generate meaningful answers. This book not only provides the key financial tools in general use, but also explains how and when they are applied. At the same time, experience has shown again and again that a proper structure and perspective for the problem to be solved are as important as the analysis techniques used.

While the tools and techniques covered in this book are discussed and demonstrated in detail, the user must not be tempted to view them as *ends* in themselves. It is simply not enough to master the techniques! Financial analysis is a process which helps answer questions that have been properly posed, and therefore it is a *means* to an end. We cannot stress enough that financial analysis is an aid which allows those responsible to make decisions. The "solutions" to financial problems depend on the point of view of the parties involved and on the relative importance of the issue as well as on the specific analytical results. In each situation the objective must be clearly stated before pencil is put to paper or computer keys are touched—otherwise the analysis becomes wasteful "number crunching."

Management has been defined as the "art of asking significant questions"; the same applies to financial analysis, which should be directed toward finding meaningful answers within the context of these significant questions, whether the results are fully quantifiable or not.

The degree of precision and refinement to which any financial analysis is carried also depends on the situation. Given the uncertain nature of many of the estimates used, it is preferable to develop ranges of potential outcomes rather than precise "answers." The qualitative aspects bearing on the problem should also be specified. Similarly, further refinement of answers that clearly suggest particular alternatives would be wasted—there is no need to belabor the obvious! Finally, effort should be directed at areas where the likely payoff from additional analysis is large—to match the amount of energy expended with the significance of the issue.

It may be helpful to review the following questions *before* any analysis is begun:

1. What exactly is the nature and scope of the issue to be analyzed? Has the problem and its relative importance been clearly spelled out, including the alternatives to be studied?
2. Which specific factors, relationships, and trends are likely to be helpful in analyzing the problem? What is the order of their importance?
3. Are there possible ways to obtain a quick ballpark estimate of the likely result, to help the analyst judge how important the data may be?
4. How reliable are the available data, and how is this uncertainty likely to affect the range of results?
5. How exact does the answer have to be relative to the importance of the problem being analyzed? Is refinement going to be worth the effort?

6. What limitations are inherent in the tools to be applied, and how is this likely to affect the range of results?

Only after having thought through these questions should actual analytical work on a problem proceed. The relatively small amount of effort expended at the beginning of the process will pay off in avoiding potential wasted effort. In effect, we are talking not only about meaningful financial analysis, but also about a rational approach to problem solving. In the end, this is what support of decision making in investment, operations, and financing is all about.

1 ASSESSMENT OF BUSINESS PERFORMANCE

The performance of a business is the result of many individual decisions made continually by its management. To assess business performance, therefore, involves analyzing the financial and economic effects of these decisions and judging the results through the use of comparative measures. Some of the decisions are major, such as investment in a new facility, raising large amounts of debt, or adding a new product or service. Such decisions may be specifically evaluated in the course of financial analysis. Most other decisions are part of an ongoing process. Their effect is seen in total when business results are examined. Throughout this book, we will view financial analysis in the *context of the major decision areas* in which management has to guide the fortunes of a business, whether large or small.

In essence, management makes decisions to *deploy resources for economic gain.* Viewed in their broadest sense, these decisions involve three areas: (1) the *investment* of resources, (2) the *operation* of the business through the use of these resources, and (3) the proper mix of *financing* with which to provide the resources. Today's business world is one of infinite variety— enterprises of all sizes engage in manufacturing, trade, finance, and provide myriad services, while having widely different legal and organizational structures. Common to all, however, is this fundamental theme of management: *Planned commitment of resources for the purpose of creating, over time, economic value sufficient to recover the resources employed and to earn a margin of profit.*

Over the long run, the result of such resource deployment should be a net improvement in the economic position of the owners—including the ability to make further resource commitments. This net improvement should be reflected in the increased value of the business as judged by the securities markets if the stock is traded publicly, or in the value recognized by potential buyers of the business. If there is no increase in value over time, the economic viability of the business is in question.

FINANCIAL STATEMENTS AND PERFORMANCE

Assessment of business performance is the most basic and common of the techniques we will present in this book. Performance assessment is normally based on an examination of the financial statements periodically issued by a business, whether that business is publicly traded or private. These financial statements, prepared according to commonly accepted accounting principles, reflect past and current effects of the decisions made by management. However, they involve some ambiguity. Financial statements are prepared according to rules that try to consistently and fairly account for business transactions. These rules by their very nature, leave the results, particularly the economic impact, open to some interpretation.

Therefore, as we begin the process of financial analysis, we must first understand the basic financial statements which normally provide the essential information for judging whether a business has performed well or poorly. This analysis involves the three areas of management decisions mentioned earlier: *investment, operations,* and *financing.* Before we begin our financial analysis it will be useful briefly to discuss the nature, relationships and limitations of the common financial statements: the **balance sheet, operating statement, funds flow statement,** and **statement of changes in owners' equity.** Then we will turn to the techniques of analysis that can be employed to judge the quality of performance as reflected in these statements.

The Balance Sheet

The balance sheet describes the *resources* employed by the business and the offsetting *financial obligations* incurred to lenders and owners *on a given date.* Also called the **statement of financial condition** or **financial position,** it must always balance, because the total assets invested in the business at any point in time are matched precisely by the sources of these assets. The sources are (*a*) financing from outside creditors, and (*b*) owners' equity, the funds contributed by the owners of the business. Balance sheets are *static* in that, like a snapshot, they reflect conditions on the date of their preparation. They are also *cumulative* in that they represent the effects of all decisions and transactions that have taken place and have been accounted for up to the date when they are prepared.

Accounting rules require that the costs of transactions be recorded when they are incurred, and retroactive adjustments are made only in very limited circumstances. As a consequence, balance sheets, being cumulative, show assets and liabilities acquired or incurred at different times. Because the current economic value of assets can change, particularly in the case of longer-lived items such as buildings and machinery, or resources such as land and minerals, the costs stated on the balance sheet may not reflect true values. Moreover, changes in the value of the currency in which the transactions are recorded can, over time, distort the balance sheet. The accounting profession has expended a great deal of effort to resolve these and other issues affecting the meaning of the balance sheet, but with only partial success. The analyst must therefore still make interpretive judgments. (We will discuss some of these as we examine analytical techniques.)

In our decisional context of investment, operations, and financing, the balance sheet can be viewed as a cumulative listing of the net effect of investment and financing decisions; while the net effect of operations in the form of profit or loss is reflected in the balance sheet account of ownership equity. Figure 1-1 shows how the balance sheet relates to our three areas of management decisions:

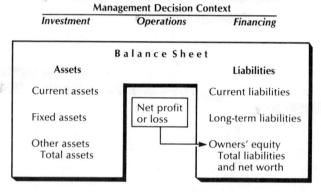

Figure 1-1
Balance Sheet in Performance Assessment

The key categories normally found on the balance sheet are listed. However, this is a simplification. In actual practice, the analyst encounters a large variety of asset, liability, and net worth accounts, because balance sheets reflect the unique nature of a given company and the business it is in. But the actual accounts can always be grouped into the basic categories listed.

As an example of the balance sheet of a major corporation, IBM's consolidated balance sheet for December 31, 1985 and December 31, 1984 is reproduced in Figure 1-2.

The Operating Statement

The operating statement reflects the effect of management's operating decisions on business performance and the resulting

Figure 1–2
INTERNATIONAL BUSINESS MACHINES CORPORATION
AND SUBSIDIARY COMPANIES
Consolidated Statement of Financial Position at December 31
($ millions)

Assets	1985		1984
Current assets:			
Cash	$ 896	$ 600	
Marketable securities, at cost, which			
approximates market	4,726	3,762	
Notes and accounts receivable-trade, net			
of allowances	9,757	7,393	
Other accounts receivable	809	718	
Inventories	8,579	6,598	
Prepaid expenses and other current assets	1,303	1,304	
Total current assets		26,070	20,375
Rental machines and parts	4,637	6,375	
Less: Accumulated depreciation	2,804	3,425	
Total rental machines and parts		1,833	2,950
Plant and other property	29,846	23,048	
Less: Accumulated depreciation	11,999	9,635	
Total plant and other property		17,847	13,413
Investments and other assets		6,884	6,070
Total assets		$52,634	$42,808
Liabilities and Stockholders' Equity			
Current liabilities:			
Taxes	$ 3,089	$ 2,668	
Loans payable	1,293	834	
Accounts payable	1,823	1,618	
Compensation and benefits	2,460	2,223	
Deferred income	391	340	
Other accrued expenses and liabilities	2,377	1,957	
Total liabilities		11,433	9,640
Long-term debt		3,955	3,269
Other liabilities		1,606	1,353
Deferred income taxes		3,650	2,057
Stockholders' equity:			
Capital stock, par value $1.25 per share	6,267	5,998	
Shares authorized: 750,000,000			
Issued: 1985—615,741,687; 1984—613,076,500			
Retained earnings	27,234	23,486	
Translation adjustments	(1,466)	(2,948)	
Total equity	32,035	26,536	
Less: Treasury stock, at cost	45	47	
Shares: 1985—323,425; 1984—390,961			
Total liabilities and stockholders' equity		31,990	26,489
		$52,634	$42,808

Source: Adapted from IBM 1985 Annual Report.

profit or loss for the owners of the business *over a clearly speci-fied period of time*. The profit or loss shown increases or decreases owners' equity on the balance sheet. The operating statement is thus a necessary adjunct to the balance sheet in explaining the components of changes in owner's equity, and it provides essential performance assessment information.

The operating statement, also referred to as the **income statement, earnings statement,** or **profit and loss statement** lists the revenues for a specific period, and the costs and expenses charged against these revenues, including write-offs and taxes. Revenues and costs involve elements such as sales for cash or credit, purchases of goods or services for resale or manufacture, payment of wages, incurring trade credit, selling activities, administration, etc. The operating statement represents the best effort of the firm's accountants to match the relevant items of revenue with the relevant items of expense. Again these efforts are governed by generally accepted accounting principles. How some costs and expenses are handled involves the accountant's judgments. Depreciation of assets being used over more periods than the one reported, the cost of goods purchased or manufactured in previous periods, and proper allocation of general expenses to a specific period are among the areas subject to accounting judgment. We will take up the more critical judgment areas later as we apply analysis techniques.

When viewed in our decisional context, the operating statement in the center column of Figure 1–3 expands the details of transactions and allocations that make up one of the key performance elements, profit or loss. Again we are providing an actual example, Figure 1–4, the consolidated operating statement of IBM for the years ending December 31, 1985 and December 31, 1984.

The combination of a balance sheet and an operating statement will provide more basic insights than the balance sheet alone. But because the operating statement covers a period of time, while the balance sheet describes conditions at the end of

Figure 1–3
Operating Statement in Performance Assessment

Management Decision Context		
Investment	*Operations*	*Financing*

	Operating Statement	
Current assets	Revenues – cost of sales	Current liabilities
Fixed assets	= Gross margin – expenses	Long-term liabilities
Other assets	= Net earnings/loss – taxes	Owner's equity
Total assets	= After tax profit/ loss	Total liabilities and net worth

a period, it is useful to have balance sheets for both the beginning and the end of the period covered by the operating statement.

Using both balance sheets, the effects of investment, operating, and financing decisions can be related to the specific period, be it a month, quarter, year, or any other time interval represented by the operating statement.

The Funds Flow Statement

Clearly, over a period of time, not only the profit and loss account will be affected. There will also be changes in assets and liabilities, particularly in the accounts making up working capital, such as cash, receivables, inventories, and payables. The statement that shows such changes in terms of the movement of funds is called a **funds flow statement.** This financial statement is a *dynamic analysis* that focuses on the *changes* in financial condition resulting from the decisions made during a given period. It is prepared from a comparison of the beginning and ending balance sheets, and is linked to the operating statement for the period. It reflects decisions involving *uses*

Figure 1–4

INTERNATIONAL BUSINESS MACHINES CORPORATION
AND SUBSIDIARY COMPANIES
Consolidated Statement of Earnings
For the Year Ended December 31
($ millions)

	1985		1984
Gross income:			
Sales	$34,404		$29,753
Services	11,536		9,605
Rentals	4,116		6,579
		$50,056	$45,937
Cost of sales	14,911		12,374
Cost of services	4,689		4,347
Cost of rentals	1,503		2,198
		21,103	18,919
Gross margin	$28,953 *57.8%*		$27,018
Selling, general and administrative			
expenses	13,000		11,587
Research, development and			
engineering expenses	4,723 *9.43%*		4,200 *9.14*
Interest expense	443		408
		18,166	16,195
		10,787	10,823
Other income, principally interest		832	800
Earnings before income taxes		11,619	11,623
Provision for income taxes		5,064	5,041
Net earnings		$ 6,555 *13.1%*	$ 6,582
Per share		$ 10.67	$ 10.77
Depreciation charged to costs			
and expenses		$ 2,894	$ 2,987
Amortization charged to costs			
and expenses		$ 425	$ 486
Cash dividends paid		$ 2,703	$ 2,507
Average number of shares			
outstanding:			
1985—614,084,568			
1984—611,426,324			
1983—606,769,848			

Source: Adapted from IBM 1985 Annual Report.

and sources of funds, that is, (*a*) commitments of funds to invest in assets or to repay liabilities, or (*b*) raising of funds through additional borrowing or reducing asset investments. One major source of funds is profitable operations in which revenues exceed costs and expenses. In contrast, unprofitable operations are a use of funds. The link between the funds flow statement and performance analysis should be clear.

The amount of detail and the format of the funds flow statement can vary widely, depending on the nature of the business and the different funds movements emphasized. One common format relates the changes in long-term assets, liabilities, and net worth to a *net* change in working capital, that is, to the difference between current assets and current liabilities. Other formats list uses and sources by major decision area. The main point about the funds flow statement, however presented, is its emphasis on the *changes in financial condition* brought about by management decisions.

One of the refinements introduced in the statement is the treatment of accounting write-offs. From a funds flow standpoint, write-offs such as depreciation and amortization merely represent bookkeeping entries that *do not affect funds*. Consequently such expense categories, insofar as they reduce net profit, are added back to profit in the funds flow statement to restore the funds from operations to their level before the write-off. Handling of this adjustment will be illustrated more specifically in Chapter 2.

The funds flow statement has the same inherent limitations as the balance sheet and the operating statement. Another limitation is the necessity of displaying the *net* change in each asset, liability, and ownership account reported, which may bury major individual transactions that offset each other. As we said before, management decisions affecting performance are made in a continuous sequence, and the balance sheets and operating statement for the period capture only their net effect. If there were material transactions, such as major investments, acquisitions, or divestitures, however, they are generally noted specifically in the company's funds flow statement. Figure 1–5 shows the funds flow statement in terms of our management decision context.

The consolidated funds flow statement of IBM for the years ended December 31, 1985 and December 31, 1984 (Figure 1–6) shows how these elements are listed in practice. A number

Figure 1–5
Funds Flow Statement in Performance Assessment

Management Decision Context

Investment	*Operations*	*Financing*
F u n d s F l o w S t a t e m e n t		
Current assets (plus or minus)		Current liabilities (plus or minus)
Fixed assets (plus or minus)	Net profit or loss	Long-term liabilities (plus or minus)
Other assets (plus or minus)	(plus or minus)	Owners' equity (plus or minus)
Total assets (plus or minus)	(Adjustments for write-offs)	Total liabilities and net worth (plus or minus)
Uses or Sources	**Sources or Uses**	**Sources or Uses**

of adjustments based on internally available information have been made by IBM to show more clearly the nature of funds movements during the periods covered.

The Statement of Changes in Owners' Equity

The fourth financial statement commonly provided by a business is an analysis of the *main changes during a specific period* in the owners' capital accounts, or net worth. We know from the earlier discussion that one of these changes is the profit or loss for the period, as displayed in the operating statement. But other management decisions may have affected owners' equity. For example, many corporations, including IBM, pay dividends on a quarterly basis. Such dividends are normally paid in cash, reducing both the cash balance and owners' equity. Another decision may be to provide additional capital through sale of common stock. A third area may involve write-offs or adjustments of asset values connected with disposition of assets or business combinations. A fourth area involves the complex adjustments related to the exchange of foreign currencies by companies doing business internationally. The net change in owners' equity may thus be selectively split into its major components to highlight the impact of these decisions.

Figure 1–6
INTERNATIONAL BUSINESS MACHINES CORPORATION
AND SUBSIDIARY COMPANIES
Consolidated Statement of Funds Flow
For the Year Ended December 31
($ millions)

	1985	1984
Funds (Cash and Marketable Securities)		
at January 1	$4,362	$5,536
Provided from (used for) Operations:		
Sources:		
Net earnings	$ 6,555	$ 6,582
Items not requiring the current use		
of funds:		
Depreciation charged to costs		
and expenses	2,894	2,987
Net book value of rental machines		
and other property retired		
or sold	867	1,483
Amortization of program		
products	425	486
Other (principally deferred		
income taxes)	1,880	1,004
	12,621	12,542
Depreciation of manufacturing		
facilities capitalized	157	228
	12,778	12,770
Uses:		
Investment in rental machines . .	313	858
Investment in plant and other		
property	6,117	4,615
	6,430	5,473
Investment in program products	785	803
Increase in investments and		
other assets	454	1,764
Net change in working capital		
(excluding cash, marketable		
securities and loans payable)	3,101	4,043
	10,770	12,083
Translation effects	677	(324)
Net provided from operations . .	2,685	363
Provided from External Financing:		
Net change in long-term debt	686	595
Net change in loans payable	459	302
Net provided from external		
financing	1,145	897
Provided from Employee and		
Stockholder Plans	133	73
	8,325	6,869
Less: Cash Dividends Paid	2,703	2,507
Funds (Cash and Marketable Securities)		
at December 31	$5,622	$4,362

Source: Adapted from IBM 1985 Annual Report.

The limitations of this special analytical statement largely depend on how much the issuing company chooses to disclose beyond what is legally required. Unless a company decides to provide specific information related to ownership accounts, the analyst may find it difficult to reconstruct the components of financial change from published data alone. Viewed in our context of performance assessment, the statement of changes in owners' equity thus can be clearly recognized as subsidiary information which helps us understand the financing sector of the balance sheet. This is suggested in Figure 1–7.

Again IBM's consolidated statement of changes in owners' (stockholders') equity for the years ended December 31, 1984, and December 31, 1985 is given as an actual example in Figure 1–8. The format used displays the principal changes very clearly.

In this portion of the chapter we have provided an overview of the nature and relationships of the financial statements as the background for analysis of these statements. The decision framework employed can be combined to help us visualize the

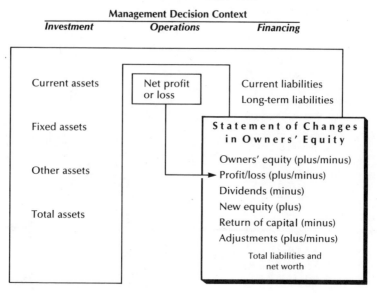

Figure 1–7
Statement of Changes in Owners' Equity
in Performance Assessment

Figure 1–8
INTERNATIONAL BUSINESS MACHINES CORPORATION
AND SUBSIDIARY COMPANIES
Consolidated Statement of Stockholders' Equity
For the Year Ended December 31
($ millions)

		Capital Stock	Retained Earnings	Translation Adjustments	Treasury Stock	Total
	Stockholders' equity, December 31, 1983	$5,800	$19,489	$(2,070)		$23,219
1984	Net earnings		6,582			6,582
	Cash dividends declared . . .		(2,507)			(2,507)
	Capital stock issued under employee plans (2,351,859 shares)	154				154
	Purchases (6,711,522 shares) and sales (6,320,561 shares) of treasury stock under employee and stockholder plans—net		(78)		(47)	(125)
	Tax reductions—employee plans	44				44
	Translation adjustments . . .			(878)		(878)
	Stockholders' Equity, December 31, 1984	5,998	23,486	(2,984)	(47)	26,489
1985	Net earnings		6,555			6,555
	Cash dividends declared . . .		(2,703)			(2,703)
	Capital stock issued under employee plans (2,664,869 shares)	173				173
	Purchases (6,346,223 shares) and sales (6,413,759 shares) of treasury stock under employee and stockholder plans—net		(104)		2	(102)
	Other (principally tax reductions—employee plans)	96				96
	Translation adjustments . . .			1,482		1,482
	Stockholders' equity, December 31, 1985	$6,267	$27,234	$(1,466)	$(45)	$31,990

Source: Adapted from IBM 1985 Annual Report.

coverage and relationship of the four financial statements. Note that the generalized overview in Figure 1–9 displays not only what the four basic financial statements cover in terms of key information, but also how they are related. (The dotted line indicates the impact of accounting write-offs.)

Figure 1–9
Generalized Overview of Financial Statements

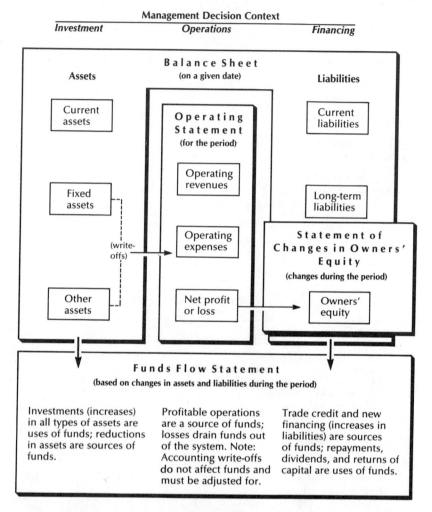

To summarize, the **balance sheet** describes the financial condition of a business at a point in time. It shows the cumulative effect of previous decisions and includes the profits or losses for preceding periods. The **operating statement** matches revenues and expenses for a specific period, including write-offs and allocations. It provides more detail about the elements making up the aftertax net profit and loss that was recorded in arriving at the owners' equity on the balance sheet. In contrast to the two previous statements, the **funds flow statement** is a dynamic look in that it highlights the *net changes* in assets, liabilities, and ownership accounts over a specific period. It allows the analyst to see the pattern of funds uses and sources that resulted from management's decisions concerning investments, operations, and financing. The statement recognizes and corrects for the fact that write-offs and amortization of assets acquired in the past are bookkeeping entries and do not affect funds. Finally the **statement of changes in ownership equity** gives more details concerning the change in ownership accounts as recorded on the beginning and ending balance sheets.

From our point of view, within the limitations of accounting rules and accountant's judgment, financial statements are an effort to reflect with reasonable consistency, all business transactions that, over time, result in a net improvement or worsening of the economic value of owners' equity. We have seen decisions and transactions as an interlinked series of movements of funds that are summarized on the financial statements. The analyst must take these statements, interpret their meaning, and apply standard techniques as well as explicit judgments in evaluating the financial and economic performance of the company under review.

RATIO ANALYSIS AND PERFORMANCE

Many analytical techniques, including those involving a variety of financial ratios, are available for performance assessment. However, the reader should be reminded that different techniques are appropriate for different purposes. Thus, before any analysis is undertaken, the analyst must clearly define the *viewpoint*, the *objectives* of the analysis, and the potential *standards* of comparison. In financial analysis there is often a temptation to "run all the numbers"—yet normally only a few relationships will yield the information and insights the analyst needs. A ratio can relate any magnitude to any other, such as net profit to total assets, or current liabilities to current assets. The choices are limited only by the analyst's imagination. The actual *usefulness* of any particular ratio, however, is strictly governed by the specific *objectives* of the analysis. Moreover, ratios are not absolute criteria: meaningful ratios serve best to point out changes in financial conditions or operating performance, and help illustrate the patterns of such change, which in turn, may indicate to the analyst the risks and opportunities for the business under review.

A further caveat is the fact that performance assessment based on financial statements deals with *past* data and conditions from which it may be difficult to extrapolate future expectations. Yet it is only the *future* that can be affected by decisions—the past is gone.

No attempt to assess business performance can provide firm answers. Insights are *relative*, because business and operating conditions vary so much from company to company and industry to industry. Differences exist in locations, types of facilities, products and services, accounting policies, capital structures, levels of efficiency, technological know-how, and caliber of management, to name but a few. The utility of comparisons and standards based on past performance has been further weakened by the growing trend toward multibusiness companies and conglomerates. Accounting adjustments for inflation present further complications. Means of specifically dealing with all of these aspects are far beyond the scope of this book. Nevertheless, the analyst must keep this background in mind when dealing with the available numerical data that reflect the effects of all of these conditions.

In this section we will discuss and characterize the key **ratios and measures** commonly applied in the financial analysis of business performance. Bear in mind that only the most important techniques will be dealt with. As mentioned before, the reason for the analysis will determine the most appropriate methods to use. Thus, our discussion will be developed around the **major viewpoints** that can be taken in performing a financial performance analysis and the usefulness of the different measures for each viewpoint.

Many different individuals and groups are interested in the success or failure of a given business. The most important are owners (investors), managers, lenders, and creditors, employees, labor organizations, government agencies, and society in general ("the public"). These groups differ in their view of business results and performance and will often go beyond financial data to include broader and more intangible values in their assessments.

Closest to the business from a day-to-day standpoint but also responsible for long-range plans is the *management* of the organization—whether professional managers or owner/managers. Managers are responsible and accountable for operating efficiency, current and long-term profitability, and the effective deployment of capital, human effort, and other resources. The various *owners* of the business, in turn, are especially interested in the current and long-term profitability of their equity investment. They expect growing earnings and dividends, and consequent growth in the economic value of their "stake." The providers of "other people's money," *lenders and creditors* who extend funds to the business for various lengths of time, are concerned about the reliability of the interest payments due them, about the ability of the business to repay the principal, and about the availability of specific residual asset values that give them a margin of protection against their risk. Other groups such as the *government, labor,* and *society,* will have specific objectives of their own—the reliability of tax payments, the ability to pay wages, stability of employment, or the financial wherewithal to meet various social and environmental obligations, for instance.

We will discuss business performance measures and tests in terms of the first three viewpoints, that is, of **management, owners,** and **lenders.** These viewpoints are, of course, interdependent and differ mainly in their emphasis. The reader should keep in mind that some of the measures are also applicable to the viewpoints of the other groups mentioned. In Figure 1–10, the principal financial areas of interest to the three groups are shown along with the ratios and measures relevant to these areas. We will follow the sequence in the table in discussing the measures and their application.

Management's Point of View

As mentioned before, management has a dual interest in the analysis of financial performance—it is used to assess both efficient and profitable operations, and the effective use of resources. The assessment of operations is largely based on analysis of the operating (income) statement, while the effective use of capital is usually measured by a combined review of the balance sheet and the income statement.

For purposes of illustration we will use the appropriate information from the sample statements of IBM for 1984 and 1985, which were reproduced as Figures 1–2, 1–4, 1–6, and 1–8. To facilitate the analysis, we have prepared a somewhat abbreviated version of IBM's balance sheet and operating statement (Figures 1–11 and 1–12), which we will employ for the remainder of this chapter and again in Chapter 2.

Figure 1–10
Financial Performance Measures by Area and Viewpoint

	Viewpoint	
Management	*Owners*	*Lenders*
Operational analysis	**Profitability**	**Liquidity**
Gross margin	Return on net worth	Current ratio
Profit margin	Return on common equity	Acid test
Operating expense analysis	Earnings per share	
Contribution		
Asset management	**Disposition of earnings**	**Leverage**
Asset turnover	Cash flow per share	Debt to assets
Working capital:	Dividends per share	Debt to capitalization
Inventory turnover	Dividend yield	Debt to equity
Accounts receivable	Payout/retention	
Accounts payable	Dividend coverage	
Profitability	**Market indicators**	**Debt service**
Return on assets	Price/earnings ratio	Interest coverage
Earnings before interest	Market to book value	Interest and principal
and taxes (EBIT), return		coverage
on assets		

Figure 1–11
INTERNATIONAL BUSINESS MACHINES CORPORATION
AND SUBSIDIARY COMPANIES
Consolidated Balance Sheet
at December 31
($ millions)

	1985	1984	Change
Assets			
Current assets			
Cash and marketable securities	$ 5,622	$ 4,362	+ 1,260
Receivables, net	10,566	8,111	+ 2,455
Inventories	8,579	6,598	+ 1,981
Prepaid expenses; other	1,303	1,304	− 1
Total current assets	26,070	20,375	+ 5,695
Plant, equipment and rental machinery	34,483	29,423	+ 5,060
Less: Accumulated depreciation	14,803	13,060	+ 1,743
Net plant and equipment	19,680	16,363	+ 3,317
Investments* and other assets	6,884	6,070	+ 814
Total assets	$52,634	$42,808	+ 9,826
Liabilities and Net Worth			
Current liabilities			
Accounts and notes payable	$ 1,823	$ 1,618	+ 205
Loans payable	1,293	834	+ 459
Accrued taxes	3,089	2,668	+ 421
Other accruals	5,228	4,520	+ 708
Total current liabilities	11,433	9,640	+ 1,793
Long-term debt	3,955	3,269	+ 686
Other liabilities	1,606	1,353	+ 253
Deferred taxes	3,650	2,057	+ 1,593
Shareholders' equity			
Capital stock	6,267	5,998	+ 269
Retained earnings(net)	25,723	20,491	+ 5,232
Total shareholders' equity	31,990	26,489	+ 5,501
Total liabilities and net worth	$52,634	$42,808	+ 9,826

*Includes program products which are amortized.

Operational Analysis.   For the business as a whole or any of its subdivisions, an assessment of operations is generally performed through a "common numbers" or percentage analysis of the operating statement. The ratios are usually based on *net sales*, that is, gross sales revenues after any returns and allowances. Use of net sales as the base provides a reasonable standard for measurement, which is particularly useful when tracing results over a series of past periods or when making comparisons between companies.

Figure 1–12
INTERNATIONAL BUSINESS MACHINES CORPORATION
AND SUBSIDIARY COMPANIES
Consolidated Operating Statement
For Years Ending December 31
($ millions)

	1985	1984	Percent of Revenues 1985	Percent of Revenues 1984
Revenues				
Sales of products	$34,404	$29,753	68.7%	64.7%
Services	11,536	9,605	23.1	21.0
Rentals	4,116	6,579	8.2	14.3
Total revenues	$50,056	$45,937	100.0%	100.0%
Costs and expenses*				
Cost of sales	$14,911	$12,374		
Cost of services	4,689	4,347		
Cost of rentals	1,503	2,198		
Cost of goods and services	21,103	18,919	42.2	41.2
Gross margin	28,953	27,018	57.8%	58.8%
Selling, gen. & admin	13,000	11,587	26.0	25.2
Research & development	4,723	4,200	9.4	9.1
Interest expense	443	408	.9	.9
Total expenses	18,166	16,195	36.3%	35.2%
	10,787	10,823	21.5	23.6
Other income	832	800	1.7	1.7
Earnings before taxes	11,619	11,623	23.2%	25.3%
Provision for income taxes	5,064	5,041	10.1	11.0
Net income	$ 6,555	$ 6,582	13.1%	14.3%
*includes depreciation	$ 2,894	$ 2,987		
*includes amortization	425	486		
Dividends paid	2,703	2,507		

The ratios derived are used both to judge the relative magnitude of selected key elements and to determine any trends towards improving or declining performance. During the analysis we must keep in mind the type of industry involved and its particular characteristics, as well as the individual trends and special conditions of the company being studied. For example, the gross margin of a jewelry store with slow turnover of merchandise and high markups will be far higher (50 percent is not uncommon) than that of a supermarket which depends for its success on low margins and high volume (gross margins of 10 to 15 percent are typical). In fact, comparison of a particular company's ratios to those of similar companies in its industry *over a period of time* will provide the best clues as to whether the company's position is improving or worsening. Many published annual overviews of company and industry performance use such ranking approaches, and often individual companies develop their own comparisons with the performance of relevant competitors.

Gross Margin and Cost of Goods Sold Analysis. One of the most common ratios in operational analysis is the calculation of cost of goods sold as a percentage of net sales (total revenues in our example). This ratio indicates the magnitude of the cost of goods purchased or manufactured in relation to the margin left over for operating expenses and profit. The ratios calculated from our sample statements appear as follows:

$$\text{Cost of goods sold} = \frac{\$21,103}{\$50,056} = 42.2\% \quad (1984: 41.2\%)$$

$$\text{Gross margin} \quad = \frac{\$28,953}{\$50,056} = 57.8\% \quad (1984: 58.8\%)$$

The cost of goods sold of 42.2 percent and the gross margin of 57.8 percent indicate the margin of "raw profit." Remember that gross margin reflects the relationship of prices, volume, and costs. Any change in gross margin can involve a combination of changes in the selling price of the product and in the level of manufacturing costs if the product was made by the company. In a trading or service organization, gross margin can be affected by the price charged for the product or service provided and the prices paid for the merchandise or services purchased on the outside. Volume of operations can be significant if, for example, a manufacturing company has high fixed costs (see Chapter 4 for a discussion of operating leverage) or a trading company has less buying power and fewer economies of scale than a larger competitor.

In the case of IBM, we calculated the costs of goods sold and the gross margin for the three major product lines *combined.* Note that the company provided both sales revenues and cost of sales for *each* of its lines: *products, services,* and *machine rentals.* Calculating the gross margin for individual areas improves the insight gained from the analysis. The results are 56.6 percent (58.4 percent) for product sales, 59.4 percent (54.7 percent) for services, and 63.5 percent (66.5 percent) for machine rentals.[1] It is significant that rentals, the smallest line of business with the highest gross margin, dropped from 14.3 percent of total company sales in 1984 to only 8.2 percent in 1985, affecting the overall gross margin adversely. At the same time, the gross margin on the largest line of business, product sales, declined almost two percentage points, causing a further reduction in the overall margin, a drop which the improved profitability of the much smaller services area was not able to overcome. The margin squeeze experienced by IBM is a reflection of the difficult competitive environment in computer markets worldwide during 1985.

There are particular complications in the analysis of manufacturing companies, because the nature of the cost-accounting system determines the specific costing of products for inventory and for current sale. The charges for a period of operations can be greatly affected by the choice of accounting methods. Significant differences can exist between the apparent performance of companies using standard full cost systems and those using direct costing. (In the latter case, fixed manufacturing costs are not allocated to individual products but charged as a block against operations.) Inflation, which affects the prices of both cost inputs and goods or services sold, further distorts the picture.

A major change in a company's cost of goods sold or gross margin over a relevant period of time would call for further analysis of the cause. The relevance of the time period depends on the nature of the business; for example, many businesses experience normal seasonal fluctuations, while others are affected by longer-term business cycles. Thus, the ratio serves as a signal rather than an absolute measure, as is the case with most of the measures to be discussed.

---

[1] Figures in parentheses represent comparable amounts for 1984.

Profit Margin.   The relationship of reported net profit after taxes (net income) to sales indicates management's ability to operate the business with sufficient success not only to recover the cost of the merchandise or services, the expenses of operating the business (including depreciation), and the cost of borrowed funds, but also to leave a margin of reasonable compensation to the owners for putting their capital at risk. The ratio of net profit (income) to sales (total revenue) essentially expresses the cost/price effectiveness of the operation. As we will demonstrate later, a more significant ratio for this purpose is the relationship of profit to the capital employed in producing it.

The calculation of the net profit ratio is simple, as figures from our IBM example show:

$$\text{Profit margin} = \frac{\$6{,}555}{\$50{,}056} = 13.1\% \quad (1984{:}\ 14.3\%)$$

A variation of this ratio uses net profit *before* interest and taxes. This figure represents the operating profit before any compensation is paid to debtholders. It is also the profit before the calculation of federal and state income taxes, which are often based on modified sets of deductible expenses and accounting write-offs. The use of this ratio rests on the assumption that it provides a "purer" view of operating effectiveness, undistorted by financing patterns and tax calculations. Called earnings before interest and taxes (EBIT), this pretax, preinterest income would be:

$$\text{Profit margin} = \frac{\$11{,}619 + \$443}{\$50{,}056} = 24.1\% \quad (1984{:}\ 26.2\%)$$

There is a sound argument, however, for considering income taxes, however calculated, as an ongoing business expense. The formula can therefore be modified by using profit *after* taxes but *before* interest—again, to focus on operating efficiency by leaving out any compensation to the various holders of capital. In terms of the figures we are using this would be:

$$\text{Profit margin} = \frac{\$\ 6{,}555 + (1 - .436)443}{\$50{,}056} = 13.6\% \quad (1984{:}\ 14.7\%)$$

For convenience in making the adjustment to aftertax profit, we assume that the interest paid during the period was fully tax deductible, and we simply add back the *aftertax* cost of interest, which is pretax interest times 1 minus the tax rate, employing either the effective (average) tax rate paid (43.6 percent in IBM's case) or, ideally, the marginal (highest bracket) corporate tax rate for the firm in question. The choice of tax rates depends on the complexity of the company's taxation pattern. Because IBM operates worldwide and therefore is subject to a variety of taxes, we are forced to rely on the effective overall rate paid. Chapter 6 contains a specific discussion of the cost of debt and the nature of the adjustments necessary.

Operating Expense Analysis. Various expense categories are routinely related to net sales. These comparisons include such items as administrative expense, selling and promotion expenses, and many others typical of particular businesses and industries. The formula used to calculate this expense ratio is:

$$\text{Expense ratio} = \frac{\text{Various expense items}}{\text{Net sales}} = \text{Percent}$$

We have shown a few expense categories in the abbreviated operating statement of IBM and calculated the ratio to sales for each. In practice, a more detailed breakdown is often desirable. Many trade associations collect extensive data from their members and publish statistics on expense ratios, as well as on most of the other ratios discussed in this chapter. These publications help provide standards of comparison and the basis for trend analysis to those interested in the industry. Some sources of industry statistics are listed in the reference section at the end of this chapter. To make the comparisons reasonable, great care is often taken to categorize the businesses within the industry by size and other characteristics, which reduces the degree of error introduced by large-scale averaging.

Contribution Analysis. This type of analysis has been used mainly for internal management, although it is increasingly applied in broader financial analysis. The process involves relating net sales to the "contribution margin" of product groups or of the total business. This calculation requires a very selective analysis or estimate of the fixed and variable costs and expenses of the business, and takes into account the effect of operating leverage. Only the directly variable costs are subtracted from net sales to show the contribution of operations to fixed costs and profits for the period. This is calculated as follows:

$$\text{Contribution to fixed cost and profit} = \frac{\text{Net sales} - \text{Direct costs(variable costs)}}{\text{Net sales}} = \text{Percent}$$

Significant differences can exist in the contribution margins of different industries, due to varying needs for capital investment and resultant cost/volume conditions. Even within a company, various lines of products or services may contribute quite differently to fixed costs and profits.

Contribution margins are useful in gauging the risk characteristics of a business, that is, the amount of leeway management enjoys in pricing its products and services, and in its ability to control costs and expenses under different economic conditions. Analysis of break-even conditions and of pricing strategies as they relate to volume achieved become important in this context. Chapter 4 contains a more extensive discussion of these points.

Asset Management.   Several ratios are useful in judging the effectiveness with which management has employed the *assets* entrusted to it. The ratios essentially involve *turnover* relationships and express, in various forms, the relative amount of capital used to support the volume of business transacted.

Asset Turnover.   The most commonly used ratios relate *net sales* to *gross assets*, or *net sales* to *net assets*. The measure indicates the size of the recorded asset commitment required to support a particular level of sales or, conversely, the sales dollars generated by each dollar of assets. While simple to calculate, overall asset turnover is a crude measure at best, because the balance sheets of most well-established companies list a variety of assets at the widely differing cost levels of past periods.

These recorded values often have little relation to current economic values, and the distortions grow with any significant change in the level of inflation. Another distortion is caused by a company's mix of product lines, as we observed in the case of IBM, where some lines are asset intensive, while others (like services), need relatively few assets to support the volume of revenues generated. Nevertheless, the turnover ratio is another of several clues that, in combination, can indicate favorable or unfavorable performance.

If gross assets are used, the calculation is as follows:

$$\frac{\text{Net sales}}{\text{Gross assets}} = \frac{\$50,056}{\$52,634} = 0.95 \qquad (1984: 1.07)$$

or

$$\frac{\text{Gross assets}}{\text{Net sales}} = \frac{\$52,634}{\$50,056} = 1.05 \qquad (1984: 0.93)$$

If net assets (*total assets* less *current liabilities*, which equals the *capitalization* of the business) are used, the calculations are either:

$$\frac{\text{Net sales}}{\text{Net assets}} = \frac{\$50,056}{\$52,634 - \$11,433} = 1.21 \qquad (1984: 1.38)$$

or

$$\frac{\text{Net assets}}{\text{Net sales}} = \frac{\$41,201}{\$50,056} = 0.82 \qquad (1984: 0.72)$$

The difference between the two sets of calculations lies in the choice of the asset total—that is, whether to use gross assets or net assets. Using net assets eliminates current liabilities from the total. The assumption is that current liabilities, which are mostly operational (accounts payable, current taxes due, current repayments of debt, and accrued obligations), are available to the business as a matter of course. Therefore the amount of assets employed in the business is effectively reduced through these ongoing trade credit relationships. Such reasoning is especially important for trading firms, where the size of accounts payable to suppliers is quite significant in terms of the total balance sheet.

Working Capital.   Among the assets of a company, the key working capital accounts—*inventories* and *accounts receivable*—are usually given special attention. The ratios used to analyze these categories attempt to establish the relative effectiveness with which inventories and receivables are managed. They aid the analyst in detecting signs of deterioration in value, or excessive accumulation of inventories and receivables. The amounts in these accounts stated on the balance sheet are generally related to the single best indicator of activity, such as sales or cost of sales (cost of goods sold), on the assumption that a reasonably close relationship exists.

Inventories cannot be judged precisely, short of an actual count, verification, and appraisal of value. Because an analyst can rarely do this, the next best step is to relate the recorded inventory to net sales or to cost of goods sold, to see whether there is a shift in magnitude over a period of time. Normally *average* inventory values are used to make this calculation (the average of beginning and ending inventories). At times, it is also desirable to use only *ending* inventories, especially in the case of rapidly growing firms where inventories are being built up to support steeply rising sales. Furthermore it is necessary to closely observe the method of inventory costing employed by the company—such as last-in, first-out (LIFO), first-in, first-out (FIFO), average costing, etc.—and any changes made during the time span covered by the analysis. (See Chapter 2 for further discussion of inventory costing.)

While the relationship of sales and inventories will often suffice as a broad measure of performance, it is usually more precise to relate inventories to *cost* of goods sold, because only then will both factors be stated on a comparable basis. The use of the net *sales* figure introduces a distortion in that recorded sales include a markup that is not included in the stated cost of the inventories. The difference in the two methods of calculation is reflected in the equation below:

$$\frac{\text{Average inventory}}{\text{Net sales}} = \frac{.5(\$8,579 + \$6,598)}{\$50,056} = 15.2\% \quad (1984: 12.0\%)$$

or

$$\frac{\text{Average inventory}}{\text{Cost of goods sold}} = \frac{\$7,588}{\$21,103} = 36.0\% \quad (1984: 29.0\%)$$

In the sample calculations we have employed total IBM sales and cost of goods and services. The information we have about the three product lines clearly suggests that a more refined analysis is necessary and possible. We know from the annual report that inventories essentially relate to manufactured products, which is the major line of business but represents only about two thirds of the annual sales volume. We also know that rental machines are listed separately among fixed assets. Consequently, we should calculate the ratios by taking *product sales* alone. The revised figures appear as follows:

$$\frac{\text{Average inventory}}{\text{Sales of products}} = \frac{\$7,588}{\$34,404} = 22.1\% \quad (1984: 18.4\%)$$

or

$$\frac{\text{Average inventory}}{\text{Cost of sales}} = \frac{\$7,588}{\$14,911} = 50.1\% \quad (1984: 44.4\%)$$

When we deal with a manufacturing company we must also be particularly aware of the problem of accounting measurements—so often encountered when using other analytical methods—because the stated value of inventories can be seriously affected by the specific cost-accounting system employed.

Instead of average inventory, the *number of times* inventory has *turned over* during the period of analysis is more commonly used in working capital analyses. In IBM's case, turnover slowed as the business environment became more difficult:

$$\frac{\text{Net sales}}{\text{Average inventory}} = \frac{\$34,404}{\$7,588} = 4.5 \text{ times} \quad (1984: 5.4 \text{ times})$$

or

$$\frac{\text{Cost of sales}}{\text{Average inventory}} = \frac{\$14,911}{\$7,588} = 2.0 \text{ times} \quad (1984: 2.3 \text{ times})$$

Generally speaking, the higher this number the better, because low inventories often suggest a minimal risk of unsalable goods, and indicate efficient use of capital. Yet inventory turnover figures which are well above industry norms may signal the risk of inventory shortages, resultant poor customer service, and thus the potential for competitive disadvantage. The final judgment depends on the specific circumstances.

The analysis of *accounts receivable* again is based on *net sales*. Here, the question arises of whether accounts receivable outstanding at the end of the period closely approximate the amount of credit sales we would expect to remain uncollected, assuming normal credit terms. For example, a business selling with terms of net/30 (payment due in 30 days) would normally expect to have as accounts receivable the sales of the prior month. If 40 or 50 days' sales were reflected on its balance sheet, this could mean that some customers had difficulty paying or were abusing their credit privileges, or that some sales had to be made on extended terms. An exact analysis of accounts receivable can only be made by examining the *aging* of the individual accounts recorded on the company's books. Aging involves classifying accounts receivable into brackets of days outstanding—10 days, 20 days, 30 days, 40 days, and so on—and relating these to the credit terms applicable in the business. Because this type of analysis requires access to inside information, financial analysts assessing the business from the outside must be satisfied with the relatively crude overall approach of restating accounts receivable in terms of daily sales. This is done as follows:

$$\frac{\text{Net sales}}{\text{Days in the year}} = \frac{\$50,056}{360} = \$139 \text{ million/day} \quad (1984: \$128 \text{ million})$$

and

$$\frac{\text{Accounts receivable}}{\text{Sales per day}} = \frac{\$9,757}{139} = 70.2 \text{ days} \quad (1984: 57.8 \text{ days})$$

A complication arises when a company's sales are normally made to different types of customers under varying terms, or when the sales are made partly for cash and partly on account. Cash and credit sales should be differentiated if possible. If no detailed information is available on this aspect and on the terms of sale used, the rough average must suffice to provide a broad indication of trends.

A similar process can be applied to judge a company's performance with regard to *accounts payable.* The analysis is a little more complicated, because accounts payable should be specifically related to the purchases made during the operating period. Normally such information is not readily available to the outside analyst, except in the case of trading companies, where the amount of purchases can be readily deduced by adding the change from beginning to ending inventories to the cost of goods sold for the period. In a manufacturing company, purchases of goods and services are buried in the cost-of-goods-sold account and in the inventories at the end of the operating period. A very crude approximation can be made in such cases by relating accounts payable to the average daily use of raw materials, if this expense element can be identified from the available information. In most cases, we can follow the process used for analyzing accounts receivable, if it is possible to approximate the average daily purchases for the period. The number of days of accounts payable is then directly related to the normal credit terms under which the company makes purchases, and serious deviations from that norm can be spotted.

Proper management of accounts payable involves paying within the terms, but not sooner, yet taking discounts where offered for early payment, such as 2 percent if the bill is paid in 10 days versus the full amount due in 30 days. Credit rating agencies can be a source of information to the analyst because they will express an opinion on the timeliness with which a company is meeting its credit obligations, including accounts payable.

Profitability.   Here the issue is the effectiveness with which management has employed the *total assets* and *net assets* as recorded on the balance sheet. This effectiveness is judged by relating *net profit*—defined in a variety of ways—to the commitment of *assets* used to generate the profit. The relationship is one of the more telling analyses, although, again, the nature and timing of the stated values on the balance sheet will tend to distort the results.

Return on Assets.   The easiest form of profitability analysis is the relationship of reported *net profit (net income)* to the *total assets* on the balance sheet. *Net assets* (total assets less current liabilities), which are equivalent to the total long-term sources on the balance sheet, may also be used. This is called *capitalization.* The calculations for both forms are as follows:

$$\frac{\text{Net profit}}{\text{Assets}} = \frac{\$6,555}{\$52,634} = 12.4\% \quad (1984: 15.4\%)$$

or

$$\frac{\text{Net profit}}{\text{Net assets (capitalization)}} = \frac{\$6,555}{\$52,634 - \$11,433} = 15.9\% \ (1984: 19.8\%)$$

While either ratio is an indicator of overall profitability, the results can be seriously distorted by changes in the company's capital structure (the proportion of interest-bearing long-term debt to owners' equity), and by federal income tax calculations applicable for the period analyzed.

EBIT Return on Assets.   As we stated before, net profit (net income) is the final operating result after interest and taxes are deducted. It is therefore affected by the proportion of debt in the capital structure and the resultant interest charges. A somewhat more meaningful result can be obtained if we eliminate *both* interest and taxes from the profit figure. (EBIT, earnings before interest and taxes, was mentioned earlier.) The revised ratio expresses the gross earnings power of the capital employed in the business independent of the pattern of financing that provided the capital. The calculation is:

$$\frac{\text{Net profit before interest and taxes (EBIT)}}{\text{Assets}} = \frac{\$12,062}{\$52,634} = 22.9\% \ (1984: 28.1\%)$$

or

$$\frac{\text{Net profit before interest and taxes (EBIT)}}{\text{Net assets (capitalization)}} = \frac{\$12,062}{\$41,201} = 29.3\% \ (1984: 36.3\%)$$

If we accept the argument that income taxes are a normal part of doing business, this result can be modified by using net profit before interest but *after* taxes. We can again employ the simple adjustment shown earlier to add back to net profit the aftertax cost of interest. If there is reason to believe that actual income taxes paid were modified for any reason and thus that the effective tax rate paid does not reflect normal conditions, we should use the marginal income tax rate to calculate the interest added back (see p. 27). The calculations are as follows:

$$\frac{\text{Net profit after taxes, before interest}}{\text{Total assets}} = \frac{\$6,805}{\$52,634} = 12.9\% \ (1984\colon 15.9\%)$$

or

$$\frac{\text{Net profit after taxes, before interest}}{\text{Net assets (capitalization)}} = \frac{\$6,805}{\$41,201} = 16.5\% \ (1984\colon 20.5\%)$$

In summary, the various ratios available for judging a business from the point of view of management deal with the effectiveness of operations, the effectiveness of capital deployment, and the profitability achieved on the assets deployed. These measures are all affected to some degree by uncertainties involving accounting and valuation methods, but together they can provide reasonable clues to a firm's performance, and also for further analysis.

We now turn to the second of the three viewpoints relevant in analyzing performance, that of the owners of a business. These are the investors to whom management is responsible and accountable. So far we have not mentioned the owners directly, even though it should be quite clear that management, in the timing, execution, and appraisal of the results of operations, must be fully cognizant of, and responsive to the owners' viewpoint and expectations, just as it must be alert to the lenders' viewpoint and criteria.

Owners' Point of View

The key interest of the owners of a business—the shareholders in the case of a corporation—is *profitability*. In this context, profitability means the returns achieved through the efforts of management, on the funds invested by the owners. The owners are also interested in the *disposition* of earnings which belong to them, that is, how much is reinvested in the business or paid out to them as dividends. Finally, they are concerned about the effect of business results on the *market value* of their investment, especially in the case of publicly traded stock. The key concepts related to this last aspect are taken up in detail in Chapters 6 and 8, and we will only make brief reference to them here.

Profitability. The relationship of profits earned to the shareholders' stated investment is watched closely by the financial community. Analysts track several key measures that express the company's performance in relation to the owner's stake. Two of these, *return on net worth* and *return on common equity* address the profitability of the total ownership investment, while the third, *earnings per share*, measures the proportional participation of each unit of investment in corporate earnings for the period.

Return on Net Worth. The most common ratio used for measuring the return on the owners' investment is the relationship of *net profit* to *net worth* (equity). In performing this calculation, we do not have to make any adjustments in net profit, because this figure has already been properly reduced by the interest charges, if any, paid to creditors and lenders. Therefore net income for purpose of this calculation is the *residual* result of operations and belongs totally to the holders of common or preferred equity shares. Within the shareholder group, only those holding common shares have a claim on the residual after obligatory preferred dividends have been paid.

The relationship is calculated as follows:

$$\frac{\text{Net worth}}{\text{Net worth (equity)}} = \frac{\$6,555}{\$31,990} = 20.5\% \quad (1984: 24.8\%)$$

Here we have used the *ending* shareholders' equity in the calculation for IBM. It is quite common, however, to use the *average* equity for this calculation, on the assumption that profitable operations build up shareholders' equity *during* the year and that therefore the annual profit should be related to the midpoint of this buildup. In fact, IBM used this method to calculate the ratio published in its annual report:

$$\frac{\text{Net profit}}{\text{Average net worth}} = \frac{\$6,555}{.5(\$26,489 + \$31,990)} = 22.4\% \ (1984: 26.5\%)$$

A possible distortion must be mentioned here. Frequently questions arise about the way a particular liability account on the balance sheet, called *deferred taxes*, should be handled in this analysis. This account shows the accumulated difference between the accounting treatment and the tax treatment of a variety of revenue and expense elements. Essentially it represents tax payments deferred due to a *timing difference* in recognizing tax deductions allowable under Internal Revenue rules. Most corporations calculate tax payments based on an operating statement that may differ in various aspects from the one appearing as the published financial report. Examples of these aspects are recognition of installment sales and the method used in various write-offs. To illustrate, if a company chooses to use accelerated depreciation for tax purposes, but reports normal depreciation for bookkeeping purposes, the difference is shown as a liability against the day that this accumulated tax benefit might be "recaptured" by the Internal Revenue Service. This would happen if the company stopped investing in depreciable assets, or if future tax laws eliminated accelerated depreciation. Some analysts argue that deferred income taxes are, in effect owners' equity set aside against future higher tax levels. Others argue that they represent a form of long-term debt. Because there is no consensus on treatment, deferred income taxes often are not included in *any* of the ratio calculations. Given that this accumulation on the liability side of the balance sheet can be quite large, material differences can result from an inclusion of deferred taxes as owners' equity or as long-term debt.

Return on Common Equity. A somewhat more refined version of the calculation of return on owners' investment is based on earnings accruing to the holders of *common* shares *only*, if there are several types of stock outstanding, such as preferred stock. Net profit is reduced by dividends paid to holders of preferred shares and by other obligatory payments, such as distributions to holders of minority interests. Net worth is likewise reduced by the amount of preferred equity and any minority elements, to yield the common equity figure. IBM has only common stock outstanding, however, and thus we will show only the formula for the calculation:

$$\frac{\text{Net profit to common}}{\text{Common equity}} = \text{Percent}$$

Return on common equity is a widely published statistic. Rankings of companies and industry sectors are compiled by major business magazines and rating agencies. Return on common equity is closely watched by stock market analysts and, in turn, by management and boards of directors. The accuracy of recorded values and earnings calculations is an issue in these ratios as well, however, and adjustments may be necessary if the analyst is aware of major inconsistencies.

Earnings per Share. The analysis of earnings from the owners' point of view centers on *earnings per share* in the case of a corporation. This ratio simply involves dividing net profit to common stock by the number of shares of common stock outstanding:

$$\frac{\text{Net profit to common}}{\text{Average number of shares outstanding}} = \text{Earnings per share}$$

Earnings per share is a measure to which both management and shareholders pay a great deal of attention. It is widely used in the valuation of common stock, and is often the basis for setting specific corporate objectives and goals as part of strategic planning. Chapter 8 contains more background on the uses and limitations of this measure. Normally the analyst does not have to calculate earnings per share because the result is readily announced by corporations large and small. In IBM's case, earnings per share were $10.67 for 1985 ($10.77 for the previous year) as stated in the annual report (see Figure 1–4). Earnings per share are available on both an annual and a quarterly basis, and are a matter of record whenever a company's shares are publicly traded.

Even though the earnings per share figure is one of the most readily available statistics reported by publicly held corporations, some complications exist nevertheless. Apart from possible unusual elements in the quarterly and annual net profit pattern, the number of shares outstanding varies during the year in many companies, either because of newly issued shares (new stock offerings, stock dividends paid, options exercised, etc.), or because outstanding old shares are retired (purchase of treasury stock). Therefore, the *average* number of shares outstanding during the year is commonly used in this calculation (see Figure 1–4).

In recent years it has become mandatory for corporations to also calculate earnings per share on a *converted* basis, if the capital structure contains convertible securities that can be turned into common stock at some future time. This is done to call attention to the *diluting* effect of such convertible securities. Moreover, any significant change in the number of shares outstanding (such as would be caused by a stock split, for example) requires retroactive adjustments in past data to ensure comparability.

Analysts are quite interested in *past* earnings per share, both quarterly and annual. *Future* projections are frequently made on the basis of past earnings. Fluctuations and trends in actual performance are compared to the projections and watched closely for indications of strength or weakness. Again, great caution is advised in interpreting these data. Allowances must be made for unusual elements both in the earnings figure and in the number of common shares outstanding.

Disposition of Earnings. The separation of earnings (net profit) into dividends paid and earnings retained is closely watched by shareholders and the financial community, because the retained residual builds up the owners' equity recorded on the balance sheet and is a source of funds for management's use. Thus, earnings are either *reinvested* in the business to support further growth, or are *paid out* in part or full as dividends. Cash dividends are the most common form of payment, although stock dividends are also frequently used. In the latter case, no cash is involved. Instead, additional fractional shares are issued to each holder of record. If there is a normal cash dividend paid as well, stock dividends result in fractionally higher cash dividends, of course.

Cash Flow per Share. A calculation approximating the cash flow per share is frequently used as a rough measure of the company's ability to pay *cash dividends*. The cash flow per share ratio is an effort to simulate the operating funds flow on a per share basis. It is developed from a *net profit* figure to which operating *write-offs* such as depreciation, amortization, and depletion have been added back. Recall from our earlier discussion of the funds flow statement that such accounting write-offs do not represent a movement of funds. Therefore, adding back these bookkeeping entries restates the net profit in a form that approximates the funds generated by operations. The calculation parallels the earnings per share ratio:

$$\frac{\text{Net profit to common plus write-offs}}{\text{Average number of shares outstanding}} = \text{Cash flow per share}$$

In the case of IBM, we know that depreciation and amortization amounted to $2,894 million and $425 million respectively. The average number of shares outstanding was given in Figure 1–4 as 614,084,568. Write-offs thus amounted to $5.40 per share, which when added to the earnings per share of $10.67, results in a cash flow per share of $16.07. Cash flow per share is used to indicate the potential availability of cash for dividends and various other disbursements. Because the uses of funds in a business are largely at the discretion of management, however, the figure is at best only a crude indication of the potential to pay dividends. A more extensive analysis of funds flow is required to judge the pattern of sources and uses, and we will discuss this further in Chapter 2.

Dividends per Share. Dividends are generally declared publicly on a *per share basis* by a corporation's board of directors, and no calculation is necessary. Dividend policy is the prerogative of the board of directors which has legal authority to set payments at any level it deems appropriate. Because the market value of common stock is in part influenced by dividends paid and anticipated, the board generally deals with this periodic decision very carefully. IBM paid dividends of $4.40 per share in 1985 and $4.10 in 1984.

Dividend Yield. Annual dividends per share can be related to current or average *share prices* to derive the dividend yield:

$$\frac{\text{Annual dividend per share}}{\text{Average market price per share}} = \text{Dividend yield}$$

This is a measure of the return on the owners' investment from cash dividends. In the case of IBM, the 52-week range of stock prices from April 1985 to March 1986 was 117⅜ to 161, with an average of 139⅛. The dividend yield of $4.40 per share thus amounts to 3.2 percent. The ratio falls short as a basis for comparison with other companies, however, because dividend policies differ widely. Even more importantly, the total economic return normally enjoyed by the shareholder is a *combination* of dividends and market appreciation of the stock. A more detailed discussion of the complex issues surrounding the value of the business and of shareholder equity can be found in Chapters 6 and 8.

Payout/Retention. A ratio commonly used in connection with dividend policy is the so-called *payout ratio*, which represents the proportion of earnings paid out to the shareholders in the form of cash during any given year:

$$\frac{\text{Cash dividends per share}}{\text{Earnings per share}} = \frac{\$4.40}{\$10.67} = 41.2\% \quad (1984: 38.1\%)$$

Because most boards of directors tend to favor paying a fairly stable dividend per share, adjusted only gradually, the payout ratio of a company may fluctuate widely in the short run in response to swings in earnings performance. Over a period of several years, however, the payout ratio can often be used to indicate the tendency of directors to reinvest funds in the business versus paying out earnings to the shareholders. There are no firm standards for this ratio, but the relationship is significant in characterizing the "style" of the corporation. High-growth companies tend to pay out relatively low proportions of earnings because they prefer to reinvest the earnings to support profitable growth. Stable or moderate-growth companies tend to pay out larger proportions. Some companies pay no cash dividends at all, or provide stock dividends. Many more factors must, of course, be considered in making judgments in this area, and the reader is directed to the references at the end of this chapter for further insight into both concepts and practices.

Dividend Coverage. Owners are also interested in the degree to which their dividends are *covered* by earnings and cash flow. Furthermore, they are concerned about the degree to which the proportion of debt in the capital structure and its associated interest and repayment requirements will affect management's ability to achieve reasonably stable and growing earnings, and to pay dividends commensurate with the owners' expectations. A variety of coverage ratios can be calculated, but they hardly differ from the ones we will take up in our discussion of the lenders' point of view.

Market Indicators. We will only briefly mention two ratios which are commonly used as indicators of stock market values, the *price/earnings ratio* and the *market to book ratio.* The subject of market valuation will be covered in detail in Chapters 6 and 8.

Price/Earnings Ratio. The simple relationship between current or expected *earnings per share* and the current *market price* of the stock is often quoted by both management and owners. The ratio is also called the *earnings multiple,* and it is used to indicate how the stock market is judging the company's earnings performance and prospects. The calculation shown, which uses the market price as of March 31, 1986, is straightforward:

$$\frac{\text{Market price per share}}{\text{Earnings per share}} = \frac{\$151\frac{1}{2}}{\$10.67} = 14.2 \text{ times}$$

The earnings multiple is used quite commonly as a rough rule of thumb in valuing companies for purposes of acquisition.

Earnings multiples vary widely by industry and by company, and are in effect a simple overall approximation of the market's current judgment of industry and company risk versus past and prospective earnings performance.

The reverse of the formula is the so-called *earnings yield*, which relates earnings per share to the market price. Although it is sometimes used to express the current yield the owner enjoys, the measure can be misleading, because earnings are not normally paid out in full as dividends. Thus, the earnings yield cannot be compared to, for example, the yield on a bond where interest payments are contractual. Additionally, as mentioned, the economic return to the shareholder is a combination of the dividends received and the appreciation of the stock, as we will discuss further in Chapter 6.

Market to Book Ratio.   This indicator relates *current market value* on a per share basis to the stated *book value* of owners' equity stated on the balance sheet, also on a per share basis. IBM's December 31, 1985 book value per share was $52.09, while the market value was three times higher. The market to book ratio leaves much to be desired as a measure of performance for many of the reasons mentioned in earlier discussions of other ratios. In addition, while in a given company the relationship between stated balance sheet values and market values may be favorable, the ratio does not truly help the analyst judge what comparable expectations should be for other firms. Thus, the measure can only be a beginning step in the appraisal of long-term performance and outlook.

In summary, the ratios pertinent to the owners' view of a company's performance are measures of the *return* owners have *earned* on their stake and the *cash* rewards they received in the form of *dividends*. These results depend on the earning power of the company and on management policies and decisions regarding the use of financial leverage and reinvestment. Ultimately, these affect the economic value of the owners' capital commitment, as reflected in stock market prices. The concepts and issues are taken up in more detail in Chapters 6 and 8.

Lenders' Point of View

While the main orientation of management and owners is toward the business as a going concern, the lender of necessity has to be of two minds. Lenders have an interest in funding the needs of a successful business that will perform as expected. At the same time, they must consider the possible negative consequences of default and liquidation. Sharing none of the rewards of success other than receiving regular payments of interest and principal, the lender must carefully assess the risk of recovering the original funds extended, particularly if they have been provided for a long period of time. Part of this assessment must be the ultimate value of the lender's claim in case of serious difficulty. The claims of a general creditor rank behind federal tax obligations and the claims of secured creditors, who lend against a specific asset, such as a building or equipment. Thus, caution dictates looking for a margin of safety in the assets held by the company, a "cushion" against default. Several ratios are used to assess this protection by testing the **liquidity** of the business. Another set of ratios tests the relative debt exposure, or **leverage** of the business in order to weigh the position of lenders versus owners. Finally, there are coverage ratios relating to the company's ability to provide **debt service** from funds generated by ongoing operations.

Liquidity.   One way to test the degree of protection afforded lenders focuses on the short-term credit extended to a business for funding operations. It involves the *liquid assets* of a business, that is, those current assets that can readily be converted into cash, on the assumption that these would form a ready cushion against default.

Current Ratio.   The ratio most commonly used to appraise the debt exposure represented on the balance sheet is the current ratio. This relates *current assets* to *current liabilities* in an attempt to show the safety of current debtholders' claims in case of default. The calculation is shown using the relevant totals from Figure 1–11:

$$\frac{\text{Current assets}}{\text{Current liabilities}} = \frac{\$26,070}{\$11,433} = 2.3:1 \quad (1984: 2.1:1)$$

Presumably the larger this ratio, the better the position of the debt holders. From the lenders' point of view, a higher ratio would certainly appear to provide a cushion against drastic losses of value in case of business failure. A large excess of current assets over current liabilities seems to help protect claims, should inventories have to be liquidated at a forced sale and should accounts receivable involve sizable collection problems. Seen from another angle, however, an excessively high current ratio might signal slack management practices. It could indicate idle cash balances, inventory levels that have become excessive when compared to current needs, and poor credit management that results in overextended accounts receivable. At the same time, the business might not be making full use of its current borrowing power.

A very common rule of thumb is the belief that a current ratio of 2:1 is "about right" for most businesses, because this ratio appears to permit a shrinkage of up to 50 percent in the value of current assets while still providing enough cushion to cover current liabilities. The problem with this concept is that the current ratio measures an essentially *static* condition and assesses a business as if it were on the brink of liquidation. The ratio does not reflect a going concern, which should be the top priority of management. The lender or creditor looking to do future business with a successful client should bear this in mind.

Acid Test. An even more stringent test, although again on a static basis, is the *acid test* or *quick ratio*, which is calculated using only a *portion* of current assets—cash, marketable securities, and accounts receivable—which are then related to current liabilities as follows:

$$\frac{\text{Cash} + \text{Marketable securities} + \text{Receivables}}{\text{Current liabilities}} =$$

$$\frac{\$5,622 + \$10,566}{\$11,433} = 1.4{:}1 \quad (1984{:}\ 1.3{:}1)$$

The key concept here is testing the *collectibility* of current liabilities in the case of a real crisis, on the assumption that inventories would have no value at all. As drastic tests of the ability to pay in the face of disaster, both the current ratio and the acid test are helpful. From an operational standpoint, however, it is better to analyze a business in terms of expected total future funds flows. The proportion of current assets to current liabilities normally covers only a small part of this total.

Leverage.   As we will discuss in greater detail in Chapters 4 and 7, successful use of debt enhances earnings for the owners of the business, because returns earned on these funds over and above the interest paid belong to the owners and thus increase owners' equity. From the lenders' viewpoint, however, when earnings do not exceed or even fall short of the interest cost, fixed interest and principal commitments must still be met. The owners' must fulfill these claims, which might then severely affect owners' equity. The positive *and* negative effects of leverage increase with the proportion of debt in a business. The risk exposure of the providers of debt grows, as does the risk exposure of the owners. From the lenders' point of view, a variety of ratios that deal with total debt, or long-term debt only, *in relation* to various parts of the balance sheet, are more inclusive measures of riskiness than leverage alone. The ratios measure the risk exposure of the lenders in relation to the available asset values against which all claims are held.

Debt to Assets.   The first and broadest test is the proportion of *total debt*, current and long term, to *total assets*, which is calculated as follows:

$$\frac{\text{Total debt}}{\text{Total assets}} = \frac{\$20,644^*}{\$52,634} = 39.2\% \quad (1984: 38.1\%)$$

*Includes deferred taxes and other liabilities.

This ratio describes the proportion of "other peoples' money" to the total claims against the assets of the business. The higher the ratio, the greater the likely risk for the lender. It is not necessarily a true test of the ability of the business to cover its debts, however, because as we have already observed, the asset amounts recorded on the balance sheet are not necessarily indicative of current economic values, or even liquidation values. Nor does the ratio give any clues as to likely earnings fluctuations that might affect current interest and principal payments.

Debt to Capitalization. A more refined version of debt proportion analysis involves the ratio of *long-term debt* to *capitalization.* The latter is again defined as the total long-term claims against the business, both debt and owners' equity, but does not include short-term (current) liabilities. This total also corresponds to net assets, unless some adjustments are made, such as ignoring deferred taxes. The calculation appears as follows:

$$\frac{\text{Long-term debt}}{\text{Capitalization (net assets)}} = \frac{\$3,955}{\$41,201} = 9.6\% \quad (1984: 9.9\%)$$

A great deal of emphasis is placed on this particular ratio, because many lending agreements of both publicly held and private corporations contain covenants regulating maximum debt exposure in terms of debt to capitalization. As we shall see later, however, there is growing emphasis on a more relevant aspect of debt exposure, namely, the ability to *service* the debt from ongoing funds flows.

Debt to Equity. A third version of debt proportion analysis involves the ratio of *total debt,* normally the sum of current liabilities and all types of long-term debt, to total *owners' equity,* or *net worth.* The debt to equity ratio is an attempt to show, in another form, the relative proportions of lenders' claims and of ownership claims, and is used as a measure of debt exposure. It is expressed as either a percentage or as a proportion. In the example shown, the figures again were taken from IBM's balance sheet in Figure 1–11:

$$\frac{\text{Total debt}}{\text{Net worth (equity)}} = \frac{\$20,644}{\$31,990} = 64.5\% \quad (1984: 61.6\%)$$

In preparing this ratio, as in some earlier instances, the question of deferred income taxes is often sidestepped by leaving this long-term claim out of the capitalization figure. We have included it here. One specific refinement of this formula uses only *long-term debt,* as related to *net worth,* while another refinement adjusts the calculation to express *long-term debt* as a proportion of total *capitalization*.

$$\frac{\text{Long-term debt}}{\text{Net worth (equity)}} = \frac{\$3,955}{\$31,990} = 12.4\% \quad (1984: 12.3\%)$$

or

$$\frac{\text{Long-term debt}}{\text{Capitalization} - \text{Long-term debt}} =$$

$$\frac{\$3,955}{\$41,201 - \$3,955} = 10.6\% \quad (1984: 10.9\%)$$

In the latter calculation, such elements as deferred income taxes and a variety of other special claims might or might not be included. We have again included them here.

Debt Service.   Regardless of the specific choice from among the several ratios we just discussed, debt proportion analysis is in essence *static* and does not take into account the operating dynamics and economic values of the business. The analysis is totally derived from the balance sheet, which in itself is a static snapshot of the financial condition of the business at a single point in time.

Nonetheless, the relative ease with which these ratios are calculated probably accounts for their popularity. Such ratios are useful as indicators of trends when they are applied over a long period of time. However, they still do not get at the heart of an analysis of debt-worthiness, which involves a company's ability to pay both interest and principal on schedule as contractually agreed upon, that is, to service its debt.

Interest Coverage.   One very frequently encountered ratio reflecting a company's debt service uses the relationship of *net profit (earnings) before interest and taxes* (EBIT) to the amount of the *interest payments* for the period. This ratio is developed with the expectation that annual operating earnings can be considered a basic source of funds for debt service, and that any significant change in this relationship might signal difficulties. Major earnings fluctuations are one type of risk considered. No hard-and-fast standards for the ratio itself exist; rather, the prospective debtholders often require covenants in the loan agreement spelling out the number of times the business is expected to cover its debt service obligations. The ratio is simple to calculate:

$$\frac{\text{Net profit before interest and taxes (EBIT)}}{\text{Interest}} = \frac{\$12{,}062}{\$443} = 27.2 \text{ times}$$
$$(1984: 29.5 \text{ times})$$

The specifics are based on judgment, often involving a detailed analysis of a company's past, current, and prospective conditions.

Interest and Principal Coverage. A somewhat more refined analysis of debt coverage relates the *net profit* of the business, *before interest and taxes,* to the sum of current *interest and principal repayments,* in an attempt to indicate the company's ability to service its debt. A problem arises with this particular analysis, because interest payments are tax deductible, while principal repayments are not. Thus we must guard against thinking about these figures on a *comparable* basis. One correction used involves converting the principal repayments into an equivalent pretax amount. This is done by dividing the principal repayment by the factor 1 minus the tax rate. The resulting calculation appears as follows:

$$\frac{\text{Net profit before interest and taxes (EBIT)}}{\text{Interest} + \dfrac{\text{Principal repayments}}{(1 - \text{tax rate})}} =$$

$$\frac{\$12{,}062}{\$443 + \dfrac{\$473^{*}}{(1 - .436)}} =$$

$$\frac{\$12{,}062}{\$443 + \$839} = 9.4 \text{ times} \qquad (1984: 9.2 \text{ times})$$

*Repayment obligations listed in supplementary data of annual report.

Another format uses operating cash flow (net profit after taxes plus write-offs), taken from Figure 1–12, to which aftertax interest has been added back. This is then compared to the sum of aftertax interest and principal repayment:

$$\frac{\text{Operating cash flow} + \text{interest (1 minus tax rate)}}{\text{Interest (1 } - \text{ tax rate)} + \text{Principal repayments}} =$$

$$\frac{\$9,874^* + \$443(.564)}{\$443(.564) + \$473} = \frac{\$10,124}{\$723} = 14.0 \text{ times} \quad (1984: \\ 13.6 \text{ times})$$

*$6,555 + $2,894 + $425.

Analysis of a company's ability to meet its debt obligations is most meaningful when a review of past profit and cash flow patterns is made over a long enough period of time to indicate the major operational and cyclical fluctuations that are normal for the company and its industry. This may involve financial statements covering several years or several seasonal swings, as appropriate, in an attempt to identify characteristic high and low points in earnings and funds needs. The pattern of past conditions can then be projected into the future to see what margin of safety remains to cover interest, principal repayments, and other fixed payments, such as major lease obligations.

If a business is subject to sizable fluctuations in aftertax cash flow, lenders may be reluctant to extend credit when the debt service cannot be covered several times at the low point in the operational pattern. In contrast, a very stable business would encounter less stringent coverage demands. The type of *dynamic* analysis involved is presented in Chapters 2, 3, and 4. It is a form of financial modeling that can be greatly enhanced both in scope and in the number of possible alternative conditions explored by using computer spreadsheets.

RATIOS AS A SYSTEM

The ratios discussed in this chapter have many elements in common, as they are derived from key components of the same financial statements. In fact, they are often interrelated and can be viewed as a system. Thus, their usefulness lies in the analysts' ability to turn a series of ratios into a dynamic display highlighting the elements that are the important *levers* used by management to affect operating performance. In internal analysis, many companies employ systems of ratios and standards that segregate into their components the series of decisions affecting operating performance, overall returns, and shareholder expectations. DuPont was one of the first to do so. Many years ago that company published a chart showing the effects and interrelationships of decisions in these areas, the first "model" of the business.

We will demonstrate the relationships between the ratios discussed using two key parameters segregated into their elements: **return on assets,** which is of major importance for judgment management performance, and **return on equity,** which serves as the key measure from the owners' viewpoint. We will leave aside the refinements applicable to each to concentrate on the *linkages.* As will be demonstrated, it is possible to model the performance of a given company by expanding and relating these ratios.

Elements of Return on Assets

The basic formula for return on assets (ROA) was:

$$\text{Return on assets} = \frac{\text{Net profit}}{\text{Assets}}$$

We also know that net profit was related to asset turnover, and in a ratio to sales. Thus, it is possible to restate the formula as follows:

$$\text{Return on assets (ROA)} = \frac{\text{Net profit}}{\text{Sales}} \times \frac{\text{Sales}}{\text{Assets}}$$

Note that the element of sales cancels out in the second formula, resulting in the original expression. But we can further expand the relationship by substituting more elements in the basic equation:

$$\text{ROA} = \frac{(\text{Gross margin} - \text{expenses})(1 - \text{tax rate})}{\text{Price} \times \text{Volume}} \times$$

$$\frac{\text{Price} \times \text{Volume}}{\text{Fixed} + \text{Current} + \text{Other assets}}$$

We can see that the relationships expressed here serve as a simple model of key decision levers management can employ to improve return on assets. For example, *gross margin* improvement is important, as is *expense* control. *Price/volume* relationships are canceled out, but are important in arriving at gross margin, as we know. (The first bracket could have been expanded to include this element.) *Asset management* is very important, because the return on assets will rise if fewer assets are employed and all the measures of effective management of working capital apply. Minimizing *taxes* within the legal options available will also improve the return.

Elements of Return on Equity

A similar approach can be taken with the basic formula for return on owners' equity:

$$\text{Return on equity} = \frac{\text{Net profit}}{\text{Equity}}$$

If we use some of the known relationships to expand the expression, the following formula emerges:

$$\text{Return on equity} = \frac{\text{Net profit}}{\text{Assets}} \times \frac{\text{Assets}}{\text{Equity}}$$

Note that in effect, the formula states that return on equity (ROE) consists of two elements: the net profit on assets and the degree of leverage or debt capital in the business. "Assets to equity" is a way of describing this proportion.

We can expand the formula even more to include components of the return on assets:

$$\text{ROA} = \frac{\text{Net profit}}{\text{Sales}} \times \frac{\text{Sales}}{\text{Assets}} \times \frac{\text{Assets}}{\text{Assets} - \text{Liabilities}}$$

Now we can again look for the key decision levers that management should use to raise the return on owners' equity. As before, improving profitability of sales (operations) comes first, combined with effective use of assets that generate sales. The added factor is the boosting effect given by debt in the capital structure. The greater the liabilities, the greater the improvement in return on equity—assuming, of course, that the business is profitable to begin with. Using other people's money is helpful until the risk of default on debt service in a down cycle becomes significant. The analyst can use this simple framework to test the impact on return of one or more changed conditions, and to test how sensitive the result is to the magnitude of change introduced.

We will return to the subject of business modeling again in Chapters 3 and 4.

IMPACT OF INFLATION

The extreme inflationary conditions in the United States beginning in the early 1970s resulted in significant distortions in many of the calculations we discussed. (Many other countries have, of course, had to deal with far more insidious levels of inflation for much longer periods of time.) In the United States, the accounting profession and the Securities and Exchange Commission have expended much effort in developing new ways to account for and disclose the impact of changes in prices of goods and services and of fluctuating exchange rates due in part to inflation. However, the intricacies and arguments abundant in this difficult area are beyond the scope of this book. We will only discuss a few of the basic mechanisms commonly employed to deal with price level changes where this is necessary to understand the impact on financial analysis. Thus, Chapters 2, 3, and 8 contain a discussion of essential price level adjustments pertaining to the subjects of operating funds management, projections, and valuation. Appendix I contains a discussion of the basic concepts underlying the inflation phenomenon.

In performance analysis, the main problem associated with inflation is the use of *historical costing* as a generally accepted accounting principle. The original cost of assets utilized in and charged to operations is reflected on the balance sheet. Depreciation and amortization reflect past values, which are often lower than current values. Financial statements of particularly heavily capitalized industries with long-lived depreciable assets and physical resources tend to overstate profits and taxes, and understate asset values. This raises the issue of comparability of companies of different ages, and certainly of comparability of whole industries. Even short-term fluctuations in values will affect companies with high inventory turnover, such as wholesalers.

Another area of distortion affects the *viewpoint of the lender.* In inflationary times, the declining value of currency will affect borrowing/lending relationships because eventual repayment will be made in less valuable dollars. Thus, the lender would be at a disadvantage unless the interest rate contracted for is high enough to offset this risk. The rise in the 1970s and fall in the 1980s of short- and long-term interest rates in response to growing and waning inflationary pressures will remain in creditors' memories, particularly long-term lenders.

Among the many methods used to deal with price level changes are replacement cost accounting, new forms of inventory valuation, and partial or full periodic restatement of financial reports. In fact, inflation has turned the deceptively simple accounting principle of matching costs and revenues into an economic and intellectual challenge. The most recent required addition to the financial statements of major corporations is a *restatement* of certain highlights of the operating statement in terms of inflation-adjusted data. An example is the statement from IBM's 1985 Annual Report, reproduced in Figure 1–13. As yet, there are no consistent ways of appraising the difference between this type of recast statement and the original accounting statements.

Figure 1–13
INTERNATIONAL BUSINESS MACHINES CORPORATION AND SUBSIDIARY COMPANIES
Consolidated Operating Statement
For Years Ending December 31
($ millions)

Information on the Effects of Changing Prices

Although inflation-adjusted information is an imprecise estimate, there are circumstances in which it can serve to emphasize the debilitating effects of inflation. It points out the importance of keeping inflation under control and sustaining public policy initiatives to encourage capital investment.

Rates of inflation continued to moderate in the United States and in many other countries throughout 1985. Despite this current positive trend, the cumulative effect of inflation over the past several years has generally eroded industry's ability to fund the replacement and expansion of productive capacity. This has not been the case with IBM.

The following supplemental information, which has been prepared in accordance with standards established by the Financial Accounting Standards Board, is intended to assist users of financial statements in understanding the impact of changing prices on the company's operations.

The data presented below reflect the effects on earnings and stockholders' equity resulting from using estimated changes in specific prices to restate the value of inventories and other properties at currently prevailing prices (current cost).

The estimates are based upon latest production costs, published price indexes, current suppliers' prices and appraised valuations. Cost of sales and depreciation expense are restated to reflect the change in the related asset values.

Discussion of Financial Results

IBM's 1985 financial results, which adjusted for changing prices, show a reduction of $246 million from reported net earnings and an increase in stockholders' equity of $2,648 million. The decrease in earnings results principally from increased depreciation expense of $270 million on plant, rental machines, and other property that have been valued at $22,487 million to approximate current cost. Current inventories have been valued at $8,480 million on a current cost basis.

Companies which retain monetary assets or liabilities, such as cash or debt, incur gains and losses in purchasing power during periods of inflation. IBM's net monetary asset position resulted in a purchasing power loss of $124 million in 1985.

The effects of translation on the changes in specific prices of IBM's net assets have been estimated without any attempt to adjust the data for general rate of inflation differences among various countries. The translation adjustments reflect changes in the valuation of assets denominated in currencies other than the U.S. dollar which result from exchange rate fluctuations.

In dollars of average 1985 purchasing power, the increase in current costs that might have been expected from general inflation exceeded IBM's specific price level changes by $838 million. Management views this positively, in that technology and productivity improvements substantially offset inflation. Similar patterns are reflected in the prior years.

Comparison of Selected Financial Data Adjusted for Changes in Specific Prices (Current Cost)

(Dollars in millions except per share amounts)	As Reported in Financial Statements 1985	In Average 1985 Dollars				
		1985	1984	1983	1982	1981
Gross income from sales, services and rentals	$50,056	$50,056	$47,576	$43,385	$38,298	$34,384
Cost of sales, services and rentals	21,103	21,156	19,762	17,916	15,355	14,151
Expenses and other income	17,334	17,527	16,084	15,118	14,038	13,001
Provision for income taxes	5,064	5,064	5,221	4,811	4,251	3,371
Net earnings	$ 6,555	$ 6,309	$ 6,509	$ 5,540	$ 4,654	$ 3,861
Loss from decline in purchasing power of net monetary assets		$ 124	$ 130	$ 83	$ 1	$ 74
Translation adjustments	$ 1,482	$ 1,597	$(1,075)	$ (976)	$ (866)	$(1,178)
Change in specific prices—net of general inflation		$ (838)	$ (707)	$ (78)	$ (342)	$(1,373)
Stockholders' equity (net assets) at December 31	$31,990	$34,638	$30,241	$28,156	$25,272	$23,360
Per share information:						
Earnings per share	$ 10.67	$ 10.27	$ 10.65	$ 9.13	$ 7.81	$ 6.57
Cash dividends per share	$ 4.40	$ 4.40	$ 4.25	$ 4.01	$ 3.83	$ 4.07
Market price at December 31		$155.50	$127.52	$131.73	$107.28	$ 67.28
Average consumer price index for all urban consumers (1967 = 100.0)		322.2	311.1	298.4	289.1	272.4

*Source: From IBM 1985 Annual Report.
The actual market price of IBM stock at December 31, for years 1981 to 1985 was $56.88, $96.25, $122.00, $123.13, and $155.50 respectively.

SUMMARY

In this chapter, we discussed essential aspects of the main **financial statements** as a basis for appraising business performance. With this background, we demonstrated that the assessment of performance is made meaningful when seen from the **points of view** of the key groups interested in the company's success.

We chose to concentrate on the particular viewpoints of three groups—**management, owners, and lenders**—which are essential to the functioning of the business. The insights of these groups are used and expanded by others for their own particular needs. All three groups are concerned about the success of the business, each from its own standpoint.

It is management's prime duty to bring about stability, growth, and reliable earnings performance with the investment entrusted to it by the owners. We found that within the wide range of ratios displayed, the crucial test is the **economic return** on the **capital** employed in the business and its attendant effect on the **value of the ownership stake.** We also found that the ratios are **linked** by their common information base, and many are directly connected through the common use of certain elements. They are best interpreted when the business is viewed as a system of interdependent conditions responding to the decisions of management. To this end, modeling and computer simulation are increasingly accepted and meaningful, because many individual ratios are, by their nature, only **static** tests that cannot do justice to the dynamics of a business.

Shortcomings in the analysis relate to the limitations of the **accounting principles** commonly used, and further distortions are introduced through **price level changes** stemming from inflation, currency fluctuations, and economic changes. No definitive ways of compensating for these problems have as yet been found to make financial analyses comparable and economically meaningful. As a result, the analyst must use **judgment.**

APPENDIX: PERSPECTIVE ON IBM

The data for IBM which we have used in this chapter and the one that follows should be put into a somewhat wider perspective. IBM has literally emerged as the world's most profitable industrial company. Founded in 1914, it has been experiencing surging growth, particularly since the 1950s. Its rapid expansion in one of today's fastest-growing business segments—computers and information handling—has led to a doubling of IBM's sales volume *and* net profit every five to six years, which is a compound annual rate of growth of about 15 percent.

IBM's worldwide market share for large computer systems was 62.6 percent in 1985, followed by Burroughs (6.5 percent), Sperry (6.1 percent), and Digital Equipment (2.8 percent). In small computer systems, IBM led the market in 1985 with 20 percent, followed by Digital Equipment (12.7 percent), Nixdorf (6 percent), and Hewlett-Packard (5.8 percent). In microsystems, which include personal computers, IBM was first with 27.7 percent, following by Apple (9 percent), Commodore (4.2 percent) and Hewlett-Packard (4.2 percent). (AT&T had a minor share in the last segment.)

While IBM now ranks among the largest industrial companies, its performance likewise stands out by any measure. In Figure 1–14 we have provided a comparison of IBM's key dimensions and ratios with those of two of its smaller competitors, Digital Equipment Corp. and Apple, and with four of the largest American companies. The data speak for themselves.

Figure 1–14
1985 Comparative Dimensions and Measures
($ millions)

	IBM	Digital Equipment	Apple	General Motors	General Electric	Du Pont	U.S. Steel*
KEY DIMENSIONS							
Net sales	$50,056	$ 6,686	$ 1,918	$96,372	$28,285	$29,483	$19,283
Net profit	6,555	383	61	3,999	2,336	1,100	313
Net worth	31,990	4,555	550	29,334	13,904	12,659	6,555
Long-term debt	3,955	837	None	2,867	753	3,284	5,448
Working capital	14,637	3,694	527	1,958	3,627	3,565	380
Total assets	52,634	6,369	936	63,833	26,432	25,140	18,446
R & D expenditures	4,700	725	73	3,625	1,075	1,150	54
Capital expenditures	6,430	575	54	6,100	2,050	3,050	1,200
No. of employees	395,000	89,000	4,200	811,000	330,000	158,000	89,000
No. of shareholders	793,000	74,835	45,000	2 million	511,000	242,000	203,000
KEY MEASURES							
•Management viewpoint							
Operating margin	28.5%	11.4%	9.9%	7.3%	14.7%	25.8%	13.7%
Profit margin	13.1%	5.7%	7.5%	4.1%	8.3%	3.7%	1.6%
Return on net assets	15.9%	7.1%	9.6%	9.6%	13.3%	5.5%	2.1%
Net asset turnover	1.21 X	1.23 X	2.99 X	2.32 X	1.62 X	1.49 X	1.30 X

Owners' viewpoint							
Return on net worth	22.4%	8.4%	11.1%	13.6%	16.8%	9.7%	4.8%
Earnings per share	$10.67	$3.18	$0.90	$12.28	$5.13	$4.52	$1.71
Cashflow per share	$15.70	$5.89	$1.67	$21.40	$7.81	$12.50	$12.04
Dividends per share	$4.40	none	none	$5.00	$2.23	$3.00	$1.10
Dividend yield	3.3%	—	—	6.9%	3.6%	5.2%	3.9%
Payout ratio	41%	—	—	40%	43%	65%	64%
Average annual P/E	12.4×	15.9×	22.1×	5.9×	12.1×	12.7×	16.4×
Book value per share	$52.09	$38.43	$8.90	$84.85	$30.49	$51.62	$43.80
1985 price range	158.8–117.4	68.4–47.7	31.1–14.3	85.0–68.4	73.9–55.6	69.4–47.6	33.0–24.4
Total Market Value 3/86	$91.7 billion	$9.6 billion	$1.7 billion	$26.5 billion	$34.6 billion	$17.4 billion	$2.8 billion
Lenders' Viewpoint							
Current ratio	2.3:1	4.3:1	3.1:1	1.09:1	1.4:1	1.7:1	1.1:1
Debt to assets	39.2%	28.1%	—	53.7%	46.9%	49.3%	63.9%
Debt to capital	9.6%	15.6%	—	28.9%	19.9%	28.2%	55.2%
Debt to equity	10.6%	18.4%	—	41.0%	25.0%	56.4%	125.2%
Interest coverage	27.2×	6.7×	—	5.9×	10×	7.7×	2.0×
	(Fiscal year ends 6/30)	(Fiscal year ends 6/30)	(Fiscal year ends 9/30)				

*Now USX

SELECTED REFERENCES

Anthony, Robert N., and Reece, James S. *Accounting: Text and Cases.* 6th ed. Homewood, Ill.: Richard D. Irwin, 1979.

Bernstein, Leopold A. *Financial Statement Analysis: Theory, Application, and Interpretation.* Rev. ed. Homewood, Ill.: Richard D. Irwin, 1978.

Graham, Benjamin. *The Interpretation of Financial Statements.* 3rd ed. New York: Harper & Row, 1975.

Robert Morris Associates. *Annual Statement Studies.*

Dun & Bradstreet. *Industry Norms and Key Business Ratios.*

Troy, Leo. *Almanac of Business and Industrial Financial Ratios.* Englewood Cliffs, N.J.: Prentice-Hall.

Van Horne, James C. *Financial Management and Policy.* 7th ed. Englewood Cliffs, N.J.: Prentice-Hall, 1986.

Viscione, Jerry A. *Financial Analysis—Principles and Procedures.* Boston: Basic Books, 1976.

Weston, J. Fred, and Copeland, Thomas E. *Managerial Finance.* 8th ed. Hinsdale, Ill.: Dryden Press, 1986.

Fraser, Lyn M. *Understanding Financial Statements: Through the Maze of a Corporate Annual Report.* Reston, Va.: Reston Publishing, 1985.

Brealey, Richard, and Myers, Stuart. *Principles of Corporate Finance.* 2nd ed. New York: McGraw-Hill, 1984, chap. 25.

SELF-STUDY EXERCISES AND PROBLEMS

(Solutions to Items 1 and 2 are provided in Appendix III)

1. Work the following exercises:
    a. A company has achieved a 1987 net profit which represents 11.4 percent of net sales. What is the company's return on net worth if asset turnover is 1.34 and the capitalization is 67 percent of total assets? How would a faster asset turnover affect the result?
    b. A company's gross margin on sales for 1987 is 31.4 percent. Total cost of goods sold amounted to $4,391,300, and net profit was 9.7 percent of sales. What are the company's total assets if the ratio of sales to assets is 82.7 percent? What is the return on capitalization if current liabilities are 21 percent of total assets?

c. What is the change in a company's current ratio of 2.2:1 (current assets are $573,100) if the following actions are taken individually? Also, how does each item affect working capital?

The company:

1. Pays $67,500 of accounts payable with cash.
2. Collects $33,000 in notes receivable.
3. Purchases merchandise worth $41,300 on account.
4. Pays dividends of $60,000, of which $42,000 had been shown as accrued (an unpaid current liability).
5. Sells machine for $80,000, on which book value is $90,000 and accumulated depreciation is $112,000.
6. Sells merchandise on account which cost $73,500. Gross margin is 33 percent.
7. Writes off $20,000 from inventory as scrap and amortizes $15,000 of goodwill.

d. From the following data calculate the outstanding days' receivables and payables for a company, using the methods shown in the chapter. What is the inventory turnover, calculated in different ways? Discuss your assumptions.

Sales for three months	$437,500
Cost of sales	298,400
Purchases	143,500
Beginning inventory	382,200
Ending inventory	227,300
Accounts receivable	156,800
Accounts payable	69,300
Normal sales terms	2/10,n/30
Normal purchase terms	n/45

2. From the following financial statement of the ABC Company for 1986 and 1987, prepare the ratios and measures discussed in this chapter.

   a. Ratios from the viewpoint of management.
   b. Ratios from the viewpoint of owners.
   c. Ratios from the viewpoint of lenders.

Comment on the changes shown between the two years, and discuss the significance of the results from the three points of view. Indicate which additional kinds of comparison you would like to make for this company, a manufacturer of electronics, and the type of information you would need.

ABC COMPANY
Balance Sheets
December 31, 1986, and 1987
($ millions)

	1986	1987
Assets		
Current assets:		
Cash	$ 82.7	$110.9
Accounts receivable (net)	92.6	146.2
Inventories	88.8	129.5
Prepaid expenses	2.8	6.2
Advances from government	5.3	2.8
Total current assets	272.2	395.6
Property, plant, and equipment	215.2	283.4
Less: Accumulated depreciation	101.2	119.6
Net property	114.0	163.8
Other assets	3.1	4.2
Total assets	$389.3	$563.6
Liabilities and Net Worth		
Current liabilities:		
Accounts payable	$ 43.4	$ 62.9
Accrued income tax	36.7	44.0
Accrued pension and profit sharing	27.1	38.4
Other accruals	21.9	31.2
Current portion of long-term debt	2.1	—
Total current liabilities	131.2	176.5
Debentures (9% due 1989)	—	94.0
Other long-term debt	7.8	4.1
Deferred income tax	5.2	7.6
Common stock ($1 par)	10.1	10.2
Paid-in surplus	25.1	27.2
Earned surplus	209.9	244.0
Total liabilities and net worth	$389.3	$563.6

ABC COMPANY
Operating Statements for 1986 and 1987
($ millions)

	1986	1987
Assets		
Net sales	$655.1	$872.7
Cost of goods and services*	460.9	616.1
Gross profit	194.2	256.6
Selling, general, and administrative expenses	98.3	125.2
Employee profit sharing and retirement	26.9	38.7
	125.2	163.9
Operating profit	69.0	92.7
Other income	1.1	1.8
	70.1	94.5
Interest paid	1.0	7.4
	69.1	87.1
Provision for income taxes	31.8	40.1
Net profit†	$ 37.3	$ 47.0
	1986	1987
*Depreciation and amortization	$28.2	$38.5
†Common dividends paid	5.5	6.0

3. Select a major manufacturing company, a retailing firm, a public utility, a bank, and a transportation firm. From an information source like
   Moody's or Standard & Poor's, develop a historical analysis of key measures you consider significant to appraise the effectiveness of management, the return to the owners, and the position of the lenders. Develop
   significant industry comparisons and comment on the relative position
   of your chosen company. Also comment on some of the assumptions and
   choices you have to make on the selection of specific accounts and data
   to work the analytical techniques.

2 MANAGING OPERATING FUNDS

This chapter deals with the key issues surrounding the **flow of funds** through a business, that is the management of operating funds. The daily decisions made by management, in one form or another, affect the company's ability to pay its bills, obtain credit from suppliers and lenders, extend credit to its customers, and maintain a level of operations that matches the demand for the company's products or services. Every decision has a monetary impact on the ongoing *cycle* of uses or sources of funds. It is management's job to maintain an appropriate balance between the inflows and outflows of funds at all times, and to allow for any *changes* in operations, caused by management decisions or by outside influences, that may affect these flows.

Managing operating funds is critical to successful business performance. New businesses often find that balancing operating funds needs and sources is a struggle for plain survival. Yet, well-established companies likewise must devote much management time and effort to operational financing. As we shall see, proper management of operating funds requires an understanding of the **systems impact** of investment, operating, and financing decisions. It further requires insight into the effect of **different operating patterns** on funds uses and sources. Funds flows are affected differently depending on the nature of the operations, whether level, growing, or declining. Finally, one must be aware that short-term **working capital management** is *not independent* of the longer-term financial structure with which the business is funded. Funds sources and uses arise as a matter of course during operations that may affect long-term investments and long-term capital sources. For this reason, the chapter focuses on the broader issue of **operating funds management,** which *includes* the specific needs for working capital, but is not *limited* by the common definition of working capital as the *net* of current assets and liabilities.

In the first chapter we looked at a variety of performance measures drawn from financial statements, which are periodic summaries of financial condition and operating results. We hinted then that these summaries often *mask peaks and valleys* of funds movements—financing needs, for example—because these took place *during* the period covered by the statements. Obviously, management of a business is an *ongoing* day-to-day process. In this chapter, we will examine how **funds** constantly **cycle** through a business, what the *implications* of these movements are, and how to identify the critical financial *variables* that must be weighed in making daily operating decisions. We will demonstrate the funds impact of **variability of operations** in different forms, and discuss key **accounting issues,** such as **inventory costing** and methods of **depreciation.** We will then return to the preparation and interpretation of **funds flow statements,** using our example of IBM's 1984 and 1985 performance, and examine the major types of analytical steps needed to make funds flow statements meaningful.

FUNDS FLOW CYCLES

Businesses vary widely in orientation, size, structure, and products or services, but they all experience *operating funds cycles* in their own fashion. Even a solitary ice cream vendor selling cones for cash has to provide an inventory on wheels which is slowly converted into cash as the day progresses. He invested his own cash at the beginning of the day to purchase the ice cream from his supplier and hopes to recoup it with a markup for profit at the end of the day. If he was short of cash, he may even have signed an IOU at the supplier's, promising to pay for the inventory after he sells it. In any event, his cycle is a short one. An initial investment in inventory, funded with cash or credit, is followed by cash sales during the day, which build up his cash balance for the next day's operations. In the morning he will either use the cash to replenish his inventory, or pay off the supplier so that he will be extended credit for the next cycle. Any profit above the cost of the goods sold will be his to keep or to invest in more inventory.

The funds cycles of larger and more structured businesses differ only in complexity, not in concept. Even for the largest conglomerate, the ultimate form of settlement of a transaction is *cash*. Meanwhile, however, the operational funds cycle involves a great variety of partially offsetting credit extensions, changes in inventories, transformation of assets, etc., that *precede* the cash collections or payments. In essence, the funds cycle arises because of a series of *lags* in the timing of business transactions. Our ice cream vendor has a lag of a few hours between the buildup of his inventory and its ultimate conversion into cash through many small transactions. A large manufacturer may have a lag of months between the time a product is made in the factory and the ultimate collection of the selling price from customers who purchased on credit. Management must always *plan for* and find *financing for the funds tied up* because of these lags.

To illustrate the nature of the concept, we will explore in some detail the funds cycle of a simplified *manufacturing* operation and the funds cycle for *selling* the products. We have separated the two processes for purposes of discussion, even though the funds cycles are *intertwined* in an ongoing business that both produces and sells products. The sales cycle *alone*, of course, applies to any retail, wholesale, or trading operation purchasing goods for resale.

The Funds Cycle for Manufacturing

For purposes of illustration, we will assume that the Widget Manufacturing Company has just begun operations and is going to produce widgets for eventual sale. Figure 2–1 shows the company's funds flow cycle. We have presented this in terms of the three decision areas discussed in Chapter 1. As we can see, the company was initially financed through owners' equity, long-term debt, and short-term debt of three kinds: (1) accounts payable due vendors of materials and supplies, (2) some short-term loans from banks, and (3) other current liabilities that have accrued. The investments made are fixed assets (i.e., plant facilities), other assets (i.e., patents and licenses), and three kinds of current assets: (1) cash, (2) raw materials inventory, and (3) finished goods inventory. The last of these is, of course, nonexistent until the plant starts producing.

We can assume that long-term debt and owners' equity are the logical sources for funds for the plant and equipment, while the short-term loan most likely provided the cash needed to start operations. Materials and supplies were bought on credit from the vendors.

Figure 2–1
Funds Flow Cycle for Manufacturing

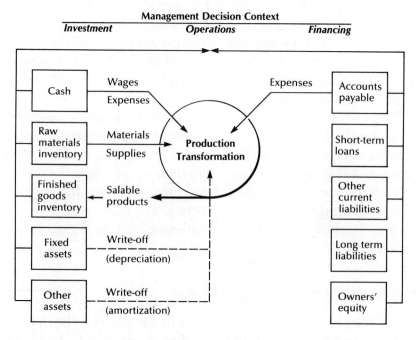

As production begins, a *transformation* process takes place. Some of the cash is used to pay weekly wages and various on-going expenses. Materials and supplies are withdrawn from inventory to be used in manufacture. Some operating inputs, like power and fuel, are obtained on credit, and are temporarily financed through accounts payable. Depreciation for the use of the plant and equipment is charged against the transformation process through an accounting write-off, and licenses are similarly amortized. As widgets are finished on the factory floor, they are moved into the warehouse and are reflected in the finished goods inventory account.

In the *absence* of sales, the production process continuously transforms cash, raw materials, and some trade credit into a growing buildup of finished goods inventory. A fraction of fixed and other assets is also transformed into finished goods—even though no funds are moved—by means of an *accounting write-off* which only affects the books.

What are the financial implications of this transformation? From the time the business was originally set up, the operational funds flow has only affected the *working capital* accounts. Cash and raw materials, which were *sources* of funds, have been drawn down. An additional source has been found in trade credit. The major *use* of the funds has been to build up finished goods inventory. Unless the company can eventually turn these finished goods into *cash* through sale to its customers, the continued inventory buildup will drain the cash and raw material accounts. These would have to be replenished by new infusions of credit or owners' equity or both. Adding to the cash drain is the obligation to at some point begin repayment of accounts payable for trade credit incurred, usually 30 or 45 days from the invoice date.

From a funds flow standpoint, several *timing lags* are significant in our example. First, a *supply* of raw materials sufficient for several days of operation has to be kept on hand to ensure uninterrupted manufacturing. Next there is a *physical* lag in the number of days required to produce a widget, which involves buildup of an inventory of work in process, that is, widgets in various stages of completion. Last, a sufficient number of widgets must be produced and kept continually in finished goods inventory to support an ongoing sales effort. The *total* of these lags has to be financed through funds provided by owners and creditors on a continuous basis. Offsetting this funds use, in part, is the length of time *credit* is extended by the suppliers. This is a favorable lag, because purchases of raw material and supplies, as well as certain other expenses, will be financed by the vendors for 30 or 45 days, or for whatever length of time is common practice in the industry. With ongoing operations, *new* credit will continue to be extended as repayments are made.

As we observed before, however, the buildup of finished goods in the warehouse cannot go on indefinitely, and *sales revenues* will be essential to replenish the cash needed for settling obligations as they become due. Thus, we must examine the funds implications of the selling process to complete the picture.

The Funds Cycle for Sales

The funds flows connected with selling the widgets produced can also be examined in terms of our decisional framework, as shown in Figure 2–2. Operations now include the main accounts in the operating statement, *sales, cost of goods sold, selling expenses,* and *net income.*

The selling cycle is based on another major *lag,* which results from the *extension of credit* to the company's customers. If the widgets were sold for cash, receipt would be instantaneous. With the extension of normal trade credit, however, the company has to *await* the collection of *accounts receivable* after 30, 45, or whatever number of days is usual in the industry. This lag, like the ones in production, has to be financed *continuously,* because for any given sales volume, an equivalent value of 30, 40, or 50 days' worth of sales will be outstanding. As collection takes place, *new* credit is extended, just as was the case with the vendors supplying the company.

Figure 2–2
Funds Flow Cycle for Sales

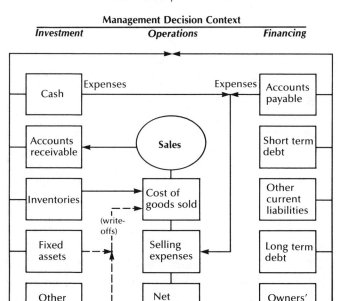

Cost of goods sold is the value of the widgets withdrawn from finished goods inventory, each of which represents a share of the labor, raw material, overhead, and other costs expended in its manufacture. *Selling expenses,* which consist of the salaries of the sales force, the marketing support staff, and advertising and promotional costs will be paid partly in cash, partly on credit. After these costs and expenses have been subtracted from sales revenue, the resulting *net income*, subject to taxes to be paid, will increase the owners' equity.

What are the funds flow implications of this picture? First of all, assuming that the company is maintaining a *level* volume of sales and manufacturing operations, management must plan for *continuous* commitment of funds invested in *working capital*, as well as for obtaining the funds necessary for *expenditures* on fixed and other assets supporting operations, and for *repayment* of debt. Sufficient funds have to be committed for raw materials and work in process to carry on production, for finished goods to support smooth sales and deliveries, and for accounts receivable to permit proper credit extension to customers. Finally, a minimum level of cash must be maintained for punctual payment of currently due obligations.

The sources of this financing will come only in part from *accounts payable*, which can support a level of raw materials, supplies, and ongoing operating expenses in line with the normal number of days' credit extended by the suppliers. The difference between the amount represented by inventories and receivables, and accounts payable must come from funds sources that are relatively permanent, such as *long-term debt* and *owners' equity.*

The dynamics of the system are such that the need for working capital funds is *constant* as long as the business operates on a *sustained* level. The amount will change, as we shall see, when operating conditions themselves change.

VARIABILITY OF FUNDS FLOWS

So far we have assumed that our company, after start-up, has reached a fairly steady level of operations. Under these conditions, the funds cycle is also *stable.* Unless there are significant changes in operating conditions or in the marketplace, the financing needed to support operations will remain a function of effective *inventory management*, sound customer *credit management*, and the prudent use of *supplier credit*, as well as reliable relations with other *lenders*, such as banks. Clearly, any worsening in collections from customers, or tightening of credit terms extended by suppliers or lenders will increase the continuous financing needed.

Rarely does a company enjoy the steady state that has made financing so predictable in our example. In reality, several major external and internal factors can affect a business. Major external forces include *seasonal* variations and *cyclical* movements in the economy. Major internal forces, among others, encompass management's ability to seize opportunities for *growth,* or inability to stem a *decline* in the company's volume of operations. Each of these conditions has its own particular implications in terms of funds flow.

Seasonal Variations

A fairly large number of industries experience distinct seasonal operating patterns, that is, specific months or weeks of high sales, followed by an often dramatic decline in demand. These ups and downs repeat themselves quite predictably. Examples are most common in retailing operations, many of which are geared to special holiday periods or specific customer segments with seasonal style or gift requirements. Producers of seasonal items like snowmobiles or bathing suits will experience high fluctuations in demand. Another seasonal pattern affects canneries that process specific crops or other seasonal foods.

Common to all seasonal businesses is a funds cycle with *large swings* over a *short period* of a year or less. The implications for management are quite obvious. During the low point of demand, ongoing operations have to be supported (unless the business can be shut down, as are some seasonal resorts). In most cases, inventories are gradually built up, either through production or through purchase from suppliers. As was the case in our simple example earlier, funds for this will have to come from credit, loans, and even owner's equity. When sales activity begins, growing amounts of receivables have to be financed. It is not until the first receivables are collected that *cash* starts flowing back into the business. The lags are usually such that collection of the receivables from peak sales will occur well *after* the peak of funding requirements has occurred.

As a result, management must make several critical decisions, among them the size of the buildup of inventories relative to anticipated demand, the level of operating and other expenditures during the cycle, and the nature of the funding to finance the bulge in requirements. Allowances must be made for contingencies such as lower than expected demand or prices, or both, and delays in collection, when arranging for short-term financing. Otherwise the business could find itself strapped because its own obligations must be met before collections are made.

The reader will recall that in Chapter 1 we discussed applying turnover relationships and the "aging" of receivables to judge the effectiveness of asset use. Under highly seasonal conditions, these relationships are unstable because lags and surges in the accounts make ratio comparisons difficult. A more illuminating evaluation of a seasonal business comes from a month-to-month analysis of funds changes and a careful assessment of changes in the funds cycle from peak to peak or trough to trough, instead of arbitrary comparisons of year-end financial statements.

Cyclical Variations

A variant of the seasonal cycle is the *cyclical pattern of funds movements* which involves changes over several years. However, these general economic as well as specific industry cycles are long term and *not* as regular and predictable as seasonal variations. The economic swings that affect a business or industry tend to bring *many more variables* into play, such as changes in raw materials prices and availability, competitive conditions in the marketplace, capital investment needs, etc. Nevertheless, the principles we observed in dealing with the seasonal pattern apply here as well.

Funds lags during a cyclical upturn or downturn tend to be *magnified* by the lag in decision making as management tries to gauge, from its day-to-day experience, whether the economy is undergoing a long-term change. For example, a sudden *downturn* in housing construction will leave many producers and wholesalers of building materials with inventories in excess of slumping demand. As sales decrease, and the prices of lumber, plywood, and other commodities fall, management is faced with a funding crisis. Ongoing production operations will transform raw material into products that cannot be sold; thus, production must be curtailed. Lower volume and prices will decrease the eventual cash flow from current sales, while collections from past higher sales are going to run out. A cyclical downturn brings several management challenges: management must *know* that the turning point has come, *manage inventories* by curtailing purchases and production, and *cut ongoing costs* wherever possible. Careful management of *credit*, both extended and received, is another vital aspect.

In a cyclical *upswing*, lags in decision making may result in insufficient inventories and production. To compensate, extra shifts or outside purchases may be used at times, even though the costs incurred may be higher than normal. Growing sales will raise the amount of credit extended to customers. Thus, a cyclical boom will likely require the infusion of *additional capital* to provide the increased working capital needed to finance increased physical operations. This may involve additional investment in plant and facilities.

Overall it may be said that a cyclical upswing will require an increase in medium- to long-term financing to support added levels of working capital and other requirements, while a downswing will first result in rising inventories—until management can adjust its operations—and then release cash if working capital and production levels are carefully managed downward.

Growth/Decline Variations

It should now be clear that a business which is *growing successfully* must continually increase its funding of working capital and other expenditures, and these funds will be *permanently* tied up. Consider the following rules of thumb: If the business sells on 30-day credit, the value of each incremental layer of sales must be added to accounts receivable, equal to 30 days. Similarly, if the business turns over its inventory nine times per year, the value of the incremental cost of the goods sold must be added to inventories, equal to 40 days ($360 \div 9$).

Offsetting this additional use of funds, but *in part only*, will be the increase in accounts payable and other minor accruals as sources. The payables credit extension will amount to the equivalent value of the additional purchases for 30 days. Because the investment in accounts receivable and inventories is normally much more than *twice* the credit from payables and accruals, it is clear that successful *growth* means *extensive funding* of new working capital. To this need must be *added* the funds required for expansion of physical facilities. What should also be clear is that this funds use is *permanent* and *growing*, and must be financed over the *long term*—quite unlike the case with the seasonal business—through the use of owners' equity and long-term debt. Normally, reinvestment of profits is not sufficient, because in a fast-growth business, the contribution from the profit margin is commonly far outweighed by these funding demands. We will demonstrate this in greater detail in Chapter 4.

A business that *declines* in volume and is managed to undergo this shrinkage efficiently can become a strong *generator of cash*. Here the opposite of the growth situation prevails. As sales decline, management should deliberately adjust operations and inventories to the lower levels, thus *releasing* the funds that had been tied up in receivables and inventories. If this is done properly, the situation is analogous to that of the seasonal business, except that the release of funds will be much *slower*. If the decline is *not* managed properly, however, the specter of inventory markdowns, operating inefficiencies, and emergency actions will negatively affect the release of funds. Thus, the ability to release funds depends on the careful removal of layers of activity that no longer need to be supported. A proportional shrinkage of receivables and inventories, partly offset by declining payables, becomes the major potential cash source, apart from the disposal of other assets no longer needed.

In summary, variability in funds flows results from *external* conditions or *management actions*, or both. A business in a steady state has a *permanent* stock of working capital as well as fixed and other assets. As a general rule of thumb, the amount of funds tied up in current assets far exceeds trade credit sources and normal short-term borrowings. Thus, the introduction of any significant *variability* in the level of operations can cause major shifts in a company's financial condition from changes in *working capital* alone. In addition, funding for other needs must be superimposed on this pattern. In Chapter 3 we will discuss these issues in the context of the techniques of forecasting funds requirements.

Generalized Funds Flow Model

At this point it is useful once again to examine the overall relationships of funds movements in a generalized framework. In Figure 2–3 we have added flow lines which show the poten-

Figure 2–3
Generalized Funds Flow Diagram

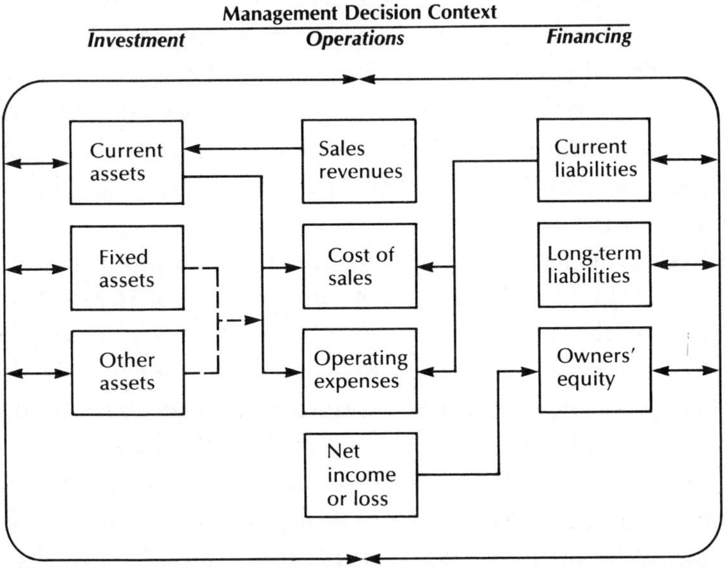

| Investments (increases) in all types of assets are uses of funds; reductions in assets are sources of funds. | Profitable operations are a source of funds; losses drain funds from the system. **Note:** Accounting write-offs do **not** affect funds and must be adjusted for. | Trade credit and new financing (increases in liabilities) are sources of funds; repayments, dividends and returns of capital are uses of funds. |

tial funds *movements* and the *linkages* between the main accounts of the balance sheet and operating statement. The diagram is applicable to any business, large or small. A summary
of *sources* and *uses* in terms of our management decision context is given at the bottom of the diagram.

This representation will be useful when we will discuss some
of the more technical aspects of constructing funds flow statements in the last section of this chapter.

Accounting Issues in Funds Flow

Several times in our discussion we commented on the impact
of accounting practices and decisions on the management of
funds. In Chapter 1 we mentioned accounting write-offs, inventory costing, and deferred taxes as issues that affect the
measures of performance analysis. At this point, it will be useful to refine our understanding of these issues a little further
because the possible alternative treatments of these matters at
times significantly affect the assessment of operations as well as
the patterns of funds created. Reviewing the key choices available to management in the areas of **inventory costing** and **depreciation methods** may help the reader in forming his or her
own judgments when faced with interpreting financial statements and funds flows.

Inventory Costing.   One accounting challenge present at
all times is the proper allocation of a portion of the costs accumulated in the inventory account to the actual goods being
sold. We can visualize layers of cost built up over time in the inventory account, which correspond to the physical movement
of raw materials, work in process, and finished goods into stor-
age. The accountant wants to *match revenues and expenses* in
the inventory account, yet from a physical standpoint, it is just
as possible to ship the oldest unit on hand as it is to ship the
most recent arrival. The warehouse supervisor can even pick
the goods at random.

If unit costs never changed, matching costs to revenues
would not be a problem, because the accountant would simply

track the number of units shipped and multiply them by the unchanged unit cost, regardless of the actual physical choices made by the warehouse supervisor. In real life, however, several problems arise. A manufacturing company may experience fluctuations that affect the *unit cost* of the products inventoried. This results in the *different layers of cost* in the inventory account. Further, the *prices* of raw materials and other inputs may be positively or negatively influenced by supply and demand. Again this affects the different layers of cost. Most cost-accounting systems provide for such variances to the extent they are predictable, but larger swings do affect costs. Finally, there is the impact of *general inflation*—or, more rarely, *deflation*. Inflation causes an upward trend in price levels for most goods and services that is brought about by monetary imbalances. The result is a weakening of the purchasing power of the currency. Under significant inflationary conditions, such as the United States experienced in the 1970s and early 1980s, prices tend to escalate above and beyond what actual supply/demand conditions for the item in question would dictate. The impact of inflation on inventories generally is a steady rise in the cost of the more recent additions, resulting in successive layers of escalating costs.

The accountant is therefore faced with a real problem in matching costs and revenues. If unit costs are growing significantly from period to period, deciding *which costs* to charge against the revenues for the same period can have significant effects on the financial statements. If the more "logical" method of removing the oldest units first is used, the oldest—and presumably lowest—unit costs will be charged against current revenues. Depending on how quickly the inventory turns over, such costs may *lag* current conditions by months and even years. Therefore, if price levels are rising, first-in, first-out inventory costing (FIFO) causes the profit on the income statement to be *higher* than it would be if current unit costs had been charged. At the same time, the balance sheet will reflect inventory values that are reasonably current, because the oldest, lowest-cost units are being removed.

If the opposite method is employed, that is last-in, first-out costing (LIFO), the income statement will be charged with current costs and thus reflect lower but more realistic profits. The balance sheet, however, will show inventory values that in time will be highly *understated*, because only the oldest and lowest layers of cost remain.

We could argue that the choice of methods does not really matter, because one of the financial statements will be distorted in *either* case. The question then becomes whether more realistic balance sheet values or more realistic reported profits are preferred. There is a significant *funds aspect*, however. The choice of methods affects the amount of *income taxes paid* for the period. The higher earnings under FIFO are taxed as income from operations, even though they contain a profit made from old inventories. Therefore, one criterion in making the choice is the difference in tax payments, which *does* affect the company's funds. LIFO is preferable from this standpoint, even though with continued inflation, inventory values stated on the balance sheet will become more and more obsolete. Yet surprisingly FIFO has remained a very common form of inventory costing, despite the fact that it can lead to a funds drain from higher tax payments. Apparently the higher reported *income* from FIFO is attractive enough to many managements to outweigh the actual tax disadvantage.

In contrast to other permissible choices of accounting methods for tax purposes, current federal tax laws do *not* allow the use of one inventory costing method for *tax calculation* and another for *bookkeeping and reporting*. Thus, the ideal combination of LIFO for tax purposes and FIFO for reporting earnings cannot be employed.

Trading firms, retailers, and manufacturing companies experiencing significant fluctuations in the current values of inventories often adjust inventory values, usually at year-end, using the conservative method of restating inventories at cost or market value, whichever is lower, and writing off the difference against current profits. Such periodic adjustments tend to *reduce* stated values, not raise them, and allow the company to reflect the negative effects of changed conditions so as not to overstate inventory values. Under inflationary conditions, this practice does not, of course, assist in resolving the inventory costing issues we have just discussed.

Depreciation Methods.   Depreciation is based on the accountant's desire to reflect as a charge against current operations some appropriate fraction of the cost of assets employed in producing revenues. Because physical assets other than land deteriorate with use and eventually wear out, the accounting challenge is to establish an appropriate period of time over which portions of the cost of the asset are charged against revenues. Moreover, the accountant has to decide on the pattern of the depreciation write-off, that is, level, declining, or variable depreciation. Another issue involves estimating any salvage value that may be realized at the end of an asset's useful life. Only the difference between asset cost and such salvage value is normally depreciated.

A similar rationale is applied to assets such as patents and licenses, which are *amortized* and charged against operations over an appropriate period of years, and to specialized assets such as mineral deposits and timber, on which *depletion* allowances are calculated.

In the case of physical assets, the depreciation write-off is shown as a charge in the operating statement, and is accumulated on the balance sheet as an offset to the fixed assets involved, in an account called *accumulated depreciation* or *reserve for depreciation*. Thus, over time, the original asset value stated on the balance sheet is reduced, as periodic charges are made against operations. For performance assessment, the significance of depreciation write-offs is in the *appropriateness* of the charges in light of the nature of the assets and industry conditions, and thus depreciation's impact on *profits* and *balance sheet values*. The significance for purposes of *funds* management involves the *tax impact* of depreciation. Under normal circumstances, depreciation is a tax-deductible expense, even though it is only an accounting allocation. The highest depreciation write-off legally possible will normally be taken by management to minimize the cash outlay for taxes, unless operating profits (including tax adjustments like operating loss carryback and carryforward, which permit making use of past losses to reduce the taxes of profitable periods) over the taxable period are not sufficient to take full advantage of the deductions.

The choice of depreciation methods is made easier by the provision in the tax laws allowing the use of *one* method for bookkeeping and reporting purposes and *another* for income tax calculation. Recall that this was not possible for inventory valuation. Thus, a company can enjoy the best aspects of both depreciation concepts: slower depreciation for reporting higher profits, and faster depreciation for paying lower taxes.

As we observed in Chapter 1, the difference between the taxes actually paid versus what would be due had the book profit been taxed is accumulated on the balance sheet as a liability called *deferred taxes*. This liability will keep growing if a company continually adds to its depreciable assets and consistently uses faster write-offs for tax purposes. If the company stops growing or changes its depreciation policies, actual tax payments in future periods will increase and the differences will begin to reduce the deferred taxes account. In Chapter 1 we stated that there is no current consensus on how to treat this often significant amount in the calculation of performance assessment measures.

What are the most common *choices* for depreciation write-offs? Historically, accounting practice favored **straight-line depreciation.** This is determined by dividing the cost of the asset (less the estimated salvage value) by its expected life. For example, an asset costing $10,000, with a salvage value of $400 and a six-year life would be depreciated at the annual rate of $1,600 (one sixth, or 16⅔ percent of $9,600). A variant of this method is *unit depreciation,* in which the allocation is based on the total number of units estimated to be produced over the life of the asset; annual depreciation is based on the number of units produced in that year.

Because many types of assets, such as automobiles, lose more of their value in early years, and also because allowing faster write-offs provides a tax incentive, several methods of **accelerated depreciation** were developed over time. The three most common methods will be mentioned here. **Double-declining balance** depreciation is calculated by using *twice* the annual rate of straight-line depreciation (33⅓ percent for a six-year life), multiplying the full original cost of the asset for the first year by this factor, and the declining balance for each successive year. In other words, in our example, one third of the remaining balance would be depreciated in each year (see Figure 2–4). The last year's depreciation is the remaining balance, and any salvage value is recognized by reducing the amount charged in the *final* year.

Sum-of-years-digits depreciation is calculated by adding the digits for all the years of the asset's life (1 + 2 + 3, etc.). The total is the denominator in a fraction. (For a six-year life this would be 21: 1 + 2 + 3 + 4 + 5 + 6.) The numerators represent each year of useful life, in *reverse* order. (In our example, the fractions are 6/21, 5/21, 4/21, 3/21, 2/21, and 1/21.) In a given year, the depreciation write-off is the asset's original cost (less salvage value) multiplied by the fraction for that year.

The most recent depreciation method is the **accelerated cost recovery system (ACRS)** mandated for federal tax purposes in 1981. It must be used if a company chooses to use accelerated

Figure 2–4
Comparative Annual Depreciation Patterns ($10,000 asset with six-year life and $400 salvage value)

	Straight-Line Method	Double-Declining Balance Method		Sum-of-Years-Digits Method	ACRS System
Year One:	$1,600	$3,333		$2,743	(One half)
Year Two:	1,600	2,222		2,286	depends
Year Three:	1,600	1,482		1,829	on
Year Four:	1,600	988		1,371	class
Year Five:	1,600	658		914	of
Year Six:	1,600	917	(net of salvage)	457	asset
Total:	$9,600	$9,600		$9,600	$9,600

depreciation for *tax* purposes, while *any other* method can be employed for bookkeeping and reporting. The ACRS system specifies the rates of depreciation to be employed for all assets, which have been divided into five classes. The first year's depreciation is specified as six months' worth at the highest rate, regardless of whether the asset was installed early or late in the company's tax year. The specifics of the system are best examined in the detailed materials provided by the Internal Revenue Service.

The different patterns of depreciation resulting from the use of the various methods are readily compared in Figure 2–4.

To summarize, we have discussed the accounting issues surrounding choices of *inventory costing* and *depreciation methods* to illustrate the impact of these elements on both performance assessment and funds management. We found that there could be a significant impact on the measurement of both profitability and balance sheet values. The analyst must assess and judge the nature of these differences and depending on the purpose of the analysis, make allowances. From a funds management standpoint, the choices are significant because of the differing *tax impact* of what are otherwise mere bookkeeping conventions. Taxes are paid in cash and thus are a use of funds. We will return to these issues when we take up the specifics of the funds flow statement in the next section.

FUNDS FLOW STATEMENT REFINEMENTS

Having provided the basic concepts of how funds flow through a business, we are now ready to examine the *construction* of actual funds flow statements. For this purpose, we will again use the 1985 IBM data shown in Chapter 1. It is critical to remember that funds flow analysis is developed from balance sheets and the operating statement, which, as we mentioned, contain a variety of write-offs and other adjustments. These must in effect, be *reversed*, or canceled out, so that only funds movements caused by management decisions during the period are shown. Therefore, we will work back from the IBM balance sheets and operating statement to develop our version of the funds flow statement, which we can compare to the one published by IBM. As we will see, some of the adjustments must be based on assumptions, because we do not have access to the detailed records of the company. Therefore, our own version of the funds flow statement will approximate, but not be identical to, the key funds figures shown in IBM's statement.

Our discussion will begin with a look at the straightforward funds movements taken directly from differences in balance sheet items. Then we will examine in greater detail three commonly encountered refinements in funds flow analysis. These areas of refinement—**adjustments to retained earnings (owners' equity), adjustments to net income,** and **adjustments to net fixed assets**—will give us greater insight into the results of management decisions in our three key areas of investments, operations, and financing. IBM's consolidated balance sheets and consolidated income statements, used in Chapter 1, are reproduced below as Figures 2–5 and 2–6, and the supplementary notes from IBM's 1985 annual report explaining the key accounting policies followed by IBM are shown in Figure 2–7.

To develop a funds flow statement, the *changes* in the accounts in the beginning and ending balance sheets for the period of analysis must be classified as *uses* and *sources*. We have done this in Figure 2–8, where increases and decreases in assets and liabilities are assigned to the appropriate categories, following the rules we developed earlier.

However, some of these categories are too broad. As a result, several of the funds flows are not specifically delineated. First of all, *net profit* from operations is not recognized as such, but is encompassed in the change in retained earnings. Although we know that *dividends* were paid, these are also included in the change in retained earnings. We also know that *depreciation and amortization* were sizable, but at this point they are buried under changes in net plant and equipment, and investments and other assets. Finally, IBM *invested* heavily in plant and equipment, a fact which still remains obscured.

Figure 2–5
INTERNATIONAL BUSINESS MACHINES CORPORATION
AND SUBSIDIARY COMPANIES
Consolidated Balance Sheet
December 31
($ millions)

	1985	1984	Change
Assets			
Current assets:			
Cash and marketable securities	$ 5,622	$ 4,362	+ 1,260
Receivables, net	10,566	8,111	+ 2,455
Inventories	8,579	6,598	+ 1,981
Prepaid expenses; other	1,303	1,304	− 1
Total current assets	26,070	20,375	+ 5,695
Plant, equipment, and rental machinery	34,483	29,423	+ 5,060
Less: Accumulated depreciation	14,803	13,060	+ 1,743
Net plant and equipment	19,680	16,363	+ 3,317
Investments* and other assets	6,884	6,070	+ 814
Total assets	$52,634	$42,808	+ 9,826
Liabilities and Net Worth			
Current liabilities:			
Accounts and notes payable	$ 1,823	$ 1,618	+ 205
Loans payable	1,293	834	+ 459
Accrued taxes	3,089	2,668	+ 421
Other accruals	5,228	4,520	+ 708
Total current liabilities	11,433	9,640	+ 1,793
Long-term debt	3,955	3,269	+ 686
Other liabilities	1,606	1,353	+ 253
Deferred taxes	3,650	2,057	+ 1,593
Shareholders' equity:			
Capital stock	6,267	5,998	+ 269
Retained earnings(net)	25,723	20,491	+ 5,232
Total shareholders' equity	31,990	26,489	+ 5,501
Total liabilities and net worth	$52,634	$42,808	+ 9,826

* Includes program products which are amortized.

What we can observe from the simple statement in Figure 2–8 is the picture of a growing company. Major *net funds uses* were the growth in net plant and equipment and other investments; the growth in cash, receivables, and inventories, the key working capital items supporting operations, were even larger. The key *net funds source* was the growth in retained earnings from profits *after* dividends. Major growth in deferred taxes due to timing differences in tax incidence, and a

Figure 2–6
INTERNATIONAL BUSINESS MACHINES CORPORATION
AND SUBSIDIARY COMPANIES
Consolidated Operating Statement
For Years Ending December 31
($ millions)

			Percent of Revenues	
	1985	1984	1985	1984
Revenues				
Sales of products	$34,404	$29,753	68.7%	64.7%
Services	11,536	9,605	23.1	21.0
Rentals	4,116	6,579	8.2	14.3
Total revenues	$50,056	$45,937	100.0%	100.0%
Costs and expenses*				
Cost of sales	$14,911	$12,374		
Cost of services	4,689	4,347		
Cost of rentals	1,503	2,198		
Cost of goods and services	21,103	18,919	42.2	41.2
Gross margin	28,953	27,018	57.8%	58.8%
Selling, general and administrative	13,000	11,587	26.0	25.2
Research and development	4,723	4,200	9.4	9.1
Interest expense	443	408	.9	.9
Total expenses	$18,166	$16,195	36.3%	35.2%
	$10,787	$10,823	21.5	23.6
Other income	832	800	1.7	1.7
Earnings before taxes	11,619	11,623	23.2%	25.3%
Provision for income taxes	5,064	5,041	10.1	11.0
Net income	$ 6,555	$ 6,582	13.1%	14.3%
* Includes depreciation	$ 2,894	$ 2,987		
* Includes amortization	425	486		
Dividends paid	2,703	2,507		

large variety of credit arrangements, including a small net increase in long-term debt, were also key sources. Although we do, at this point, have a certain amount of insight into IBM's sources and uses of funds, we can further refine our analysis of the company's funds flow pattern.

Adjustments to Retained Earnings

The net change in *retained earnings* usually contains at least two elements of interest. The first is *net profit or loss* from op-

Figure 2–7
International Business Machines Corporation
and Subsidiary Companies
Notes to 1985 Consolidated Financial Statements

Significant Accounting Policies

Principles of Consolidation

The consolidated financial statements include the accounts of International Business Machines Corporation and its U.S. and non–U.S. subsidiary companies, other than the wholly owned IBM Credit Corporation and non–U.S. finance subsidiaries, for which the equity method is used. Investments in joint ventures, and other companies in which IBM has a 20 to 50 percent ownership, are accounted for by the equity method. Investments of less than 20 percent are accounted for by the cost method.

*Translation of
Non-U.S. Currency Amounts*

For non–U.S. subsidiaries which operate in a local currency environment, assets and liabilities are translated to U.S. dollars at year-end exchange rates. Income and expense items are translated at average rates of exchange prevailing during the year. Translation adjustments are accumulated in a separate component of stockholders' equity. For non–U.S. subsidiaries and branches which operate in U.S. dollars or whose economic environment is highly inflationary, inventories and plant, rental machines, and other property are translated at approximate rates prevailing when acquired. All other assets and liabilities are translated at year-end exchange rates. Inventories charged to cost of sales and depreciation are remeasured at historical rates. All other income and expense items are translated at average rates of exchange prevailing during the year. Gains and losses which result from remeasurement are included in earnings.

Gross Income

Gross income is recognized from sales or sales-type leases when the product is shipped, or in certain cases upon customer acceptance, from rentals under operating leases in the month in which they accrue, and from services over the contractual period or as the services are performed. Rental plans include maintenance service and contain discontinuance and purchase option provisions. Rental terms are predominantly monthly or for a two-year period. IBM equipment offered under term leases by IBM's finance subsidiaries is accounted for by IBM as outright sales.

Program Products

Costs related to the conceptual formulation and design of licensed programs are expensed as research and development. Costs incurred subsequent to establishment of technological feasibility to produce the finished product are generally capitalized as program products assets. The assets are amortized based on the estimated revenue distribution over their revenue-producing lives, but not in excess of six years. Ongoing costs to support or service licensed programs are expensed.

Figure 2–7 *(concluded)*

Depreciation	Plant, rental machines, and other property are carried at cost and depreciated over their estimated useful lives. Depreciation of assets acquired subsequent to December 31, 1983 is computed using the straight-line method. Depreciation of assets acquired prior to January 1, 1984 is computed using the sum-of-the-years digits method for rental machines, and either accelerated methods or the straight-line method for plant and other property.
Goodwill	The excess of the cost over the fair value of the net assets of purchased businesses is recorded as goodwill and amortized on a straight-line basis over 20 years. Goodwill related to equity investments is included in the investment and amortized on a straight-line basis over 20 years.
Retirement Plans and Other Postretirement Benefits	Current service costs of retirement plans are accrued currently. Prior service costs resulting from improvements in the plans are amortized generally over 15 years. Postretirement health-care and life insurance benefits are fully accrued when the employee retires.
Selling Expenses	Selling expenses are charged against income as they are incurred.
Income Taxes	Income tax expense is based on reported earnings before income taxes. It thus includes the effects of timing differences between reported and taxable earnings that arise because certain transactions are included in taxable earnings in other years. Investment tax credits are deferred and amortized as a reduction of income tax expense over the average useful life of the applicable classes of property.
Inventories	Raw materials, operating supplies, finished goods and work in process are included at the lower of average cost or market.

Source: From IBM 1985 Annual Report.

erations, as reflected on the operating statement. The second is *dividends paid* to the various classes of shareholders. Both normally represent major funds movements that should be shown separately, one as a source and the other as a use. Often certain *adjustments* have been made to the retained earnings account, however. These may include changes in balance sheet reserves, value adjustments in selected accounts, goodwill adjustments, and currency translation adjustments. Such adjustments should be highlighted if they are significant.

In the case of IBM we know from the operating statement that net profit (income) for 1985 was $6,555 million. This

Figure 2–8
INTERNATIONAL BUSINESS MACHINES CORPORATION
AND SUBSIDIARY COMPANIES
Statement of Balance Sheet Changes
For the Year Ended December 31, 1985
($ millions)

Sources:	
Decrease in prepaid expenses	$ 1
Increase in accounts and notes payable	205
Increase in loans payable	459
Increase in accrued taxes	421
Increase in other accruals	708
Increase in long-term debt	686
Increase in other liabilities	253
Increase in deferred taxes	1,593
Increase in capital stock	269
Increase in retained earnings	5,232
Total sources	$9,827
Uses:	
Increase in cash and marketable securities	$1,260
Increase in receivables	2,455
Increase in inventories	1,981
Increase in net plant and equipment	3,317
Increase in investments and other assets	814
Total uses	$9,827

amount must have been added to the retained earnings account. The operating statement also indicated that cash dividends paid were $2,703 million. The net of these two figures is $3,852 million. Yet we can see from the statement of balance sheet changes that retained earnings increased by $5,232, or almost $1.5 billion *more* than we would have expected from the figures in the operating statement. Where did the remaining retained earnings come from?

In Figure 2–9, we show a section of IBM's 1985 statement of changes in owners' equity. From this we learn that the major additional element was a currency translation adjustment of $1,482 million, and some minor transactions in treasury stock held under employee and stockholder plans, netting a negative $102 million. Thus funds flow in terms of retained earnings are adjusted as follows:

	Sources	Uses
Net income for 1985	$6,555	
Cash dividends declared		$2,703
Translation effects	1,482	
Other adjustments (treasury stock transactions)		102
Totals	$8,037	$2,805
Net source	$5,232	

With this information at hand, we can include these detailed funds flow elements into an expanded version of our simple funds flow statement. This is done in Figure 2–10, which also reflects certain other adjustments still to be discussed.

Some additional comments will be useful here. Had the company made significant bookkeeping adjustments in its reserve accounts or goodwill carried on the balance sheet and re-

Figure 2–9
INTERNATIONAL BUSINESS MACHINES CORPORATION
AND SUBSIDIARY COMPANIES
Consolidated Statement of Stockholders' Equity
For the Year Ended December 31, 1985
($ millions)

	Capital Stock	Retained Earnings	Translation Adjustments	Treasury Stock	Total
Stockholders' Equity, December 31, 1984	$5,998	$23,486	$(2,948)	$(47)	$26,489
Net earnings		6,555			6,555
Cash dividends declared		(2,703)			(2,703)
Capital stock issued under employee plans (2,664,869 shares)	173				173
Purchases (6,346,223 shares) and sales (6,413,759 shares) of treasury stock under employee and stockholder plans—net		(104)		2	(102)
Other (principally tax reductions—employee plans)	96				96
Translation adjustments			1,482		1,482
Stockholders' Equity, December 31, 1985	$6,267	$27,234*	$(1,466)*	$(45)*	$31,990

*All related to retained earnings of $25,723 million.

Source: Adapted from IBM 1985 Annual Report.

flected these changes in retained earnings, the analyst could choose to in effect, cancel out the amounts involved by adjusting both accounts to their level before the write-off. Whether to do this "reversing" is a matter of judgment and depends on what the funds flow statement is used for. Unless the amounts involved are truly significant, the extra refinement is probably not worth the effort. Stock dividends, which some companies pay in lieu of or in addition to cash dividends, can be handled similarly. Stock dividends, strictly speaking, involve no change in economic value. They simply increase the number of shares outstanding by a fraction without affecting the stated value of the total owners' equity. It is important that such refinements do not divert us from the key purpose of the analysis, which is to gauge the *effect on funds* of *major management decisions* made during the period.

Adjustments to Net Income

As we know, net income is derived after a number of bookkeeping *write-offs* are taken, the largest of which normally is depreciation. Other write-offs involve amortizing patents and licenses, and depletion of mineral deposits and standing timber. Any items of significance should be recognized and added back to income (thus canceled out) in the funds flow statement to achieve a closer approximation of the funds movements.

In IBM's case, depreciation and amortization were shown in the operating statement at $2,894 million and $425 million respectively. Normally depreciation and amortization are listed in the funds flow statement as "sources of funds" after net income. However, this practice results in the common misconception of seeing depreciation and amortization as *actual* sources of funds. We must remember that depreciation itself does *not create any funds;* it is only an accounting entry. Nonetheless, it must be recognized and *added back* to the extent that it previously *reduced* net income. This *cancels out* (reverses) the effect of depreciation and is achieved by listing depreciation as a source along with net income. Depreciation does, of course, affect the amount of *taxes* paid, but this positive funds effect has already been recognized in the amount of income taxes which were deducted before arriving at net income.

One factor to remember while adjusting for depreciation and amortization is that a *corresponding* adjustment should be made in the asset accounts from which they arose. We recall that depreciation charges for a period are recorded as a *reduction* in net fixed assets through the vehicle of accumulated depreciation. Amortization is normally charged directly against the asset account being written off. When we show depreciation and amortization as "sources," we are in effect increasing net income. But we must also *restore* the same amount to the relevant asset account. Otherwise our funds flows will not balance. (We will return to the specifics of this adjustment in the next section.)

Deferred taxes are another major funds flow element that affect net income. As we discussed earlier, taxes may be deferred because some revenues and expenses, particularly depreciation, are timed differently for tax purposes than for reporting purposes. Taxes *paid* are therefore lower than taxes *provided for* on the income statement. The amount of the difference is shown as a liability on the balance sheet. Reported income consequently does *not* reflect the funds benefit from the lower taxes actually remitted. Therefore, as in the case of depreciation, we should show the increase in deferred taxes as a *source* in our funds flow statement, in effect adding it to reported net income. Because we can take the change in deferred taxes directly from the balance sheet, there is no need to make any further adjustments. In 1985, IBM's deferred taxes rose by $1,593 million, which should be reflected as a source in conjunction with the reported net income of $6,555 million.

Other elements in the net income picture will sometimes result from adjustments of assets and liabilities on the balance sheet. Normally these amounts are not significant enough to warrant special attention. If they are substantial, the analyst can again choose to reverse them to keep the funds flow analysis "pure." The relevance of the item to the analysis must be the overriding factor in this decision.

Finally, net income is often affected by gains and losses from the sale of capital assets. This will be discussed in detail in the next section.

Adjustments to Net Fixed Assets

The change in net fixed assets—*property, plant, and equipment*—results from shifts in a variety of funds and non–funds flow items. It consists of changes in the gross fixed assets account, and changes in accumulated depreciation. Nonrecurring asset adjustments from retirement of various fixed assets often also have an effect. In most cases, funds flow analysis is more meaningful when at least the major elements of the net change in fixed assets are recognized. Normally the funds flow pattern behind the change in net fixed assets is significant enough to warrant this special attention. At the same time, fixed asset effects are among the more difficult aspects of financial analysis for newcomers to understand. This is partly because fixed assets represent the *net* of an asset and a reserve account. Another part of the problem is the mystique surrounding depreciation and asset write-offs.

The easiest approach to this difficult subject is to lay out the components of the fixed asset account and to observe the relevance of the figures. Then we can look for additional information in other parts of the published statements. Some of this information may be available only to the insider, however. In such cases we must make do with reasonable assumptions.

In our IBM example, the balance sheet in Figure 2–5 provides the following information:

	12–31–85	12–31–84	Change
Gross plant, equipment and rental machinery	$34,483	$29,423	+ $5,060
Less: Accumulated depreciation ...	14,803	13,060	+ 1,743
Net plant and equipment	$19,680	$16,363	+ $3,317

Our basic task is to identify the relevant *individual* funds sources and uses which in combination, amounted to the *net use* (net increase) of $3,317 million shown. Quite obviously, there was an increase of $5,060 million in gross plant and equipment, which must have been due to new investments (a use). At the same time, accumulated depreciation rose by $1,743 million, which is largely due to current write-offs (a source, as we discussed before). In some cases, this coarse breakdown of sources and uses is sufficient and many analysts will let the matter rest here. Yet we already know, for instance, that *actual* depreciation for the period as shown on the operating statement was $2,894 million, far *more* than the change in accumulated depreciation. There must have been other elements affecting the picture. As a result, depending on the depth of analysis desired, the following questions arise:

1. What are the relevant elements of funds flow, in the *accumulated depreciation* account, one of which was the reported amount of depreciation for the year?

2. What was the *total* amount of *new investment* in plant, equipment, and rental machines—a major aspect of the management decision process?

3. Were there any divestitures and asset retirements (i.e., reduction in gross plant and equipment) that significantly affected the company's funds flow?

These questions are interrelated and can be handled at two levels of complexity. The *simpler* approach is to assume that the amount of depreciation normally taken for the year ($2,894 million in the case of IBM) will *equal* the amount by which accumulated depreciation has increased. If this in fact is *not* the case, as we discovered in our example, then there must have been some reduction in the accumulated depreciation account which, for simplicity, we can assume to represent the *abandonment* of *fully depreciated* assets during the period.[1] We thereby imply that no proceeds at all were received. This simple but often adequate approach also eliminates the problem of having to deal with any gains or losses on the *sale* of capital items. The adjustments involved in this simpler level of analysis modify our funds flow layout as follows:

	(1) 12-31-84	(2) Additions	(3) Deductions	(4) 12-31-85	(5) Change
Gross plant, etc.	$29,423	+ $6,211*	− $1,151†	$34,483	+ $5,060
Less: Accumulated depreciation	13,060	+ 2,894	− 1,151‡	14,803	+ 1,743
Net plant and equipment	$16,363	$3,317	−0−	$19,680	+ $3,317

*Derived figure.
†Must be same as in accumulated depreciation if fully depreciated assets were abandoned.
‡Assumed figure in order to balance the change in the account.

Because we must reconcile the data with the net changes in the accounts on the balance sheet, our simple assumption has given us the necessary data to complete the funds flow analysis: we recognize the actual depreciation write-off of $2,894 million as a source (column 2), and accept the *derived* amount of $6,211 as the new capital investment, a use. The process relies on the *assumed* write-off of $1,151 million of fully depreciated assets, which under normal accounting practice, equally reduces *both* the asset *and* the accumulated depreciation accounts (column 3). This practice is observed in our analysis. We are ignoring possible tax implications that would tend to confuse the issue, but do little to improve the accuracy of our analysis.

From a funds flow point of view, we now have all the elements needed to identify and separate the sources and uses behind the change in the net plant and equipment account as reflected in Figure 2–8:

---

[1]Fully depreciated assets, when scrapped, are removed by an accounting entry that credits (reduces) assets by the amount of the recorded value, and debits (reduces) accumulated depreciation by the same amount.

Source: Depreciation for the period .	$2,894	
Use: New investment	6,211	
Adjusted net use	$3,317	

It is obvious that our relatively simple adjustment of the net balances in the two accounts has improved our assessment of one of the most important management decisions: the amount of *new asset investment*. Our original version in Figure 2–8 reflected only a fraction of this sizable commitment for future growth.

We can now assemble a modified funds flow statement from the information originally displayed in Figure 2–8, which is improved by the adjustments we have made in owners' equity, net income, and plant and equipment. In Figure 2–10, we have arranged the funds flow data in terms of our three familiar areas of management decision—operations, financing, and investment—to provide a picture of the effect of IBM management decisions in 1985. We can see that operational decisions resulted in a net funds source of $7,565 million, which is net of an increase in working capital of $3,902 million (a $5,695 million increase in current assets minus a $1,793 million increase in current liabilities) needed to support the company's steady growth. Funds flows from financing decisions netted out almost evenly, while the sizable investments in plant and equipment, rental machines, and program products (shown as other investments) were, in effect, funded by the operational flows. We have shown dividends paid as part of the investment section, but could also have shown this item in the operational area, in the sense that dividends represent a sharing of profits.

Yet we are *still* short of a fully accurate picture because we made one simplifying assumption—that *fully depreciated* assets were abandoned and written off. A check of the company's annual report reveals that the actual 1985 capital investment made by IBM in plant and equipment and rental machines was $6,430 million ($6,117 million and $313 million respectively), which differs by $219 million from our derived total figure of $6,211 million.

Figure 2-10
INTERNATIONAL BUSINESS MACHINES CORPORATION
AND SUBSIDIARY COMPANIES
Modified Funds Flow Statement
For the Year Ended December 31, 1985
($ millions)

	Sources	Uses
Operational funds flows:		
Net income	$ 6,555	$ —
Depreciation (nonfunds item)	2,894	—
Amortization (nonfunds item)	425	—
Deferred income taxes	1,593	—
Increase in current liabilities	1,793	—
Increase in current assets	—	5,695
Total operational flows	13,260	5,695
Net operational flows	$ 7,565	
Financing funds flows:		
Increase in long-term debt	$ 686	$ —
Increase in other liabilities	253	—
Increase in capital stock	269	—
Adjustments in retained egs	1,380	—
Dividends paid	—	2,703
Total financing flows	2,588	2,703
Net financing flows		$ 115
Investment funds flows:		
Investments in plant and equipment	—	$6,211
Other investments	—	1,239
Total investment flows	—	7,450
Totals	$ 7,565	$7,565

If we are interested in reconciling our analysis with this added bit of information, we must follow a second, *more complex* level of analysis. In effect, we have to dig more deeply and try to understand the accounting adjustments that were probably made in these fixed asset accounts. Our assumption about fully depreciated assets left out the possibility of receiving any proceeds, or of recognizing gains or losses from the disposition of property and other fixed assets. Normally the amounts involved are relatively minor, as is proportionately true in this example (only about a 3 percent adjustment is necessary). But it will nevertheless be useful to work through the implications of a possible gain or loss from depreciated assets for better understanding.

If in fact there had been *proceeds* from assets sold—and this can be ascertained through examination of published financial data for most larger companies—there must have been three effects on the company's statements. First, the write-off in the gross property account, and in accumulated depreciation must have *differed* by the amount of any remaining *book value* of the assets disposed of. This expectation slightly complicates our basic data.

Second, any gain or loss resulting because cash proceeds are larger or smaller than the remaining book value would have affected *net income*. If such gains or losses were material, they will be reflected in the operating statement. For purposes of funds flow analysis, net income can therefore be split into operating earnings as one source, and the reported *gain or loss* as another source or use.

Third, proceeds received from disposition of the asset will have been buried in the *cash* account. Yet, if these proceeds had differed substantially from the book value of the assets, they should be recognized as a source if they were material. Unless there is a specific indication in the operating statement about gains or losses, we simply *assume* that the *proceeds* received exactly *matched* the remaining *book value*. Consequently, the reduction in gross plant and equipment this represents must have been a cash *source* for the period.

How can we deal with this adjustment? First of all, it will be helpful again to sort out our basic data, this time to include all the details we now have:

	(1) 12–31–84	(2) Additions	(3) Deductions	(4) 12–31–85	(5) Change
Gross plant and equipment .	$29,423	+ $6,430	− $1,370*	$34,438	+ $5,060
Less: Accumulated depreciation	$13,060	+ 2,894	− 1,151	14,803	+ 1,743
Net plant and equipment . .	$16,363	+ 3,536	− $ 219†	$19,680	+ $3,317

*Derived figure, because both additions are now known.
†Proceeds from sale of assets, corresponding to their remaining book value.

The effect on funds flow of this refinement is a somewhat *higher* amount of investment recognized as a use, and the offset is the proceeds for the remaining book value as a source. When we now separate the elements of the final adjustment, the following picture emerges:

Sources:	
Depreciation	$2,894
Proceeds from sale of assets*	219
	$3,113
Use:	
Investment in plant and equipment	6,430
Net change in plant, equipment and rental machines	$3,317
*Remaining book value.	

We have now reconciled the analysis with our information about investment, depreciation, and the change in the balance sheet accounts related to these funds flows. We have not been able to determine whether there were other, *internal* adjustments that were too detailed to be reflected in the highly abbreviated version of the financial statements published in the annual report. But we have succeeded in reflecting the *major funds implications* of the *decisions* made by IBM's management. In fact, we have come very close to the *actual* funds flow statement published by the company in its annual report shown in Chapter 1 and reproduced below in Figure 2–11.

We can incorporate this last adjustment in our modified statement (Figure 2–10), as shown in Figure 2–12. Note that the only change in that statement is the modification of the *investment* funds flow sector because of the $219 million adjustment for assumed asset proceeds.

When we compare IBM's statement (Figure 2–11) to ours, we find that, apart from differences in presentation, most of the figures we have developed are reflected there as well. In Figure 2–11, amounts in the company's statement that correspond exactly to ours are marked by an asterisk. The only items on which the statements disagree require more detailed knowledge than is normally available in published statements. Proceeds from assets sold (net book value) is higher by $648 million in IBM's statement. Clearly, our second level of analysis

Figure 2–11
INTERNATIONAL BUSINESS MACHINES CORPORATION
AND SUBSIDIARY COMPANIES
Consolidated Statement of Funds Flow
For the Year Ended December 31
($ millions)

	1985	1984
Funds (Cash and Marketable Securities)		
at January 1	$4,362†	$5,536
Provided from (used for) Operations:		
Sources:		
Net earnings	$ 6,555*	$6,582
Items not requiring the current use of funds:		
Depreciation charged to costs and expenses	2,894*	2,987
Net book value of rental machines and		
other property retired or sold	867	1,483
Amortization of program products	425*	486
Other (principally deferred income		
taxes)	1,880	1,004
	12,621	12,542
Depreciation of manufacturing		
facilities capitalized	157	228
	12,778	12,770
Uses:		
Investment in rental machines	313	858
Investment in plant and other property . . .	6,117	4,615
	6,430*	5,473
Investment in program products	785*	803
Increase in investments and other		
assets	454*	1,764
Net change in working capital		
(excluding cash, marketable securities		
and loans payable)	3,101†	4,043
	10,770	12,083
Translation effects	677	(324)
Net provided from operations	2,685	363
Provided from External Financing:		
Net change in long-term debt	686*	595
Net change in loans payable	459†	302
Net provided from external financing	1,145	897
Provided from Employee and Stockholder Plans	133	73
	8,325	6,869
Less: Cash Dividends Paid	2,703*	2,507
Funds (Cash and Marketable Securities)		
at December 31	$5,622†	$4,362

Source: Adapted from IBM 1985 Annual Report.
*Matches figures on final modified statement, Figure 2–12.
†Net matches Figure 2–12 net change in current assets & liabilities ($5,622 − $4,362 + $3,101 − $459 = $3,902) = ($5,695 − 1,793 = $3,902).

Figure 2–12
INTERNATIONAL BUSINESS MACHINES CORPORATION
AND SUBSIDIARY COMPANIES
Final Modified Funds Flow Statement
For the Year Ended December 31, 1985
($ millions)

	Sources	Uses
Operational funds flows:		
Net income	$ 6,555	$ —
Depreciation (nonfunds item)	2,894	—
Amortization (nonfunds item)	425	—
Deferred income taxes	1,593	—
Increase in current liabilities	1,793	—
Increase in current assets	—	5,695
Total operational flows	13,260	5,695
Net operational flows	$ 7,565	
Financing funds flows:		
Increase in long-term debt	$ 686	$ —
Increase in other liabilities	253	—
Increase in capital stock	269	—
Adjustments in retained earnings	1,380	—
Dividends paid	—	2,703
Total financing flows	2,588	2,703
Net financing flows		$ 115
Investment funds flows:		
Investments in plant and equipment	$ —	$6,430
Other investments	—	1,239
Proceeds from assets sold	219	—
Total investment flows	219	7,669
Net investment flows		$7,450
Totals	$ 7,565	$7,565

was based on the assumption of *no gain or loss* from the sale of depreciated equipment, and we had no information to the contrary. It is possible that the company put these transactions into the single category shown. But it is really not necessary to speculate about this fact.

The item titled "other," which principally encompasses deferred taxes, is *larger* than the increase in deferred taxes we showed as $1,593 million. There must have been additional unspecified adjustments that brought the figure up. We also differ in capitalized depreciation, probably because facilities are being remodeled or expanded and are not currently in operation. We could not have known about this directly, and the company correctly added this element to its sources from operations to reflect the adjustment. Part of the translation effects which were *netted out* in Figure 2–9 are shown here separately as a use. Again, we cannot expect to understand these internal adjustments. Finally, only part of the capital stock transactions related to employee and stockholder plans is shown here, $133 million versus $269 in our statement. All in all, however, the refinements provided by the company do not significantly alter the picture of funds flows we were able to construct ourselves.

The company's presentation shows the *change in liquid funds*, cash, and marketable securities, and relates the other funds flows to this change. The approach is quite common, as is the practice of focusing on the *total change* in working capital. In any event, the end result is quite comparable to our own form of structuring the results of funds flow analysis.

To summarize, in this section we constructed a funds flow statement that goes beyond simply listing the changes readily observable from a comparison of beginning and ending balance sheet accounts. This was achieved by making informed adjustments in several of the accounts. The *purpose* of the refinements was to highlight significant results that reflect management decisions involving investments, operations, and financing. If a funds flow statement is not made available as a matter of course, the analyst can *approximate* the statement an insider could prepare by going through the adjustment process demonstrated. We must usually examine three areas in depth: the components of the change in *owners' equity*, the elements in *net income* (particularly those relating to accounting write-offs), and the various components of change in the *fixed asset* accounts and related accumulated depreciation. Under most conditions, the analyst will be able to come close enough to the actual figures to be able to construct a funds flow statement that is meaningful in format and content.

SUMMARY

In this chapter we demonstrated the funds flow cycle involved in any business, large or small, and its implication for management. We discussed **operating funds cycles** from a manufacturing and sales standpoint, and observed the nature and behavior of **working capital.** We highlighted the impact of **variability of operations,** and demonstrated the effect of **funds lags** on the nature and duration of financing required to support a business. The insights gained included the need to consider the **permanence** of basic working capital requirements, the financial drain of even successful **growth,** and the potential funds release from **decline** in volume. Several key questions arise as funds movements are analyzed. Most relate to the **types of funds commitments** (uses) made compared to the **sources of funds available.** Have enough long-term funds been provided to fund ongoing growth in working capital and fixed asset expansion? Are most sources of funds temporary loans and credit extension? Is the business counting on **profits** to fund peaks of need that may **exceed** such expectations? In essence, funds flow analysis is a broad, **dynamic** view of the financial management of the business, that relates **changes** in conditions to the key financial **implications** by reconstructing the major funds transactions during the period. The techniques are simple, requiring only basic accounting knowledge to provide this **extra dimension** in assessing balance sheets and operating statements.

SELECTED REFERENCES

Anthony, Robert N., and Reece, James S. *Accounting Principles.* 4th ed. Homewood, Ill.: Richard D. Irwin, 1979.

Brealey, Richard, and Myers, Stewart. *Principles of Corporate Finance.* 2nd ed. New York: McGraw-Hill, 1984.

Moore, Carl L., and Jaedicke, Robert K. *Managerial Accounting.* 5th ed. Cincinnati, Ohio: South-Western Publishing Co., 1980.

Seitz, Neil. *Financial Analysis: A Programmed Approach.* 3rd ed. Reston, Va.: Reston Publishing, 1984.

Vancil, Richard F., and Makela, Benjamin R., eds. *The CFO Handbook.* Homewood, Ill.: Dow Jones-Irwin, 1986.

Van Horne, James C. *Financial Management and Policy.* 7th ed. Englewood Cliffs, N.J.: Prentice-Hall, 1986.

Weston, J. Fred, and Copeland, Thomas E. *Managerial Finance.* 8th ed. Hinsdale, Ill.: Dryden Press, 1986.

SELF-STUDY EXERCISES AND PROBLEMS

(Solutions to Items 1, 2a and b, and 4 are provided in Appendix III)

1. Develop a funds flow statement from the balance sheets and income statements of the CBA Company (shown below) for the year 1987. Make appropriate assumptions and comment on the results.

CBA COMPANY
Balance Sheets
December 31, 1986, and 1987

	1986	1987
Assets		
Current assets:		
Cash	$ 39,700	$ 27,500
Marketable securities	1,000	11,000
Accounts receivable (net)	81,500	72,700
Inventories	181,300	242,000
Total current assets	303,500	353,200
Fixed assets:		
Land	112,000	112,000
Plant and equipment (net)	445,200	464,800
Total fixed assets	557,200	576,800
Other assets	13,300	21,500
Total assets	$874,000	$951,500
Liabilities and Net Worth		
Current liabilities:		
Accounts payable	$ 71,200	$ 83,000
Notes payable	50,000	140,000
Accrued expenses	33,400	36,300
Total current liabilities	154,600	259,300
Long-term debt:		
Mortgage payable	106,000	90,800
Net worth:		
Common stock	225,000	230,000
Earned surplus	388,400	371,400
Total net worth	613,400	601,400
Total liabilities and net worth	$874,000	$951,500

CBA COMPANY
Operating Statements for 1986 and 1987

	1986	1987
Net sales	$1,113,400	$1,147,700
Cost of goods sold*	742,500	813,300
Gross margin	370,900	334,400
Expenses:		
Selling expense	172,500	227,000
General and administrative ...	65,500	71,800
Other expenses	11,200	25,000
Interest on debt	9,700	14,300
Total expenses	258,900	338,100
Profit (loss) before taxes	123,000	(3,700)
Federal income tax	56,600	(1,700)
Net income (loss)†	$ 66,400	$ (2,000)

*Includes depreciation of $31,500 for 1986 and $32,200 for 1987.
†Dividends paid were $30,000 for 1986 and $15,000 for 1987.

2. Work the following exercises:
   a. The following data about the ABC Company's operations and conditions for the year 1987 are available from a variety of sources:

Depreciation for 1987	$ 21,400
Net loss for 1987	14,100
Common dividends paid	12,000
Amortization of goodwill, patents	15,000
Inventory adjustment—write-down	24,000
Investments in fixed assets	57,500
Loss from abandonment of equipment	4,000
Balance of earned surplus, 12–31–86	167,300

   Which of the items above affect earned surplus during 1987 (the only surplus account of the company), and what is the balance of earned surplus as of December 31? Which of the items above are funds sources, and which are funds uses? Can depreciation be considered a funds flow item if the operating results are negative? What would be different if the $4,000 loss from abandonment had been a gain from sale of assets instead? Discuss.

   b. The following items, among others, appear on the funds flow statement of DEF Company for the year 1987:

Outlays for properties and fixed assets	$1,250,500
Profit from operations after taxes	917,000
Funds from depreciation	1,613,000

   The only other information readily available is as follows:

Gross property and fixed assets, 12–31–86	$8,431,500
Gross property and fixed assets, 12–31–87	8,430,000
Accumulated depreciation, 12–31–87	3,874,000

Determine the change in the *net* properties and fixed assets accounts from this information, and spell out your assumptions. How significant would be the likely effect on the results if you used some possible alternative assumptions? Discuss.

c. The XYZ Company experienced the transactions and changes listed below, among many others, during 1987, and these affected its balance sheet as follows:

Fixed assets recorded at $110,000 were sold for $45,000 (gain reflected in net income.)

Accumulated depreciation on these specific assets was $81,000.

Accumulated depreciation for the company as a whole decreased by $5,000 during 1987.

Total depreciation charged during 1987 was $78,500.

Balance of gross fixed assets were as follows: 12–31–86, $823,700, and 12–31–87, $947,300.

From this information, determine the amount of new investment in fixed assets for 1987 which should be shown in the funds flow statement. What was the amount of change in the *net* fixed assets account during 1987? Which other items shown above or derived from these should be shown on the funds flow statement? What assumptions are necessary? Discuss.

3. Develop a funds flow statement from the balance sheets, income statements, and earned surplus statements of the FED Company, shown below, for the year 1987. Make appropriate assumptions and comment on the results. If you net out changes in working capital accounts into one figure, will significant information be obscured? Will it be helpful to assign uses and sources to key management decision areas? Discuss.

FED COMPANY
Balance Sheets, December 31, 1986, and 1987
($000)

Assets	1986	1987	Change
Current assets:			
Cash	$ 12	$-0-	– $12
Marketable securities	18	-0-	– 18
Accounts receivable (net)	68	73	+ 5
Notes receivable	30	50	+ 20
Inventories	131	138	+ 7
Total current assets	259	261	+ 2
Fixed assets:			
Land	25	25	-0-
Plant and equipment	268	283	+ 15
Less: Accumulated depreciation	157	160	+ 3
Net plant and equipment	111	123	+ 12
Total fixed assets	136	148	+ 12

FED COMPANY *(concluded)*

	1986	1987	Change
Other assets:			
Prepaid expenses	12	14	+ 2
Patents, organization expense	30	27	− 3
Total other assets	42	41	− 1
Total assets	$437	$450	+$13
Liabilities and Net Worth			
Current liabilities:			
Bank overdraft	$–0–	$ 4	+$ 4
Accounts payable	73	97	+ 24
Notes payable	100	70	− 30
Accrued expenses	13	22	+ 9
Total current liabilities	186	193	+ 7
Long-term liabilities:			
Secured notes payable	40	20	− 20
Net Worth:			
Deferred income taxes	25	27	+ 2
Preferred stock	35	39	+ 4
Capital surplus	90	109	+ 19
Earned surplus	51	51	–0–
Common stock	10	11	+ 1
Total net worth	211	237	+ 26
Total liabilities and net worth	$437	$450	+$13

Other data: (1) sold fully depreciated machinery for $4,000, (2) issued $20,000 of common stock ($1 par) to reduce note payable, and (3) issued $4,000 of preferred stock to outsiders.

FED COMPANY
Operating Statement for 1986 and 1987
($000)

	1986	1987
Sales	$1,115	$1,237
Cost of goods sold:		
Material	312	345
Labor	274	341
Depreciation	24	26
Overhead	158	210
Cost of goods sold	768	922
Gross profit	347	315
Expenses:		
Selling and administrative		
expense	268	297
Interest on debt	9	7
Total expenses	277	304
Profit before taxes	70	11
Income taxes	32	5
Net income	$ 38	$ 6

FED COMPANY
Statement of Earned Surplus for 1987
($000)

Balance, 12–31–86		$51
Additions:		
Net income from 1987 operations	$6	
Gain from sale of fixed assets	4	10
		61
Deductions:		
Preferred dividends	2	
Common dividends	5	
Patent, other amortization	3	10
Balance, 12–31–87		$51

4. The ZYX Company, a vegetable packing plant, operates on a highly seasonal basis, which affects its financial results during various parts of its fiscal year and forces a financial planning effort in tune with these fluctuating requirements. From the nine quarterly balance sheets shown in the table, which cover two fiscal years of the ZYX Company, develop a funds flow analysis which will appropriately reflect the funds requirements and sources as balanced by the company management.

Data you may need in addition to that shown in the table on the next page include (1) purchases of machinery, $48,000 in April 1987 and $50,000 in April 1988; (2) depreciation charged at $6,000 per quarter through April 1987, at $7,000 through April 1988, and at $8,000 through July 1988; and (3) dividends paid at $15,000 per quarter through October 1987 and at $18,000 per quarter through July 1988.

Comment on the various alternative ways this analysis can be developed, and state your reasons for the choices you made. What are your key findings?

ZYX COMPANY
Balance Sheets by Fiscal Quarters
July 31, 1986, to July 31, 1988
($000)

	1986		1987				1988		
	7-31	10-31	1-31	4-30	7-31	10-31	1-31	4-30	7-31
Assets									
Cash	$ 21	$ 30	$ 74	$ 91	$ 7	$ 28	$ 90	$103	$ 16
Accounts receivable	114	247	319	128	141	293	388	151	103
Inventories	231	417	315	131	271	467	351	98	310
Net plant and equipment	239	233	227	269	262	255	248	291	283
Other assets	15	16	16	15	15	14	18	18	17
Total assets	$620	$943	$951	$634	$696	$1,057	$1,095	$661	$729
Liabilities and Net Worth									
Accounts payable	$ 68	$297	$121	$103	$ 79	$ 314	$ 188	$ 97	$ 84
Notes payable	35	126	294	—	63	178	342	—	80
Mortgage payable	80	80	75	75	70	70	65	65	60
Preferred stock	100	100	100	100	100	100	100	100	100
Common stock	100	100	100	100	125	125	125	125	125
Earned Surplus	237	240	261	256	259	270	275	274	280
Total liabilities and net worth	$620	$943	$951	$634	$696	$1,057	$1,095	$661	$729

3 PROJECTION OF FINANCIAL REQUIREMENTS

Up to this point we have discussed the appraisal of performance and the management of operating funds in the context of *past* business decisions involving investments, operations, and financing. This chapter represents a shift in emphasis to a *forward look* at likely future conditions. We will discuss the concepts and techniques of *projecting operating performance* and the resulting *financial requirements*. Such projections normally involve alternative plans developed for different conditions.

The projection of financial requirements is only *part* of the business planning process with which management positions the company's future activities relative to the expected economic, competitive, technical, and social environment. When business plans are developed, they are usually structured around specific goals and objectives cooperatively set by the organization and its subgroups. The plans normally spell out strategies and actions for achieving desired short-term, intermediate, and long-term results. These, in turn, are quantified in financial terms, in the form of *projected financial statements (pro forma statements)* and a variety of *operational budgets*. Often detailed *cash budgets* and *funds flow statements* are included to provide greater insight into the funds implications of the projected activities. The concepts and techniques discussed in Chapters 1 and 2 are, as we will see, necessary tools with which to quantify projected conditions.

The scope of this book allows us to focus only on the *major* methods and formats of financial projection. We cannot explicitly take into account the broader strategic planning framework through which the future direction of the company should be explored before financial quantification can become fully meaningful. At the same time, financial projection techniques by themselves can be useful simulations of the likely results of broad assumptions about a variety of future conditions. The ease with which pro forma financial statements can be developed makes them attractive as approximations from which refinements are possible with additional information and insights, as alternatives for action are narrowed down.

The use of planning models and computer-generated spreadsheets has grown explosively in the 1980s, as has the availability of a large selection of software packages offering financial simulation and projection capabilities. While these commercial offerings differ in their specific orientation and degree of sophistication, they are built around the very concepts we will be discussing in this chapter. Computer speed and multiple tracking capabilities have eliminated much of the drudgery of tracing investment, operational, and financing assumptions through the financial framework of a business. Yet the analyst must first *understand* and be comfortable with the basic *financial techniques and relationships* embodied in the computer models in order to take advantage of the capabilities of the available software. Therefore, this book focuses not on programming spreadsheets, but on the financial techniques themselves.

The main techniques of financial projection fall into three categories: **pro forma financial statements, cash budgets,** and **operating budgets.** Pro forma statements, as the name implies, are projected financial statements embodying a set of assumptions about a company's future performance and funding requirements. Cash budgets are detailed projections of the specific incidence of cash moving in and out of the business. Operating budgets are detailed projections of departmental revenue and/or expense patterns, and they are *subsidiary* to both pro forma statements and cash flow statements. All three categories involve an organized arrangement of financial and economic data for the purpose of assessing future performance and funds requirements. As we will see, all three methodologies are also **interrelated.** This interrelationship can be exploited to achieve consistent financial forecasts. We will also examine **financial modeling** and the use of **sensitivity analysis** for testing the impact of changes in critical assumptions underlying the financial projections.

PRO FORMA FINANCIAL STATEMENTS

The most comprehensive look at the likely future financial performance of a company can be obtained by developing a set of pro forma statements. These statements are merely an *operating statement* and a *balance sheet* extended into the future. The pro forma operating statement represents an *"operational plan"* for the business as a whole, while the pro forma balance sheet reflects the anticipated *cumulative* impact of assumed future decisions on the *financial condition* of the business. Both statements are prepared by taking the most readily available estimates of future activity and projecting, account by account, the assumed results and conditions. A third statement, a pro forma *funds flow statement*, adds further insight into the funds movements expected during the forecast period.

Pro forma projections can be done at any level of detail desired. In summarized form, the statements are one of the most widely used ways of quickly making estimates. They are particularly favored by bank loan officers, who must assess the credit-worthiness of the client company from a total financial standpoint. Detailed plans are not needed to construct complete pro forma statements, even though a formal planning process would increase the degree of precision. Instead, ratios can be used to produce statements that are entirely satisfactory, particularly as a first look. As we will demonstrate, an important aspect of pro forma analysis is the ability to find the *funds requirements* necessary for the company as of the date the pro forma balance sheet is prepared.

To show how pro forma statements are assembled, we will use the example of a fictitious manufacturing company called XYZ Corporation. The company makes and sells three products, A, B, and C, has a seasonal pattern with the low point occurring in December, and is currently profitable. The most recent actual results available are for the third quarter of 1987. These statements are the initial set of data which allows us to project ahead. But we can also ask management for additional information as needed. The pro forma projection is to be made for the last quarter of 1987, and the objective is to determine the level of profit for the quarter and the amount of additional funds needed as of the end of the year.

Pro Forma Operating Statement

We begin the process with the *pro forma operating statement* for XYZ Corporation. The operating statement is normally prepared first, because the amount of aftertax profit developed there must be reflected in the pro forma balance sheet as retained earnings. The starting point for the operating statement is a projection of the unit and dollar volume of *sales*. This can be estimated in a variety of ways, ranging from trend-line projection to detailed departmental sales forecasts built up from field estimates. In the absence of any other information we may, of course, make our own "guesstimates" based on past results. In the case of XYZ Corporation, we know that a seasonal pattern exists, and that sales can be expected to decline in the last quarter. In Figure 3–1 we have shown the actual operating statement for the third quarter of 1987. Dollar amounts are given as well as a breakdown into percent of sales, or "common numbers." The statement will become the basis for the series of assumptions we must make.

Company statistics from past years suggest that an 18 to 20 percent drop in sales volume from the third quarter is normal.

We will take the midpoint of this range as a beginning assumption. After calculating a 19 percent drop in sales volume, we make the further assumption that *prices* and *product mix* will remain unchanged. It is possible, of course, to make different assumptions about volume, prices, and mix in order to reflect specific insights or to test the impact of "what if" questions. In our case, an inquiry to sales management will confirm that this set of assumptions about sales matches their own forecast.

Next we turn to *cost of goods sold.* The actual third-quarter operating statement provides details on the main components—*labor, materials, overhead,* and *delivery*—in cost of goods sold. We can calculate the proportion of cost that each of these elements represents and assume that the same proportions will hold during the fourth quarter. But we must also remember that the last quarter is the company's seasonal low point, and we can assume that some inefficiencies are likely to raise overall production costs as operations slow. Without more data we can assume a rise of something like 1 percentage point in the ratio of cost of goods sold to sales as a quick way to allow for the seasonal distortion. The dollar penalty of this assumption is a reduction in gross margin of 1 percent of $10,250,000, or $102,500. Other levels of cost of goods sold could, of course, be tested. Note that cost of goods sold and gross margin can be estimated *directly* without the detailed cost breakdown (labor, materials, etc.) given in the third quarter operating statement.

The main *expense* categories can be estimated by again examining the actual statement for the third quarter. The figures provided there might simply be accepted as our projection. *Selling expense* is shown as $875,000. Given that the fourth quarter has lower sales activity, we can assume a small decrease, such as $50,000. A reduction fully proportional to the 19 percent drop in volume would not be realistic, however, given that many of the costs, such as salaries of marketing personnel, are essentially fixed in the near term. *Administrative expense* is rounded off a little higher for purposes of our projection because of expected nonrecurring year-end expenses. Note that both expense elements now represent a higher proportion

Figure 3–1
XYZ CORPORATION
Pro Forma Income Statement
For the Quarter Ended December 31, 1987
($000)

	Actual Quarter Ended 9–30–87		Pro Forma* Quarter Ended 12–31–87		Assumptions and Sources of Information
Units sold	137,000		111,000		Last quarter is seasonal low; past data show 18 to 20 percent decline from third quarter
Net sales	$12,650	100.0%	$10,250	100.0%	Projected 19 percent lower volume with same price and mix
Cost of goods sold:					
Labor	2,210		1,810		21.5% of cost of goods as before
Materials	2,045		1,680		20.0% of cost of goods as before
Overhead	5,685		4,660		55.5% of cost of goods as before
Delivery	305		250		3.0% of cost of goods as before
Cost of goods sold . . .	10,245	81.0	8,400	82.0	
Gross margin	2,405	19.0	1,850	18.0	Increase of 1 percentage point to simulate operating inefficiencies

Expenses:					
Selling expense	875	6.9	825	8.1	Assume drop of $50, to show lower activity
General and administrative expenses	585	4.6	600	5.9	Assume slight increase for year-end costs
Total expenses	1,460	11.5	1,425	14.0	
Operating profit	945	7.5	425	4.0	Shows effect of less efficient operations
Interest	190	1.5	175	1.7	Based on outstanding debt.
Profit before taxes	755	6.0	250	2.3	Projected at 46%.
Income taxes	347	2.7	115	1.1	
Net income	408	3.3	135	1.2	
Dividends	100	0.8	-0-	-0-	No payment of dividends scheduled.
Retained earnings	308	2.5%	135	1.2%	Carried to balance sheet.
Depreciation added back	575		600		From *fixed asset records* (assume tax and book depreciation are the same)
Cash flow after dividends	$ 883		$ 735		Rough measure of cash from operations (should add back any dividends to reflect operations only).

* All projections are rounded off.

of sales than was true for the actual prior quarter. If in the analyst's judgment, this result seems out of line it may, of course, be modified. Even if highly detailed historical information were available, we must remember that the projection deals with the future, and that the purpose of the exercise is to make the most realistic assumptions possible. The estimates will *remain* assumptions, however, until actual experience supersedes them.

As a result of our assumptions, the fourth quarter *operating profit* falls by half a million dollars, and the profit ratio drops to almost half its former level. This is due mostly to the 19 percent drop in sales volume and the associated loss in profit contribution. This reduction represents $2.4 million of sales which, with a normal cost of goods sold of 81 percent, would have contributed $456,000. Moreover, we assumed certain inefficiencies in operations and only a partial ability to reduce what are mostly fixed expenses. As we stated before, the analyst can examine this result and judge its appropriateness.

Interest is charged according to the provisions of the outstanding debt, and this information must be provided by the financial officer. The operating statement can be completed once we calculate *income taxes* (assumed here at the top rate of 46 percent) to arrive at *net income*. We note that net income has dropped significantly in response to the slowdown in operations. A further assumption needs to be made about *dividends* to arrive at retained earnings, which have to be reflected in the pro forma balance sheet. No dividends have been scheduled, according to the financial officer. As a last step and for convenience, we have added back the *depreciation* for the period to approximate the *cash flow from operations*. This is a quick estimate which we will review in the context of all other expected funds movements.

Pro Forma Balance Sheet

Armed with the data about expected operations, we can now develop the *pro forma balance sheet*, which is illustrated in Figure 3–2. Again we must make specific assumptions about each account on the statement, working from the actual balance sheet at the beginning of the forecast period and additional information we can obtain from management. We have relative freedom to make and vary our estimates, except that there *must* be *consistency* between the assumptions affecting *both* the operating statement and the balance sheet. The objective is not accounting precision, of course, but rather to develop an indication of approximate funds needs three months hence and of the overall financial condition of the company at that time.

We begin the calculations with the first account, *cash*, and make the assumption that three months from now the company would need to keep only the minimum working balance in its bank accounts. The source for this figure ($1,250,000) again is the financial officer. In the absence of such specific information, we could assume a level of cash that is common among companies of this size. As we will see later, the desired amount of cash on hand will affect the amount of funds the company may have to borrow. Cash maintained on the balance sheet is an *investment* like any other.

Next we turn to *accounts receivable*. If the company sells its products on terms of net 30, it can expect to have at least 30 days' sales outstanding; more, if some of its customers are late in payment. On the December 31 balance sheet receivables would represent the sales for the whole month of December. We do not have the exact December sales estimate because our pro forma operating statement shows sales for the last *three* months *combined*. In the absence of specific *monthly* sales estimates, we could assume that one third of the projected quarterly sales would be outstanding at the end of the quarter. In our case, that would be one third of the $10,250,000 in Figure 3–1, or $3,417,000. But after some discussion with sales management we learn that given the *seasonal low* in December, the company's sales force projects the month's sales at only $3,050,000. This then is the 30-day amount of sales we can assume to be outstanding as accounts receivable at the end of the year.

Figure 3–2
XYZ CORPORATION
Pro Forma Balance Sheet as of December 31, 1987
($000)

Assets	Actual 9–30–87	Change	Pro Forma 12–31–87	Assumptions and Sources of Information
Current assets:				
Cash	$ 1,450	– 200	$ 1,250	Cash set at estimated minimum balance.
Accounts receivable	4,250	– 1,200	3,050	Represents 30 days' sales (from December sales projection).
Raw materials	1,500	–0–	1,500	Safety level; requirements purchased as needed.
Finished goods	4,050	– 750	3,300	Reduced production by 19 percent.
Total current assets	11,250	– 2,150	9,100	Drop reflects seasonal pattern.
Fixed assets:				
Land	2,500	–0–	2,500	No change assumed.
Plant and equipment	20,800	– 1,500	19,300	Sale of machines with original cost of $1,500 and accumulated depreciation of $950.
Less: Accumulated depreciation	8,350	– 350	8,000	Depreciation for period $600, per income statement.
Net plant and equipment	12,450	– 1,150	11,300	
Total fixed assets	14,950	– 1,150	13,800	
Other assets	1,250	–0–	1,250	No change assumed.
Total assets	$27,450	– 3,300	$24,150	

Liabilities and Net Worth

Current liabilities:				
Accounts payable	$ 1,120	– 410	$ 710	45 days' purchases (from November/December purchase estimates).
Notes payable	3,000	– 1,500	1,500	Repayment as scheduled.
Due contractor	3,400	– 2,900	500	From payment schedule.
Accruals	1,250	– 285	965	Tax payments (– $400) and tax accrual (+ $115).
Total current liabilities	8,770	– 5,095	3,675	Reflects heavy current repayments of obligations.
Long-term liabilities	8,500	–0–	8,500	No change.
Common stock	4,250	+ 250	4,500	Sale of stock under option.
Retained earnings	5,930	+ 135	6,065	Retained earnings per income statement (no payment of dividends).
Total liabilities and net worth	$27,450	– 4,710	22,740	
Funds required		+ 1,410	1,410	"Plug" figure representing financing need as of 12–31–87, the same as in Figure 3–4.
		– 3,300	$24,150	

Raw material inventory could be projected by using the monthly withdrawal and purchase patterns, information that the company could provide. Manufacturing management informs us that for reasons of continuity, they like to keep on hand at all times $1.5 million worth of raw materials, and thus frequent purchases are made as required to maintain that level.

Finished goods inventory is likely to decline in response to lower sales and production activity, and we have calculated a 19 percent reduction. If we considered this an optimistic assumption, because of the precision required in adjusting production exactly to the seasonal low, a higher amount can, of course, be specified. The consequence would be a *lesser* amount of *funds released* from declining inventories.

When we add up all our changes in the *current asset accounts* we find that the total is projected to decline by over $2 million, releasing these funds for other uses. Such a pattern reflects the normal funds flow expectations from seasonal operations, as discussed in Chapter 2.

Fixed assets are affected by several events. While *land* remains unchanged, we are told that some machines will be sold during the last quarter. Their original cost was $1.5 million, against which $950,000 of depreciation has been accumulated. They are to be sold for book value, which involves no gain or loss. To reflect the transaction, the plant and equipment account on our pro forma balance sheet must be reduced by the original cost, while accumulated depreciation must be reduced by the $950,000 of past write-offs reflected there. We also know from the pro forma operating statement that normal depreciation for the period will be $600,000. This amount has to be reflected as an addition to the accumulated depreciation account. Thus, accumulated depreciation will decline by a *net* of $350,000 as a result of the two changes. *Other assets* are assumed to be unchanged.

On the liability side, *accounts payable* are assumed to decline in response to lower activity in the last quarter. The payables are mostly related to purchases of raw material. We could approximate accounts payable, which we are told have terms of net 45, by assuming that about one half of the 90-day raw materials use indicated on the pro forma operating statement would be outstanding ($840,000). But we have additional inside information on the level of *purchases* scheduled, and our assumption can be refined to show all of December's purchases ($460,000) and one half of November's ($250,000) to be outstanding as total accounts payable at year-end ($710,000).

Other current liabilities must be analyzed in terms of specific payment schedules. We are informed that *notes payable* have a provision for repayment of $1.5 million during the quarter. The *due contractor* account requires XYZ Corporation to make a payment of almost $3 million owed on past construction. *Accruals* largely involve income tax and other tax payments. We already know from the pro forma operating statement that taxes due for the quarter will be $115,000. We are also told that the company must make an estimated tax payment of $400,000 during the quarter. These two items will net out to a reduction in accruals of $285,000. Note that total current liabilities are estimated to be reduced by about $5 million, a significant *use of funds* over the forecast period.

Long-term liabilities are assumed to remain unchanged, while the value of *common stock* is expected to increase by $250,000, as stock options are exercised. Finally, *retained earnings* will increase by the net profit (income) of $135,000 calculated on the pro forma operating statement.

When the results are added up, the pro forma balance sheet *will not balance.* This is not surprising inasmuch as we did not use double-entry bookkeeping to balance our calculations. Instead, we made a variety of independent assumptions about many of the accounts, taking care only to be *consistent* with the related projections in the pro forma *operating statement.* Having done so, and given that we are reasonably satisfied with our assumptions, the *balancing figure* required to make assets equal liabilities represents the *funds need,* or the *excess funds* of the company on the pro forma balance sheet date. This "plug" figure, as it is often called, serves as a quick estimate of what additional indebtedness the company will face on the date of the statement, or what excess funds it will have at its disposal. It will *not* indicate, however, the peaks and valleys in funds requirements that may have occurred during each month of the quarter. These could be found by generating *intermediate* balance sheets more frequently than every 90 days. In other words, we could do this by taking financial "snapshots" in more closely spaced intervals. As we will see shortly, the cash budget is a more direct way of tracing the ups and downs of funds requirements within the forecast period. Before turning to the cash budget, however, we will briefly discuss the further interpretation of balance sheet changes by means of funds flow analysis.

Pro Forma Funds Flow Statement

As we observed in Figure 3–2, there were some very significant changes between the beginning and ending balance sheets of the forecast period. A *pro forma funds flow statement* will help us to highlight the funds movements reflected in these changes and their impact on the company's financial condition. Using the techniques discussed in Chapter 2, we can take the changes in the balance sheet and the key information from the operating statement to construct the pro forma funds flow analysis shown in Figure 3–3. We have divided the funds flows into working capital changes, funds from operations, and financing changes. From the data displayed, it becomes quite obvious that the reduced operations are expected to release a significant amount of working capital, almost $1.5 million. This is in addition to the net funds flow from operations, almost $0.75 million.

These sources are outweighed by significant financing changes, however. In terms of meeting financial obligations, $4.4 million are scheduled for repayment. The $1.5 million notes payable represents repayment of a *seasonal* funds need, made possible by the release of *working capital* as the seasonal low approaches. Repayment of the construction loan, however, is a consequence of major *capital investment*. It is unlikely to be covered by the *operational* funds flows from just three

Figure 3–3
XYZ CORPORATION
Pro Forma Funds Flow Statement
For the Quarter Ended December 31, 1987 ($ millions)

	Sources	Uses
Changes in working capital		
Decrease in cash	$ 200	$ —
Decrease in receivables	1,200	—
Decrease in finished goods	750	—
Decrease in payables	—	410
Decrease in accrued taxes	—	285
Totals	2,150	695
Net change in working capital	1,455	
Funds from operations		
Net income	135	
Depreciation (noncash charge)	600	
Net funds from operations	735	
Net operational funds flow	2,190	
Changes in financing		
Repayment of notes	—	1,500
Repayment of construction loan	—	2,900
Proceeds from stock option	250	—
Proceeds from sale of machinery	550	—
Totals	800	4,400
Net change in financing		3,600
Funding requirement as of 12/31/87	1,410	—
	$3,600	$3,600

months, and *other financing* must eventually be arranged. The sale of machinery and the proceeds from the exercise of stock options assist somewhat in this, but the gap left is still $1.4 million. It should be clear that if we make any *changes* in the assumptions behind the pro forma projections, the size of the funding gap will be affected. In fact, it is often very helpful to test the sensitivity of the projected conditions to changes in key assumptions, such as sales volume, collection patterns, and major cost deviations.

Funding stresses *during* the forecast period still have not been dealt with, however. These occur because the gradual *release* of operating funds from the operating slowdown during the quarter will *lag the decline in volume.* Thus the exact scheduling of the repayments within the three-month period could cause significant shortfalls. If all repayments came due in *October,* for example, the funding gap would be much *higher during that month* than the pro forma statements suggest for the end of December. As we will see, only a detailed cash budget will reveal such hidden fluctuations.

To summarize, pro forma statements are a convenient and relatively simple way of projecting *expectations* about a company's performance. To create these statements requires maintaining *consistent* assumptions in preparing the operating statement and the balance sheet, but otherwise a great degree of *subjective judgment* is involved. The balancing element in the pro forma balance sheet is the *funds need* or *funds excess* resulting from the conditions assumed. This *"plug"* will vary as assumptions are changed. Pro forma funds flow statements help highlight the funds movement implied by changes in the balance sheet. Pro forma analysis is *limited* by the *static* nature of the balance sheet which shows funds needs only at a specific point in time, and not their ebb and flow. More dynamic *intraperiod* analysis requires either generating several short-term pro forma statements at key decision points, or the budgetary forecast embodied in the cash budget.

CASH BUDGETS

Cash budgets, or **cash flow statements,** are very specific month-by-month or even week-by-week planning vehicles normally prepared by the financial staff of a company. They focus exclusively on the specific *incidence* of cash receipts and payments. The financial manager who uses a cash budget is very interested in observing the *changing levels* of the cash account, which must be maintained at a level sufficient to allow timely payment of amounts due. As a consequence, the financial manager must plan *cash activity* to reflect in very specific detail the *timing* of the inflows and outflows of cash in response to planned operational and investment activities.

As we will see, cash budgets again show the level of funds needs or excesses. The level at the *end of the period* will exactly *match* the level shown on the *pro forma balance sheet,* if the cash budget was prepared using the *same* basic assumptions employed in generating the pro forma statements.

Cash budgeting, in principle, is quite simple. It is quite similar to personal budgeting, where bills due are matched with receipts from paychecks, dividend checks, bank interest payments, and so on. This matching is necessary to determine funds requirements as they affect the cash balance available for payment. The cash balance will probably fluctuate from day to day, week to week, or month to month. If a company's collections from credit sales tend to lag for weeks while wages and purchases must be paid currently, serious cash shortages can occur. (The reader will recall the discussion in Chapter 2, where the concept of lags was explored in relation to funds flows.) Similarly, cash payments for nonrecurring items, such as outlays for capital equipment, may cause temporary funding problems that must be met. Given its detail, the cash budget is the ultimate expression of funds flow analysis, because in the end, *all funds movements have a cash effect.*

In preparing a cash budget, a *time schedule* of estimated receipts and payments of cash must be laid out. This schedule shows, period by period, the net effect of projected activity on the cash balance. The selection of the time *intervals* covered by the cash budget depends on the nature of the business and the trade terms under which it operates. If daily fluctuations are likely to be large, as in the banking business, day-by-day projections will be necessary. In other cases weekly, monthly, or even quarterly projections will suffice.

Let us now turn to the data of XYZ Corporation and prepare a *monthly* cash budget for the last quarter of 1987. This will increase our understanding of the funds flow picture over that provided by the pro forma analysis. In Figure 3–4 we have presented some of the basic data of the company's operations regarding sales, production, and purchases. We show two months of actual activities *prior to* the forecast period, because due to the credit terms of sales and purchases, the *cash lag* from these past months will influence the three months being projected.

Figure 3–4
XYZ CORPORATION
Sample Cash Budget for the Quarter Ended December 31, 1987
($000)

	August	September	October	November	December	Total for Quarter
Basic data:						
Unit sales	48,000	46,000	42,000	36,000	33,000	111,000
Unit production	50,000	50,000	35,000	34,000	31,000	100,000
Change in inventory	+2,000	+4,000	−7,000	−2,000	−2,000	−11,000
Sales volume (on credit)	$4,450	$4,250	$3,850	$3,350	$3,050	$10,250
Purchases (on credit)	760	740	520	500	460	1,480
Cash receipts:						
Collection of receivables—prior months' sales; normal terms of 30 days assumed			$4,250	$3,850	$3,350	$11,450
Proceeds from sale of stock options			−0−	250	−0−	250
Proceeds from sale of used machines at book value (original cost, $1,500)			−0−	−0−	550	550
Total cash receipts			4,250	4,100	3,900	12,250

Cash disbursements:

Payment for purchases*	750	630	510	1,890
Production payroll (from operating budget)	560	545	500	1,605
Manufacturing expenses (from operating budget)	1,265	1,260	1,235	3,760
Selling and delivery expenses (from sales budget)	350	345	335	1,030
General overhead expenses (from administrative budget)	200	200	200	600
Interest payment on debt	-0-	-0-	175	175
Principal payment on note payable	1,500	-0-	-0-	1,500
Federal tax payment	400	-0-	-0-	400
Payments on construction of new plant	-0-	2,000	900	2,900
Total cash disbursements	5,025	4,980	3,855	13,860
Net cash receipts (disbursements)	(775)	(880)	45	(1,610)
Cumulative net cash flow	$ (775)	$(1,655)	$(1,610)	

Analysis of cash requirements:

Beginning cash balance	$1,450	$ 675	(205)	$ 1,450
Net cash receipts (disbursements)	(775)	(880)	45	(1,610)
Ending cash balance	675	(205)	(160)	(160)
Minimum cash balance	1,250	1,250	1,250	1,250
Cash requirements	$ 575	$ 1,455	$ 1,410	$ 1,410

*Normal terms of 45 days assumed. Payments therefore represent one month's purchases prior to last 1.5 months (e.g., half of August and half of September paid during October).

The lag effect can be clearly demonstrated in the first of the *cash receipts*, collection of receivables. On the assumption that the company's customers will continue to remit within the 30-day terms, cash receipts for any month should be the sales made in the *prior* month. In contrast, if there were a *60-day* collection period, collections would represent the sales made *two* months earlier. Thus, any expected change in customer behavior or in the credit terms themselves must be reflected in a different receipts pattern. It is often helpful to draw a scale of time periods on which the days, weeks, or months of sales are recorded when made. Using this scale, any assumed collection experience can be simulated by "staggering" (that is, delaying) the *receipts* according to the appropriate number of days. For example, a schedule of sales and collections on 30-day credit would appear as follows:

	January	February	March	April	May	June
Credit sales	$25,000	$30,000	$40,000	$42,000	$35,000	$30,000
Collections	(Dec. sales)	25,000	30,000	40,000	42,000	35,000

The *proceeds* from the exercise of stock options and from the sale of used machinery have been budgeted in their respective months of incidence. The *total* cash receipts for each month show a declining pattern which lags the declining sales, but this is moderated somewhat by the nonoperating proceeds from options and sale of used machinery.

As we turn to the disbursements, we encounter another lag in payments for purchases made on credit. Under normal credit terms of 45 days, we can assume that the company's payments will lag by 45 days. Consequently, purchases made in the second half of August and the first half of September will be paid for in October, with a similar pattern repeating itself in November and December. In other words, one month's worth of purchases staggered by 45 days will be paid in a given month. Again a time scale with 15-day intervals will help illustrate this pattern of payment.

Inasmuch as the last quarter of 1987 is projected in a *declining pattern* to December's seasonal low in sales and manufacturing activities, the staggered timing due to credit terms shifts both somewhat higher cash receipts and payments into a period of low operating activity. Funds are *released* in the process, as we would expect when we recall the discussion of changes in operations and their funds impact in Chapter 2. This funds result matches what we observed in the totals provided by the pro forma analysis. Had there instead been a *rising* volume of operation, lower cash incidence would have resulted, and additional funds would be required. In that case, the cash budget would have reflected the lag effect of the lower activities of the earlier months. It should be apparent by now that there is a critical need for careful cash budgeting in a business where operating levels and payments swing widely.

Other cash disbursements *(payroll, manufacturing expenses, selling and delivery, and general overhead)* are shown without lags, on the assumption that payments for these expenses and obligations are made within the month they are incurred. This assumption could be slightly incorrect in the case of payroll disbursements and certain manufacturing expenses. Such items could indeed lag by one or two weeks. How such lags are dealt with is a function of the seriousness of the cash flow problems they reflect.

Production-related payments, such as payroll and manufacturing expenses, are based on the declining pattern of *production* shown in the basic data section of Figure 3–4, which also reflects a gradual inventory reduction. Yet, in the pro forma operating statement for the period, cost of goods sold is normally based on the pattern of *selling* activities to make projection easier. Thus, the pro forma statement and the more detailed cash budget may differ because the assumptions concerning sales and production are different. To ensure complete consistency it is therefore necessary to carefully determine whether the pattern of production is projected on a different basis than the pattern of sales.

As an example of such a potential difference, it is entirely possible that the seasonal low could be used by management to build up inventories in advance of the expected resurgence of sales. If that were so, the inventory assumption for the pro forma balance sheet would have to be modified to show the *buildup* of inventories and the resultant additional funds need. The cash budget, in turn, would have to reflect the higher expenditures involved in producing for inventory. Recognizing differences in production and selling patterns is a key to refining the projection of company performance, and to making cash budgeting results consistent with the pro forma statements.

The final result of our cash budget is a picture of the monthly cash effect of the operating plans on which it is based, and the net funds needs or excesses each month. Note that the funds need in December of $1,410,000 matches the indication from the pro forma statements, because the same assumptions were used throughout.

To summarize, cash budgets lay out in specific detail the exact *incidence* of cash receipts and disbursements. Like household budgets, they allow us to watch for *peaks and valleys* in cash availability and to schedule additional financing or repayments as needed. Unlike pro forma statements, which are limited to the beginning and end of a specific period, cash budgets can be drawn up for as many *intervals* as desired *within* a period to simulate the fluctuations in cash flow. Given the *same assumptions* in terms of the volume of production and sales, and the handling of receipts, payments, and credit, etc., the cash budget and pro forma statements will *agree* in terms of the funds needs or excesses at the *end* of the period covered.

OPERATING BUDGETS

The pro forma statements and cash budget we prepared for XYZ Corporation provide an *overall view* of the company's future performance. But in any sizable company, a hierarchy of more specific *operating budgets* are normally prepared. Operating budgets are essentially internal documents. As expressions of ongoing operations, such budgets are linked closely to the organizational structure and to the type of performance measurement used by the particular company. These budgets are part of the planning process we mentioned earlier, and are very useful as a background for pro forma and cash flow projections when a higher degree of detail and accuracy is desired.

Most managements structure their companies into manageable parts, for each of which an executive or manager is held responsible. The structure may be by *functions*, that is, sales, production, purchasing, and so on. In other cases, the organization may be composed of a set of smaller *"profit centers,"* each of which is expected to make a profit contribution to total company performance. Even though there are countless variations of organizational structure, the principles of budgeting and financial projection are straightforward and commonly applicable. Projection of operating results must take a form that reflects the *scope* of the business unit involved. It must be related to the elements *controllable* by the responsible manager, and should be the basis on which the manager's *performance* is measured. These criteria obviously require that operating budgets be carefully designed to fit the particular unit's conditions and the management style of the company as a whole. This means that there is a great deal of difference in the approaches taken by various companies, even within the same industry, and there may be differences within the same company in terms of operating budgets for different organizational units. A growing body of literature has recognized the criteria and impact of what is called *responsibility accounting* within a given organization.

For purposes of our discussion, a few illustrations of basic operational budgeting will suffice. Among the various internal operating budgets routinely prepared by XYZ Corporation are the *annual sales budget by quarters* and *a quarterly factory budget*. The sales budget is designed to show the sales unit's projected contribution to total corporate profits, while the factory budget reflects expected output and the total costs incurred in producing the forecast volume. There are many other types of profit and expense budgets, but we will limit our discussion to these two, showing how they are used to provide background information for the financial analyst preparing and analyzing pro forma statements and cash budgets.

Sales Budget

As is shown in Figure 3–5, the sales manager must first project the level of *unit sales* expected in the market territories served. The projection is made by major product line. Most likely this forecast will be built up from the individual judg-

Figure 3–5
XYZ CORPORATION
Sample Quarterly Sales Budget
Year Ended December 31, 1987

	Quarter				
	First	Second	Third	Fourth	Total
Basic data:					
Unit sales (number of units):					
Product A	2,700	2,900	3,000	2,800	11,400
Product B	8,000	8,500	10,000	8,000	34,500
Product C	17,500	18,500	21,000	16,000	73,000
Price level (per unit):					
Product A	$ 145	$ 145	$ 150	$ 150	—
Product B	92	92	95	95	—
Product C	74	74	74	74	—
Number of salespersons	25	25	25	26	—
Operating budget ($000):					
Sales revenue	$ 2,423	$ 2,572	$ 2,954	$ 2,364	$10,313
Less: returns, allowances	25	26	28	24	103
Net sales	2,398	2,546	2,926	2,340	10,210
Cost of goods sold	1,916	2,051	2,322	1,868	8,157
Margin before delivery	482	495	604	472	2,053
Delivery expense	56	60	68	54	238
Gross margin	426	435	536	418	1,815
Selling expense (controllable):					
Salespersons' compensation	94	94	94	98	380
Travel and entertainment	32	32	32	33	129
Sales support costs	23	23	26	24	96
Total selling expenses	149	149	152	155	605
Gross contribution	277	286	384	263	1,210
Departmental period costs	18	18	18	18	72
Net contribution	259	268	366	245	1,138
Corporate support (transferred):					
Staff support	23	25	25	27	100
Advertising	50	50	75	50	225
General overhead	63	63	63	63	252
Total corporate support	136	138	163	140	577
Profit contribution (before taxes)	$ 123	$ 130	$ 203	$ 105	$ 561

ments of the persons closest to current and potential customers. Economic conditions will likely be factored in, as will the marketing strategies XYZ Corporation and its competitors are likely to follow.

Next the *price levels* for each product must be estimated. Prices commonly are a function of three factors: industry pricing practices, the competitive environment, and the cost effectiveness of the company's manufacturing operations. Once price is established, *sales revenue* can be calculated. Then the *cost of goods sold* for products transferred internally or possibly purchased on the outside must be determined. The difference between revenue and cost is the *margin before delivery* achieved by the sales unit. Next are the projected *delivery costs* to the customers, if these are borne by the company. Controllable *selling expenses* include *compensation* to sales personnel, *travel and entertainment*, and *sales support costs*. The result is *gross contribution* from selling activities, which must be reduced by estimated *departmental period costs* (like rent, managers' salary, and other items that do not vary with short-term fluctuations in volume) to arrive at the *net contribution* provided by the department. After deducting allocated *corporate support costs*—staff support, advertising, and general overhead—the *profit contribution* for the period is established. In making all of these estimates the sales manager can use past relationships and selected ratios, tempered by his or her judgment concerning changes in future conditions.

In our example, both basic data and dollar elements are broken down by quarters and estimated for the entire year. However, other formats are possible depending on the specific needs of the organization. Generally, a company prescribes the format for its managers to follow in preparing projected activity budgets, both to maintain a degree of uniformity and to lessen the accounting problem of consolidating the projections when preparing overall financial forecasts. From the standpoint of financial projection, the sales and contribution data in our example are the raw material which goes into the total operating plan of the company.

Factory Budget

The sales budget we just discussed is basically a projection of *profit contribution*. However, companies also must make forecasts for operations or activities that involve only *costs* or *expenses*. An example of this type of projection, a cost budget for a factory, is shown in Figure 3–6. This time the data are given for each month. We have included three months and the total for the quarter. The period shown is the second quarter, during which sales and production are expected to increase. Again the

Figure 3–6
XYZ CORPORATION
Sample Factory Budget
For the Quarter Ended June 30, 1987

	April	May	June	Total
Basic data:				
Number of shifts (5-day week)	3	3	3	3
Days worked	20	21	22	63
Hourly employees per shift	33	33	33	33
Number of machines	35	35	34	—
Unit production:				
Product A	1,000	1,050	1,100	3,150
Product B	2,400	2,510	2,640	7,550
Capacity utilization	94%	94%	96%	95%
Down time for repairs (hours)	–0–	36	–0–	36
Operating budget:				
Direct costs (controllable):*				
Manufacturing labor	$ 57,600	$ 60,500	$ 63,400	$181,500
Raw materials	53,800	56,400	59,200	169,400
Operating supplies	6,500	6,900	7,300	20,700
Repair labor and parts	7,300	12,400	6,500	26,200
Power, heat, light	4,200	4,500	4,800	13,500
Total direct costs	129,400	140,700	141,200	411,300
Period costs (controllable):				
Supervision	5,500	5,500	5,500	16,500
Support labor	28,500	28,500	28,500	85,500
Insurance, taxes	8,700	8,700	8,700	26,100
Depreciation	20,500	20,500	20,500	61,500
Total period costs	63,200	63,200	63,200	189,600
Total controllable costs	192,600	203,900	204,400	600,900
General overhead (allocated)	72,000	72,000	72,000	216,000
Total cost	$264,600	$275,900	$276,400	$816,900

*Where appropriate, unit costs can be shown.

amount of detail included and the presentation format are chosen to suit the particular needs and preferences of the organization. This time we chose to arrange the headings and data to show that certain cost items (both direct and period costs) are under the *control* of the local manager. (Other costs, like *allocated* general overhead, are transferred in from corporate headquarters and thus beyond the local manager's control.) This arrangement will also be useful if the operating plan serves as a control device with which to measure the performance of the unit.

Both sales and cost budgets commonly include additional columns in which *actual* as opposed to projected figures are recorded. In addition, *variance* columns are frequently used to measure deviations from plan. We will not go into such refinements here, because our examples were only meant to show the type of internal budgeting and projection used formally or informally in most organizations preparatory to developing an overall financial forecast.

INTERRELATIONSHIP OF FINANCIAL PROJECTIONS

It should be obvious by now that the various types of projection presented in this chapter are closely related. If all three forecasts—pro forma statements, cash budgets, and operating budgets—are based on the *same* set of assumptions about receipts and collections, repayment schedules, operating rates, inventory levels, and so on, they will all precisely *fit together* in the fashion illustrated in Figure 3–7. The plans and the projected funds need or excess will *differ* only if different *assumptions* concerning funds flow are used, particularly in the pro forma statements and the cash budget. It is quite easy to reconcile pro forma statements and cash budgets, however, by carefully thinking through the key assumptions, one by one, and by laying out formats that contain sufficient detail and background data.

The diagram shows how the various operating budgets flow into a combined cash budget, which in turn is reinforced by

Figure 3–7
Interrelationship of Financial Projections

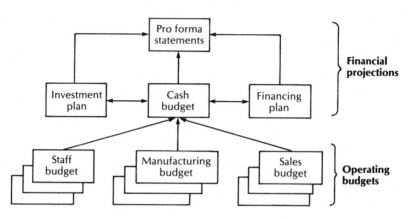

specific data from the investment and financing plans (see below). The combined information supports the pro forma statements at the top of the diagram. Thus, pro forma statements
are the all-encompassing expression of the expected conditions
for the period ahead. As a consequence, if we choose to make
pro forma statements *direct overall estimates,* as we discussed,
rather than building them up from the budgets and plans of
the company, they in effect will *imply specific assumptions*
about *all* the other elements in the diagram.

We have not yet discussed some of the elements shown in
Figure 3–7. **Staff budgets** are spending plans based on the expected cost of operating various service functions of a company. These budgets are prepared and used in the same fashion
as other expense budgets.

Investment plans are projections of new outlays for land,
buildings, machinery and equipment, and related incremental
working capital, as well as major outlays for new products and
services, expanding markets, new technology, etc. They may
also contain plans to *divest* any of the company's fixed assets.
We recall that XYZ Corporation made a minor reduction in its
capital investments by selling some used machines, while a recently constructed plant was still being paid for, as evidenced
by the current liability "due contractor." This existing invest-

ment was already reflected on the actual balance sheet of September 30, 1987, and only the payment currently due was properly scheduled as a pro forma cash disbursement.

Financing plans are schedules of proposed future additions to or reductions in indebtedness or ownership funds during the forecast period. They may involve significant expansion or restructuring of a company's capital structure, depending on the projected capital requirements. In the case of XYZ Corporation, no specific future financing was planned, but provisions would have to be made for financing the funds need established through the pro forma analysis.

FINANCIAL MODELING AND SENSITIVITY ANALYSIS

In recent years, the computer software available for financial modeling has vastly expanded the financial analyst's ability to explore the consequences of different assumptions, conditions, and plans. In principle, these software packages are no more than mathematical representations of key financial accounting relationships, ratios, and formats, supported by automatic subroutines that calculate, update, and display data and results in whatever form is desired. The process is based on the *very same* steps and reasoning discussed in this chapter. A full-fledged financial model encompasses elements such as the company's accounting procedures, depreciation schedules, tax calculations, debt service schedules, debt covenants and restrictions, inventory policies, and so on. With financial modeling and spreadsheets, the data, assumptions, and format can be "custom tailored" so that the financial analyst can reflect the specific characteristics of a given company. With the help of such a model, the analyst can calculate the projected results of conditions expected by the company. Ease of operation allows the analyst to examine several sets of assumptions and assess alternative outcomes.

The major difference between the projection techniques discussed in this chapter and the use of spreadsheets and computer models basically only involves the *degree of automation* of the process. A cash budget done by hand is essentially a model of the cash flow pattern of the company. In constructing such a budget, the analyst must take into account corporate policies regarding accounting methods, tax reporting, and other detailed operating rules. These constraints can also be incorporated into a basic financial planning software package. The difference is that the computer can "run" different options, while simultaneously tracking all important interrelationships much more easily and quickly than is possible when an analysis is done by hand.

The financial modeling software available on the market is constantly evolving, and the reader should familiarize him- or herself with the latest offerings available. In scope, the modeling packages range all the way from spreadsheets with which to calculate simple condensed pro forma statements to highly sophisticated representations of a company's financial accounting system. In the latter case, the generalized model is extensively refined, with the help of the company's financial staff, to reflect the company's specific situation. Some companies have developed models that not only calculate the results of specific sets of assumptions, but also contain "optimizing routines" that select the most desirable alternative investment and financing patterns according to stipulated criteria. Other models include statistical projection programs that can be used to project key variables from past trends.

It is clearly beyond the scope of this book to treat in detail the vast number of concepts and specialized techniques involved in the building and use of computerized financial models. However, Figure 3–8 depicts the relationships represented in a full-fledged model. The central element is the software program that governs the calculations and displays, with the inputs coming from various sources and the outputs grouped into our familiar categories of analysis.

Sensitivity Analysis

One of the advantages of modeling is the ability to perform *sensitivity analysis* with considerable ease. This type of analy-

Figure 3–8
Financial Modeling:
An Overview of Relationships between the Elements of Input and Output

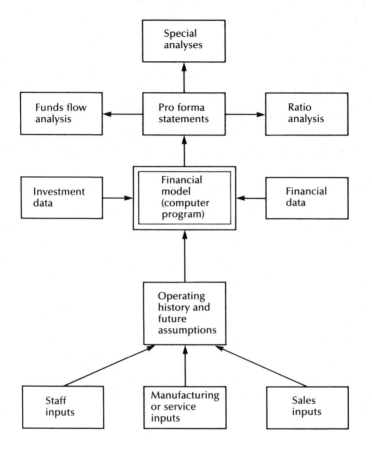

sis involves selecting a few key conditions and altering them to determine the sensitivity of the result to such changes. For example, one of the key assumptions in our pro forma analysis of XYZ Corporation was the usual seasonal pattern of an 18 to 20 percent decline in sales volume in the last quarter. If there were reason to believe that a more serious drop might occur, the analyst could estimate the dollar decline in contribution from each additional 1 percent decrease in volume. If all other conditions were to remain the same, that dollar decline would be the *lost contribution* from the units left unsold. The impact on funds needs would be traced by adjusting aftertax profits, and by recognizing that there would be a change in working capital because sales levels are lower, except in inventory where the unsold units might remain. If prices were considered unstable, a series of assumptions about the effect of lower prices for one or all of the product lines could be traced. In every case, the critical test would be the sensitivity to the changes of the funds need in *each* of the three months. Clearly, many other tests could be made and related to the altered result brought about by the change in a given assumption.

The key to this type of reasoning is the analyst's judgment as to which elements in the operating and financial patterns being projected are *most subject* to variability. Then the task is to simulate how sensitive the desired result is to each change. Given such a range of results, the decision maker using the analysis can judge the *riskiness* of the proposed course and adjust operating and financial policies accordingly. A computer model is *not critical* to making such sensitivity test. Even our simple pro forma statements and cash budgets can be modified to answer basic questions of this sort. Nonetheless, with relevant software, the analyst can examine many more possibilities and examine the impact of a far greater number of assumptions. Sensitivity tests can be performed on more than one variable *simultaneously,* and whole *scenarios* can be developed, with the financial impact reflected in the output. We will return to sensitivity analysis again in later chapters.

SUMMARY

The principles of financial projection discussed in this chapter revolve around the use of **pro forma statements** and **budgets.** We observed that financial projection is only *part* of the broader process of **business planning.** Financial projection is expressed in the familiar form of financial statements and many specifically tailored budget formats. The process is *simple* in that it represents an orderly way of sorting out the financial impact of investment, operational, and financing decisions. The process is *difficult* in that judgments about *future* conditions are fraught with uncertainty, as planning of any sort must be. It is here that the use of **sensitivity analysis,** the calculation of the impact of *alternative assumptions*, can narrow the range of uncertainty. Financial projection basically is modeling of the future in the context of operational and procedural constraints. To the extent that more detail and more options for future plans are desired, automation of the process with the help of computer-based **modeling** can yield the significant benefits of speed, accuracy, and greater insight.

SELECTED REFERENCES

Anthony, Robert N., and Reece, James S. *Accounting: Text and Cases.* 6th ed. Homewood, Ill.: Richard D. Irwin, 1979.

Rivett, Patrick. *Model Building for Decision Analysis.* Chichester (Eng.): John Wiley and Sons, 1980.

Vancil, Richard F., and Makela, Benjamin R. eds. *The CFO Handbook.* Homewood, Ill.: Dow Jones-Irwin, 1986.

Van Horne, James C. *Financial Management and Policy.* 7th ed. Englewood Cliffs, N.J.: Prentice-Hall, 1986.

Vatter, Paul A., Bradley, Stephen P., Frey, Sherwood, Jr. and Jackson, Barbara B. *Quantitative Methods in Management.* Homewood, Ill.: Richard D. Irwin, 1978.

Weston, J. Fred, and Copeland, Thomas E. *Managerial Finance.* 8th ed. Hinsdale, Ill.: Dryden Press, 1986.

SELF-STUDY EXERCISES AND PROBLEMS

(Solutions to Items 1, 2, 4, 6, and 7 are provided in Appendix III)

1. Complete the following exercises, based on these selected data about a company. Consider each exercise separately.

Total assets on 12–31–87	$2,750,000
Sales for the year 1987	9,137,000
Current assets on 12–31–87	1,315,000
Long-term debt on 12–31–87	210,000
Current ratio on 12–31–87	2.4:1
Cost of goods sold for 1987	83% of sales
Purchases during 1987	$5,316,000
Depreciation for 1987	174,000
Net profit after taxes for 1987	131,000
Taxes on income for 1987	112,000

a. Currently the company's accounts receivable outstanding are 18 days' sales. To meet competitive pressures in 1988, the company will have to extend credit to an average of 40 days' sales to maintain operations and profits at 1987 levels. No other changes are contemplated for the next year, and sales and operations are expected to continue at 1987 rates. What is the impact of this change in credit policy on corporate funds needs? Will the company have to borrow? What if credit had to be extended to 60 days? Discuss.

b. The inventory levels maintained by the company have averaged $725,000 during 1987, with little fluctuation. If turnover were to slow to seven times (average inventory in cost of goods sold) due to a switch to a consignment policy, what would the financial impact be? Assume no change in sales levels. What other changes are likely to take place, and how would these affect the company's financial stance? What if turnover rose to 11 times? Discuss.

c. Payment for purchases has been made under normal trade terms of 2/10, n/30 with discounting done as a matter of policy. Suppliers anxious for business are beginning to offer 2/15, n/45 terms, which will become universal during the coming year. What would the financial impact of this change be if the company were to follow its policy of discounting purchases? What trade-off has to be considered? Discuss.

d. If the company is planning capital expenditures of $125,000 and simultaneously is planning to pay dividends at the rate of 60 percent of net profits, what are the financial implications, assuming all other elements are unchanged?

e. If sales are expected to grow 10 percent for the following year, with all *normal* relationships under *(a)* through *(c)* unchanged, what financial considerations arise? How would the intentions of *(d)* look then? Discuss.

2. In September 1988, ABC Company, a manufacturing firm, was making budget plans for the 12 months beginning November 1, 1988. Projected sales volume was $4,350,000, as compared to an estimated $3,675,000 for the fiscal year ended October 31, 1988. The best estimates of the operating results for the current year are shown in the operating statement.

The projected increase in volume of operations was expected to bring improvements in efficiency, while at the same time some of the cost factors would continue to rise absolutely, in line with past trends. Following this statement are the specific working assumptions with which to plan financial results for the next year.

ABC COMPANY
Estimated Operating Statement
For the Year Ended October 31, 1988
($000)

	Amount		Percent	
Net sales		$3,675		100%
Cost of goods sold:				
Labor	$919		25.0	
Materials	522		14.2	
Overhead	743		20.2	
Depreciation	133	2,317	3.6	63.0
Gross profit		1,358		37.0
Selling expense	305		8.3	
General and administrative expenses	323	628	8.8	17.1
Profit before taxes		730		19.9
Income taxes		336		9.1
Net income		$ 394		10.8%

Assumptions for fiscal year 1989:

Manufacturing labor would drop to 24 percent of direct sales, because volume efficiency would more than offset higher wage rates.

Materials cost would rise to 14.5 percent of sales, because some price increases would not be offset by better utilization.

Overhead costs would rise above the present level by 6 percent of the 1988 dollar amount, reflecting higher costs, and additional variable costs would be encountered at the rate of 11 percent of the incremental sales volume.

Depreciation would increase by $10,000, reflecting the addition of some production machinery.

Selling expenses would rise more than proportionately, by $125,000, because additional effort would be required to increase sales volume.

General and administrative expense would drop to 8.1 percent of sales.

Income taxes were estimated at 46 percent of pretax profits.

Develop a pro forma operating statement for the ABC Company and discuss your findings.

3. In December 1988, the DEF Company, a distributor of stationery products, was planning its financial needs for the coming year. As a first indication, the firm's management wished to have a pro forma balance sheet as of December 31, 1989, to gauge funds needs at that time. Estimated financial condition as of December 31, 1988 was reflected in this balance sheet:

DEF COMPANY
Estimated Balance Sheet,
December 31, 1988

Assets

Current assets:		
Cash	$ 217,300	
Receivables	361,200	
Inventories (pledged as security)	912,700	
Total current assets	1,491,200	
Fixed assets:		
Land, buildings, trucks, and fixtures ..	421,500	
Less: Accumulated depreciation ...	217,300	
Total fixed assets	204,200	
Other assets	21,700	
Total assets	$1,717,100	

Liabilities and Net Worth

Current liabilities:		
Accounts payable	$ 612,300	
Note payable—bank	425,000	
Accrued expenses	63,400	
Total current liabilities	1,100,700	
Term loan—properties	120,000	
Capital stock	200,000	
Paid-in surplus	112,000	
Earned surplus	184,400	
Total liabilities and net worth	$1,717,100	

Operations for the ensuing year were projected using the following working assumptions to plan the financial results:

Sales were forecast at $10,450,000, with a gross margin of 8.2 percent.

Purchases were expected to total $9,725,000, with some seasonal upswings in May and August.

Accounts receivable would be based on a collection period of 12 days, while 24 days' accounts payable would be outstanding.

Depreciation was expected to be $31,400 for the year.

Term loan repayments were scheduled at $10,000, while bank notes payable would be allowed to fluctuate with seasonal needs.

Capital expenditures were scheduled at $21,000 for trucks and $36,000 for warehouse improvements.

Net profits after taxes were expected at the level of 0.19 percent of sales.

Dividends for the year were scheduled at $12,500.

Cash balances were desired at no less than $150,000.

Develop a pro forma balance sheet and discuss your findings.

4. In September 1988, the XYZ Company, a department store, was planning for cash needs during the last quarter of 1988 and the first quarter of 1989. The Christmas buying season always meant a considerable strain on finances, and the first planning step was development of a cash budget. The following data were available for this purpose:

Projected sales (half for cash, half charged on 90-day account):

October	$ 770,000	January	$650,000
November	690,000	February	580,000
December	1,010,000	March	720,000

Projected purchases (half on n/45; 40 percent on 2/10, n/30; 10 percent for cash):

October	$610,000	January	$320,000
November	535,000	February	450,000
December	290,000	March	480,000

Projected payments on purchases as of 9–30–88:

Due by October 10 (2% discount)	$ 60,000
Due by October 31 (net 45)	257,000
Due by November 15 (net 45)	113,000
Total	$430,000

Projected collections of receivables as of 9–30–88:

Due in October	$215,000
Due in November	245,000
Due in December	265,000
Total (bad debts negligible)	$725,000

Projected financial data:

Minimum cash balance required	$75,000
Beginning cash balance (October 1)	95,000
Mortgage payments (monthly)	7,000
Cash dividend due December 31	40,000
Federal taxes due January 15	20,000

Projected operations: salaries and wages average 19 percent of sales, cash operating expenses average 14 percent of sales.

Develop a monthly cash budget to show the seasonal funds requirements. Discuss your findings.

5. A newly formed space technology company, the ZYX Corporation, was in the early stages of planning for the first several months of operations. The initial capital put up by the founders and their associates amounted to 250,000 shares of $1 par value stock. Furthermore, patents estimated to be worth $50,000 were provided by two of the principals in exchange

for 50,000 shares of common stock. Equipment costing $175,000 was purchased with the funds, and organization expenses of $15,000 were paid. Operations were to start February 1, 1988.

Orders already in hand amounted to $1,400,000 of electronic devices, which, at an estimated monthly output of $400,000 (sales value), represented almost four months' sales. More orders were expected from contacts made. Monthly operating expenses and conditions were estimated as follows:

Manufacturing labor	$ 60,000
Rent for building	18,500
Overhead costs	76,000
Depreciation	6,000
Write-off of patents	500
Selling and administrative expenses	55,000
Purchases of materials, supplies	125,000
Sales terms	n/30
Collection experience expected	45 days
Purchase terms	n/30
Raw materials inventory level	$ 60,000
Finished goods inventory level	145,000
Prepaid expenses (average)	12,000
Accrued wages	1 week's
Accrued taxes (40% effective rate)	As incurred

If the company wanted to maintain a minimum cash balance of $40,000, what would the financial situation be after six months of operations? Develop pro forma statements and discuss the likely timing of any funds needs. How are the next six months likely to affect this picture? Discuss your findings.

6. The ABC Supermarket's management expected the next six months (January 1, 1988, through June 30, 1988) to bring a variety of cash requirements beyond the normal operational outflows. A monthly cash budget was to be developed to trace the specific funds needs. The following projections were available for the purpose:
   a. Cash sales projected:

January	$200,000	April	$200,000
February	190,000	May	230,000
March	220,000	June	220,000

   b. Cost of goods sold averages 75 percent of sales.
   c. Purchases closely scheduled with sales volume. Payments average a 15-day lag behind purchases. December purchases were $168,000.
   d. Operating expenses projected:

1. Salaries and wages at 12 percent of sales, paid when incurred.
2. Other expenses at an average 9 percent of sales, paid when incurred.
3. Rent of $3,500, paid monthly.
4. Income tax payments of $2,000 due in January, March, and June, and $3,500 due in April.
5. Cash receipts from sale of property at $6,000 per month due in March, April, and May.
6. Payments on note owed local bank due as follows: $3,000 in February and $5,000 in May.
7. Repayments of advances to principals of the firm due at $3,000 each in January, March, and May.
8. New store fixtures of $48,000 acquired, and four payments of $12,000 each due in February, March, April, and May.
9. Old store fixtures with a book value of $4,500 scrapped, to be written off in January.
10. Rental income from a small concession granted on the premises to begin at $300 per month in March.

Develop a cash budget as requested and show the effect of the operations and other elements described above on the beginning cash balance of $42,500. The principals of the firm would like to keep a cash balance of not less than $20,000 at any one time. Will additional funds be required? If so, when? Discuss your findings.

7. The XYZ Company, a fast-growing manufacturing operation, found its inventories in 1988 increasing faster than growth in sales. (As additional territories and customers had been developed, production schedules were stepped up in an effort to provide excellent service levels.) Also, collections had deteriorated, and the company's receivables represented two months' sales compared to normal 30-day terms. Because both conditions caused considerable pressures on the company's finances, a change to a level production schedule was considered beginning October 1, 1988, to allow inventories to be worked off while still providing employment to the company's full-time workers. Also, more effort would be expended on collections. A six-month trial of the new policy was to be analyzed in September before implementation, and the following assumptions and data were provided:
   a. Current sales and forecast:

August	$1,925,000	December	$2,450,000
September (est.)	2,050,000	January	2,625,000
October	2,175,000	February	2,750,000
November	2,300,000	March	2,850,000

b. Current purchases and forecast (terms n/45):

August	$ 750,000	December	$ 650,000
September (est.)	675,000	January	650,000
October	650,000	February	650,000
November	650,000	March	650,000

c. Collection period, current and forecast:

August 31	63 days	December 31	40 days
September 30 (est.)	60	January 31	40
October 31	50	February 28	40
November 30	50	March 31	40

d. Materials usage beginning October: $825,000 per month.

e. Wages and salaries, beginning October: $215,000 per month, paid as incurred.

f. Other manufacturing expenses, beginning October: $420,000 per month, paid as incurred.

g. Depreciation: $43,000 per month.

h. Cost of goods sold has consistently averaged 70 percent of sales.

i. Selling and administrative expenses: October and November, 15 percent of sales; December and January, 14 percent of sales; and February and March, 12 percent of sales.

j. Payments on note payable: $750,000 each in November and February.

k. Interest due in January: $300,000.

l. Dividends payable in October and January: $25,000 each.

m. Income taxes due in January: $375,000.

n. Most recent balance sheet (estimated) is shown on the next page.

From the data given, develop a cash budget for the six months ended March 31, 1989, and pro forma statements for the quarters ended December 31, 1988, and March 31, 1989. Assume income taxes to be 50 percent, do not detail cost of goods sold, and assume no changes in accounts not specifically analyzed or projected here. What funds needs arise, and when? What if the collection speedup effort were unsuccessful and receivables stayed at 60 days? Discuss your findings about the policy changes being considered.

XYZ COMPANY
Estimated Balance Sheet
For September 30, 1988
($000)

Assets

Current assets:

Cash		$ 740
Accounts and notes receivable		3,975
Inventories:		
Raw materials	$ 2,725	
Finished goods	6,420	9,145
Total current assets		13,860
Plant and equipment	12,525	
Less: Accumulated depreciation	5,315	7,210
Other assets		1,730
Total assets		$22,800

Liabilities and Net Worth

Current liabilities:

Accounts payable	$ 1,050
Notes payable	4,120
Accrued liabilities	2,875
Total current liabilities	8,045
Long-term debt	5,250
Preferred stock	1,750
Common stock	5,000
Earned surplus	2,755
Total liabilities and net worth	$22,800

4 DYNAMICS OF THE BUSINESS SYSTEM

In this chapter we will integrate the concepts we have discussed so far. In previous chapters we frequently mentioned the need to see business as a *system* of interconnected conditions, objectives, and policies. For the most part it was necessary, however, to discuss key techniques of financial analysis *separately* in order to highlight and explain the concepts involved. With this approach as a background, we can now provide an *overview* of the business system in terms of applying selected analytical approaches to broad financial and operational planning areas. All along we have distinguished between decisions involving investment, operations, and financing. In this chapter we will provide a format with which to examine those key decisions *as they affect each other.* In other words, the overview presented here is a *dynamic* closed system rather than merely a *static* look at any one set of conditions. We will further expand on two specific dynamic elements of the system, **operating leverage** and **financial leverage**, which were briefly mentioned earlier. We will also enlarge our discussion of the effect of the *disposition of profits* on financial plans, and how the ability to make *investments* is affected by the level of retained earnings and debt capacity. Finally, we will test the *constraints* under which specific financial objectives, such as growth in owners' equity, or growth in earnings, must be planned. There the emphasis will be on **financial planning,** and on a framework that highlights the effect of specific financial policy constraints on the performance objectives set by management.

THE BUSINESS SYSTEM: AN OVERVIEW

Figure 4–1 is a modification of the conceptual framework we have used in earlier chapters. It illustrates the notion of a *closed business system* within which the cycle of decisions and ensuing funds flows continuously revolves. The system is aligned to four key areas of strategy: (1) **investment strategy,** (2) **conduct of operations,** (3) **disposition of profits,** and (4) **financing strategy.** Three of these correspond to the management decision areas we identified and used for analytical purposes in earlier chapters. The fourth, disposition of profits, was added because of its direct impact on a business's ability to grow in the future.

Investment Strategy

This segment covers the area of **capital budgeting,** that is, the selection of new investment alternatives. The investments chosen must match not only the operational characteristics and needs of the business, but also the financial policies management deems acceptable. Various types of capital outlays must be analyzed and integrated in a company's strategic plans. For example, the selection of current and potential markets, a strategic choice, will affect how new facilities will be deployed. The opposite of investment, *disinvestment,* is also part of capital budgeting. Disinvestment is a significant option when withdrawal from markets or activities and more advantageous redeployment of the funds are economically justified. The selection and mix of new investments and disinvestments can be analyzed using a variety of techniques based on *present value* concepts. These will be discussed in greater detail in Chapter 5.

Figure 4-1
The Business System: An Overview

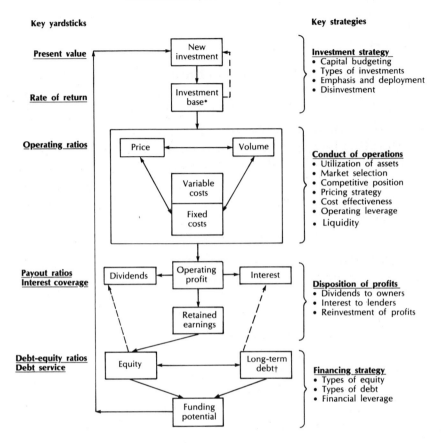

Key yardsticks

Present value

Rate of return

Operating ratios

Payout ratios
Interest coverage

Debt-equity ratios
Debt service

Key strategies

Investment strategy
• Capital budgeting
• Types of investments
• Emphasis and deployment
• Disinvestment

Conduct of operations
• Utilization of assets
• Market selection
• Competitive position
• Pricing strategy
• Cost effectiveness
• Operating leverage
• Liquidity

Disposition of profits
• Dividends to owners
• Interest to lenders
• Reinvestment of profits

Financing strategy
• Types of equity
• Types of debt
• Financial leverage

*Assumes an amount *equal* to depreciation continuously reinvested here, to maintain existing investments in good order.
†Assumes continuous rollover, or refinancing, with no reduction through repayments.

Investment strategy is the driving force of the business system. Therefore, management must direct the deployment of the existing investment base as well as new investments to achieve appropriate economic returns. Rate of return measures are helpful in judging the effectiveness with which the existing asset base is employed. Whether plant and machinery, various other physical resources, labor deployment, working capital increments, or promotional outlays are involved, investment is the operational "trigger" for action in almost every kind of business.

Conduct of Operations

Here the key strategies involve the *effective utilization* of assets in serving *selected markets*, and finding appropriate *pricing and service* policies for competitive success. Operations must also be made and kept *cost effective*. This depends in part on **operating leverage**, that is, the effect on profitability of the level and proportion of fixed (period) costs necessary, versus the variable (direct) costs expended on manufacturing, service, or trading operations. The interplay of these forces results in the operating profit for a period. Operating profit depends on the effect of *market selection* and *competitive position* on *pricing*, on the *price/volume trade-off* caused by the competitive environment, and on the *operating efficiency* resulting from management actions and leverage conditions. (Leverage will be taken up in the next section.)

The key assessment measures in this area include certain operating ratios, such as the return on net assets (capitalization) before interest as an overall indicator of the effectiveness of capital deployment. The now familiar range of ratios from gross margin to specific expense and profit indicators, as discussed in Chapter 1, apply here. (The impact of operating leverage on these results will be demonstrated shortly.)

Disposition of Profits

This "new" area of analysis involves the three-way split of profits between owners, lenders, and reinvestment. Each element is affected by current or past management decisions and policies. The payment of *dividends* to owners, as we observed before, is at the discretion of the board of directors in a corporation. The *rate* of payout directly affects the possible use of the residual profit for reinvestment and growth. The payment of *interest* to lenders is a matter of contractual obligation. The *relative* amount of interest payments incurred, however, is a function of management policies and actions regarding the use of debt—the higher the proportion of debt in the capital structure, the greater the demand on profit dollars for use as interest compensation. High proportions of debt generally cause lenders to demand somewhat higher interest to compensate for the potentially higher risk exposure. *Retained earnings* are residual profits for the period, after payment of interest and dividends, which, combined with any new capital provided by investors and lenders, are used to fund additional investment and growth. The key measures used for assessment in this area are payout ratios and coverage of interest and debt service.

Financing Strategy

This involves the selection and balancing of the relative proportions of *ownership* and *debts* funds which, after taking into account *business risk* and *debt service* obligations, should result in an acceptable level of profitability. Numerous types of equity can be employed (as discussed in Chapter 7), and the choices of debt instruments are similarly varied. The key concept in terms of the instrument chosen is the impact of **financial leverage**, which will be discussed in detail shortly. This type of leverage involves prudent use of fixed-cost debt obligations to finance investment opportunities with earnings that are potentially higher than the cost of the interest. Key measures in the financial strategy area include debt/equity ratios, return on equity, and various debt service coverage ratios.

Internal Assumptions

Our simplified model of the business system contains two key assumptions that should be highlighted. First, *depreciation* is not recognized as such, because we have assumed that an amount *equal* to the annual depreciation write-off will be *reinvested* each year in order to maintain the productive capacity of the business, but without providing any incremental profits. Consequently, Figure 4–1 shows the smaller item, *operating profit*, instead of *cash flow from operations*, as one of the funds sources for profit disposition and new investment. Second, we assume that the amount of existing *long-term debt* outstanding remains *unchanged*, that is, there is no provision for *paying off* this debt. Instead, we assume a *continuous rollover* of expiring debt (new financing is arranged as principal becomes due). This is the only way to maintain the debt/equity ratio, because as the amount of owners' equity *grows* with profitable operations, management will likely wish to match this increase with an appropriate incremental amount of *new debt*, unless a change in policy is desired. If *existing* debt were repaid, the debt/equity ratio would *fall*. These simplifying but realistic assumptions let us develop meaningful financial plans without having to simulate complex financing details. A more specific and detailed approach involving the use of operating cash flow, targeted investments for maintaining the current level of operations, and scheduled repayments of debt can, of course, be used.

Interrelationships of Key Strategic Areas

It should be obvious by now that our concept of the business system forces us to recognize and deal with the *interrelationships* of the key variables and the policies governing them. For example, it would be ineffective for a company to establish ambitious objectives for its operations while at the same time restricting itself to a set of rigid and conservative financial policies. Similarly, high payout levels of current profit in the form of dividends together with restrictive debt policy would *clash* with an objective of fast growth, because adequate funds for new investment would simply not be available. The basis for successful management and for proper financial analysis and planning is a *consistent set of business strategies, operating goals,* and *financial policies* that will reinforce each other rather than conflict. A modeling approach based on the systems diagram allows us to recognize these interrelationships and to test plans and decisions accordingly.

LEVERAGE

We now turn to a more detailed discussion and analysis of the importance of *leverage* in operations and financing. Once we have covered this final point, we can combine the key concepts into a simplified version of a long-term financial plan. Leverage, as mentioned, refers to the often favorable condition of having a *stable element of cost support a wide range of profit levels.* **Operating leverage** means part of the costs of the business are fixed over a broad range of operating volume. As a consequence, profits are boosted or depressed more than proportionally for changes in volume. Similarly, **financial leverage** occurs when a company's capital structure contains obligations with fixed interest rates. The effect of this condition is similar to the case of operating leverage. Again, earnings after interest are boosted or depressed more than proportionally as operating volume fluctuates. In principle, operating and financial leverage are one and the same. However, there are differences in the specific elements involved and in the methods of calculating each type of leverage. *Both* operating and financial leverage can be present in a business, and their respective impact on net profit will tend to be mutually *reinforcing.*

Operating Leverage

Distinguishing between fixed and variable costs, that is, those costs that vary with time and those that vary with the level of activity, is an old idea. This distinction is the basis for **break-even analysis.** The concept of "breaking even" essentially springs from the simple question of how many units of product or service a business must sell in order to *"cover" its fixed costs.* Presumably, prices are set at a level high enough to recover all direct (variable) costs and leave a margin of *contribution* towards fixed costs and profit. Once sufficient units have been sold to accumulate the amount needed to *offset fixed*, or period *costs*, any *additional* units sold will turn into pure profit. An understanding of this principle will improve our insight into how the operating aspects of a business relate to financial planning and projections. In a broader sense, it will also allow us to appreciate the *distorting effect* which significant operating leverage may exert on the measures and comparisons of financial analysis.

As mentioned, the introduction of fixed costs into the operation of a business tends to *magnify* profits at higher levels of operation. This is due to the incremental *contribution* each additional unit provides over and above the strictly variable costs incurred in producing it. Depending on the *proportion* of fixed and variable costs in the company's cost structure, the incremental contribution from the added units can result in a sizable *overall jump in profit*. Once all fixed costs are recovered by the contributions from a sufficient minimum number of units, profits grow *proportionately faster* than the growth in volume. Unfortunately, the same effect holds for *declining* volumes of operations, which result in a *decline in profit* and acceleration of losses *disproportionate* to the rate of volume reduction. Leverage is definitely a two-edged sword!

The formal way of describing these conditions is quite simple. We are interested in the effect on profit (I) of changes in volume (V). The elements which bear on this are unit price (P), unit variable costs (C), and fixed costs (F). The relationship is as follows:

$$I = VP - (VC + F)$$

This formula can be rewritten as:

$$I = V(P - C) - F$$

which illustrates that profit depends on the number of goods or services sold times the difference between unit price and unit variable cost—which is the contribution to the constant element, fixed costs. As unit volume changes, the unit contribution $(P - C)$ times the change in volume will be equal to the total change in profit. The constant, fixed costs (F), will remain just that, under normal conditions. The relative changes in profit for a given change in volume will, of course, be magnified as long as the fixed element remains. Another way of stating the leverage relationships is to use profit as a percent of sales (s), one of the ratios developed in Chapter 1. Using the previous notation,

$$s = \frac{I}{VP}$$

and defining I in terms of its components, the formula becomes:

$$s = \frac{V(P - C) - F}{VP}$$

and slightly rewritten:

$$s = \left(I - \frac{C}{P}\right) - \frac{F}{VP}$$

This indicates that the profit-to-sales ratio depends on the contribution per unit of sales, less fixed costs as a percent of sales revenue. We observe that, to the extent fixed costs are present, they cause a reduction in the profit ratio. The larger F, the larger the reduction. A change in volume, price, or unit cost, however, will tend to have a disproportional impact on s because F is constant.

Let us examine how the process works using some concrete examples. Figure 4–2 shows the cost/profit conditions for a simple business with relatively high fixed costs of $200,000 in relation to volume of output and variable costs per unit. The company has a maximum level of production of 1,000 units, and for simplicity, we assume that there is no lag between production and sales. Units sell for $750 each, and variable costs of materials, labor, and supplies amount to $250 per unit. As a consequence, each unit provides a contribution of $500 toward fixed costs and profit.

The *break-even chart* is a simple representation of the conditions just outlined. At zero volume, fixed costs amount to $200,000, and these remain level as volume is increased until full capacity has been reached. Variable costs, on the other hand, accumulate by $250 per unit as volume is increased until a level of $250,000 has been reached at capacity, for a total cost

Figure 4–2
ABC CORPORATION
Simple Operating Break-Even Chart: Basic Conditions

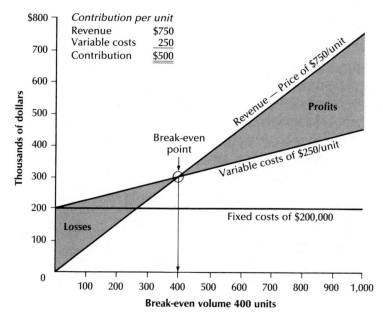

Break-even volume 400 units

Profits and Losses as a Function of
Volume Changes of 25 Percent

Volume	Increase	Profits	Increase
400	—	–0–	—
500	25%	$ 50,000	Infinite*
625	25	112,500	125%
781	25	190,500	69
976	25	288,000	51

Volume	Decrease	Losses	Increase
400	—	–0–	—
300	25%	$ 50,000	Infinite*
225	25	87,500	75%
169	25	115,500	32
127	25	136,500	18

*Infinite because the base is zero.

at capacity of $450,000. Revenue rises from zero, in incre-
ments of $750, until the total revenue has reached $750,000 at
capacity.

Where the revenue and variable cost lines cross (at 400 units
of output), a *break-even condition* of no profit and no loss has

been reached; the total cumulative revenue of $300,000 at that point is just sufficient to offset the fixed costs of $200,000 and the total variable costs of 400 units at $250 each ($100,000). If operations increase beyond this point, profits are generated; while at volumes less than 400 units, losses are incurred. The break-even point can be found numerically, of course, by simply dividing the total fixed costs of $200,000 by the unit contribution of $500, which results in 400 units, as we expected:

$$\text{Break-even point } (I = 0) : \frac{F}{P - C} = V$$

$$\text{Zero profit } = \frac{\$200,000}{\$500} = 400 \text{ units}$$

The most interesting aspect of the break-even chart, however, is the clear demonstration that increases and decreases in profit are *not proportional*. A series of 25 percent increases in volume above the break-even point will result in much larger percentage jumps in profit growth. The relevant figures for our example are displayed in the table under the chart. They show a gradual decline in the growth rate of profit from infinite to 51 percent. Similarly, as volume decreases below the break-even point in 25 percent decrements, the growth rate of losses goes from infinite to a modest 18 percent, as volume approaches zero. Thus, changes in operations *close* to the break-even point, whether up or down, are likely to produce *sizable* swings in earnings. Changes in operations well above or below the break-even point will cause lesser fluctuations.

We must be careful in interpreting these changes, however. As in any percentage analysis, the specific results depend on the starting point and the relative proportions of the components. It is easy to exaggerate the meaning of profit fluctuations unless they are carefully interpreted in the context of a company's cost structure and its normal level of operations. Nevertheless, the concept should be clear—the *closer* a firm is to its *break-even point*, the more dramatic will be the profit impact of volume changes. The financial analyst assessing the company's performance or making financial projections must attempt to understand where the level of the company's current operations is relative to normal volume and the break-even point, and interpret the results of the analysis accordingly.

Furthermore, the greater the relative level of *fixed costs*, the more powerful the effect of leverage becomes. Our need to understand this aspect of the company's cost structure increases commensurately. In capital-intensive industries, such as steel, mining, forest products, and heavy manufacturing, most of the costs of production are fixed for a wide range of volumes. This condition tends to accentuate profit swings as such companies move away from break-even operations. Another example is the airline industry, which from time to time substantially increased the capacity of its flight equipment, e.g., from the 727 to the 747 jumbo jet. The fixed costs associated with owning and operating these aircraft caused sharp drops in profit for most airlines. As business and private travel rose to approach the new levels of capacity, several airlines experienced dramatic improvements in profits. In contrast, service industries, such as consulting firms, can directly influence their major cost—manpower—by adjusting the number of employees as *demand changes*. Thus, they are much less subject to the effects of the operating leverage phenomenon.

As we observed earlier, there are three main elements that management can *influence* in the operating leverage relationship: *fixed costs*, *variable costs*, and *price*, all of which are in one way or another related to *volume*. We shall demonstrate the effect of changes in all three by *varying* the basic conditions in our example.

Effect of Lower Fixed Costs.   If management can lower *fixed costs* through energetic reductions in overhead or by using facilities more intensively, the effect can be a significant lowering of the break-even point. As a consequence, profits will begin to be made at a lower level of operations. This change is shown in Figure 4–3. Note that lowering fixed costs by one eighth has led to a corresponding reduction in break-even volume. It will now take one-eighth fewer units contributing $500 each to recover the lower fixed costs. From the table

Figure 4–3
ABC CORPORATION
Simple Operating Break-Even Chart: Effect of Reducing Fixed Costs
(reduction of $25,000)

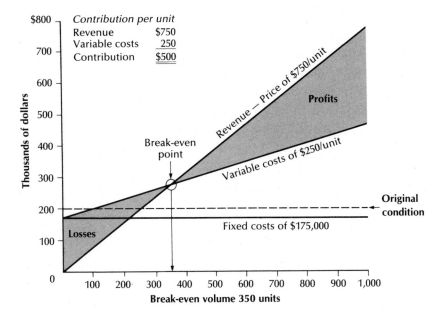

Profits and Losses as a Function of
Volume Changes of 25 Percent

Volume	Increase	Profits	Increase
350	—	-0-	—
438	25%	$ 44,000	Infinite*
547	25	98,500	125%
684	25	167,000	69
855	25	252,500	51
Volume	Decrease	Losses	Increase
350	—	-0-	—
262	25%	$ 44,000	Infinite*
196	25	77,000	75%
147	25	101,500	32
110	25	120,000	18

*Infinite because the base is zero.

we can observe that 25 percent volume changes from the reduced break-even point lead to increases or decreases in profit
quite similar to those in our first example in Figure 4–2. Reducing fixed costs, therefore, is a very direct and effective way

of lowering the break-even point to improve the firm's profit performance.

Effect of Lower Variable Costs. If management is able to reduce the *variable* (direct) *costs* of production—thereby increasing the contribution per unit—the action can similarly affect profits at current levels and influence the movement of the break-even point itself. In Figure 4–4 we have shown the resulting change in the *slope* of the variable cost line, which in effect *widens* the area of profit. Loss conditions are similarly reduced. However, the change in break-even volume resulting from a 10 percent change in variable costs is *not* as dramatic as the change experienced when fixed costs were lowered by one eighth. The reason is that the reduction applies only to a small portion of the total production cost, because variable costs are relatively low in this example. (This illustrates the point we made earlier about having to consider the relative proportions in this type of analysis.) Only at full capacity of 1,000 units does the profit impact of $25,000 correspond to the effect of the reduction of $25,000 in fixed costs in the earlier example. At lower levels of operations, lower unit volumes and the lesser impact of variable costs combine to minimize the effect. Nevertheless, the result is clearly an improvement in the break-even condition, and a profit boost is achieved earlier on the volume scale. Again, 25 percent incremental changes are tabulated to show the specific results.

Effect of Lower Prices. Up to this point we have concentrated on the effects of costs, which are largely under the control of management. In contrast, *price changes* are to a large extent dependent on the firm's competitive environment. As a result, changed prices normally affect the competitive equilibrium and will directly influence the unit sales volume of a business. Thus, it is not enough to trace the effect of raised or lowered prices on the break-even chart. We must also anticipate the likely change in *volume* resulting from the price change. In other words, raising the price may more than proportionately affect the volume the company will be able to sell competitively, and the price action may actually bring about *lower total prof-*

Figure 4–4
ABC CORPORATION
Simple Operating Break-Even Chart: Effect of Reducing Variable Costs
(reduction of $25 per unit)

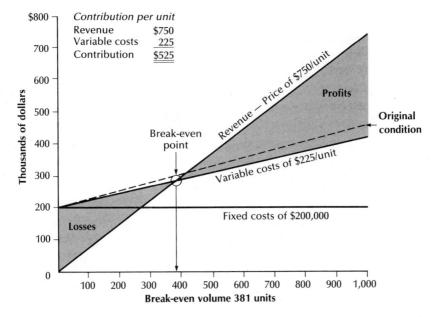

Break-even volume 381 units

Profits and Losses as a Function of
Volume Changes of 25 Percent

Volume	Increase	Profits	Increase
381	—	–0–	—
476	25%	$ 49,900*	Infinite†
595	25	112,375	125%
744	25	190,600	69
930	25	288,250	51

Volume	Decrease	Losses	Increase
381	—	–0–	—
286	25%	$ 50,150	Infinite†
215	25	87,125	75%
161	25	115,475	32
121	25	136,475	18

*First 25 percent change not exactly equal due to rounding.
†Infinite because the base is zero.

its. Conversely, lowering the price may more than compensate for the lost contribution per unit by boosting the total unit volume that can be sold.

Figure 4–5 demonstrates the effect of lowering the price by $50 per unit, a 6.7 percent reduction. Note that this raises the required break-even volume by about 11 percent, to 444 units. In other words, the company needs to sell 44 additional units *just to recoup* the loss in contribution of $50 from the sale of *every* unit. For example, if current volume were 800 units, with a contribution of $400,000 and a profit of $200,000, the price drop of $50 would require the sale of enough *additional* units to recover 800 times $50, or $40,000. This must be done to cover a *lower* per unit contribution of $450. Consequently, 89 additional units have to be sold at the lower price—which represents a volume increase of 11 percent. Note that this results in a *more than* proportional change in unit volume (11 percent) versus the change in price (6.7 percent).

Price changes affect the internal operating results, but they may have an even more pronounced and lasting impact on the competitive environment. If a more than proportional volume advantage—and therefore improved profits—can be obtained over a significant period of time after the price has been reduced, this may be a wise move. Otherwise, if price reductions can be expected to be quickly matched by other competitors, the final effect may simply be a drop in profit for everyone, because little if any shift in relative market shares would result. This is not the place to discuss the many strategic issues involved in pricing policy; the intent is merely to show the effect of this important element on the operating system and to provide a way of analyzing likely conditions.

Multiple Effects on Break-Even Conditions. In the foregoing analysis, cost, volume, and price implications and their impact on profit were analyzed separately. In practice, the many conditions and pressures encountered by a business often affect these variables *simultaneously.* Cost, volume, and price for a single product may all be changing at the same time in

Figure 4–5
ABC CORPORATION
Simple Operating Break-Even Chart: Effect of Reduction in Price
(reduction of $50 per unit)

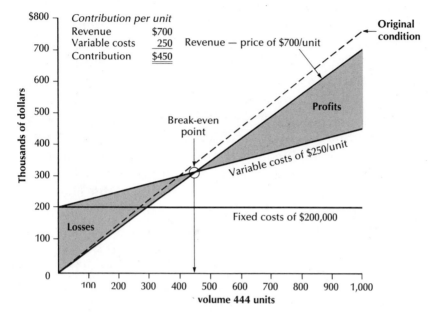

Profits and Losses as a Function of Volume Changes of 25 Percent

Volume	Increase	Profits	Increase
444	—	–0–	—
555	25%	$ 49,750*	Infinite†
694	25	112,300	125%
867	25	190,150	69
1084	25	287,800	51

Volume	Decrease	Losses	Increase
444	—	–0–	—
333	25%	$ 50,150*	Infinite†
249	25	87,950	75%
187	25	115,850	32
140	25	137,000	18

*First 25 percent change not exactly equal due to rounding.
†Infinite because the base is zero.

subtle and often unmeasurable ways. Analysis is further complicated when *several products* are involved, as is the case with all major companies. In such cases, changes in the sales mix can introduce many complexities. Moreover, our simplifying assumption that production and sales are *simultaneous* does not necessarily hold true in practice; the normal lag between production and sales has a significant effect and must be taken into account. In a manufacturing company, sales and production can be widely out of phase. Some of the implications arising from this condition were discussed in Chapter 2, when we dealt with funds flow conditions under varying levels of operations, and in Chapter 3 when we examined the relationship of cash budgets and pro forma operating statements.

Up to this point, we have assumed that operating conditions were essentially *linear*, which allowed us to simplify our analysis of leverage and break-even conditions. A more realistic framework is suggested in Figure 4–6. The chart shows potential changes in both fixed and variable costs over the full range of operations. Possible changes in price/revenue relationships are also reflected. In other words, changes in *all three* factors affecting operating leverage are reflected at the *same time.* The chart further indicates that the simple straight-line relationships used in Figures 4–2 through 4–5 are normally only approximations of the "step functions" and the gradual shifts in cost and price often encountered under realistic circumstances. Inflationary distortions arising over time must also be considered. A few of the possible changes in conditions and sample reasons for these are described below the chart.

The fixed/variable cost relationship can also be used to examine the effect of various proportions of debt in the financial structure of a company, that is, to analyze financial leverage.

Financial Leverage

As we stated earlier, there is a close similarity between operating and financial leverage in that both present an opportunity to gain from the fixed nature of certain costs in relation to in-

Figure 4–6
Generalized Break-Even Chart: Allowing for Changing Cost and
Revenue Conditions

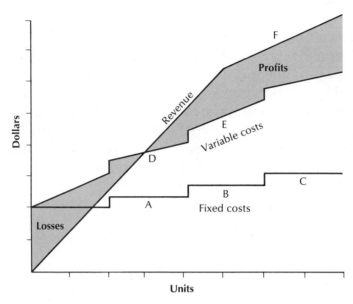

A. A new layer of fixed costs is triggered by growing volume.
B. A new shift is added, with additional requirements for overhead costs.
C. A final small increment of overhead is incurred as some operations require overtime.
D. Efficiencies in operations reduce variable unit costs.
E. The new shift causes inefficiencies and lower output, with more spoilage.
F. The last increments of output must be sold on contract at lower prices.

crements of profit. With *financial leverage*, the advantage
arises from the possibility that funds borrowed at a *fixed interest rate* can often be used for investment opportunities earning a rate of return *higher* than the interest paid. The difference, of course, accrues to the owners of the business. Given
the ability to make investments that consistently provide returns *above* the going rate of interest, it will be to a company's
advantage to "trade on equity." This means borrowing as
much as prudent debt management will permit, and thereby
boosting the return on owners' equity by the difference between the rate of return achieved and the rate of interest paid.
The opposite effect will, of course, apply if the company fails
to earn higher returns.

Figure 4–7 shows the leverage effect on return on equity of three different levels of return on net assets. All three curves are based on the assumption that funds can be borrowed at 4 percent per year *after taxes*. If the normal return on the company's capitalization *before* interest and *after* taxes is 20 percent (curve A), growing proportions of debt cause a dramatic rise in return on equity. This return jumps to infinity as debt nears 100 percent. Curves B and C show the leverage effect under more modest earnings conditions. While somewhat lessened, the return on equity still shows sharp increases as the proportion of debt rises. As we observed before, leverage also works in the opposite direction. This is suggested by the fact that the distances between curves A, B, and C increase with higher debt levels. Should earnings drop, the plunge in return on equity can be massive.

Figure 4–7
Return on Equity as Affected by Financial Leverage
(aftertax interest on debt is 4 percent)

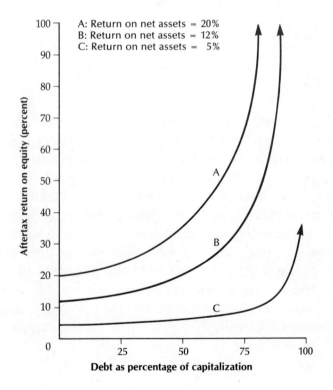

To express the financial leverage relationships we begin by defining the components, as we did in the case of operating leverage. Profit after taxes (I) now has to be related to equity (E) and long-term debt (D). We also single out return on equity (R), and return on net assets (capitalization) before interest and after taxes (r). Finally, the interest rate after taxes (i) must be noted. First, we define the return on equity as

$$R = \frac{I}{E}$$

and the return on capitalization (the sum of equity and debt) as

$$r = \frac{I + Di}{E + D}$$

We now restate profit (I) in terms of its components,

$$I = r(E + D) - Di$$

which represents the difference between the return on the total capitalization $(E + D)$ and the aftertax cost of interest on outstanding debt. We then find that our first formula becomes:

$$R = \frac{r(E + D) - Di}{E}$$

which we can restate as

$$R = r + \frac{D}{E}(r - i)$$

This formulation shows that the leverage effect is represented by the positive expression, that is, the proportion of debt to equity, multiplied by the difference between the earnings power of net assets and the aftertax cost of interest. Thus, to the extent that debt is introduced into the capital structure, the return on equity is boosted as long as interest cost does not exceed earnings power.

When we apply the formula to one set of conditions which pertained in the graph of Figure 4–7, the results can be calculated as follows. Given $i = 4\%$, and $r = 12\%$, then for

(1) $D = 0$, $E = \$100$ R equals 12.0%
(2) $D = \$25$, $E = \$75$ R equals 14.7%

(3) $D = \$50$, $E = \$50$ R equals 20.0%
(4) $D = \$75$, $E = \$25$ R equals 36.0%

In this illustration, we have four different debt/equity ratios, ranging from no debt in the first case to a 3:1 debt/equity relationship in the fourth case. Given an aftertax cost of interest of 4 percent and the normal ability to earn 12 percent after taxes on net assets invested, the return on equity in the first case is also 12 percent after taxes, because no debt exists and the total capitalization is represented by equity. As increasing amounts of debt are introduced into the capital structure, however, the return on equity is boosted considerably, because in each case, the return on investments far exceeds the cost of interest paid to the debtholders. This was, of course, demonstrated in the graph of Figure 4–7. The reader is invited to work through the opposite effect, that is, interest charges in excess of the ability to earn a return on the investments.

We are also interested in the impact of leverage on the return on capitalization (r), which we obtain by first reworking the formula:

$$R = r + \frac{D}{E}(r - i)$$

into

$$r = \frac{RE + Di}{E + D}$$

Given $i = 4\%$, and $R = 12\%$, we can determine the *minimum* return on capitalization necessary to obtain a return on equity of 12%, for

(1) $D = 0$, $E = \$100$ r equals 12%
(2) $D = \$25$, $E = \$75$ r equals 10%
(3) $D = \$50$, $E = \$50$ r equals 8%
(4) $D = \$75$, $E = \$25$ r equals 6%

This is a useful way of testing the expected return from new investments. Such an approach simply turns the calculation around by fixing the return on equity and letting the expected return on investment vary. The calculation is straightforward. Note that the required amount of earnings on net assets (capitalization) drops sharply as leverage is introduced, until it begins to approach the 4 percent aftertax interest cost. It will never quite reach this figure, however, because normally some small amount of equity must be maintained in the capital structure.

While it is simple to work out the mathematical relationships, the translation of these conditions into the appropriate financial strategies is much more complex. No management is completely free to vary the capital structure at will, and there are practical as well as legal and contractual constraints on any company to maintain some "normalcy" in the liability side of the balance sheet. While no absolute rules exist, the various tests of credit-worthiness run the gamut of the ratios discussed in Chapter 1, particularly the measures oriented to the *lenders' point of view*. With enlightened self-interest in mind, lenders will impose upper limits on the amount of debt capital to be utilized by a potential borrower. For manufacturing companies, the amount of long-term debt will normally range between 0 and 50 percent of their capitalization, while public utilities will range between 30 and 60 percent. Trading companies with highly liquid assets may have even higher debt proportions.

As stated before, we are interested in the effects of *financial leverage* on the broader area of *financial planning* for a company. In these terms, financial leverage is only one of several aspects affecting performance. In the next section, we will integrate financial leverage and the other key factors into a broader financial plan.

FINANCIAL GROWTH PLANS

Most managements aspire to successfully building ever *larger* businesses, whenever the opportunities in the marketplace permit this. Typically, investor expectations also target for *growing economic benefits* derived from owning shares of the company. Thus, it is not surprising that one important dimension of financial planning is continual testing of the *effects of growth on investment, operations, and financing.* The financial policy choices open to management have different impacts on the expected results, and therefore must be tested along with the operational aspects of the plans. Management can set a variety of *financial objectives* and *financial policies* to direct and constrain the company's planning effort and the specific financial projections based on these plans. Foremost among the financial objectives is, of course, *return on shareholders' equity.* But this objective in turn is derived from specific objectives concerning *growth in earnings per share, growth in total profits, growth in dividends, growth in market value, and growth in shareholders' equity.* None of these objectives can singly be used as an overall standard, of course.

Foremost among the *financial policies* is the amount of financial leverage the company considers prudent, and subsidiary to it are the various measures of credit-worthiness that management will wish to observe as constraints.

To demonstrate the buildup of an **integrated financial plan** that enables us to observe the effect of growth and its relationship to financial objectives and policies, we will begin by selecting *one* of the objectives named above to work through a simple *conceptual model* of a hypothetical company. The format of this model is the framework that will allow us to later build a more detailed integrated financial plan.

A simple way of demonstrating the interrelated elements that affect growth in the business system is to use the objective of growth in owners' equity, as recorded on the balance sheet. Not only is this particular element easy to calculate, but it also indirectly encompasses the effects of profit growth and dividend payout.

Table 4–1 is a simplified financial model that allows us to trace the several aspects affecting growth in a company, namely, leverage, profitability, earnings disposition, and financing. With its help we can demonstrate the effect of *different financial policies* on the objective of growth in owners' equity. Three cases have been worked out. The first shows an *unlever-*

Table 4–1
Financial Growth Model: Three Different Policies ($000)

	Case I	Case II	Case III
Capitalization:			
Debt/equity ratio	0:1	1:1	1:1
Debt	–0–	$250	$250
Equity	$500	$250	$250
Net assets	$500	$500	$500
Profitability (after taxes):			
Gross return on net assets*	10%	10%	10%
Amount of profit	$ 50	$ 50	$ 50
Interest at 4%	–0–	10	10
Profit after interest	50	40	40
Earnings disposition:			
Dividend payout	0%	0%	50%
Dividends paid	–0–	–0–	$ 20
Reinvestment	$ 50	$ 40	$ 20
Financing:			
Additional debt	–0–	$ 40	$ 20
New investment possible	$ 50	$ 80	$ 40
Results (in percent):			
Net return on net assets (capitalization)†	10%	8%	8%
Return on equity	10	16	16
Growth in equity‡	10	16	8

*Profits *before* interest, *after* taxes related to net assets (capitalization) as a measure of operational return on assets.

†Profits *after* interest and taxes related to net assets, as often shown in financial reports.

‡The growth in recorded equity based on earnings reinvested after payment of dividends.

aged company with $500,000 in equity which pays no dividends and reinvests all of its profits in operations similar to its present activities. The second case shows the same company, but in a leveraged condition with a 1:1 *debt/equity ratio.* In the third case, we take the conditions of case II, but assume a *dividend payout* of 50 percent of earnings. All other financial conditions are assumed to remain constant.

Let us trace through the data for Case I. Given a gross return on net assets of 10 percent after taxes, the amount of profit generated for the year is $50,000, all of which can be reinvested in the company's activities in the form of new investment for expansion, profit improvements, and so on.[1] The results of Case I

---

[1] As we assumed in our business system overview, the reinvestment of annual depreciation is considered necessary to maintain present facilities in operating condition. Depreciation funds therefore do *not* represent investments in *new* profit opportunities.

are a net return on net assets (capitalization) of 10 percent, a return on equity of 10 percent, and thus a growth in equity of 10 percent, because all of the profits for the period are assumed to be reinvested in the business. In Table 4–2 we have calculated three additional periods for the operations of this particular company, without changing the assumptions. We can quickly observe that given stable policies and conditions, equity growth will indeed continue at 10 percent per year.

The second case differs only with regard to the use of *debt financing*. Because $250,000 has been borrowed at 4 percent after taxes, $10,000 of aftertax interest must be deducted from profit on net assets, which reduces the amount available for reinvestment to $40,000. If management wants to maintain its policy of a 1:1 debt-equity ratio, an additional $40,000 can be borrowed. This raises the funds available for new investment to $80,000. Compared to Case I, the results have changed in several ways. Net return on capitalization has dropped to 8 percent because interest charges were introduced. As we expected, however, return on equity was boosted to 16 percent when leverage was introduced. Under these conditions, growth in equity can be similarly maintained at a level of 16 percent as long as all of the internally generated funds are reinvested and matching additional borrowings are made for new investments.

In the third case, the introduction of *dividends* is the only change involved. A 50 percent payout reduces the internal funds available for reinvestment to $20,000 and also reduces the available additional debt to $20,000, under a 1:1 debt/equity ratio. Total funds for new investment have thus been reduced to $40,000. The dividend action seriously affects our assumed objective of growth in equity, which is now half the level in Case II.

This very simple model illustrates the effects of a combination of decisions about investment, operations, earnings disposition, and financing strategy. It permits easy analysis of changes. Clearly the conditions have been oversimplified, but any refinements in the assumptions about such items as return

Table 4-2

Financial Growth Model: Results of Three Different Policies Held Constant over Three Periods

	Case I			Case II			Case III		
	Period 1	Period 2	Period 3	Period 1	Period 2	Period 3	Period 1	Period 2	Period 3
Capitalization:									
Debt/equity ratio	0:1	0:1	0:1	1:1	1:1	1:1	1:1	1:1	1:1
Debt	-0-	-0-	-0-	$250	$290	$336.4	$250	$270	$291.6
Equity	$500	$550	$605	$250	$290	$336.4	$250	$270	$291.6
Net assets	$500	$550	$605	$500	$580	$672.8	$500	$540	$583.2
Profitability (after taxes):									
Gross return on net assets*	10%	10%	10%	10%	10%	10%	10%	10%	10%
Amount of profit	$50	$55	$60.5	$50	$58.0	$67.28	$50	$54.0	$58.32
Interest at 4%	-0-	-0-	-0-	10	11.6	13.46	10	10.8	11.66
Profit after interest	$50	$55	$60.5	$40	$46.4	$53.82	$40	$43.2	$46.66
Earnings disposition:									
Dividend payout	0%	0%	0%	0%	0%	0%	50%	50%	50%
Dividends paid	-0-	-0-	-0-	-0-	-0-	-0-	$20	$21.6	$23.33
Reinvestment	$50	$55	$60.5	$40	$46.4	$53.82	$20	$21.6	$23.33
Financing:									
Additional debt	-0-	-0-	-0-	$40	$46.4	$53.82	$20	$21.6	$23.33
New investment possible	$50	$55	$60.5	$80	$92.8	$107.64	$40	$43.2	$46.66
Results:									
Net return on net assets (capitalization)†	10%	10%	10%	8%	8%	8%	8%	8%	8%
Return on equity	10	10	10	16	16	16	16	16	16
Growth in equity‡	10	10	10	16	16	16	8	8	8
Growth in total profit (after interest)	—	10	10	—	16	16	—	8	8

*Profits before interest, after taxes related to net assets (capitalization) as a measure of operational return on assets.
†Profits after interest and taxes related to net assets, as often shown in financial reports.
‡The growth in recorded equity based on earnings reinvested after payment of dividends.

on net assets, dividend payout ratios, and increments of additional borrowing, to name but a few, will only be variations on the basic theme expressed here.

If growth in ownership equity were indeed considered to be the chief objective in our illustration, it would be useful to express the relationships on the basis of formulas similar to those used earlier.

In Case I, when no debt was employed and no dividends were paid, the following relationship held:

$$g = r$$

where g is growth in equity and r is the aftertax rate of return on capitalization. This formula simply expresses the fact that under these basic conditions, return on capitalization is equal to return on equity, and growth in equity is *equal* to return on equity.

In Case II, debt is introduced to the capital structure, and we add the leverage effect to the formula as we did before:

$$g = r + \frac{D}{E}(r - i)$$

where D is debt, E is equity, and i the interest rate after taxes. Leverage, as we discussed earlier, is a direct function of the proportion of debt in the total capital structure and the size of the margin between the return on investment and the interest cost of the funds, both after taxes. Because all earnings are reinvested, the rate of *growth* in equity must be equal to the rate of *return* on equity—which is a combination of the return on net assets and the boost from leverage.

In Case III, the introduction of dividends slows the growth in equity, because only the earnings *retained* can be reinvested. We have to adjust each of the two components to reflect this change, and p stands for the proportion of earnings retained as a percentage of total earnings. The resulting formula is shown below:

$$g = rp + \frac{D}{E}(r - i)p$$

We now have a generalized formula for the rate of growth in equity that can be *sustained* by a business if *stable* conditions and policies hold. It is called the **sustainable growth formula.** If the business, over the long run, is able to invest its funds at the return indicated, if management maintains the debt/equity ratio indicated, and if interest costs and payout ratios do not change, then the growth in equity obtained will *stabilize,* as expressed in the formula.

As we stated before, growth in equity is only one of several different types of financial objectives. Table 4–2 shows the applicability of such modeling to another objective growth in earnings. As the last line of "Results" indicates, under our stable sets of policies, growth in total earnings (profit after taxes) stabilizes at the same rate as growth in equity. In fact, the formula used for growth in equity applies to this objective as well, because profit growth depends on the same variables. As changes in policies are introduced, however, the fluctuations in year-to-year profit can be severe. The reader is invited to test the formulation, using these and other possibilities.

Similar models can be developed for the conditions affecting earnings per share, dividends per share, debt service, or any other financial area of the business. We will not attempt to go into detail about these, but rather let growth in equity and growth in earnings serve as examples.

We can now turn to an illustration of an integrated financial plan, which in concept and format is based on the models in Tables 4–1 and 4–2. This time the focus is on taking a set of operating and financial assumptions and working them through this format. The XYZ Company is considering a number of changes in its financial policies, and management wants to study the impact of the combination of operating projections and policy modifications on the company's rate of growth and profitability over the next five years. The resulting integrated financial plan is shown in Table 4–3. It encompasses changes in debt/equity proportions, return on net assets, interest cost (changing as debt proportions rise), and dividend payout. One of the key benefits of displaying the interrelationships in this

Table 4–3

XYZ CORPORATION

Integrated Financial Plan:

Sample Five-Year Projection of Effect of Policy Changes

($000)

	Year 1	Year 2	Year 3	Year 4	Year 5
Capitalization:					
Debt/equity ratio	0.5:1	0.75:1	0.75:1	1:1	1:1
Debt	$300	$ 468	$ 489	688	$ 728
Equity	600	624	652	688	728
Net assets	$900	$1,092	$1,141	$1,376	$1,456
Profitability (after taxes):					
Return on net assets	8%	7%	8%	8%	9%
Amount of profit	$ 72	$ 76	$ 91	$ 110	$ 131
Interest after taxes	4%	4%	4%	4.5%	4.5%
Amount of interest	$ 12	$ 19	$ 20	$ 31	$ 33
Profit after interest	$ 60	$ 57	$ 71	$ 79	$ 98
Earnings disposition:					
Dividend payout	60%	50%	50%	50%	40%
Dividends paid	$ 36	$ 29	$ 35	$ 39	$ 39
Reinvestment	$ 24	$ 28	$ 36	$ 40	$ 59
Financing and investment:					
New debt, old ratio	$ 12	$ 21	$ 27	$ 40	$ 59
New debt, revised ratio	156	–0–	172	–0–	–0–
New investment	$192	$ 49	$ 235	$ 80	$ 118
Results:					
Net return on net assets*	6.7%	5.2%	6.2%	5.7%	6.7%
Return on equity	10.0	9.1	10.9	11.5	13.4
Growth in equity	4.0	4.6	5.5	5.8	8.1
Earnings per share					
(100,000 shares)	$0.60	$ 0.57	$ 0.71	$ 0.79	$0.98
Dividends per share	0.36	0.29	0.35	0.39	0.39

*Return after taxes and interest.

way is that any obviously inconsistent conditions will show up
in the results. As undesirable effects occur, the analyst can explore them with more tenable assumptions and calculate the
effect of such changes. Planning frameworks of this kind are
now easily obtainable either in preset form or through readily
adaptable spreadsheets for use on personal computers. Again,

we stress that computerization *does not obviate the need to understand the relationships* we are demonstrating here.

XYZ Corporation starts with a debt/equity ratio of 0.5:1 and a total capitalization of $900,000. Current return on net assets after taxes but before interest is 8 percent, which provides a profit of $72,000. Interest after taxes requires $12,000, which leaves a profit after interest of $60,000. With a dividend payout of 60 percent, cash dividends of $36,000 are required, which leaves $24,000 for reinvestment. Because the debt-equity ratio is to be maintained at 0.5:1, new debt of $12,000 can be incurred, supported by the increased equity.

In anticipation of expansion plans, management has decided to *raise* its debt/equity ratio to 0.75:1 for the Year 2. This would necessitate additional borrowing of $156,000 at the end of the first year beyond the increase of $12,000 under the old debt/equity ratio. For simplicity, we have assumed that all changes take place at year-end. The results for the first year show a net return on capitalization of 6.7 percent, a return on equity of 10 percent, and a growth in equity of 4 percent. Earnings per share are $0.60; and dividends are $0.36. The influx of new funds at the beginning of Year 2 capitalization to well over $1 million.

For Year 2, the assumption about returns earned is *lowered* to reflect some inefficiencies as the new funds are invested; the overall return on net assets is thus 7 percent. After making proper allowance for interest, profits available are $57,000. A change in dividend payout to 50 percent calls for only $29,000 in dividends, leaving $28,000 for reinvestment. This is matched by $21,000 of new debt under the existing debt/equity ratio of 0.75:1. These funds are added to the investment base for the Year 3.

The process is repetitive, as changes in policies are anticipated at the end of each year's operations. For example, we find a sizable *new influx of capital* into Year 4, as debt/equity proportions are changed to 1:1. Some additional interest cost due to higher rates charged by lenders is assumed, as the capital structure becomes more leveraged and thus more risky. At the same time, however, the effectiveness of employing capital (return on net assets) has been left at 8 percent in Years 3 and 4, but raised to 9 percent in Year 5, allowing some time for the effect of the new investments.

The results at the bottom of the exhibit indicate some fluctuations in net return on capitalization over the years, as either profitability or interest cost is changed. The return on equity, however, after dropping in Year 2, rises steadily to a sizable 13.4 percent in Year 5. Growth in equity jumps, after some intermediate boosts, to about double the original 4 percent rate in Year 5, that is, to 8.1 percent. Changes in total profit after interest are quite sizable, as the policy changes from year to year take effect. Similarly, growth in earnings per share fluctuates while dividends per share are somewhat diminished— showing little or no growth for most years.

Results obtained using such a model raise some realistic questions. For example, it may not be prudent to change the dividend payout ratio in sizable steps as was done. We observe a drop in dividends per share of almost 20 percent in the second year. In the absence of general economic problems, the corporation's directors might be very reluctant to produce this result because a consistent dividend pattern is generally considered desirable. Therefore, the dividend payout for Year 2 might be maintained at the original level; dividend payout would be lowered only as earnings rise sufficiently to avoid a sharp drop in dividends per share. At the same time, it might be useful to refine assumptions about return on net assets. We have used an overall percentage. It would be more realistic if we split the analysis into return on *existing* assets and return on *incremental* assets, taking into account the *lag* in expected returns on the new assets. Such a refinement might be particularly useful if a company were diversifying its operations and expecting a highly *different return* from some of these new activities. More attention might also be paid to the assumption that depreciation *will be reinvested* without generating additional profits.

A company consolidating some of its ongoing operations to free funds for redeployment in more diversified lines of business might *not be willing* to reinvest the equivalent of depreciation in old product lines.

The main purpose of this illustration is to show the overall usefulness of financial planning. By observing the key results of interest, the analyst can arrive at a set of assumptions and recommendations that fairly reflect management's desires and capabilities. Many more refinement formats are, of course, possible, and the process is greatly enhanced by the use of computer spreadsheets, as discussed in Chapters 1 and 3.

SUMMARY

In this chapter we have attempted to integrate some of the key concepts discussed in the earlier parts of the book into a *dynamic framework*. We added an expanded treatment of *operating* and *financial leverage* to demonstrate the important impact of fixed-cost elements on changing operating conditions. Through the use of a simplified **systems overview** of financial relationships and a financial **modeling** approach we demonstrated the need for *consistency* in operating and financial objectives and policies. We applied the modeling approach to the needs of a company and developed an **integrated financial plan** with which we tested the impact of the different policies on the company's growth and performance.

In the end, the key test of financial analysis is the *viability of the methods* and results as *predictors* of future activity, which was a major point made in the earlier chapters. Often the optimal approach is the use of quite detailed and sensitive financial models of the business. Yet the outside analyst, and even insiders, will often be well served by *simplified yardsticks and models* which can sufficiently approximate solutions to planning alternatives. In this sense, the chapter draws together many of the points of earlier materials to give the reader an *overall*, albeit simplified, framework for analysis.

SELECTED REFERENCES

Break-Even and Leverage Concepts

Anthony, Robert N., and Reece, James S. *Accounting: Text and Cases.* 6th ed. Homewood, Ill.: Richard D. Irwin, 1979.

Moore, Carl, and Jaedicke, Robert K. *Managerial Accounting.* 5th ed. Cincinnati, Ohio: South-Western Publishing, 1980.

Rosen, L., ed. *Topics in Managerial Accounting.* Toronto and New York: McGraw-Hill Ryerson, 1974.

Van Horne, James C. *Financial Management and Policy.* 7th ed. Englewood Cliffs, N.J.: Prentice-Hall, 1986.

Weston, J. Fred, and Copeland, Thomas E. *Managerial Finance.* 8th ed. Hinsdale, ILL.: Dryden Press, 1986.

Financial Strategy and Planning

Childs, John F. *Profit Goals and Capital Management.* Englewood Cliffs, N.J.: Prentice-Hall, 1968.

Donaldson, Gordon. *Strategy of Financial Mobility.* Boston: Division of Research, Graduate School of Business Administration, Harvard University, 1969 (a classic).

Henderson, Bruce D. *Henderson on Corporate Strategy.* Cambridge, Mass.: Abt Books, 1979.

Porter, Michael E. *Competitive Strategy.* New York: Free Press, 1980.

Vancil, Richard F., and Makela, Benjamin R. eds. *The CFO Handbook.* Homewood, ILL.: Dow Jones-Irwin, 1986.

SELF-STUDY EXERCISES AND PROBLEMS

(Solutions are provided in Appendix III)

1. The ABC Corporation, a manufacturing company, sells a product at a price of $5.50 per unit. The variable costs involved in producing and selling the product are $3.25 per unit. Total fixed costs are $360,000. Calculate the break-even point and draw an appropriate chart.
   a. Calculate and demonstrate the effect of leverage by noting the profit impact of moving from the break-even point in 20 percent volume increments and decrements.

b. Calculate and graph separately the impact of a 50-cent drop in price, a 25-cent increase in variable cost, and an increase of $40,000 in fixed cost.

c. Draw a graph and discuss the implications if an increase in fixed costs of $30,000 occurs after 175,000 units of production, the average price drops to $5.25 per unit after 190,000 units are produced, and variable costs drop to an average of $3 after 150,000 units. How are the calculations for break-even affected?

2. Calculate the effect of financial leverage under the following two conditions:

a. Interest rate is 5 percent after taxes; return on net assets is 8 percent after taxes.

b. Interest rate is 6 percent after taxes; return on net assets is 5 percent after taxes.

Develop the effect on return on equity in each case for debt as a percent of capitalization at 0 percent, 25 percent, 50 percent, and 75 percent. Discuss.

3. Develop a five-year financial plan for a company based on the following assumptions:

	Year 1	Year 2	Year 3	Year 4	Year 5
Net assets (000)	$1,500	—	—	—	—
Debt/equity	0.25:1	0.25:1	0.50:1	0.50:1	0.50:1
Return on net assets					
(after taxes)	8%	9%	10%	10%	10%
Interest rate (after taxes)	4.5	4.5	5.0	5.0	5.0
Dividend payout	⅔	⅔	⅔	½	½
Number of shares	200,000	—	—	—	—

a. Calculate all relevant financial results, such as earnings per share, return on equity, growth in equity, and growth in earnings, and discuss your assumptions and findings.

b. Demonstrate the sensitivity of earnings per share, return on equity, and growth in equity by varying the conditions in Year 5 as follows: debt/equity, 0.75:1; return on net assets, 11 percent; interest rate, 4.5 percent; and dividend payout, two thirds. Discuss your findings.

5 ANALYSIS OF CAPITAL INVESTMENT DECISIONS

The first four chapters of this book dealt with the basic concepts and techniques used in analyzing ongoing businesses: ratio analysis, funds flow techniques, projections, leverage, and financial modeling of the total business system. We focused on the *results* and the *funds implications* of management decisions, but not on the *rationale* behind them. We specifically assumed that appropriate analytical methods were used for decisions about investments required to operate the business, and also for the choice of appropriate financing alternatives to cover the company's funds needs.

In this chapter, and throughout the rest of the book, we will change our focus, examining in some detail the *conceptual and practical reasons* behind capital investment and funding decisions. From time to time it will be desirable to provide some basic conceptual background by describing applicable portions of financial theory. In keeping with the scope of this book, however, we will avoid the esoteric in favor of the practical and useful. At the end of each chapter we will summarize, in a separate list, the key conceptual issues underlying the analytical approaches covered, both as a reminder and as a guide for the interested reader in exploring the references listed.

The topic of this chapter, the analysis of decisions about new *capital investments,* is part of a complex set of issues and choices that must be resolved continuously by management.

We have earlier called capital investments the driving force of any business. Such investments in resources, facilities, working capital, research, promotion, and other areas make possible the provision of goods and services to the customers of the company. Because capital investments, in contrast to *operational spending*, are normally relatively long-term commitments, they must be *compatible* with the *overall strategy* of a given company. Therefore, decisions about capital investment outlays must first be evaluated from the **strategic perspective** of the business. Further, the financial analysis underlying the decisions must be made within a **framework** of accepted conceptual and practical guidelines. Finally, there are several key **components of analysis** in the evaluation of capital investment alternatives that must be understood and made explicit as well as comparable so that a proper choice of investments can be made.

Our emphasis will be on the latter two areas as we take up the various **methods of analysis** used to choose among capital investments; these methods include the important topic of risk analysis. Building on these methods, we will examine certain **refinements** in the analytical process. Some comments about **further considerations** in making investment decisions will follow, and we will close with a checklist of **key issues** affecting capital investment analysis.

STRATEGIC PERSPECTIVE

Investments in land, productive equipment, buildings, natural resources, research facilities, and other assets for future economic gain are part of a company's strategic direction which management must periodically reevaluate. Business investment decisions cannot be made lightly, because normally a significant commitment of funds is made over the *long term*. It is therefore necessary that investment choices reflect the desired *direction* the company wishes to take, with due consideration given to expected *economic conditions*, the outlook for the company's specific *industry or business segment*, and the *competitive position* of the company.

An almost infinite variety of business investments are available to most firms. A company may invest in new facilities for *expansion*, with the rationale that the higher profits from the new volume will make the investment economically desirable. Investments may also *upgrade* worn or outmoded facilities to improve cost effectiveness. Here the savings in operating costs are the justification. Some plans call for entering *new markets*, which could involve entirely new facilities, or even a major *repositioning* of existing facilities through rebuilding or through sale and reinvestment. Other strategic proposals might involve establishing a *research* facility, justified on the basis of its potential for developing new products or processes. Capital investment could also involve significant *promotional* outlays, targeted toward raising the company's market share over the long term—and with it the profit contribution from higher volumes of operation.

Through the process of strategic planning, these and other choices are conceived and examined within the context and constraints of corporate and divisional *objectives and goals*. Then the various alternatives must be narrowed down to those options that should be given serious analysis. In most companies, the flow of ideas within the organization is greater than the firm's desire or ability to fund the potential projects. Thus, periodic spending plans are prepared which cover those capital outlays that have been selected and approved. The many steps involved in identifying, analyzing, and selecting capital investment opportunities are collectively known as **capital budgeting.** The process includes everything from broad ideas to very refined economic analyses. In the end, the company's *capital budget* contains an acceptable group of projects that individually and collectively are expected to provide economic returns that meet the goals set by management.

In a sense, the task of corporate management in capital budgeting is similar to what is involved in managing a financial investment portfolio. In both cases, the basic challenge is to find those investments that promise to give the desired level of economic reward within the constraint of the degree of risk that is acceptable. In an investment portfolio, current outlays are *traded off* against future inflows of cash in the form of dividends, interest, and return of principal. In the business setting, the trade-off involves cash outlays and future cash inflows from higher profits and the potential recovery of a portion of the capital committed.

However, the analogy carries only so far. In a going business, the situation is complicated by the need not only to select a portfolio of investments, but also to *operate* the facilities or other assets invested in. In addition, analyzing potential investments in a business context is far more complex because the outlays often involve multiple expenditures spread over a period of time. The construction and equipping of a new factory is an example. Determining the economic benefits derived from the outlay is even more complex. An individual investor generally receives specific contractual interest payments or dividend checks. In contrast, while a business investment generates additional profits from higher volume, new products, or cost reduction, the specific profit from the investment may be difficult to identify, because it is *intermingled* in the company's reports with other accounting information. As we will see, the analysis of potential capital investments involves a fair degree of *economic* reasoning and projection of *future conditions* that goes beyond merely using normal financial statements.

If we follow the analogy between a capital budget and an investment portfolio to its logical conclusion, then, ideally, capital budgeting would involve arraying all business investment opportunities in the order of their expected economic returns, and choosing a combination that would meet the desired portfolio return within the constraints of risk and funding sources. In fact, the theoretical concepts for business investment that have been developed and refined in the last two decades rely heavily on *portfolio theory,* both in terms of *risk evaluation* and the trade-off between *investment returns* and the *cost of capital* incurred in funding the investments. These concepts are highly structured and dependent on a series of underlying assumptions. Not easy to apply in practice, they continue to be the subject of much learned argument. In simple terms, business investments should be accepted up to the point at which incremental benefits equal incremental cost, given appropriate risk levels.

In reality, this theory entails several problems. First, at the time the capital budget is prepared, it is not possible to forecast *all* investment opportunities, because management is faced with a *revolving* planning horizon over which new opportunities keep appearing, while known opportunities may fade as conditions change. Second, capital budgets are prepared annually in most cases. As a result of time lags, actual *implementation* may not occur, because circumstances can change. Third, economic criteria, such as rate of return and cost of capital, are merely *approximations*, and moreover, *not the only* basis for the decision. The broader context of strategy, the competitive environment, the ability of management to implement the investment, organizational considerations, and other factors come into play as management weighs the *risk* of an investment against the potential *economic* gain. Thus, there is nothing automatic and simple in making decisions about the continuous stream of potential investments that flow from an organization.

Our task in this chapter will be to explore in depth the decisional framework and the analytical techniques that *support* the decision process in capital budgeting. We will not delve into the broader conceptual issues of capital budgeting and portfolio theory, except to point out the key issues. However, the reader interested in these topics is directed to the references at the end of the chapter. The important question of the *cost of capital* as related to capital budgeting will be taken up in the next chapter. In Chapter 7 the analytical reasoning behind the *choice of potential funding* of capital investments will be dealt with.

THE DECISIONAL FRAMEWORK

To carry out an effective analysis of capital investments, we must be very conscious of the many dimensions involved. We need a series of ground rules to ensure that our results are consistent and meaningful. These ground rules have to do with *problem definition*, with the *nature of the investment*, with estimates of *future costs and benefits*, with *incremental cash flows*, and with *relevant accounting data*.

Problem Definition

We begin our evaluation by stating *what* the investment is supposed to accomplish. Careful definition of the problem to be solved (or the opportunity presented) by the investment, and identification of any potential *alternatives* to the proposed action are critically important to proper analysis. Unfortunately, this elementary point is often overlooked and even ignored. But the importance of appropriate definition cannot be stressed too much. This is because in most cases, there are several alternatives available and examination of the specific circumstances may reveal an even greater number. As an example, the decision of whether to replace a machine nearing the end of its useful life appears to be a relatively straightforward "either/or" problem. The most obvious alternative is *to do nothing*, that is, to continue patching up the machine until it falls apart. The ongoing costs incurred with that option are compared with the cost pattern of a new machine to make a decision about replacement.

Yet there are some *not-so-obvious* alternatives. Perhaps the company should stop making the product altogether! This "go out of business" option should at least be considered—painful as it may be—before new resources are committed. While the improved efficiency of a new machine or a new facility may raise the product's profit performance from poor to average, there may indeed be different alternatives *elsewhere* that would yield greater profit from the amount invested. And even if it is decided to continue making the product, there *still* are several alternatives. Among these are replacement with the same machine, or with a larger, more automated model, or with equipment employing a different manufacturing process altogether.

A simple diagram can help us to visualize the key options for a replacement decision, as shown in Figure 5–1. This basic "decision tree" for a relatively simple decision strongly suggests the need to think through the many alternatives usually surrounding a major capital outlay. It is crucial to select the appropriate alternatives for analysis and to structure the problem in such a way that the analytical tools are applied to the real issue to be decided.

Figure 5–1
Options for Replacement Decision

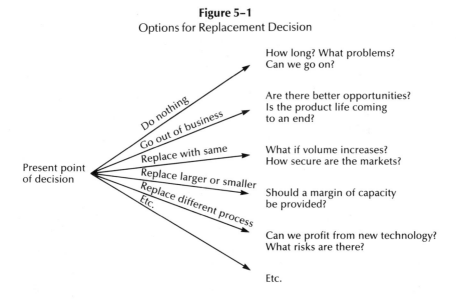

Present point
of decision

Do nothing
Go out of business
Replace with same
Replace larger or smaller
Replace different process
Etc.

How long? What problems?
Can we go on?

Are there better opportunities?
Is the product life coming
to an end?

What if volume increases?
How secure are the markets?

Should a margin of capacity
be provided?

Can we profit from new technology?
What risks are there?

Etc.

Nature of the Investment

Most capital investments tend to be **independent** of each other, that is, the choice of any one of them does not preclude also choosing any other. In that sense they can be viewed as a portfolio of choices, and the analysis and reasoning behind each decision will be relatively unaffected by past and future choices. There are, however, circumstances in which investments compete with each other to the extent that choosing one will preclude the other. Typically, this arises when two alternative ways of solving the same problem are being considered. Such investment projects are *mutually exclusive*. The significance of this condition will become apparent when we discuss the measures used to judge economic desirability. This condition can also arise when management sets a strict limit on the amount of spending—capital rationing—which will preclude investing in some worthy projects once others have been accepted.

Another type of investment involves *sequential* outlays beyond the initial expenditures. Any major capital outlay for plant and equipment usually also entails further future outlays for major maintenance, upgrading, and partial replacement some years hence, which should be considered when the decision is made. The most logical evaluation of such investments comes from taking into account all major consequences of the decision, even though future individual decisions concerning each of the consequences are possible.

Future Costs and Benefits

It is essential to recognize that the economic calculations used to justify, for example, a new machine, the replacement of an outmoded factory, or the purchase of a plot of land for development must be based on projections and forecasts of *future revenues and costs*. It is simply not enough to assume that the past operating costs will continue unchanged, or that past experience will be applicable to a new venture. While this may seem obvious, there is a practical temptation to *extrapolate* past conditions instead of carefully *forecasting* likely developments. The past is at best a rough guide, and at worst irrelevant for analysis. The success of investments with time horizons of 5, 10, and even 25 years rests entirely on future events and the *uncertainty* surrounding them. It therefore behooves the analyst to explore as much as possible the uncertainty surrounding the estimates. If potential deviations are great, it may be useful to run the analysis under different assumptions, thus testing the *sensitivity* of the result to changes in particular variables, such as product prices, raw material costs, and so on. The reader will recall our references to this type of analysis in the earlier chapters.

The uncertainty of future conditions surrounding an investment is the *risk* of not meeting expectations—the degree of risk being a function of the relative uncertainty of the key variables of the project. Careful estimates and research are often warranted to narrow the margin of error in the predicted conditions on which the analysis is based.

Incremental Cash Flows

The economic reasoning behind any capital outlay is based strictly on the *incremental* changes resulting from an investment. Moreover, the analysis recognizes only **cash flows**, that is, those funds movements traceable to cash inflows and outflows, not mere *accounting* transactions. Thus, the basic questions to be asked are: What *additional funds* will be required to finance the chosen alternative? For example, the investment proposal may entail the sale or other disposal of assets that will no longer be used, in addition to the outlay for the new equipment. Here it is the *net outlay,* after any applicable taxes, that counts.

Similarly, the next question is: What *additional* revenues will be created over and above any existing ones? If an investment results in *new* revenues, but at the same time some *existing* revenues are lost, only the *net impact*, after taxes, is relevant for economic analysis. A further question concerns the costs that will be *added* or *removed* as a result of the investment. The only relevant items here are those costs, including taxes, that will go up or down *as a consequence of* the investment decision; anything that remains the *same* before and after the investment has been made is *not relevant* for the analysis. This is why we say that the economic analysis of investments is an *incremental* process. The approach is relative rather than absolute, and is tied closely to carefully defined alternatives and the differences between them. The specific data used in the analysis therefore are the *differential* funds commitments as well as revenues and costs caused by the decision, all viewed in aftertax *cash flow* terms.

Relevant Accounting Data

Investment analysis involves the use of data derived from accounting records. However, not all accounting data are *relevant* for the purpose. For example, some changes in financial statements reflect accounting conventions and not actual changes in cash flows. As a result, particularly with investments that cause changes in costs, a clear distinction must be made between those items that *do vary* with the operation of the new investment and those which only *appear to vary.* The latter are often **accounting allocations** which may change in magnitude but do not necessarily represent a true change in costs incurred. For example, for accounting purposes, general overhead costs (administrative costs, insurance, etc.) may be allocated based on operating volume. Thus, a new machine with higher output will be charged with a higher share of overhead than was the machine it replaces. Yet there has likely been *no actual change* in general overhead attributable to the substitution of one machine for the other. Therefore, the change in *allocation* is not relevant for purposes of analysis. Investment analysis constantly requires making judgments as to whether there has been a change in the *true* cash outlays and revenues, not whether the accounting system is *redistributing* the existing costs differently.

There is also the common temptation to include in the analysis of a new investment some outlays that occurred in the *past*, perhaps preparatory to making the new commitment. Economic analysis does *not* permit backtracking to expenditures that have already been made and recorded on the books. Such **sunk costs,** even if they are connected in some way to the decision at hand, cannot be altered by making the investment now. If, for example, significant amounts were spent on research and development of a new product, the current decision about whether to invest in the facilities to produce the product should be in *no way* affected by those sunk costs. Economic decisions are *forward looking* and involve *only* those things that can be *changed* by the action decided upon. This is the essential test of relevance for any element to be included in the analysis of a capital investment decision.

COMPONENTS OF ANALYSIS

Bearing in mind the strategic perspective and the ground rules just enumerated, we can now turn to the basic components common to all business investment proposals. In essence, capital is invested for one basic reason: to obtain sufficient future economic returns to warrant the original outlay, that is, sufficient cash receipts over the life of the project to justify the cash spent. Analytical methods should take into account in one way or another, this basic *trade-off* of current cash outflow against future cash inflow.

To judge the attractiveness of any investment we must consider the following elements: the amount expended, that is, the **net investment**, the potential benefits, that is, the **operating cash flows,** and the time period over which it will provide those benefits, that is, the **economic life** of the investment. A proper economic analysis must relate these three elements to provide an indication of whether the investment is worthy of consideration or not. We can use a simple example to show how this is done. An outlay of $100,000 for equipment needed to manufacture a new product is expected to provide aftertax cash flow benefits of $25,000 over a period of six years, without significant annual fluctuations. Although the equipment will not be fully worn out after six years, it is unlikely that more than scrap value will be realized at this time, due to technical obsolescence. The cost of removal is expected to offset this scrap value. Straight-line depreciation over the six years ($16,667 per year) has been appropriately reflected in the cash flow figure of $25,000, by being added back.

Net Investment

The first element in the analysis, the investment involved, normally consists of the gross capital requirements for the new assets *less* any capital recovered from the resulting trade or sale of existing assets. Such recoveries must be adjusted for the tax change arising from any gain or loss from the disposal of existing assets. It is the amount of *net investment* that will be committed to the decision. Because no assets were replaced in our simple case, the net investment is $100,000.

Particularly when the investment is for new products or an increased volume of existing products, increased *working capital* has to be considered in the analysis. Normally, such incremental working capital is added to net investment. For our first example this refinement is ignored, but we will demonstrate how working capital is handled later in the chapter.

Further capital outlays might also be necessary *during* the life of the investment project. This potential consequence of the initial decision must also be considered as part of the investment proposal. We will demonstrate the method of dealing with such sequential elements later on. Similarly, if there were a substantial *recovery* of capital from eventual disposal at the end of the economic life (beyond the minor scrap value assumed here) such amounts would have to be made part of the analysis. Again we will demonstrate the handling of this element later on.

Operating Cash Flows

These revenue and cost changes are the period-by-period *net* economic benefits over the economic life of the investment, after taking into account their impact on income taxes. They include such elements as operating savings caused by a machine replacement, the additional profits from a new product line, the increased profits from plant expansion, or the profits created by developing land or other natural resources. These economic benefits normally appear as an increase in the profits reported in the periodic operating statements. From a cash standpoint they will improve the company's *aftertax cash flow,* which we know from earlier chapters to consist of aftertax profit plus depreciation.

We will later give numerous examples of how project cash

flows are derived, but for our example we will assume the annual operating cash flow after taxes to be a *level* $25,000, representing new product profits of $8,333, adjusted for depreciation of $16,667. As we will see, however, a *variable* pattern of annual or periodic cash flows can significantly influence the results of our analysis. Level periodic flows are easiest to deal with, but are rare in practice. Uneven cash flows are more common and make the analysis more complex, but can be handled readily, as we will see.

Economic Life

The third element, the *time period* covered by the analysis is commonly referred to as the *economic life* of the investment project. For analysis purposes, the only relevant time period is the economic life, as distinguished from the *physical* life of equipment, or the *technological* life of a particular process. Even though a building or a piece of equipment may be perfectly usable from a physical standpoint, the economic life of the investment has ceased if the market for the product or service has disappeared. At that point, any usable resources will have to be repositioned—which requires another investment decision—or disposed of for their recovery value. The net investment in the case where usable resources are *reinvested* in another project would, of course, be the estimated recovery value after taxes. Similarly, the economic life of any given technology is bound up with the economics of the marketplace—the best process is useless if the resulting product can no longer be sold.

The *depreciation life* used for accounting or tax purposes does not normally reflect an investment's true life span. As we discussed earlier, such write-offs are based on standard accounting and tax guidelines, and do not necessarily represent the economic usefulness of the investment. In our simple example, we have assumed a six-year economic life, the period over which the product manufactured with the equipment investment will be sold.

To summarize, up to this point in the chapter, we have laid the groundwork for analyzing a capital investment by describing the *strategic perspective,* the *decisional framework,* and the *components* of the analysis. This background was needed because the reader must be aware that analyzing a capital investment is not the simple matter that it appears to be. The points covered so far in the chapter establish *what* must be analyzed. We now turn to the question of *how* this is done—the methods and criteria of analysis.

METHODS OF ANALYSIS

How do we relate the three basic elements—net investment, operating cash flow, and economic life—to determine the project's attractiveness? We will first deal with *simple methods* of analysis. These are essentially rules of thumb that intuitively grapple with the trade-off between investment and operating cash flows. Two measures of the desirability of an investment will be discussed, **payback** and **accounting rate of return,** which are still being used in practice despite their demonstrable shortcomings. We will then turn to the concept of the **time value of money,** which enables the analyst to deal with the relevant cash flows in **equivalent** terms, that is, regardless of the timing of their incidence. The key measures in this area are **net present value,** the **profitability index,** and the **internal rate of return (yield).** Next we will turn to **risk analysis,** and discuss **present value payback, annualized net present value, ranges of estimates, simulation, probabilistic reasoning,** and **risk adjusted rates.**

Simple Measures

Payback. Payback measures the direct relationship between annual cash inflow from a project and the net investment required.

$$\text{Payback} = \frac{\text{Net investment}}{\text{Average annual operating cash flow}} = \frac{\$100,000}{\$25,000} = 4 \text{ years}$$

The result of the calculation is the number of years required for the original outlay to be repaid. The payback period is commonly used as an indication of whether the investment will be repaid within its economic life span. In our simple example this is true, as payback is achieved in four years versus an estimated economic life of six years.

While the payback period is easy to calculate—which probably accounts for its popularity—some difficult questions arise when it is applied. First, the measure tests the recovery of the original investment on, so to speak, an installment basis. "How long will it be until I get my money back?" is the implied query. To recover the capital is not enough, of course, because from an economic viewpoint, one would hope to earn a profit on the funds while they are invested. To illustrate, we can draw an analogy to a savings account in which $100 is invested, and from which $25 is withdrawn at the end of each year. After four years, the principal will have been repaid. However, the saver would be very upset, indeed, if the bank statement showed that the account was now depleted. The investment was made with the expectation of earning 5 or 6 percent *every year* on the declining balance in the account. The saver would certainly demand payment of the accumulated interest.

In the case of our machine investment, the payback period of four years calculated above similarly implies that no economic return has been earned on the funds committed. Four years is just sufficient to recover the *original outlay*. Thus, we must look to the years *beyond* the payback point to provide an economic return. In fact, if the economic life and the payback period were to coincide precisely, an *opportunity loss* would have been suffered, because the same funds invested elsewhere would probably have earned some return every year—at least savings account interest! This point is demonstrated in Table 5–1. Here we again assume that our $100,000 capital investment provides an annual operating cash flow after taxes of $25,000. If our hypothetical company typically earned 10 percent after taxes on its investments, part of every year's cash flow would have to be considered as this normal return, while

Table 5–1
Amortization of $100,000 Investment at 10 Percent

Year	(1) Beginning Balance	(2) Normal Earnings at 10 Percent	(3) Operating Cash Flow	(4) Ending Balance to be Recovered
1	$100,000	$10,000	$(25,000)	$85,000
2	85,000	8,500	(25,000)	68,500
3	68,500	6,850	(25,000)	50,350
4	50,350	5,035	(25,000)	30,385 (payback)
5	30,385	3,039	(25,000)	8,424
6	8,424	842	(25,000)	(15,734)

the remainder would be applied to reducing the outstanding balance. The first column shows the beginning balance of the investment for each year. Normal earnings of 10 percent are calculated on these balances in the second column. The operating cash flows in the third column, reduced by the normal earnings, are applied against the beginning balances to calculate every year's ending balance. The result is an amortization schedule for our simple investment that extends to the *sixth* year—two years longer than the payback measure would suggest.

Strictly for simplicity we have assumed that earnings are calculated on the *beginning* balance of the investment, and operating cash flows are received at the *end* of the period. A more precise simulation would not materially affect the result. From the figures in the table it is quite obvious that a payback of four years would mean an opportunity loss of about $30,000, if the project ended at this point. With an economic life of five years, the opportunity loss vis-à-vis the normal expectation of earning 10 percent would be reduced to about $8,400, while at six years there would be a sizable advantage of $15,700.

This brief illustration points up one of the important short-comings of the payback measure. It is relatively *insensitive* to the economic life span and thus not a truly meaningful criterion for determining earnings power. The speed with which the initial investment is repaid is neither a convenient nor a sufficient way to appraise profitability. All we can say about our example in payback terms is that the project pays out in four years, with two "extra" years for profit. Moreover, the payback measure would also give a "4 years plus something extra" reading on other projects with similar cash flows but 8- or 10-year economic lives, even though those projects may be clearly superior to our example.

Another shortcoming of the payback measure is that it implicitly assumes *level* annual operating cash flows. Projects with rising or declining cash flow patterns—although very common—cannot properly be evaluated using payback. An investment in a new product, for example, may yield cash flows that slowly rise during the early years, but that eventually level out and decline sharply in the late stages of the product's economic life. A machine replacement, in contrast, will normally generate ever-growing improvements in operating costs as the existing machine deteriorates. Moreover, any additional sequential investments during the period, or capital recoveries at the end of the economic life will cause distortions in this rule of thumb measure. Table 5–2 illustrates the insensitivity of the payback measure to variations in cash flow.

Table 5–2
Payback Results under Varying Conditions

	Project 1	Project 2	Project 3
Net investment	$100,000	$100,000	$100,000
Average annual operating cash flow	$ 25,000	$ 25,000	$ 33,333
Economic life	6 years	8 years	3 years
Payback	4 years	4 years	3 years
Cash flow pattern (years):			
1	$ 25,000	$ 20,000	$ 16,667
2	25,000	30,000	33,333
3	25,000	50,000	50,000
4	25,000	40,000	–0–
5	25,000	30,000	–0–
6	25,000	15,000	–0–
7	–0–	10,000	–0–
8	–0–	5,000	–0–
Total	$150,000	$200,000	$100,000
Cumulative first four years	$100,000	$140,000	n.a.
Average first four years	$ 25,000	$ 35,000	n.a.

n.a. = not applicable.

If we assume similar risks for each of the three projects shown in the table, we would chose Project 2 over Project 1, because over its economic life, it will return $50,000 more than Project 1. Yet the payback is the same for both projects. Project 3, on the other hand, appears to be the most favorable one if judged *only* by the payback period of three years. Yet it is obvious that Project 3 involves an opportunity loss, because the operating cash flows during its three-year economic life are just sufficient to recover the original outlay, without providing any economic return. The difference in the cash flow patterns of Projects 1 and 2 is also masked by the payout criterion. Although both projects pay back the initial investment in four years, the cumulative operating cash flows are higher for Project 2 than for Project 1. Average annual cash flows are $35,000 versus $25,000 during the first four years. Thus, Project 2 clearly provides significantly higher operating cash flows early on and is therefore more desirable.

A modification of the payback measure substitutes *average accounting profit after taxes* as the denominator in the formula instead of aftertax cash flow. Here the rationale is that the net income improvement (in accounting terms) attributable to the investment, which has been lowered by the annual depreciation allowance, implicitly provides for *both* the return of principal *and* a periodic profit. According to this reasoning, the amount of depreciation charged against net income is assumed to roughly simulate the recovery of principal—as we had done more precisely in our amortization table earlier—while the net profit improvement is considered as earnings on the original investment. In the simple example we have used so far, the average aftertax cash flow is $25,000, composed of an average accounting profit improvement of $8,333 plus annual depreciation of $16,667 ($100,000 depreciated straight-line over six years). When we use this figure in the revised formula, the payback jumps to 12 years, clearly a distortion of what we would expect to be the economic return:

$$\frac{\text{Net investment}}{\text{Average annual aftertax profit}} = \frac{\$100,000}{\$8,333} = 12 \text{ years}$$

This result, based on a crude implied simulation of amortizing the investment, simply cannot represent the "cash-in, cash-out" reasoning that underlies economic investment analysis. We must be very careful not to let changes in accounting profits and associated depreciation write-offs take the place of the *economic cash flow trade-offs* in our analytical framework, because each is designed for a valid but different purpose. Table 5–1 demonstrated that the project was desirable if its economic life was five years or better. A 12-year payback is clearly unreasonable, even if we raised the company's normal earnings expectations significantly above the assumed 10 percent aftertax return built into the amortization table. The degree of distortion introduced by the use of accounting profits will, of course, vary depending on the circumstances, particularly with changes in a project's economic life.

By now it should be obvious that the payback measure must be used with considerable caution. It is an effective device for selecting investments *only* if it is applied to an array of projects with *similar* cash flow patterns and *similar* economic lives. For example, the method would be applicable for a company facing routine replacement of machines in large numbers. If cash flow and economic life are dissimilar, however, a more viable and flexible analysis is necessary.

Accounting Rate of Return. A few comments should be made about a measure that is an outgrowth of the payback method. In fact, this measure is the inverse of the payback formula. The accounting rate of return states the economic desirability of an investment in terms of a percentage return on the *original* outlay. The method shares all of the shortcomings of the payback method, however, because it again relates only two of the three critical aspects of any project, net investment and operating cash flows, and ignores the economic life:

$$\text{Return on investment} = \frac{\text{Average annual operating cash flow}}{\text{Net investment}} = \frac{\$25,000}{\$100,000} = 25\%$$

All this measure indicates is that $25,000 happens to be 25 percent of $100,000. This is the only conclusion that can be drawn because there is no reference to economic life and also no recognition of the fact that, as is true with a savings account, regular cash benefits will draw down the balance of the principal. Note that using the rate of return calculation, the *same* answer would be given if the economic life were 1 year, 10 years, or 100 years. In fact, the return indicated in the formula would be valid in an economic sense only if the investment provided $25,000 per year *in perpetuity*. Only then could we say the return was truly 25 percent.

A slightly more meaningful version of the accounting rate of return uses aftertax accounting profit as the numerator. A much more credible result emerges in the case of our example:

$$\text{Return on investment} = \frac{\text{Average annual aftertax profit}}{\text{Net investment}}$$

$$= \frac{\$8,333}{\$100,000} = 8.3\%$$

Apart from being employed to generate a simulated economic criterion for use in capital investment decisions, this version of accounting rate of return also simulates the impact the project would have on corporate financial statements. It normally will approximate the resulting changes in the operating statement and the balance sheet, at least for the early part of the project's life. As an economic measure it is still subject, however, to all the other shortcomings we have discussed because it is merely the inverse of the payback formula. Therefore, meaningful comparisons can be made using the accounting rate of return *only* if the alternatives being evaluated have *quite similar* operating cash flow patterns and economic lives.

As mentioned, the methods discussed above are relatively easy to calculate, which in part accounts for their popularity. However, with the increasing availability of computer-aided analytical methods, more sophisticated analyses can be performed with comparative ease. These methods, which involve the *time value of money*, more accurately reflect the true economic trade-offs and returns.

The Time Value of Money

Earlier we described investment analysis as the process of weighing the trade-off between current dollar outlays and the future benefits expected over a period of time. This concept applies to all kinds of investments made by individuals and businesses alike. In the following section, we will examine how the relationship between an investment and the resulting future benefits is established. We will begin by discussing how the basic principles of **compounding** and **discounting** can be used to derive *equivalent* monetary values irrespective of timing. Then we will discuss certain *key measures* of investment analysis that involve applying these principles to the *economic* choice among investment propositions.

Compounding, Discounting, and Equivalence. Common sense tells us that a person will not be indifferent between two investment propositions that are exactly alike in all aspects except for a *difference in timing* of the future benefits. Our investor will obviously prefer the one providing more immediate benefits. The reason for this preference, of course, is that more immediately available funds offer an individual or a company the *opportunity to invest* these funds at a profit—be it in a savings account, a government bond, a loan, a new facility, or any one of a great variety of other economic possibilities. Thus, having to wait for a period of time until funds become available entails an *opportunity cost* in the form of lost earnings. Conversely, common sense dictates that given a choice between making an expenditure now versus making the same expenditure some time in the future, it is advantageous to *defer the outlay.* Again the reason is the normal opportunity to earn a profit on the funds in the meantime. Stated another way, the value of money is affected directly by the *timing* of its receipt or disbursement, and this in turn is related to the *opportunity* of *earning a profit* during the interval.

A simple example will help illustrate this point. If a person normally uses a savings account to earn interest of 5 percent per year, a deposit of $1,000 made today will grow to $1,050 in one year. (For simplicity we ignore the practice of daily or monthly compounding commonly used by banks and savings institutions.) If for some reason the person had to wait one year to deposit the $1,000, the opportunity to earn $50 in interest would be lost. Without question, a sum of $1,000 offered to the person one year hence has to be worth *less* than the same amount offered immediately. Specifically, *today's value* of the delayed $1,000 must be related to the person's earnings opportunity of 5 percent. Given this earnings opportunity, we can calculate the **present value** of the $1,000 to be received in one year's time as follows:

$$\text{Present value} = \frac{\$1,000}{1.05} = \$952.38$$

What the equation shows is that given a return of 5 percent, $1,000 received one year from now is the *equivalent* of $952.38 today. This is so because $952.38 invested at 5 percent today will grow into $1,000 at the end of one year. The calculation therefore expresses the economic trade-off between dollars received today versus those received in the future, a trade-off which is based on the *length of time* involved and the *earnings opportunity* available. If for the moment, we ignore risk, it also follows that our investor should be willing to pay $952.38 *today* for a financial contract that will deliver $1,000 in one year, given that the investor normally has the opportunity to earn 5 percent on invested funds.

Similarly, the longer the waiting period, the lower the present value of a sum of money becomes, because for each additional year of delay, more opportunity to earn a return is forgone. Principal and interest left in place would have *compounded*, earning an annual return on the total for every year. Conversely, the opportunity to defer an expenditure as long as possible allows the individual to earn a return each year on the amount *not spent* plus the interest left in place. This reduces the impact of the eventual expenditure in today's terms. The process of calculating this change in value is quite simple when we know the time period and the earnings opportunity rate.

For example, a sum of $1,000 to be received at the end of five years will be worth only $783.53 today, because that amount invested today at 5 percent compounded annually would grow to $1,000 five years hence, if the earnings are left to accumulate and interest is earned on the growing balance each year. The calculation is as follows:

$$\text{Present value} = \frac{\$1,000}{(1 + 0.05)^5} = \frac{\$1,000}{1.27628} = \$783.53$$

The result of $783.53 was obtained by relating the **future value** of $1,000 to the **compound earnings factor** of 5 percent in five years, shown in the denominator as 1.27628, which is simply 1.05 raised to the fifth power. Through dividing the future value by the compound earnings factor, we have in effect *discounted* the future value into a lower *equivalent present value*. Note that the mathematics are straightforward in achieving what we described earlier. The value of a future sum is lowered in precise relationship to the earnings opportunity and the timing incidence. The earnings opportunity is our assumed 5 percent compound interest, while the timing is reflected in the number of times the interest is compounded to express the number of years during which earnings were forgone. The reduction in value is achieved by dividing the earnings factor into the future value.

We refer to the calculation of present values as *discounting*, while the reverse, the calculation of future values is called *compounding*. With the help of the very basic mathematical relationships involved, we can derive the *equivalent value* of any sum to be received or paid at any point in time, either at the present moment, or at any specified future date.

The process of compounding and discounting is as old as money lending and has been used by financial institutions from time immemorial. Even though the application of this methodology to business investments is of more recent vintage, the techniques have become commonplace. The advent of handheld electronic calculators with compounding and discounting capability has made the derivation of equivalent values and time-adjusted investment measures routine.

The discount factors are also listed in so-called **present value tables,** which were used by analysts to calculate present values before programmed calculators and personal computers were available. Two of these tables are provided at the end of this chapter. Even though they are no longer necessary for making actual calculations, they provide a visual demonstration of the effect of discounting. With their help we can clarify a few points. Table 5–10 contains the factors that translate into equivalent present values a *single sum* of money received or disbursed at the end of any period, under different assumptions about the rate of earnings. It is based on this general formula:

$$\text{Present value} = \frac{1}{(1 + i)^n}$$

where i is the applicable earnings rate (discount rate) and n the number of periods over which discounting takes place. The table covers a range from 1 to 60 periods, and discount rates from 1 to 50 percent. The rates are related to the *periods,* in that if the periods represent years, the rates are annual, while if months are used, the rates are monthly earnings. The present value of a sum of money therefore can be found by simply multiplying the amount involved by the appropriate factor in the table:

$$\text{Present value} = \text{Factor} \times \text{Amount}$$

Note that the results from our savings account example can be found in Table 5–10 in the 5 percent column, lines 1 and 5.

Table 5–11 is a variation of Table 5–10 that allows the user to directly calculate the present value of a *series* of *equal* receipts or payments occurring over a number of periods. Such series are called *annuities.* The same result could be found by using Table 5–10 and repetitively multiplying the periodic amount by the appropriate series of factors and adding all of the results. Table 5–11 lists a set of *additive* factors, however, which allow the analyst to obtain the present value of an annuity in the single step of multiplying the periodic receipt or payment by the appropriate factor:

$$\text{Present value} = \text{Factor} \times \text{Annuity}$$

These basic tables, which correspond to the programs in most calculators, can be used for practically all investment problems normally encountered. There are many possible variations and refinements in timing, such as more frequent discounting (monthly, weekly), or an assumption that the annuity is received or disbursed in weekly or monthly increments rather than at the end of the period. Such a forward shift in timing would result in slightly higher present values, both for single sums and annuities. This more continuous flow of receipts or disbursements more closely approximates the cash incidence from such changes in operations as savings in labor and materials and other daily, weekly, or monthly changes.

Many discounting refinements also relate to specific financial instruments, such as mortgages, bonds, charge accounts, etc., which involve specific practices, such as daily discounting or compounding. For the practical purpose of analyzing business capital investments, such refinements are not critical, because the imprecise nature of many of the estimates easily outweighs the possible increments in precision that might be obtained using more refined techniques. The periodic discounting embodied in the present value tables is quite adequate for most analytical needs. With this in mind, we can now turn to the application of the time value of money and the basic principles of discounting to business investment analysis.

Measures Using Time Value of Money

We will discuss the most common measures that apply the principles of discounting to business investment analysis. They are **net present value**, the **profitability index**, and the **internal rate of return (yield)**. As always, we will describe the basic rationale on which these measures are based, and their applicability as well as their shortcomings.

Net Present Value. Net present value is used simply to weigh the elements of the trade-off between investment outlays and future benefits in *equivalent* terms, and to determine whether the net balance of the present values is favorable or unfavorable. A rate of discount must be specified, and appropriate present value factors applied to both inflows and outflows over the economic life being analyzed. When the present values of all inflows and outflows are summed, the *net present value* is the *difference* between the two amounts. The figure can be positive or negative, depending on whether there is a net inflow or outflow over the economic life of the project. The net present value indicates whether an investment, over its life, will achieve the earnings standard desired. Inasmuch as present value depends on both timing and earnings opportunity, a *positive* net present value indicates that over its economic life, the cash flows generated by the investment will recover the original outlay (as well as any future ones considered in the analysis), earn the desired return standard on the outstanding balances, *and* in addition provide a "cushion" of excess value. Conversely, a *negative* result indicates that the project is not achieving the earnings standard and thus will cause an *opportunity loss*. Obviously, the *level* of earnings desired, the *timing* of the cash flows, and the relative *magnitudes* involved all will affect the result.

A word should be said at this point about the rate of discount to be used. From an economic standpoint, this should be the rate of return the investor normally enjoys from investments of similar nature and risk. In effect, it is an **opportunity rate of return.** In the corporate setting, the choice of a discount rate is complicated by the variety of investments available and by the types of financing provided by both owners and lenders. The corporate earnings standard used to discount capital investment cash flows should reflect the minimum return requirement that will leave the shareholder as well off as before, while taking advantage of financial leverage. The standard most commonly employed is the overall corporate **cost of capital,** which takes into account shareholder expectations, business risk, and leverage. Often the corporate earnings standard is broken down into a set of multiple discount rates that reflect the specific risks of different lines of business within a company. We will deal with these concepts in greater depth in the next chapter. For present purposes we will assume that management has chosen an appropriate earnings standard with which to discount investment cash flows, and we will focus on how present value measures are used to assess potential investments on an economic basis.

To illustrate, we will return to the simple investment example we used earlier in the chapter. As a first step, it is generally helpful to lay out the pertinent information period by period to give us a time perspective. A horizontal time scale can be used, on which the periods are marked off and the positive and negative cash flows inserted.

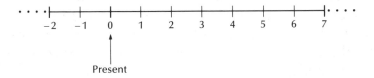

When we represent the timing of cash flows on a scale, the present is normally considered the "0" point, with periods marked off in positive increments into the future, and negative increments into the past, as applicable to the particular problem. The information can also be shown in the format used in Table 5–3.

The net investment of $100,000 at point 0 and the six annual benefit inflows of $25,000 each result in a net present value of almost $16,000, on the assumption that a company considers 8 percent after taxes to be a normal earnings standard. All of the initial outflow will have been recovered over the six-year period, while 8 percent after taxes will have been earned on the declining investment balance outstanding during the project life. An additional cushion of $15,575 in equivalent present value dol-

Table 5–3
Net Present Value Analysis by Period at 8 Percent

Time Period	Investment (outlays)	Benefits (inflows)	Present Value Factors at 8 Percent*	Present Values	Cumulative Net Present Value
0	$100,000	—	1.000	− $100,000	− $100,000
1	—	$ 25,000	0.926	+ 23,150	− 76,850
2	—	25,000	0.857	+ 21,425	− 55,425
3	—	25,000	0.794	+ 19,850	− 35,575
4	—	25,000	0.735	+ 18,375	− 17,200
5	—	25,000	0.681	+ 17,025	− 175
6	—	25,000	0.630	+ 15,750	+ 15,575
	$100,000	$150,000		+ $ 15,575	

*To illustrate the use of Table 5–10, assuming that benefits occur at year-end. We could instead use a factor from Table 5–11: 4,623 times $25,000, because the annual inflows are equal. The result for the total present value of the inflows is identical. (The factors for years 1 through 6 total 4.623.)

lars can be expected *if* the cash flow estimates are correct *and* the project does live out its economic life. We note a similarity to the payback concept discussed earlier, where we found the recovery of the investment and "something extra." The critical *difference* between payback and net present value, however, is the fact that the net present value concept has a built-in earnings requirement *in addition* to the recovery of the investment. Thus, the cushion implicit in a positive net present value is truly an economic gain that goes beyond satisfying the required earnings standard.

If a higher earnings standard had been required, say 12 percent, the results would be those shown in Table 5–4. The net present value remains positive, but the size of the cushion has decreased to only $2,800. We would expect a decrease, because at a higher discount rate, the present value must decline, with all other circumstances unchanged. At an earnings rate of 14 percent, the net present value shrinks further and in fact, is transformed into a negative result ($25,000 × 3.889 − $100,000 = − $2,775). This demonstrates the sensitivity of the net present value result to the choice of earnings standards.

The importance of the length of the economic life of the investment is demonstrated in the last column of both Table 5–3 and 5–4. There we can see that as the earnings standard was raised, the time required for the cumulative present value to

Table 5–4
Net Present Value Analysis by Period at 12 Percent

Time Period	Investment (outlays)	Benefits (inflows)	Present Value Factors at 12 Percent*	Present Values	Cumulative Net Present Value
0	$100,000	—	1.000	− $100,000	− $100,000
1	—	$ 25,000	0.893	+ 22,325	− 77,675
2	—	25,000	0.797	+ 19,925	− 57,750
3	—	25,000	0.712	+ 17,800	− 39,950
4	—	25,000	0.636	+ 15,900	− 24,050
5	—	25,000	0.567	+ 14,175	− 9,875
6	—	25,000	0.507	+ 12,675	+ 2,800
	$100,000	$150,000		+ $ 2,800	

*As in Table 5–3, we could use 4.112 times $25,000 from Table 5–11.

turn positive was lengthened. At 8 percent the economic life had to be about five years for the switch to occur (the net present value after the benefits of year 5 is just about zero), while at 12 percent most of the sixth year of economic life was necessary for the measure to turn positive (about $10,000 of negative present value at the end of year 5 has to be recovered from benefits of year 6).

The net present value measure thus appears to correctly reflect the trade-off of equivalent cash outlays and cash inflows over time, while allowing for both the recovery of the investment outlay (principal) and for earnings on the declining balance at a stipulated rate. In our example, we have assumed a *level* operating cash inflow of $25,000. Uneven cash flow patterns will have a notable impact on the results, although the method of calculation remains the same. The reader is invited to test this, using a cash inflow pattern that rises from, say, $15,000 to $40,000, and one that falls from $40,000 to $15,000, each totaling $150,000 over six years.

The best use of net present value is as a screening device that indicates whether the minimum earnings standard can be met by a capital investment over its economic life. When net present value is positive, there is potential for earnings in excess of the standard; when net present value is negative, the minimum earnings standard and capital recovery cannot be achieved with the projected cash flows over the investment's economic life. When net present value is close to or exactly zero, the earnings standard has just been met, but on the assumption that the earnings estimate and the projected life are quite certain.

While it is a useful tool in evaluating investments, the concept of net present value does not answer all our questions about the economic attractiveness of capital outlays. For example, when comparing different projects, how do we evaluate the size of the "cushion" calculated with a given return standard, particularly if the amount of investment differs significantly? Also, to what extent is achievement of the projects' economic lives a factor in such comparisons? Furthermore, how do we quantify the potential error inherent in the cash flow estimates, and how does the measure help making investment choices if such deviations are significant? Finally, what specific return will the project *yield* if all estimates are in fact realized? Further measures and analytical methods are necessary to answer these questions, and we will show how a combination of techniques helps to narrow the choices to be made.

Profitability Index. After we have calculated net present value on a series of projects, we may be faced with a choice involving several alternative investments of *different* size. In such a case, we cannot be indifferent to the fact that even though the net present values of the alternatives may be close or even equal, they involve commitments of widely varying amounts. In other words, it does make a difference whether an investment proposal promises a net present value of $1,000 for an outlay of $10,000, or whether in another case the same $1,000 calls for an investment of $25,000, even if we assume equivalent economic lives and equivalent risk. In the first case, the cushion (excess benefit) is a much larger fraction of the net investment than it is in the second, which makes the first investment clearly more attractive.

The profitability index is a formal way of expressing this *cost/benefit* relationship:

$$\text{Profitability index} = \frac{\text{Present value of operating inflows (benefit)}}{\text{Present value of net investment (cost)}}$$

The present values in this formula are the same amounts we used earlier to derive the net present value, although then we *subtracted* inflows from outflows. In the case of the profitability index the question is simply: How much in present value benefits is being created for each dollar of net investment? The two cases we cited above would yield the following results:

1. Profitability index $= \dfrac{\$11,000}{\$10,000} = 1.10$

2. Profitability index $= \dfrac{\$26,000}{\$25,000} = 1.04$

The higher the index, the better the project. As we expected, the first project is much more favorable, given the assumption that all other aspects of the investment are reasonably comparable. If the index is 1.0 or less, the project is just meeting or is below the minimum earnings standard used to derive the present values. An index of *exactly 1.0* corresponds to a *zero* net present value, based on the definition of the mathematical relationship.

The example in Table 5–3 has a profitability index of 1.16 at 8 percent ($115,575 ÷ $100,000), and 1.03 at 12 percent in Table 5–4 ($102,800 ÷ $100,000). Thus, the profitability index measure does provide additional insight. It also, as mentioned, allows us to choose between investment alternatives of differing size. But it still leaves several points unanswered, and there are theoretical issues involved which we will point out later in the chapter.

Internal Rate of Return (Yield).   The concept of the "true" return yielded by an investment over its economic life (often referred to as the **discounted cash flow return, or DCF**) has already been mentioned in the earlier discussion of net present value. This **internal rate of return** is simply that unique discount rate which, when applied to both cash inflows and cash outflows over the investment's economic life, provides a *zero net present value*—that is, the present value of the inflows is exactly equal to the present value of the outflows. Stated another way, the principal can be amortized over the economic life, while it earns the exact return implied by the underlying discount rate. Thus, the project may *yield* the earnings standard desired, but *only if* the underlying rate happens to *coincide* with the standard.

Naturally, the result will vary with changes in economic life and cash flows. In fact, the internal rate of return is found by letting it be a *variable* that is dependent on cash flows and economic life. With net present value and the profitability index, we employed a *specified* earnings standard to discount the investment's cash flows. In contrast, with the internal rate of return, we turn the problem around to *find the discount rate* that makes cash inflows and outflows equal. We can again employ our simple formula (Present value = Factor × Annuity), if the project is simple enough to involve a *single* investment outlay and *level* annual cash inflows. The formula is then:

$$\text{Factor} = \frac{\text{Present value (investment)}}{\text{Annuity}}$$

This factor can then be located in the present value table for annuities (Table 5–11). The economic life is a given. Therefore, we can find the rate of return by moving along the proper period row to the column with a factor that approximates the formula result. To illustrate, our earlier investment example has a factor of 4.0 ($100,000 ÷ $25,000). We find that on the six-period line of Table 5–11, the factor 4.0 lies almost exactly between 12 percent (4.112) and 14 percent (3.889). Approximate interpolation suggests that the result is about 13 percent. Again, the use of electronic calculators with discounting capability will eliminate the need for the table.

If a project has a more complex cash flow pattern, a trial-and-error approach is necessary when the analysis is done using present value tables. Successive application of different discount rates to all cash flows over the investment's economic life must be made until a close approximation of a zero net present value has been found. With some experience, an analyst will find that usually no more than two trials are necessary, because the first result will show the *direction* of any refinement needed. A positive net present value indicates the need for a *higher* discount rate, while a negative one calls for the opposite. We observed this effect in our earlier example, when the net present value was reduced as the discount rate was raised from 8 to 12 percent (see Tables 5–3 and 5–4). Again, programmed calculators will arrive at the result directly.

Internal rate of return is fairly accurate and much superior to the simple methods (payback and accounting return) discussed earlier. The method is not without problems, however. The first is the mathematical possibility that a complex project with many varied cash inflows and outflows over its economic life may result in *two different* internal rates of return because of the pattern and timing of the various cash inflows and outflows. While relatively rare, such a result can be an inconvenience. More important is the practical issue of choosing among alternative projects that involve widely differing net investments and internal rates of return that are inverse to the size of the project. (The smaller investment has the higher return.) A $10,000 investment with an internal rate of return of 50 percent cannot be directly compared to an outlay of $100,000 with a 30 percent internal rate of return, particularly if the risks are similar and the company normally requires a 15 percent earnings standard. While both exceed the desired return, it may indeed be better to employ the larger sum at 30 percent than the smaller sum at 50 percent, unless *both* projects can be undertaken. If the economic life of alternative projects differs widely, it may similarly be advantageous to employ funds at a lower rate for a longer period of time than to opt for a brief period of higher return, *if* a choice must be made between two investments, both of which *exceed* the corporate standard.

From these comments it should be apparent that this measure of investment desirability, like the others, must be used with caution. Inasmuch as it provides the analyst with a *unique* ("true") rate of return inherent in each project, the measure appears to be simple and direct and seems to permit ranking potential investments by a single "number." When we recall our earlier discussion of present value and the fact that it is based on *an earnings standard* that reflects the company's expectations from such investments, however, another issue arises. The internal rate of return approach solves for an earnings rate *unique to each project*, while the net present value approach solves for the trade-off of cash inflows and outflows using a *general* earnings rate. When the internal rates of return of different projects are compared, there is the *implied assumption* that the cash flows thrown off during each project's economic life can be *reinvested* at that unique rate. We know, however, that the company's earnings standard is an expression of the long-run earnings power in the company, even if only approximate. Thus, a company management applying a 15 or 20 percent return standard to investments must realize that cash flows from a project with an internal rate of return of, say, 30 percent cannot be assumed to be *reinvested* at this unique higher rate. Instead, funds thrown off by capital investments can only be expected to be reemployed over time at the *lower* average rate—the company's return standard. This does not invalidate the internal rate of return measure, but makes its use less automatic than its deceptive simplicity would suggest.

Later in this chapter we will compare the measures discussed and develop basic rules for their application. In the meantime, Table 5–5 summarizes the key elements of investment analysis employed in both the simple and the time-adjusted measures. It also lists the type of result given by each measure, which may help the reader to visualize the analytical components that make up each yardstick, and which indicates the relative applicability and shortcomings of the measures. The reader is also invited to turn to the references listed at the end of the chapter for more exhaustive discussions of the many theoretical and practical arguments surrounding the use of present value, particularly in the case of the internal rate of return.

Risk Analysis

The estimates used to analyze capital investments are projections of *future* conditions. Therefore, as we stated before, capital investments involve *risk* because of the uncertainties surrounding the key variables involved in the analysis. Consequently, the analyst making the investment calculations and management using these results for decision purposes must allow for a whole range of possible outcomes. Even the best estimates can go wrong as events unfold, yet the decisions have to be made ahead of time.

As a result, the risk inherent in the variations must be ascertained. Such risk analysis can take many forms. In earlier chapters we mentioned **sensitivity analysis** as a formal means of testing the impact of changes in key assumptions. This can be very informal, back-of-the-envelope reasoning, or it can involve systematically working through the impact of assumed changes in revenues, operating savings, costs, size of outlays, recovery of capital, and so on, either singly or in combination. We also discussed *ranges of estimates*, either for the total result or for individual key variables. These allow management to examine the most optimistic and pessimistic cases as well as the most likely figures, and are superior to single-point estimates.

Time-adjusted measures help management ascertain how much risk is allowable with a given project while still meeting the desired return standards. In this section, we will discuss two such measures, **present value payback** and **annualized net present value**, both of which are related to the *net present value* criterion discussed earlier. We will also discuss the use of **ranges of estimates**, and their refined application in **probabilistic simulation**. Finally we will touch on **risk adjusted rates**. Only the first two measures will be taken up in detail, while the other areas will be covered just enough to indicate to the reader the potential value of studying these concepts further.

Present Value Payback.   This measure derives the *minimum life* necessary for an investment to operate as expected to meet the earnings standard of the present value analysis. In

Table 5–5
Comparison of Elements Used in Key Investment Measures

Elements Used	Simple Measures		Time-Adjusted Measures			
	Payback	Accounting Rate of Return	Net Present Value	Profitability Index	Internal Rate of Return (yield)
Net investment	Comparable	Comparable	Comparable	Comparable	Comparable
Sequential investments	Possible to use rough approximation	Possible to use rough approximation	Exact sequence and timing	Exact sequence and timing	Exact sequence and timing
Recovery of terminal value	Not possible	Not possible	Specific economic impact	Specific economic impact	Specific economic impact
Average accounting profit	Rough approximation of pattern	Rough approximation of pattern	Not relevant	Not relevant	Not relevant

Average operating cash flow	Approximation of relevant pattern	Approximation of relevant pattern	Not applicable	Not applicable	Not applicable
Year-by-year operating cash flow pattern	Cannot accommodate	Cannot accommodate	Exact economic impact	Exact economic impact	Exact economic impact
Economic life	Not considered	Not considered	Integral to analysis	Integral to analysis	Integral to analysis
Result	Years to recover the initial net investment	Percent return on initial net investment	Net balance of equivalent cash inflows and outflows	Ratio of equivalent cash inflows and outflows	Yield—rate of discount equating inflows and outflows

other words, the present value payback is achieved in the period in which the cumulative sum of the positive present values equals the present value of the outlays. It is the point in the project's life at which the original investment and sequential outlays have been amortized *and* a return equal to the earnings standard has been achieved on the declining balances—the point at which the project becomes economically attractive.

In Tables 5–3 and 5–4 we included a column giving the cumulative net present value of the project. It served as a visual check for determining the point at which net present value turned positive. The present value payback with a discount rate of 8 percent was about five years, while a 12 percent standard required almost six years, just about the full economic life of the investment. The minimum time needed to recover the investment and earn the return standard on the declining balance, when compared to the economic life, is an overall expression of potential risk. The measure does not specifically address the *nature* of the risk, but rather serves as a risk *allowance*. Management can then judge whether the risk entailed in the combined elements of the project, or in any one key variable in particular, is likely to outweigh the cushion of safety implied in the additional time the project may operate once it has passed the present value payback point. It is important to remember, however, that the measure focuses on the *life* of the project, with the implicit assumption that the estimated operating *conditions* will hold.

If uneven and complicated cash flows are projected, a condition we will examine later, the minimum life or present value payback requires a year-by-year accumulation of the negative and positive present values, as was done in simplified form in Tables 5–3 and 5–4. If a project is a straightforward combination of a single outlay at point zero and level annual operating cash inflows, we can make use of the annuity factors in Table 5–11 to quickly identify minimum life and present value payback. Again, programmed calculators will do the job for us directly. But to illustrate, the following relationship is utilized:

$$\text{Present value} = \text{Factor} \times \text{Annuity}$$

We are looking for the condition under which the present value of the outflows is *exactly equal* to the present value of the inflows. Inasmuch as net investment (outflow) must be recovered by the inflows, we can change the formula to:

$$\text{Net investment} = \text{Factor} \times \text{Annuity}$$

Because we know the annuity, which is represented by the annual operating cash inflows, we can find the factor that satisfies the condition:

$$\text{Factor} = \frac{\text{Net investment}}{\text{Annuity}}$$

For our investment example, we can calculate the following results: $100,000 ÷ $25,000 = 4.0. We can look for the closest factor in the 8 percent column of Table 5–11. The answer lies almost exactly on the line for period 5(3.993), which indicates that the project's minimum life under the assumed operating conditions must be five years to achieve the standard 8 percent return. If the standard were 12 percent, the minimum life has to be approximately 5⅔ years, which is an interpolation between 3.605 and 4.112.

The test for present value payout or minimum life with any given return standard thus becomes one more factor in assessing the margin for error in project estimates. It sharpens the analyst's understanding of the relationship between economic life and acceptable performance, and is a much improved version of simple payback. The measure is a useful companion to the net present value criterion. It does not, however, address specific risk elements and in fact, leaves the assessment of any favorable difference between the minimum standard and economic life to the judgment of management.

Annualized Net Present Value.   Another approach to making an *allowance* for risk involves estimating how much of an annual shortfall in operating cash inflows is permissible over the *full economic life* of the project while still meeting the minimum return standard. We know that the net present value calculation normally results in either a cumulative excess or deficiency of present value benefits vis-à-vis the investment outlays. If the net present value is positive, the amount can be viewed as a "cushion" against any error in estimating future cash inflows. Unless a project has highly irregular annual flows, it is often useful to transform this net present value cushion into an **equivalent annuity** over the project's economic life. These annual equivalents, which express the allowable margin of error, can than be *directly compared* to the raw estimates of annual operating cash inflow. This is possible because the overall net present value cushion has in effect been "reconstituted" into equivalent annual cash flows on the *same basis* as the estimates themselves, that is, in terms of annual flows *unadjusted* for time value. To illustrate, we can transform the net present value shown in Table 5–3, $15,575, into an annuity over the six-year life of the project by simply again employing the present value relationship:

$$\text{Present value} = \text{Factor} \times \text{Annuity}$$

As we are interested in finding the annuity represented by the net present value, and wish to do so over a known economic life and at a specified rate—which is the earnings standard employed in the net present value calculation in the first place— we can transform the annuity formula as follows:

$$\text{Annuity} = \frac{\text{(Net) present value}}{\text{Factor}}$$

Our example has the following result:

$$\text{Annuity} = \frac{\$15,575}{4.623} = \$3,369$$

The annual operating cash inflows were originally *estimated* at $25,000. Given the result above, the *actual* cash flow could be *lower* by about $3,400 per year and the project would still meet the *minimum* standard of 8 percent. Note, however, that the investment has to operate over its *full* economic life for this to be true.

In this case, the risk allowance directly translates into a downward adjustment of operating cash inflows of 13 percent. More important, we know that cash flow consists of aftertax operating profit to which depreciation has been added back. In view of the sizable depreciation allowance of $16,667 contained in the cash flow figure, which is *not* subject to uncertainty, the permissible reduction in the *aftertax profit* of $8,333 amounts to a hefty 40 percent! As we can see, the use of this type of analysis permits a *more direct* approach to judging the allowable risk in the key variables than did the present value payback.

Annualization has a more general application as a very practical and quick *preliminary test* of the desirability of an investment project that has not yet been fleshed out in detail. In effect, the method *reverses* the normal investment analysis by finding the *approximate* annual operating cash flow required to justify an estimated capital outlay when the *specific* operating benefits have not yet been established. Given an estimate of the economic life and an earnings standard, we can employ the formula:

$$\text{Operating cash flow} = \frac{\text{Net investment}}{\text{Factor}}$$

to find the annual cash flow equivalent that will be the average *minimum target*. The analyst must be careful to interpret this figure properly. Because it is an aftertax cash flow, the result has to be properly modified by the assumed annual depreciation to arrive at the *minimum pretax operating improvement* necessary to justify the outlay. The concept is a useful tool for arriving at a first assessment of the chance that an investment will "be in the ballpark." As such it is a first crude assessment of risk. The process simply involves working "backward" through the analysis, recognizing that cash flow by definition consists of the sum of aftertax operating profit and annual depreciation. We can apply the example from Table 5–3 as follows:

First, we find the target cash flow over six years at 8 percent, using the appropriate factor from Table 5–11:

$$\frac{\$100,000}{4.623} = \$21,631$$

Next we transform this aftertax cash flow into its equivalent pretax operating improvement:

Aftertax cash flow	$21,631
Less: depreciation	16,667
Aftertax profit	$ 4,964
Tax at 46% of pretax profit	4,229
Pretax profit	$ 9,193
Add back depreciation	16,667
Minimum pretax operating improvement . . .	$25,860

Thus, our investment has to provide a minimum of almost $26,000 in direct operating improvements such as lower costs, incremental revenues, and so on. The process allows a quick calculation of the magnitude of pretax profit improvement required and the likely potential of the investment to realize that profit.

Needless to say, annualization is quickly performed using a programmed calculator so that present value tables are unnecessary. While a calculator makes the process "automatic," working the calculation through as we have just done, will give the reader a feeling for the reasoning behind the method.

Ranges of Estimates. Risk can be defined as the degree to which all possible cash benefit levels of an investment can *vary*. The greater the range of these possibilities, the greater the risk. Therefore, using a range of estimates is a more direct approach to investment risk analysis. This effort may not be necessary for all types of investments, however, because degrees of risk vary widely among business and financial investments.

The risk involved in holding a U.S. government bond, for example, is very small indeed, because default on the interest payments is extremely unlikely. Therefore, the range of possible benefits from the bond investment is narrowly focused on the contractual payments—in effect no range at all. In contrast, the risk of a business investment for a product or service is a function of the whole range of possible benefit levels that may go from very positive cash flows to negative loss conditions. The uncertainty surrounding these outcomes poses a challenge to the analyst and the decision maker.

The "single point" estimates of annual cash flow projections we have used so far are the *expected* results based on the best judgment of the analyst and the information available. In effect, they are the average of the possible outcomes, implicitly weighed by their respective probabilities. By introducing a range of "high," "low," and "expected" levels of annual cash inflows and outflows, the analyst can use a form of *sensitivity analysis* to indicate the consequences of expected fluctuations in the annual results—and thus the degree of risk. At times, past experience can provide clues to the range of future outcomes, but essentially the projection of future conditions has to be judgmental and based on specific estimates.

The decision maker must assess the likelihood that the range of outcomes estimated fairly expresses the characteristics of the project, and that the expected outcome is sufficiently attractive to compensate for the possibility that the actual results may vary as defined. Risk assessment in essence comes down to how comfortable the decision maker is with the possibility of adverse results—that is, a very personal *risk preference.* Stipulating a range helps the responsible person or group to visualize the possible extremes in the expected results.

Probabilistic Simulation.   A more refined approach involves estimating ranges not only for the annual cash flows, but also for the individual *key variables* making up these cash flows. Probability distributions are then assigned to the likelihood of the outcomes for each of the variables; any interdependencies between variables are defined; and the outcomes of the project can then be *simulated* by running many iterations on the computer. The method is an extension of sensitivity analysis in that the possibilities of changes in many variables are *simultaneously* evaluated.

The result is a range of possible annual cash inflows in the form of a probability distribution, or even a range of net present values or internal rates of return arrayed by probability. Such a "risk profile" allows the decision maker to think about the relative attractiveness of a project in terms of statements such as "chances are 9 out of 10 that the project will meet the minimum standard of 10 percent," or: "there is a probability of 60 percent that the net present value of the project will be at least \$1 million or better." Cumulative probability distributions such as those shown in Figure 5–2 can be drawn up as an aid.

The relative ease with which computer simulation can be done does not eliminate either the *practical* issues involved in assigning probability distributions to the individual variables in the first place or the problem of *interpreting* the final results. As we said before, judging both the likelihood of an event and the decision maker's own attitude toward the risk thus expressed are highly personal and defy precise quantification. Investment decisions in a business setting are as much a function of complex personal and group dynamics as they are of the analytical results, the quality of presentation, and the specific economic data.

Risk Adjusted Return Standards.   Another way of adjusting for risk is to *modify* the return standards to include a **risk premium** where warranted. In a sense, the reasoning behind this is quite simple—the greater the risk, the higher the return desired from the investment. This approach is intuitively attractive to business decision makers, because the process parallels the way we think about personal investments. Thus, in-

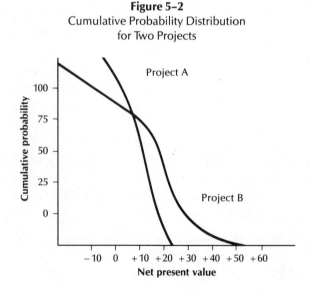

Figure 5–2
Cumulative Probability Distribution
for Two Projects

vestments in businesses subject to wide profit swings and competitive pressures would command a premium above the return standard, while with fairly predictable businesses a less-than-average return might be acceptable. The concept rests on the assumption that a diversified company can derive a range of standards that, in combination, represent an appropriate return to the shareholders and also fairly reflect the relative risk of the individual lines. We will return to earnings standards in the next chapter, and discuss both the conceptual and practical issues involved in deriving them.

REFINEMENTS OF INVESTMENT ANALYSIS

So far we have used very basic and simplified examples to illustrate the concepts and methodology of investment analysis. We will now turn to more realistic and complex examples which will enable us to refine both the *components* of analysis and the *methodology* itself. We will not introduce any *new* concepts, but rather use the expanded examples to help the reader work through the implications of many of the points we have only mentioned in passing so far. By going through two realistic examples step by step, the essentials of investment analysis should become firmly implanted in the reader's mind. We cannot stress enough the need to fully understand the reasoning behind *defining the problem* and the rationale for deriving the *net investment, operating cash flows,* and the *economic life.* Once these are determined, the calculation of the appropriate yardsticks becomes almost automatic.

Example One: A Machine Replacement

A company is studying whether to replace an existing five-year-old machine with a more automatic and faster model. A new machine of some sort is the only reasonable alternative under the circumstances, as the product fabricated using it is expected to continue to be profitable for at least 10 years, and the company could sell as much as one-third greater volume.

The old machine is estimated to have 5 years' life left before it becomes physically worn out, while the new machine will operate acceptably for 10 years before it has to be scrapped. The old machine originally cost $25,000 and has a current book value of $12,500 (depreciated straight-line at $2,500 per year). It can be sold for $15,000 cash.

The new machine will cost $40,000, will be depreciated straight-line over 10 years, and will likely be salable at book value if it is disposed of before the end of its physical life. It has an annual capacity of 125,000 units, compared to 100,000 units on the present equipment, and it will produce at lower unit costs for both labor and materials. In fact, the new machine will involve lower *total* labor costs because it will require fewer setups, releasing the time of the skilled mechanics for other productive tasks in the plant. Two operators are required as before. Materials use will be more efficient due to lower spoilage. The company expects no difficulty in selling the additional volume at the current price of $1.50, and will only incur some incremental selling and promotional expense in the process.

Such a set of conditions is very common and realistic. As we analyze this project, we will expand on several aspects of capital investment analysis and draw generalized conclusions where appropriate.

Net Investment Refined.   We recall that net investment was defined as the *net change* in funds committed to a project. Two changes in funds must be considered in this case. First, there is the *outlay* of $40,000 for the new machine, which is a straightforward cash commitment. Second, there is the current *recovery* of cash from the sale of the old machine, which is a *direct result* of the decision to replace, and therefore is *relevant* to the analysis. The amount received for the old machine will be *less* than its $15,000 cash value, however, because the gain from the sale is taxable. (We recall that the book value was only $12,500; therefore, the company will be taxed on the difference of $2,500.) For simplicity we will assume that the applicable tax rate is the top rate of 46 percent, which amounts to a tax outlay of $1,150.

We now have all the components of the initial net investment figure relevant for this example:

Cost of the new machine	$40,000
Cash from sale of old machine	(15,000)
Tax payable on capital gain	1,150
Net investment	$26,150

The economic analysis does not recognize, *except for tax purposes,* the remaining *book value* of the old machine. As we observed before, what was spent in the past is irrelevant because it is a *sunk cost.* Here we are interested only in the *changes* that are caused by the decision to be made *now.* Therefore, the proceeds from the sale and the tax outlay resulting from the transaction are relevant elements. Had the old machine been unsalable despite the stated book value of $12,500, the only item of relevance would be the *tax savings* from the capital loss recognized under that assumption. Yet, it is not uncommon to confuse accounting practice with economic analysis and include book values even though they are not relevant.

The net investment shown represents a net balance of *cash* movements, both in and out, caused by the investment decision. Were there any reason to assume that the decision caused *working capital* to rise, due to the higher volume of product being sold, this increase would also be relevant for our analysis. Similarly, if *further investments* in later years were a direct consequence of this decision, such amounts would have to be recognized in the analysis. We will show how these two elements are handled in the second example.

Operating Cash Flows Refined.   As we discussed before, the operating cash flows are net *aftertax cash changes* caused by the investment decision. In our replacement example, we must carefully sort out the relevant conditions to identify *differential revenues and costs* that should be included in the analysis. As we examine each element we must ask whether the decision to replace will make a *cash* difference in operating conditions.

The decision to replace has two major effects: First, the new machine will bring about greater efficiency which should cause *operating savings*. Second, the additional volume of product produced will result in additional *profit contribution* from the assumed successful sales effort. In addition, we must allow for the *tax* impact of the *change* in the level of *depreciation*. The calculations in Table 5–6 are carried out to illustrate how to deal with these elements in successive stages.

Stage One: Operating Savings. Operating savings for the *existing* level of output (100,000 units) are determined by simply comparing the *annual* costs of operating the two machines. Each requires two operators, but setup costs for the new machine are $1,000 less. We were told earlier that materials use is more efficient with the new machine, and the amount of savings from this is estimated to be $2,000. Overhead changes, in contrast, are *not relevant* for this comparison, because the fig-

Table 5–6
Differential Cost and Revenue Analysis

	Old Machine	New Machine	Relevant Annual Differences
1. Operating savings from current volume of 100,000 units:			
Labor (2 operators plus setup)	$ 31,000	$ 30,000	$1,000
Material	38,000	36,000	2,000
Overhead (120% of direct labor)	37,200	36,000	—*
	$106,200	$102,000	3,000
2. Contribution from additional volume of 25,000 units:			
25,000 units sold at $1.50 per unit		$ 37,500	
Less:			
Labor (no additional operators)		—	
Material cost at 36¢/unit		(9,000)	
Additional selling expense		(10,500)	
Additional promotional expense		(13,000)	$5,000
Total savings and additional contribution			$8,000
3. Differential depreciation (additional expense; for tax purposes only)	$ 2,500	$ 4,000	$(1,500)
Taxable operating improvements			6,500
Tax at 46%			2,990
Aftertax profit improvement			3,510
Add back depreciation			1,500
Aftertax operating cash flow			$5,010

*Not relevant, because it represents an allocation only.

ures represent *allocations* at the rate of 120 percent of direct labor. The fact that labor cost has gone down slightly does not mean that *spending* on overhead has changed. What *has* changed is the *basis* of allocation, which in this case happens to be the cost of labor. The plant manager and the office staff still receive the same salaries, and other overhead costs are not affected. Only if the decision to replace in fact caused a change in overhead *spending*, such as higher property taxes, insurance premiums, additional maintenance, technical support, etc., would a change be reflected in the calculation. Under those conditions, we would estimate the annual expenditures before and after the installation of the new machine, and develop the *differential* cost to be included in the analysis.

As a general rule in dealing with operating cost comparisons, it is usually conceptually easier to use *annual* costs or revenues rather than *per unit* figures. The latter increases the analyst's chances of inadvertantly applying *accounting allocations*, which are generally irrelevant for economic analysis, even though they are necessary and appropriate for costing purposes (determining cost of goods sold, inventory values, price estimating, etc.)

Stage Two: Contribution from Additional Volume. Now we are ready to determine the *incremental contribution* from the higher output level. This is an additional benefit resulting from the decision to replace, because the old machine was limited to 100,000 units of production. The additional *sales revenue* from the extra 25,000 units available to be sold at $1.50 each is relevant here, as are any additional *costs* incurred because of this incremental volume. We know that the original two operators are able to produce the higher volume, and thus no additional *labor* cost is incurred. The higher volume will require additional *materials*, however, which are charged at the usage rate of the more efficient machine, i.e., 36 cents per unit. We had been told that the higher volume will result in additional *selling and promotional* expenses, and these are also relevant here. Using the relevant figures, savings and incremental profit from the additional volume total $8,000.

Stage Three: Tax Effect. The only remaining relevant item is the *tax impact of differential depreciation.* As we discussed in Chapters 1 and 2, depreciation *as such* is not relevant to funds flows. For purposes of our analysis, it merits attention only because depreciation is tax deductible. Because depreciation charges normally reduce tax payments, they are called a "tax shield." If an investment decision causes higher or lower depreciation charges, such a difference must be reflected as a *change in the tax shield.*

For our replacement example the *differential* depreciation for the next five years will be $1,500, an increase due to the higher cost of the new machine. We are assuming straight-line depreciation is used for tax purposes here, to keep the calculations simple.

As shown in Table 5-6, the analysis results in taxable operating improvements of $6,500, and a change in aftertax profit of $3,510. The applicable tax rate is normally the rate a company would be paying on any incremental profit. The differential depreciation is *added back* as the final step to arrive at the aftertax operating cash flow of $5,010. In doing this we have correctly reflected a tax reduction from the differential depreciation, but then removed depreciation from the picture to leave us with the *economic cash effect* of the investment. We could have obtained the same result by doing the analysis in two steps: (1) determining the tax on the operating improvement *before* depreciation, and (2) directly determining the tax shield effect of the differential depreciation. This would appear as follows:

Taxable operating improvement	$8,000
Tax at 46 percent	3,680
Aftertax operating improvement	$4,320
Tax shield at 46%* of depreciation of $1,500 . . .	690
Aftertax operating cash flow	$5,010

*Each dollar of depreciation provides a tax shield of $1 times the applicable tax rate.

and the result is exactly the same.

Economic Life Refined.   Earlier we defined economic life as the length of time over which an investment yields economic benefits. Now we find that a complication has been introduced because of the assumed *difference* in the lives of the two machines. Inasmuch as the old machine is expected to wear out in 5 years while the new will last for 10, the two investments are *comparable* only over the next 5 *years*. After that, the original alternative no longer exists, and a decision would *have* to be made at that point in any case. The situation is illustrated in Figure 5–3.

Differential revenues and costs can be defined *only* as long as both alternatives exist *together*. After five years, the old machine will be gone, which means that we *cannot* analyze the situation *beyond* five years without making some assumptions about the remaining life of the new machine. While the product is likely to be salable for at least the total 10-year life of the new machine, the economic comparison for the replacement decision can be made only over 5 years.

There are two ways of handling this problem. First, we can *cut off* the analysis at the end of year 5 and assign an assumed recovery value to the new machine at that point, because the machine should be able to operate well for another five years. This "terminal value" estimate must be counted as a *capital recovery* in year 5, that is, its present value should be counted as a benefit. The approach is widely used in practice, and the terminal value is usually estimated as *at least* the book value. If

Figure 5–3
Overlapping Economic Life Spans

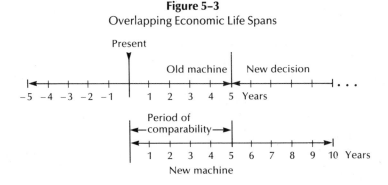

the value of the asset is quite predictable, as is the case with automobiles or trucks, an estimated sales value is stipulated and entered in the present value analysis as a benefit.

An alternative way of dealing with the problem is to assume that the old machine would be *replaced* by a new one in year 5, and a similar replacement would be made in year 10 when the current new machine wears out. This approach involves a great deal of guessing about replacement conditions 5 and 10 years in the future. In spite of this effort, the economic lives of the two machines would still not be the same. Admittedly, the power of discounting would make the estimates of the later years almost immaterial. On balance, unless there are compelling reasons to develop such a series of replacement assumptions, the cutoff analysis described earlier is far more straightforward and less fraught with judgmental traps.

Capital Additions and Recoveries. The treatment of terminal values deserves a few more comments here. It is quite common for larger projects to involve a series of additional capital outlays and, later on, actual or assumed recoveries. As a practical matter, such increments of capital committed or recovered should be entered as *cash outflows* or *cash inflows* in the present value framework at the point in time when they occur. This also applies to incremental *working capital* commitments, which should be shown as a present outflow, and assumed to be recovered in total or in part at the end of the economic life of the project.

In our replacement example we have made no provision for additional working capital. The assumed value of the new machine after five years, however, would be treated as a *capital recovery* and entered as a positive cash inflow at the end of year 5. For simplicity we will assume that its economic value will be equal to its book value. This would amount to $20,000 ($40,000 less five years' depreciation at $4,000 per year), with no taxable gain or loss expected. The amount would have to be modified, of course, if the circumstances indicated a higher or lower value due to changes in technology or other conditions. Book value is frequently used because it is easy to do, causes no taxable gains or losses, and also because the need for precision in terminal values is reduced by the exponential impact of discounting in later years.

Analytical Framework for Example One.   With the basic data at hand, we can now lay out the framework for a present value analysis. We will assume a 10 percent return standard and again set up the figures in a tabular format. The results in Table 5–7 show that there will be a sizable net present value of better than $5,200 if all of our assumptions are borne out in fact. This would suggest that on a numerical basis the replacement is desirable.

Note that the analysis is significantly affected by the assumed recovery of the book value of $20,000 in year 5, which amounts to a present value inflow of $12,420, and in effect reduces the net investment to only $13,730 in present value terms. For purposes of economic analysis, this value had to be considered an *inflow* at the end of year 5, even though there is no intention of actually selling the machine at that point. The relevance for today's decision is that the company would have the *option* of selling at the end of year 5 and realizing this economic value. After the five years are over, the alternative of selling could, of course, be compared with the alternative of recommitting the realizable value of $20,000 in order to pre-

Table 5–7
Present Value Analysis of Machine Replacement

Time Period	Investment	Operating Cash Inflows	Present Value Factors at 10 Percent*	Present Values of Net Investment	Present Value of Operating Inflows
0	– $26,150	—	1.000	– $26,150	—
1	—	+ $ 5,010	0.909	—	+ $ 4,554
2	—	+ 5,010	0.826	—	+ 4,138
3	—	+ 5,010	0.751	—	+ 3,763
4	—	+ 5,010	0.683	—	+ 3,422
5	—	+ 5,010	0.621	—	+ 3,111
5 (end)	+ 20,000	—	0.621	+ 12,420	—
	– $ 6,150	+ $25,050		– $13,730	+ $18,988
				Net present value	+ $ 5,258

*For years 1 to 5, we could use 3,791 from Table 5–11.

serve the profitable business at the level of 125,000 units. But these considerations deal with a future set of decisions and therefore are not relevant today.

The *profitability index* of the project is positive, as we might expect from the sizable net present value of + $5,258. Dividing $13,730 into $18,988 results in an index of 1.38, which should give the project a favorable ranking if the return from the company's investment opportunities average only 10 percent. Some analysts prefer to express the profitability index by relating the *original net investment* to the total of *all inflows*, including capital recoveries. In our example, the result would be $31,408 ÷ $26,150 = 1.20, again a favorable showing when a more stringent test is applied. While arguments can be made for and against both methods, consistent application of either will be satisfactory.

The *internal rate of return* has to be found by trial and error if we use the present value tables, because the capital recovery at the end of year 5 complicates an otherwise straightforward annuity. The problem can be handled as shown in Table 5–8. The trial at 15 percent indicates a still positive net present value of $584, but at 16 percent this reverses to a negative $227. Thus, the result is slightly less than 16 percent.

A *risk analysis* can be made by calculating the *present value payback* (minimum life) and the *annualized net present value*.

Table 5–8
Present Value Analysis to Find Internal Rate of Return

Time Period	Cash Flows	Present Value Factors at 15 Percent	Present Values at 15 Percent	Present Value Factors at 16 Percent	Present Values at 16 Percent
0	− $26,150	1.000	− $26,150	1.000	− $26,150
1					
2					
3	+ 5,010/yr.	3.352*	+ 16,794	3.274*	+ 16,403
4					
5					
5 (end)	+ 20,000	0.497	+ 9,940	0.476	+ 9,520
	+ $18,900		+ $ 584		− $ 227

*From Table 5–11.

For the former we must cumulate the present values of the operating cash inflows until they approximate the net investment of $13,730. A quick addition shows that this will happen after about 3 1/3 years, which leaves a cushion of 1 2/3 years against uncertainty. A technical question arises here concerning whether the assumed recovery at year 5 should be brought forward in time to obtain a more precise calculation of minimum life. This would involve a process of *iteration*, because not only would the present value of the recovery rise, but the sales value of the machine would also be higher in earlier years. Such a refinement is normally not called for even though it can be handled through computer simulation.

The *annualized net present value* in this case is $5,258 ÷ 3.791, or approximately $1,400 per year. All other aspects being equal, the project would still be acceptable if the annual operating cash inflows over the five years dropped from $5,010 to only $3,623, a possible shrinkage of $1,387 or almost 30 percent. If we remove the tax shield of $690 from this test, the drop in the pure aftertax operating improvement could be as much as one third ($1,387 against $4,320).

Another way of looking at the net present value cushion would be to ask how sensitive the result would be to a *reduction* in the expected capital recovery at the end of year 5. This answer can be readily found by *reconstituting* at the end of year 5 a dollar amount that has the equivalent present value of the cushion of $5,258. To find this *future* dollar amount we simply divide the present value of $5,258 by the single sum factor given in Table 5–10 for 10 percent in period 5, which is 0.621. We see that the expected recovery of $20,000 could be reduced by about $8,500 and the project would still be acceptable, given that all other conditions hold.

While perhaps a little complex, the step-by-step process we have just completed has exposed us to most of the practical issues encountered in investment analysis. Let us turn to one more illustration which additionally shows the handling of working capital and successive investments.

Example Two: Business Expansion

The cash flow patterns in Table 5–9 show the kinds of commitments and recoveries normally associated with a major business expansion. In the early life of the project, we find not only an outlay for facilities, but also a buildup of working capital during the first and second years. Additional equipment outlays are required at the end of years 4 and 6, while recoveries of equipment and working capital are made as the economic life comes to an end. All cash flows are assumed to have been adjusted for tax consequences along the lines we discussed in our first example. The operating cash flows show a growth stage, peak in the middle years, and decline as the end of the economic life approaches.

Nothing new is required to deal with this investment proposition. *Working capital* (additional inventories and receivables less new trade obligations) represents a commitment of capital just as definite as an expenditure for buildings and equipment, except that no depreciation write-off is involved. If all inventories and receivables can be expected to be liquidated at the end of the economic life, this capital (net of payables) will be an inflow at that point, *a capital recovery.* If we assume some fraction to be unsalable or uncollectible, the figure must be lowered.

Additional capital expenditures for equipment during the life of the project are simply recognized as cash outflows when incurred. Care must be taken, however, to reflect the additional *depreciation* pattern in each case as a tax shield during future operating periods. Uneven cash flows present no problems when programmed calculators are used to find the present value of each period's flows. But to demonstrate how the calculations are made, we have employed the present value tables to find the factors, including those for *partial annuities.*

As shown in Table 5–9, the expected result of the project is a positive *net present value* of almost $12 million. The *profitability index* is about 1.07, while the *internal rate of return* is approximately 13 percent. This leaves little margin for error, indeed. One expression of risk allowance is the annualized net

Table 5-9
Present Value Analysis of Complex Expansion Project
(thousands of dollars)

Time Period	Investments	Operating Cash Inflows (all tax adjustments made)	Present Value Factors at 12 Percent	Present Value of Investments	Present Value of Operating Inflows
0	−$130,000 (facilities)		1.000	$130,000	—
1	− 25,000 (working capital)	+$ 20,000	0.893*	− 22,325	+$ 17,860
2	− 20,000 (working capital)	+ 40,000	0.797*	− 15,940	
3	—	+ 40,000 ⎱	2.144†	—	+ 85,760
4	—	+ 40,000 ⎰			
4 (end)	− 15,000 (additional equipment)‡	—	0.636*	9,540	
5		+ 50,000 ⎱	1.075†		+ 53,750
6		+ 50,000 ⎰			
6 (end)	− 10,000 (equipment overhaul)‡	—	0.507*	5,070	
7		+ 20,000	0.452*		+ 9,040
8		+ 10,000	0.404*		+ 4,040
8 (end)	+ 25,000 (equipment recovery)	—	0.404*	+ 24,240	
8 (end)	+ 35,000 (working capital recovery)**	—	—		
	−$140,000	+$270,000		−$158,635	+$170,450
			Net present value	+$ 11,815	

*From Table 5-10.
†From Table 5-11, representing the difference between the annuity factors applicable: 3.037–.893, and 4.112–3.037, respectively.
‡Additional depreciation has been reflected in cash inflows.
**Assume loss in liquidation of $10,000.

Table 5-10
Present Value of Single Sum of $1 Received or Paid at End of Period

Period of Receipt or Payment	1%	2%	4%	5%	6%	8%	10%	12%	14%	15%	16%	18%	20%	22%	24%	25%	26%	28%	30%	35%	40%	45%	50%
1	0.990	0.980	0.962	0.952	0.943	0.926	0.909	0.893	0.877	0.870	0.862	0.847	0.833	0.820	0.806	0.800	0.794	0.781	0.769	0.741	0.714	0.690	0.667
2	0.980	0.961	0.925	0.907	0.890	0.857	0.826	0.797	0.769	0.756	0.743	0.718	0.694	0.672	0.650	0.640	0.630	0.610	0.592	0.549	0.510	0.476	0.444
3	0.971	0.942	0.889	0.863	0.840	0.794	0.751	0.712	0.675	0.658	0.641	0.609	0.579	0.551	0.524	0.512	0.500	0.477	0.455	0.406	0.364	0.328	0.296
4	0.961	0.924	0.855	0.823	0.792	0.735	0.683	0.636	0.592	0.572	0.552	0.516	0.482	0.451	0.423	0.410	0.397	0.373	0.350	0.301	0.260	0.226	0.198
5	0.951	0.906	0.822	0.784	0.747	0.681	0.621	0.567	0.519	0.497	0.476	0.437	0.402	0.370	0.341	0.328	0.315	0.291	0.269	0.223	0.186	0.156	0.132
6	0.942	0.888	0.790	0.746	0.705	0.630	0.564	0.507	0.456	0.432	0.410	0.370	0.335	0.303	0.275	0.262	0.250	0.227	0.207	0.165	0.133	0.108	0.088
7	0.933	0.871	0.760	0.711	0.665	0.583	0.513	0.452	0.400	0.376	0.354	0.314	0.279	0.249	0.222	0.210	0.198	0.178	0.159	0.122	0.095	0.074	0.059
8	0.923	0.853	0.731	0.677	0.627	0.540	0.467	0.404	0.351	0.327	0.305	0.266	0.233	0.204	0.179	0.168	0.157	0.139	0.123	0.091	0.068	0.051	0.039
9	0.914	0.837	0.703	0.645	0.592	0.500	0.424	0.361	0.308	0.284	0.263	0.225	0.194	0.167	0.144	0.134	0.125	0.108	0.094	0.067	0.048	0.035	0.026
10	0.905	0.820	0.676	0.614	0.558	0.463	0.386	0.322	0.270	0.247	0.227	0.191	0.162	0.137	0.116	0.107	0.099	0.085	0.073	0.050	0.035	0.024	0.017
11	0.896	0.804	0.650	0.585	0.527	0.429	0.350	0.287	0.237	0.215	0.195	0.162	0.135	0.112	0.094	0.086	0.079	0.066	0.056	0.037	0.025	0.017	0.012
12	0.887	0.788	0.625	0.557	0.497	0.397	0.319	0.257	0.208	0.187	0.168	0.137	0.112	0.092	0.076	0.069	0.062	0.052	0.043	0.027	0.018	0.012	0.008
13	0.879	0.773	0.601	0.530	0.469	0.368	0.290	0.229	0.182	0.163	0.145	0.116	0.093	0.075	0.061	0.055	0.050	0.040	0.033	0.020	0.013	0.008	0.005
14	0.870	0.758	0.577	0.505	0.442	0.340	0.263	0.205	0.160	0.141	0.125	0.099	0.078	0.062	0.049	0.044	0.039	0.032	0.025	0.015	0.009	0.006	0.003
15	0.861	0.743	0.555	0.481	0.417	0.315	0.239	0.183	0.140	0.123	0.108	0.084	0.065	0.051	0.040	0.035	0.031	0.025	0.020	0.011	0.006	0.004	0.002
16	0.853	0.728	0.534	0.458	0.394	0.292	0.218	0.163	0.123	0.107	0.093	0.071	0.054	0.042	0.032	0.028	0.025	0.019	0.015	0.008	0.005	0.003	0.002
17	0.844	0.714	0.513	0.436	0.371	0.270	0.198	0.146	0.108	0.093	0.080	0.060	0.045	0.034	0.026	0.023	0.020	0.015	0.012	0.006	0.003	0.002	0.001
18	0.836	0.700	0.494	0.416	0.350	0.250	0.180	0.130	0.095	0.081	0.069	0.051	0.038	0.028	0.021	0.018	0.016	0.012	0.009	0.005	0.002	0.001	0.001
19	0.828	0.686	0.475	0.396	0.331	0.232	0.164	0.116	0.083	0.070	0.060	0.043	0.031	0.023	0.017	0.014	0.012	0.009	0.007	0.003	0.002	0.001	
20	0.820	0.673	0.456	0.377	0.312	0.215	0.149	0.104	0.073	0.061	0.051	0.037	0.026	0.019	0.014	0.012	0.010	0.007	0.005	0.002	0.001	0.001	

21	0.811	0.660	0.439	0.359	0.294	0.199	0.135	0.093	0.064	0.053	0.044	0.031	0.022	0.015	0.011	0.009	0.008	0.006	0.004	0.002	0.001
22	0.803	0.647	0.422	0.342	0.278	0.184	0.123	0.083	0.056	0.046	0.038	0.026	0.018	0.013	0.009	0.007	0.006	0.004	0.003	0.001	0.001
23	0.795	0.634	0.406	0.326	0.262	0.170	0.112	0.074	0.049	0.040	0.033	0.022	0.015	0.010	0.007	0.006	0.005	0.003	0.002	0.001	
24	0.788	0.622	0.390	0.310	0.247	0.158	0.102	0.066	0.043	0.035	0.028	0.019	0.013	0.008	0.006	0.005	0.004	0.003	0.002	0.001	
25	0.780	0.610	0.375	0.295	0.233	0.146	0.092	0.059	0.038	0.030	0.024	0.016	0.010	0.007	0.005	0.004	0.003	0.002	0.001	0.001	
26	0.772	0.598	0.361	0.281	0.220	0.135	0.084	0.053	0.033	0.026	0.021	0.014	0.009	0.006	0.004	0.003	0.002	0.002	0.001		
27	0.764	0.586	0.347	0.268	0.207	0.125	0.076	0.047	0.029	0.023	0.018	0.011	0.007	0.005	0.003	0.002	0.002	0.001	0.001		
28	0.757	0.574	0.333	0.255	0.196	0.116	0.069	0.042	0.026	0.020	0.016	0.010	0.006	0.004	0.002	0.002	0.002	0.001	0.001		
29	0.749	0.563	0.321	0.243	0.185	0.107	0.063	0.037	0.022	0.017	0.014	0.008	0.005	0.003	0.002	0.002	0.001	0.001	0.001		
30	0.742	0.552	0.308	0.231	0.174	0.099	0.057	0.033	0.020	0.015	0.012	0.007	0.004	0.003	0.002	0.001	0.001	0.001			
35	0.706	0.500	0.253	0.181	0.130	0.066	0.036	0.019	0.010	0.008	0.006	0.003	0.002	0.001							
40	0.672	0.453	0.208	0.142	0.097	0.046	0.022	0.011	0.005	0.004	0.003	0.001	0.001								
45	0.639	0.410	0.171	0.111	0.073	0.031	0.014	0.006	0.003	0.002	0.001	0.001									
50	0.608	0.372	0.141	0.087	0.054	0.021	0.009	0.003	0.001	0.001	0.001										
60	0.550	0.305	0.095	0.054	0.030	0.010	0.002	0.001													

1. To find present value (PV) of future amount:
   PV = Factor × Amount
2. To find future amount representing given PV:
   Amount = PV/Factor

3. To find period given future amount, PV and yield:
   Factor = PV/Amount; locate in column
4. To find yield given future amount, PV and period:
   Factor = PV/Amount; locate in row

Table 5–11
Present Value of $1 per Period Received or Paid at End of Period (Annuity)

Number of Periods	1%	2%	4%	5%	6%	8%	10%	12%	14%	15%	16%	18%	20%	22%	24%	25%	26%	28%	30%	35%	40%	45%	50%
1	0.990	0.980	0.962	0.952	0.943	0.926	0.909	0.893	0.877	0.870	0.862	0.847	0.833	0.820	0.806	0.800	0.794	0.781	0.769	0.741	0.714	0.690	0.667
2	1.970	1.942	1.886	1.859	1.833	1.783	1.736	1.690	1.647	1.626	1.605	1.566	1.528	1.492	1.457	1.440	1.424	1.392	1.361	1.289	1.224	1.165	1.111
3	2.941	2.884	2.775	2.722	2.673	2.577	2.487	2.402	2.322	2.283	2.246	2.174	2.106	2.042	1.981	1.952	1.923	1.868	1.816	1.696	1.589	1.493	1.407
4	3.902	3.808	3.630	3.545	3.465	3.312	3.170	3.037	2.914	2.855	2.798	2.690	2.589	2.494	2.404	2.362	2.320	2.241	2.166	1.997	1.849	1.720	1.605
5	4.853	4.713	4.452	4.329	4.212	3.993	3.791	3.605	3.433	3.352	3.274	3.127	2.991	2.864	2.745	2.689	2.635	2.532	2.436	2.220	2.035	1.876	1.737
6	5.795	5.601	5.242	5.075	4.917	4.623	4.355	4.112	3.889	3.784	3.685	3.498	3.326	3.167	3.020	2.951	2.885	2.759	2.643	2.385	2.168	1.983	1.824
7	6.728	6.472	6.002	5.786	5.582	5.206	4.868	4.564	4.288	4.160	4.039	3.812	3.605	3.416	3.242	3.161	3.083	2.937	2.802	2.508	2.263	2.057	1.883
8	7.652	7.325	6.733	6.463	6.210	5.747	5.335	4.968	4.639	4.487	4.344	4.078	3.837	3.619	3.421	3.329	3.241	3.076	2.925	2.598	2.331	2.108	1.922
9	8.566	8.162	7.435	7.108	6.802	6.247	5.759	5.328	4.946	4.772	4.607	4.303	4.031	3.786	3.566	3.463	3.366	3.184	3.019	2.665	2.379	2.144	1.948
10	9.471	8.983	8.111	7.722	7.360	6.710	6.145	5.650	5.216	5.019	4.833	4.494	4.192	3.923	3.682	3.571	3.465	3.269	3.092	2.715	2.414	2.168	1.965
11	10.368	9.787	8.760	8.307	7.887	7.139	6.495	5.937	5.453	5.234	5.029	4.656	4.327	4.035	3.776	3.656	3.544	3.335	3.147	2.752	2.438	2.185	1.977
12	11.255	10.575	9.385	8.863	8.384	7.536	6.814	6.194	5.660	5.421	5.197	4.793	4.439	4.127	3.851	3.725	3.606	3.387	3.190	2.779	2.456	2.196	1.985
13	12.134	11.343	9.986	9.393	8.853	7.904	7.103	6.424	5.842	5.583	5.342	4.910	4.533	4.203	3.912	3.780	3.656	3.427	3.223	2.799	2.468	2.204	1.990
14	13.004	12.106	10.563	9.898	9.295	8.244	7.367	6.628	6.002	5.724	5.468	5.008	4.611	4.265	3.962	3.824	3.695	3.459	3.249	2.814	2.477	2.210	1.993
15	13.865	12.849	11.118	10.379	9.712	8.559	7.606	6.811	6.142	5.847	5.575	5.092	4.675	4.315	4.001	3.859	3.726	3.483	3.268	2.825	2.484	2.214	1.995
16	14.718	13.578	11.652	10.838	10.106	8.851	7.824	6.974	6.265	5.954	5.669	5.162	4.730	4.357	4.033	3.887	3.751	3.503	3.283	2.834	2.489	2.216	1.997
17	15.562	14.292	12.116	11.274	10.477	9.122	8.022	7.120	6.373	6.047	5.749	5.222	4.775	4.391	4.059	3.910	3.771	3.518	3.295	2.840	2.492	2.218	1.998
18	16.398	14.992	12.659	11.690	10.828	9.372	8.201	7.250	6.467	6.128	5.818	5.273	4.812	4.419	4.080	3.928	3.786	3.529	3.304	2.844	2.494	2.219	1.999
19	17.226	15.678	13.134	12.086	11.158	9.604	8.365	7.366	6.550	6.198	5.877	5.316	4.844	4.442	4.097	3.942	3.799	3.539	3.311	2.848	2.496	2.220	1.999
20	18.046	16.351	13.590	12.463	11.470	9.818	8.514	7.469	6.623	6.259	5.929	5.353	4.870	4.460	4.110	3.954	3.808	3.546	3.316	2.850	2.497	2.221	1.999

21	18.857	17.011	14.029	12.821	11.764	10.017	8.649	7.562	6.687	6.312	5.973	5.384	4.891	4.476	4.121	3.963	3.816	3.551	3.320	2.852	2.498	2.221	2.000
22	19.660	17.658	14.451	13.163	12.042	10.201	8.772	7.645	6.743	6.359	6.011	5.410	4.909	4.488	4.130	3.970	3.822	3.556	3.323	2.853	2.498	2.222	2.000
23	20.456	18.292	14.857	13.489	12.303	10.371	8.883	7.718	6.792	6.399	6.044	5.432	4.925	4.499	4.137	3.976	3.827	3.559	3.325	2.854	2.499	2.222	2.000
24	21.243	18.914	15.247	13.799	12.550	10.529	8.985	7.784	6.835	6.434	6.073	5.451	4.937	4.507	4.143	3.981	3.831	3.562	3.327	2.855	2.499	2.222	2.000
25	22.023	19.523	15.622	14.094	12.783	10.675	9.077	7.843	6.873	6.464	6.097	5.467	4.948	4.514	4.147	3.985	3.834	3.564	3.329	2.856	2.499	2.222	2.000
26	22.795	20.121	15.983	14.375	13.003	10.810	9.161	7.896	6.906	6.491	6.118	5.480	4.956	4.520	4.151	3.988	3.837	3.566	3.330	2.856	2.500	2.222	2.000
27	23.560	20.707	16.330	14.643	13.211	10.935	9.237	7.943	6.935	6.514	6.136	5.492	4.964	4.524	4.154	3.990	3.839	3.567	3.331	2.856	2.500	2.222	2.000
28	24.316	21.281	16.663	14.898	13.406	11.051	9.307	7.984	6.961	6.534	6.152	5.502	4.970	4.528	4.157	3.992	3.840	3.568	3.331	2.857	2.500	2.222	2.000
29	25.066	21.844	16.984	15.141	13.591	11.158	9.370	8.022	6.983	6.551	6.166	5.510	4.975	4.531	4.159	3.994	3.841	3.569	3.332	2.857	2.500	2.222	2.000
30	25.808	22.396	17.292	15.372	13.765	11.258	9.427	8.055	7.003	6.566	6.177	5.517	4.979	4.534	4.160	3.995	3.842	3.569	3.332	2.857	2.500	2.222	2.000
35	29.408	24.999	18.665	16.374	14.498	11.654	9.664	8.176	7.070	6.617	6.215	5.539	4.992	4.541	4.164	3.998	3.845	3.571	3.333	2.857	2.500	2.222	2.000
40	32.835	27.355	19.793	17.159	15.046	11.925	9.779	8.244	7.105	6.642	6.234	5.548	4.997	4.544	4.166	3.999	3.846	3.571	3.333	2.857	2.500	2.222	2.000
45	36.094	29.490	20.720	17.774	15.456	12.108	9.863	8.282	7.123	6.654	6.242	5.552	4.998	4.545	4.166	4.000	3.846	3.571	3.333	2.857	2.500	2.222	2.000
50	39.196	31.424	21.482	18.256	15.762	12.234	9.915	8.304	7.133	6.661	6.246	5.554	4.999	4.545	4.167	4.000	3.846	3.571	3.333	2.857	2.500	2.222	2.000
60	44.955	34.761	22.623	18.929	16.161	12.376	9.967	8.324	7.140	6.665	6.249	5.555	5.000	4.545	4.167	4.000	3.846	3.571	3.333	2.857	2.500	2.222	2.000

1. To find present value (PV) of series of equal receipts or payments:
   PV = Factor × Annuity
2. To find annuity representing given PV.:
   Annuity = PV/Factor

3. To find number of periods to recover investment:
   Factor = Investment/Annuity; locate in column
4. To find yield of annuity given investment:
   Factor = Investment/Annuity; locate in row

present value which suggests that the annual operating cash inflows can be off by only $11,815 ÷ 4.968, or about $2.4 million per year. The minimum life (present value payback) is about six years, when capital recoveries are included. This is as far as we can carry the analysis with the data at hand. The various judgments leading to the final decision call for much more insight into the nature of the product, the technology, the markets, the competitive setting, etc., as we outlined in the first section of this chapter.

When to Use the Investment Measures

In discussing the various investment measures, we have cautioned the reader about shortcomings and various interpretive issues. Here we will review and expand upon some of these caveats.

Basically, the measures have been developed to assist analysts and management in determining whether an investment project *meets* the earnings standard established for the business. Also, they assist them in *ranking* the relative desirability of a group of proposals during capital budgeting. Given the assumption that the projects being considered are *independent of each other,* the time-adjusted measures of *net present value, profitability index,* and *internal rate of return* will singly or in combination properly reflect the relative economic desirability of such projects and result in an appropriate ranking in order of desirability. In contrast, the simple measures, *payback* and *accounting rate of return,* are quite *limited* in their use as indicators of economic desirability, and they will serve as proper ranking devices *only* if the cash flow patterns and economic lives of the projects are quite similar.

Uneven lives of capital investments pose complications that are handled by adjusting the analysis to *equalize* the time spans for purposes of comparison. This can be achieved by *truncating* the life of a project with an assumed recovery of capital from disposal of the investment at an earlier point, as we did in our replacement example, or by *extending* the shorter alternative assuming repeated investment. Alternatively, competing (mutually exclusive) projects with different lives can be compared by *annualizing* their net present values over their respective lives to arrive at an annual equivalent benefit or cost. This process simply involves dividing the net present value by the relevant annuity factor or by using the appropriate computer program.

Mutually exclusive projects, such as those that represent two or three ways of achieving the same objective but involve different levels of investment and different operating cash flows, or which have different life spans, pose a special problem. In each case, only *one* of the alternatives can be undertaken. The various investment measures may show somewhat different rankings, and the analyst is faced with deciding how to optimize the value to the company. Normally, the *profitability index* will give a fair assessment, but the choice has to be seen in terms of the relative size and life of the commitment as well. If only one alternative can be taken, a large investment with a somewhat lower profitability index and internal rate of return may be preferable to a smaller investment *if* both alternatives show benefits *well above* normal. In other words, it may be better to earn an 18 percent return on a $10 million investment for 12 years than to earn 20 percent on $6 million for a shorter period, if, for example, normal returns are 15 percent.

Another way of analyzing mutually exclusive alternatives that entail different-sized investments is the use of *incremental* analysis. The analyst starts with the least costly option to establish the desirability of the investment per se, and then successively tests the desirability of each increment of investment versus the increment of operating benefits it provides. Again the results have to be viewed in the broader context of the other opportunities for earning returns on the same funds.

If a company's projects exceed the limits of the funds available, which is a fairly common condition, the issue of *capital rationing* arises. This forces choosing among projects that might all be acceptable if funds were unconstrained. The investment measures used here have to rank relative desirability.

Essentially, the company should choose that group of projects within the budget limit which will generate the highest *aggregate net present value*. Projects can be ranked in declining order of their *profitability index* until the budgeted amount has been exhausted. Essentially, the company should maximize the present value benefits achieved *per dollar* of investment, because investment funds are the limiting factor. In practice, capital budgets are rarely so precise that truly attractive projects which were rejected because of funds limitations could not at least be reconsidered.

Let us remember that there is nothing automatic about the use of investment measures. However, the seemingly precise results achieved with present value calculations can tempt us to "let the numbers decide." In practice, many more elements have to be weighed, as we observed at the beginning of the chapter. In addition to the constraints imposed by the uncertain nature of economic estimates, management must also consider competitive, technical, human, societal, and other constraints before significant investment decisions are made.

SOME FURTHER CONSIDERATIONS

Several topics that involve more specialized aspects of capital investment analysis have been mentioned only briefly so far. A detailed treatment would go beyond the scope of this book; yet, for completeness, we will add some further comments on the subjects of **leasing**, the impact of **accelerated depreciation** on present value analysis, and the impact of **inflation**. Finally, we will once more put into perspective the degree of **accuracy** warranted in the calculations.

Leasing

Leasing is a popular means of obtaining a wide variety of capital assets and is used by businesses as well as individuals. In the context of this chapter, the topic warrants some discussion. The most important point to consider is that leasing is one *form of financing* which should be considered *after* analysis has shown that an investment is acceptable. This is consistent with our approach in that we have considered the desirability of capital investments *separately* from the way they are to be *financed*. When leasing is employed to fund an investment, the periodic charges incurred by the lessee involve elements of interest, risk, obsolescence, maintenance costs, and profit to the owner, the pattern depending on which type of lease contract is selected from among the wide variety available. All along we have viewed investment analysis as a cash flow trade-off *independent* of the compensation paid for the funds that finance the asset. Leases are similarly handled—by eliminating from the cash charges incurred the financing costs implicit in the arrangement. Therefore, we must test whether the company is better off financing the asset through leasing *as compared to* acquiring the asset outright and financing the amount through normal means.

The most common of the several techniques now commonly available in computer programs strips the *imputed financing charges* from the leasing cash outflows, before cash flow patterns from leasing versus ownership are compared. Because of the special complexities involved in these analytical methods, the reader is referred to the references at the end of the chapter for detailed discussion and illustration.

Accelerated Depreciation

In this chapter, for simplicity, we used straight-line depreciation to derive the tax shield effect of depreciation charges. However, we also referred to the accelerated write-offs allowed under the Internal Revenue Code, which at the time of this writing are based on the ACRS system (see Chapter 2). From a present value standpoint, accelerated depreciation *increases* project benefits, because the *earlier* the tax shield is incurred, the *more valuable* it is when discounted—assuming, of course, that the company has sufficient taxable profits to take advantage of the write-offs. In view of the changing nature of the tax provisions, the reader is encouraged to seek out the most current information published by the IRS to ascertain the proper depreciation class and write-off patterns for the assets being analyzed.

Inflation Impact

The severe inflation in the 1970s and early '80s raised the issue of how to account for its impact in the economic analysis of investments. As this book is being written, inflation has moderated dramatically, which means that potential distortions are somewhat less important. Nevertheless, the issue cannot be ignored, because even moderate inflation experienced over a long time period of time will compound into an appreciable distortion of stated dollar values. Taking inflation into account in investment analysis entails two problems. The first is whether projections should *include* rising prices and costs that reflect expected levels of inflation. The second concerns the level of the discount rate—whether it should be explicitly adjusted upwards for inflation. Furthermore, there is the tendency to confuse *underlying inflation*, that is the *general decline* in the value of the dollar, with *specific price movements* that are due to the demand/supply conditions for the goods or services in question.

The most common method of projecting is to include expected price changes in costs and revenues, which are then discounted by an earnings standard that implicitly includes inflation expectations. As we shall see in the next chapter, the derivation of cost of capital for use as an earnings standard implicitly assumes that a company's cost of funds has a built-in inflation component. A less frequently used method of projection employs **constant dollar** estimates, which recognize *only* those price changes in revenues and costs that are due to changes in supply/demand patterns, and *not* those due to general inflation. For consistency, the discount factor in constant dollar analysis similarly has to be adjusted for the *general* inflation component. The results of this type of analysis are probably "purer," but harder to interpret. The many complexities involved are beyond the scope of this book. The references at the end of the chapter and Appendix I at the end of the book which deals briefly with the nature of inflation will give the reader further insights.

Accuracy

We must remember at all times that the *implied precision* of the mathematical basis of capital investment analysis should be viewed with extreme caution. As we have pointed out before, the very nature of cash flow estimates is *uncertain* because they are based on expectations, forecasts, projections, and sometimes plain guesses. Only rarely does the analyst deal with contractual sums, such as interest or lease payments—and even these are subject to a degree of uncertainty. It therefore makes no sense to generate very precise results in the course of an analysis or to allow the precise ranking to take on undue importance. In our examples we have been more precise than we probably needed to be, but the main intention was to give the reader enough detail to be able to follow, step by step, the methods being used. In practice, *liberal rounding* of the various calculations, and certainly of the final results, is advisable to keep the process from overwhelming the realistic judgments required.

The need to keep accuracy in perspective is even greater when we realize that the power of discounting is such that even widely different estimates for time periods far in the future are often so severely reduced in present value terms that they have relatively minor effects on the final result. A glance at the present value tables will confirm that shrinkage of factors accelerates for periods further in the future and at higher discount rates.

KEY ISSUES

The following is a recap of the key issues raised directly or indirectly in this chapter. They are enumerated here to help the reader keep the analysis techniques discussed within the perspective of financial theory and business practice.

1. Business investment decisions are continuously made in the larger context of strategy that evolves over time, and the portfolio of potential investments never remains constant.

2. The trade-off between outlays and benefits must be made with the objective of improving shareholder wealth, that is, the return standards employed in measuring this trade-off must reflect the earnings potential expected from the given business.

3. Cost of capital is a way of incorporating shareholder return expectations into an earnings yardstick that reflects the appropriate level of compensation to all providers of long-term capital.

4. Investment measures must take into account the timing of inflows and outflows of an investment and relate economic attractiveness to established return expectations.

5. Economic analysis of investment decisions must be based on judging the incremental differences in cash flows caused by an investment decision, and not changes merely due to accounting convention.

6. Risk is inherent in all estimates of future conditions due to uncertainty about most variables affecting an investment, and it must be expressed consistently in cash flows and investment measures alike.

7. Inflation and specific price changes in revenues and cost complicate both estimating and investment measures and must be handled consistently in both.

8. Capital budgets are neither absolute limits on investment nor are they automatically affected by project ranking on purely quantitative grounds.

9. Financing patterns affect investment capability and risk tolerance due to leverage effects and the need to cover fixed obligations.

10. Analytical techniques can provide ranges of results and quantitative insights of considerable sophistication, but qualitative business judgments must be applied to any investment decision.

SUMMARY

In this chapter we provided the basic analytical framework for investment analysis in the context of capital budgeting. The **strategic context** of this activity was highlighted before the techniques themselves were discussed. The emphasis was on the use of **time-adjusted** measures, relegating simple rules of thumb to the limited cases where they can be useful. We stressed, however, that the *critical* aspect of the process was the analysis *preceding* the application of the techniques. We emphasized the need to *define the problem,* including the development and selection of alternatives, and the careful preparation of *relevant* data about the investment, operating cash flows, and capital recoveries. We found *conceptual problems* in all of these, particularly the investment measures themselves. Working through increasingly complex examples, we provided the reader with a basic ability to solve problems in investment analysis. But these results were only inputs to the broader management task of strategic planning—the matching of long-range investment commitments with appropriate funds sources, in the light of defined corporate objectives and goals.

SELECTED REFERENCES

Analytical Process

Anthony, Robert N., and Reece, James S. *Accounting: Text and Cases.* 6th ed. Homewood, Ill.: Richard D. Irwin, 1979.

Grant, Eugene L.; Ireson, W. Grant; and Leavenworth, Richard S. *Principles of Engineering Economy.* 6th ed. New York: Ronald Press, 1976.

Horngren, Charles T. *Cost Accounting, a Managerial Emphasis.* 4th ed. Englewood Cliffs, N.J.: Prentice-Hall, 1977.

Moore, Carl, and Jaedicke, Robert K. *Managerial Accounting.* 5th ed. Cincinnati, Ohio: South-Western Publishing, 1980.

Pappas, James L., and Brigham, Eugene F. *Managerial Economics.* 3d ed. Hinsdale, Ill.: Dryden Press, 1979.

Rosen, Lawrence R. *Dow Jones-Irwin Guide to Interest: What You Should Know about the Time Value of Money.* Rev. ed. Homewood, Ill.: Dow Jones-Irwin, 1981.

Broader Framework of Capital Budgeting

Bierman, Harold Jr., and Smidt, Seymour. *The Capital Budgeting Decision.* 5th ed. New York: Macmillan, 1980.

Hull, J. C. *The Evaluation of Risk in Business Investment.* Elmsford, N.Y.: Pergammon Press, 1980.

Kaufman, Mike, ed. *The Capital Budgeting Handbook.* Homewood, Ill.: Dow Jones-Irwin, 1985.

Van Horne, James C. *Financial Management and Policy.* 7th ed. Englewood Cliffs, N.J.: Prentice-Hall, 1986.

Weston, J. Fred, and Copeland, Thomas E. *Managerial Finance.* 8th ed. Chicago: Dryden Press, 1986.

Specialized Areas

Present Value Tables

Gushee, Charles II., ed. *Financial Compound Interest and Annuity Tables.* 6th ed. Boston: Financial Publishing, 1980.

Thorndike, David. *The Thorndike Encyclopedia of Banking and Financial Tables, 1980 Yearbook.* Boston: Warren, Gorham & Lamset.

MAPI Method

Terborgh, George. *Business Investment Management.* Washington, D.C.: Machinery and Allied Products Institute, 1967.

Probability Analysis

Hertz, David B. "Risk Analysis in Capital Investment." *Harvard Business Review,* September–December 1979, pp. 42–49.

Levy, Haim, and Sarna, Marshall. *Capital Investment and Financial Decisions.* Englewood Cliffs, N.J.: Prentice-Hall, 1978.

Leasing

Prichard, Robert E., and Hindelang, Thomas J. *The Lease/Buy Decision.* New York: AMACOM, 1980.

SELF-STUDY EXERCISES AND PROBLEMS

(Solutions to Items 1, 3, 5, and 6 are provided in Appendix III)

1. An investment proposition costing $60,000 is expected to result in the following aftertax cash flows over seven years:

Year	
1	$10,000
2	15,000
3	15,000
4	20,000
5	15,000
6	10,000
7	5,000

   a. Calculate the net present value at 10 percent and at 16 percent.
   b. Determine the internal rate of return (yield) of the proposition.
   c. If the annual cash flows were an even $13,000 per year for seven years, what would be the net present value at 10 percent?
   d. What level annual cash flows would be required to yield a 16 percent return?
   e. How would the results of (*a*) and (*b*) change if there were a capital recovery of $10,000 at the end of year 7?
   f. How would the result of (*d*) change if there were a capital recovery of $10,000 at the end of year 7?

2. After having spent and written off against expenses of past periods an estimated $1,150,000 of research and development funds on a new product, the ABC Company is faced with the decision of whether to invest a total of $1,500,000 in a large-scale initial promotional and advertising campaign to bring the product to market. The campaign will be conducted over a six-month period, and all costs will be charged off as expenses in the current year. The effect of the campaign is an estimated average incremental profit of $400,000 per year for at least the next five years, before taxes and without the initial promotional costs. The likely pattern of profits is estimated to be $200,000 in the first year, $300,000 in the second, $600,000 in the third, $500,000 in the fourth, and $400,000 in the fifth year.

Assume that income taxes on incremental profits are paid at the rate of 46 percent and that the company normally has the opportunity to earn 12 percent after taxes. Calculate the various measures of investment desirability, first on the average profit and then on the annual pattern expected. Determine the simple payback and return on investment, average return, net present value, present value index, present value payback, annualized net present value, and internal rate of return (yield). What is the effect of the research and development expenditures on these results? Discuss your findings.

3. After careful analysis of a number of possible investments, a trustee of a major estate is weighing the choice between two $100,000 investments considered to be of equal risk. The first (a) will provide a series of eight year-end payments to the estate of $16,500 each, while the second (b) will provide a single lump sum of $233,000 at the end of 11 years. Which proposition provides the higher yield? If the normal return experienced by the estate for investments of this risk category is 6 percent, which investment is preferable? Should the pattern of cash flows be a consideration here, and how would this affect the choice? Ignore taxes and discuss your findings.

4. In an effort to replace a manual operation with a more efficient and reliable automatic process, the DEF Company is considering the purchase of a machine which will cost $52,800 installed and has an expected economic life of eight years. It will be depreciated over this period on a straight-line basis for both book and tax purposes, with no salvage value foreseen. The main benefit expected is a true reduction in costs due to the elimination of two operator positions and less materials spoilage. There will be some additional costs such as power, supplies, and repairs. The net annual savings are estimated to be $12,100, and the machine will be scrapped at the end of its life.

Assume that income taxes on incremental profits are paid at the rate of 46 percent and that normal opportunities return 10 percent after taxes. Calculate the simple payback and return on investment, average return, net present value, present value index, present value payback, annualized net present value, and internal rate of return (yield). Discuss your findings.

5. The strategy of the XYZ Corporation includes the periodic introduction of a new product line, which involves investments in research and development, promotion, plant, equipment, and working capital. Now the company has readied a new product after an expenditure of $3.75 million on research and development during the past 12 months. The decision to be made is whether to invest $6.3 million for the production of

the new line. The economic life of the product is estimated at 12 years, while straight-line depreciation will be taken over 15 years. At the end of 12 years, the book value of the equipment is expected to be recovered through sale of the machinery. Working capital of $1.5 million will have to be committed to the project during the first year, and $1.25 million of this amount is expected to be recovered at the end of the 12 years. An expenditure of $1 million for promotion will have to be made and expensed in the first year as well.

The best estimate of profits before depreciation, promotion expenses, and income taxes is $1.9 million per year for the first three years, $2.2 million per year for the fourth through eighth years, and $1.3 million per year for years 9 through 12. Assume that income taxes on incremental profits are paid at the rate of 46 percent and that the company normally earns 10 percent after taxes on its investments. Calculate the various measures of investment desirability. Which of these best indicates the attractiveness of the project? Should the company plan to develop similar opportunities by spending research and development funds? How much margin for error exists in this project? Discuss your findings.

6. The ZYX Company has found that after only two years of using a new machine for a semiautomatic production process, a more advanced and faster model has arrived on the market which not only will turn out the current volume of products more efficiently but will allow an increased output of the item. The original machine had cost $32,000 and was being depreciated straight-line over a 10-year period, at the end of which it would be scrapped. The market value of this machine currently is $15,000, and a buyer is interested in acquiring it.

The advanced model now available costs $55,500 installed, and because of its more complex mechanism is expected to last eight years. A scrap value of $1,500 is considered reasonable.

The current level of output of the old machine, now running at capacity, is 200,000 units per year, which the new machine would boost by 15 percent. There is no question in the minds of the sales management that this additional output could be sold. The current machine produces the product at a unit cost of 12 cents for labor, 48 cents for materials, and 24 cents for allocated overhead (at the rate of 200 percent of direct labor). At the higher level of output, the new machine would turn out the product at a unit cost of 8 cents for labor (because one less operator is needed), 46 cents for materials (because of less spoilage), and 16 cents for allocated overhead. Differences in other operating costs, such as power, repairs, and supplies, are negligible at both volume levels.

If the new machine were run at the old 200,000-unit level, the operators would be freed for a proportionate period of time for reassignment in other operations of the company.

The additional output is expected to be sold at the normal price of $0.95 per unit, but additional selling and promotional costs are expected to amount to $5,500 per year.

Assume that income taxes are paid at the rate of 46 percent and that the company normally earns 15 percent after taxes on its investments. Calculate the various measures of investment desirability and select those that are most meaningful for this analysis. What major considerations should be taken into account in this decision? Discuss your findings.

7. The UVW Company, a small but growing oil company, was about to invest $275,000 in drilling development wells on a lease near a major oil field with proven reserves. Since other companies were also drilling in the vicinity, the volume of the flow of oil expected could not be predicted except within wide limits. Nevertheless, some oil would be obtained for a period of 12 years, in the best judgment of the geologists. After careful evaluation of the market and distribution aspects, company management decided that the major uncertainty lay in the physical yield, with lesser risk in the other areas. Consequently, an assessment was made of the range of aftertax cash flows (after considering depletion, depreciation, etc.) at various levels of production and the likelihood of occurrence of these levels was estimated. There was believed to be a 5 percent chance that the cash flow would be $15,000 yearly over the life of the project, a 15 percent chance that it would be $35,000 yearly, a 40 percent chance that it would be $45,000 yearly, a 25 percent chance that it would be $50,000, and a 15 percent chance that it would be $60,000 per year. It was expected that oil would flow at any given level for the full life of the project, although there was the risk that the wells could run dry sooner. Would this be a worthwhile project if the company normally earned 10 percent after taxes? What considerations are critical? Discuss your findings.

6   ASSESSMENT OF COST
OF CAPITAL

As we have pointed out repeatedly, the economic nature
of business decisions involves a cost/benefit trade-off. Up to
this point, we have focused mainly on the economic benefits
from investing in and operating a business. Yet there are economic costs incurred with every business decision. For example, in Chapter 4, during our discussion of leverage, we encountered the special effect on profits caused by the cost of
long-term debt funds. We demonstrated how this fixed obligation introduces magnified earnings fluctuations at different
levels of profitability. In Chapter 5 we referred to the overall
cost of long-term capital as a criterion by which to judge the
desirability of business investments, because projects that provide a return at or above the cost of capital will leave shareholders at least as well off as before.

In this chapter we will discuss in greater detail the cost of
various types of capital employed in the business, examine how
this cost is measured, and in what form and for which purposes
this economic concept affects business decision making. We
will begin by sketching out the **types of decisions** for which cost
of capital considerations are important. Then we will discuss
the cost of the different types of capital, including **operating
funds, long-term debt,** and **owners' equity,** that is *preferred
stock* and *common equity.* Given the costs of each of these
types of capital, we will derive an approach to determining the

265

overall corporate **weighted cost of capital,** and discuss the use of cost of capital in relation to various **return standards** for business investments. The chapter will end with a list of **key issues.**

COST OF CAPITAL AND FINANCIAL DECISIONS

The reader will recall the *decisional* context we used in the first four chapters, which stressed the interrelationship of investment, operations, and financing. We observed that over time, most decisions made by management caused *funds movements.* However, we did not deal directly with the *sources* of these funds and their respective *costs.* The dynamics of the business system are such that at any time there is temporary and/or permanent utilization of funds from a variety of sources, both *external,* e.g., borrowing or raising new equity, or *internal,* e.g., profitable operations or shifts in existing uses of funds. We also stated that the basic purpose of investing in, operating, and funding a business was to increase the economic value of the owners' stake over time. Thus the decisions made should create economic value that is *higher* than the cost of the inputs. Among these clearly are the costs of the sources of financing. As we will see below, cost of capital must be considered in terms of each of these elements in our decisional context.

Investment Decisions

In Chapter 5 we discussed various measures used to ascertain the desirability of an investment, most of which were based on the requirement that the project provide an *economic return.* We did not address the cost of the *specific* funds to be used for financing the investments, although an economic return implies that *all costs* must be recovered. These costs include compensation to all providers of funds. We also said that minimum standards for investments had to be set high enough to compensate *both* for the specific risk of the project *and* for the opportunity loss of forgoing the returns and *alternative uses* of the funds invested. Such alternative investments in the company's normal activities were assumed to adequately compensate *both* shareholders and lenders for providing their capital. We then suggested that the company's *overall cost of capital*, when used to measure the economic desirability of investments, implicitly embodied all of these requirements.

The *analytical* methods we used in Chapter 5 did not directly include financing costs; rather, the cash outflows and inflows were developed in terms of capital outlays on the one hand, and incremental *operating* benefits and capital recoveries obtained on the other. These were then discounted at a standard of return that *implicitly* allowed for recovery of all actual and opportunity costs combined. The economic results from an investment had to be sufficiently attractive to justify allocation of part of the long-term funds available to the company. Normally, investment funds come from a *pool* of different sources, none of the elements of which can or should be specifically identified with the particular project under review. Instead, any use of investment funds should reflect a company's *overall* cost of capital. Capital expenditures are backed by the long-term capital structure of a company, which may include different degrees of leverage and a whole range of financial instruments. Thus a *weighted* cost of capital measure, which we will discuss shortly, is an important criterion in the capital budgeting context.

Operational Decisions

The time horizon for *operational* decisions involving funds movements is generally *shorter* than that of the typical capital investment. Nonetheless, the operational finance aspects of a business, such as increases or decreases in trade credit, both used and extended, and swings in cash balances and accruals do involve *costs*, both out-of-pocket charges and opportunity costs. Near-term decisions on taking purchase discounts offered, for example, may involve significant economic benefits when weighed against any incremental borrowing necessary to take advantage of the discount. Cash management decisions to minimize bank balances can eliminate the opportunity costs resulting from tying up idle funds. In fact, there are myriad circumstances in which near-term decisions cause or eliminate the cost of employing funds, as these decisions are often directly connected with incremental sources that entail *specific* costs. We will discuss some of these shortly.

Financing Decisions

There are costs connected with obtaining and compensating for various sources of funds, both short-term and long-term, which must be considered by management in making any financing decisions. Clearly, all types of funds entail an economic cost to the company in one form or another. One of management's obligations is to develop a pattern of funding that both matches the risk/reward profile of the business and is sufficiently adapted to meeting the evolving needs of the company. We will discuss the financing choices and the framework used to analyze them in the next chapter.

COST OF OPERATING FUNDS

In the course of its operations, a business commonly employs many forms of debt, including trade obligations (in the form of accounts and notes payable), intermediate-term credit, notes payable to banks or individuals, tax payments due various government agencies, wages due, payments due on installment purchases, and lease obligations. For all types of debt, including long-term obligations in the company's capital structure, the *specific cost* of borrowing can be determined rather easily. Normally, debt arrangements carry stated provisions that call for interest payments during the debt period, at its end, or as an advance deduction from principal. The last of these provisions is called discounting. In all of the cases, the *specific cost* of debt is simply the cost of this interest commitment.

We must also remember that interest payments of all kinds are *tax deductible* for corporations. Because of this feature, the *net* cost of interest to corporations (at least for those with sufficient profits that they are liable for taxes or able to apply tax-averaging provisions) is the annual interest multiplied by a factor (f) of one minus the applicable tax rate. For example, if a corporation pays 9 percent per year on the principal of a note and its effective tax rate (t) for any incremental revenue or cost is 46 percent, the net annual effective interest cost (i) of this note will be:

$$f = 1 - t$$
$$f = 1 - 0.46 = 0.54$$
$$i = 9.0 \times 0.54 = 4.86\% \text{ (after taxes)}$$

This tax deductibility *reduces* the cost of debt to a *net amount* after the prevailing tax rate is applied, *if* the company is in a position where changes in net income affect taxes due. This tax advantage may also be enjoyed by individuals in many circumstances. Deductibility of the specific cost does *not* apply to other forms of capital, however, as we will see later.

We can define operating debt as short- or intermediate-term *revolving* obligations incurred in the ordinary daily operations of most businesses. Some of these debt funds are provided by creditors *free of charge* for short periods, under trade terms generally accepted in the industry or service in which the company operates. Foremost in this category are *accounts payable,* which are the amounts owed for goods or services purchased. Depending on the terms of the purchase agreement, the company being billed for goods and services can hold off payment for 10 or 15 days, or as long as 45 or even 60 days. In the interim, it can make use of the funds without incurring any specific cost. We recall from Chapter 2 that such trade credit is in fact a significant funds source that is *rolled over continuously,* and which grows or declines with the volume of operations.

In most cases, suppliers offer a discount for early payment. For example, the terms may provide for a 2 percent reduction if payment is received within 10 days (2/10), or 3 percent within

15 days (3/15) of the date of the invoice. This common practice allows the customer effectively to *reduce* the original cost of the goods or service by the specified amount. The arrangement is intended to speed up the vendor's collections and thus to reduce the level of funds tied up in credit extended. If the buyer lets the discount period lapse, however, the invoice amount becomes due and payable at the end of the period specified (n/30, n/45. etc.). Failure to take advantage of the trade discount, and thereby prolonging the time during which the buyer can make alternative use of the funds, results in a very definite *opportunity cost*, however. While often ignored, this cost can be *quite sizable*. For instance, if the credit terms are 2/10, n/30, the cost of using the funds for the extra 20 days amounts to 2 percent of lost cash discount, or an annual rate of 36 percent!

$$\frac{360 \text{ days}}{20 \text{ days}} \times 2\% = 36\% \text{ (before taxes)}$$

In effect the company loses, as taxable income, the cash discount it would otherwise have earned. To arrive at the net cost, the cash discount must be reduced by the taxes that would have been paid on the lost income. If we assume taxes to be 46 percent, the *net cost* for using the creditor's funds for the extra 20 days amounts to:

$$1 - 0.46 = 0.54$$
$$2.0\% \times 0.54 = 1.08\% \text{ (after taxes)}$$

On an *annualized* basis, this cost is still sizable, especially when compared to the prime interest rate—which is the rate normally charged large corporations of impeccable credit rating—or even to the higher interest rates smaller companies pay to borrow operating funds. The annualization is calculated as follows:

$$\frac{360 \text{ days}}{20 \text{ days}} \times 1.08\% = 19.44\% \text{ (after taxes)}$$

Some companies, especially small and rapidly growing enterprises, make it a practice to use accounts payable as a convenient source of credit, often unilaterally *exceeding* the outside limits of credit terms by extended periods. The longer the funds are kept, of course, the lower the specific cost of accounts payable becomes, as trade creditors normally do not charge interest unless the receivable has to be renegotiated. In extreme cases, unpaid accounts may be converted into notes payable due on specific dates, with or without interest. This is usually done at the request of a trade creditor who wishes to establish a somewhat stronger claim against the debtor's resources. It is clearly a poor practice for a borrower to violate stipulated trade credit agreements, both from the standpoint of business reputation and for continuing credit-worthiness. Prospective creditors will obviously take such tardy performance into account when evaluating the customer's credit, as such data are readily available from credit rating agencies. This implicit economic cost must be added to the specific monetary cost incurred with trade credit.

Another form of operating debt includes *short-term notes* and *installment contracts*, in which interest is either charged ahead of time or is added to the amount of principal stated in the contract. For example, a one-year, $1,000 note which carries an interest rate of 9 percent will provide the debtor with only $910 if the note is "discounted" by deducting the interest in advance. The *effective cost* before taxes now becomes *higher* than the stated interest, because the company is in effect paying $90 for the privilege of borrowing $910 for one year:

$$\frac{\$90}{\$910} = 9.89\% \text{ (before taxes)}$$

The adjustment for income taxes is handled exactly as shown in the last example. In the case of an installment contract for, say, $1,000 payable in four equal quarterly installments, with annual interest of 10 percent on the original balance, the effective cost of interest is far higher than stated, because *decreasing* amounts of principal will be outstanding over the term of the contract as the quarterly payments amortize the principal while providing interest on the declining balance. The precise cost of 15.7 percent can be easily calculated with a preprogrammed microcomputer, using the present value approach discussed in Chapter 5.

A quick method of determining the *approximate* effective cost is found in an *averaging* process. Over the term of the contract, the amount of principal will decline from $1,000 to zero, with an average outstanding of roughly one half of this range, or $500. The contractual interest was 10 percent on $1,000, or $100, one quarter of which was added to each of the four payments. When we relate the *total* interest paid to the *average* amount of funds used by the borrowing company during the term of the contract, the *approximate* cost doubles, as follows:

$$\frac{\$100}{\$500} = 20\% \text{ (before taxes)}$$

The actual result of 15.7 percent was lower because in our example, the interest is in effect paid on the installment basis. (The adjustment for income taxes is the same as before.) If the contract ran for more than one year, the interest cost must be *annualized,* that is, the amount of interest must be allocated to the specific time period involved to derive the true cost *per year,* which is the normal period of comparison.

More complex financial arrangements are normally handled using present value techniques. Banks and other lending institutions use tables and computers to precisely calculate the payments and charges, and are legally bound to disclose the effective cost of the arrangement on an annualized basis. The simple averaging technique is useful in many circumstances, including personal finance, for approximating the effective cost of credit with which to make initial comparisons.

The discussion so far has focused on determining the *specific cost* of operational debt, which can range from zero to substantial annual rates of interest. This specific cost is not the only aspect of debt, however. As already mentioned in earlier chapters, *repayment of principal* has to be made, which commits the company's future *cash flow.* The obligation to repay the principal in a timely fashion forces the financial manager to forecast and plan *cash receipts and disbursements* with care. Expectations could be such that *refinancing* may be desirable when the principal becomes due. The basic techniques for making funds flow projections, discussed in Chapter 3, are applicable here.

Another element of the debt burden, as already mentioned, is the impact of the various forms of debt obligations on the *credit-worthiness* of a company contemplating current and future funding requirements. In other words, the balance between owners' equity and "other people's money" may become precarious and forestall borrowing of any kind for some time until the company has worked itself out from under its debt obligations. Having "closed off the top," as debt-heavy operations are often described, can be costly, both in terms of the risk of not meeting obligations as they fall due, and in having to turn to much more expensive sources of credit or equity funds as additional needs arise.

COST OF LONG-TERM DEBT

Most companies employ at least some type of long-term debt obligations to support part of their permanent financing needs arising from major capital outlays, growth of operations, or replacement of other types of capital. This type of debt, exemplified by bonds of various types issued by a company and traded in the financial markets, or long-term borrowing arrangements with banks and other financial institutions, becomes *integral to the capital structure* of the company. Management must make well-planned decisions, weighing the *cost, risk,* and *debt service* involved in relation to the prospective uses of the funds. Commitments to long-term debt by their very nature have a much more lasting impact on a company's situation than do short-term working capital financing or intermediate-term loans.

The *specific cost* of long-term debt is expressed in the stated annual interest rate of the financial instrument involved. Thus, for example, a 9 percent "debenture" bond, which is an unsecured (no specific assets are pledged) general debt obligation of the company has a specific cost of:

$$9\% \times (1 - .46) = 4.86\%$$

if we assume that the company is able to take advantage of the interest deductibility. An incremental tax rate of 46 percent was used. In addition, we will assume that the bond had been sold at a price that *nets* the company its **par value** (face value). The *stated annual interest rate* (**coupon rate**) of a bond is based on the par value, or 100 percent of the principal due at a specified future date, regardless of the *actual proceeds* received by the issuing company. Proceeds vary because marketable debt securities are generally sold at the best possible price obtainable in the market through underwriters who take some or all of the risk of marketing the issue for a small percentage of the gross receipts. Legal and registration expenses are also borne by the company. Therefore, depending on the *issue price*, which is related to prevailing interest yields and to the quality of the company's credit rating, the company may actually receive net proceeds *below* par value, or it may receive a small *premium* over par.

In either case, the specific cost has to be *adjusted* to allow for the actual proceeds. The effect is similar to the case with the short-term loan discussed earlier, on which the interest was due in advance and which therefore entailed a specific cost somewhat *higher* than the stated rate. If we assume that instead of 100 percent of par value the company received 95 percent for its debentures after all expenses and commissions, the *effective cost* with a 9 percent *coupon rate* is as follows:

$$.09(1 - 46) \times \frac{1}{.95} = 5.12\%$$

Apart from the specific cost of interest, long-term debt also involves repayment of the principal. There are many types of repayment provisions, generally structured to fit the nature of the company and the type of risks the debtholder visualizes. Periodic repayment requirements may be met through a **sinking fund** set aside for that purpose. Partial or full principal payments due at the end of the lending period are called **balloon payments**. The point to remember, however, is that debt instruments, even if long term, must in some form and at some time be *repaid*. The cost of this repayment is implicit in the need to carefully plan future cash flows, and also to consider the company's ability to achieve future refinancing if the funds needs are likely to continue or even grow. The reader will recall the discussion of funds projections in Chapter 3.

Another implicit cost of long-term debt involves the nature and degree of *restrictions* normally embodied in the debt agreement (**indenture**). Such provisions may limit management's ability to use other forms of credit, e.g., leasing; or may specify *minimum levels* of some financial ratios, e.g., working capital proportions or debt service coverage; or they may *limit* the amount of dividends that can be paid to shareholders. At times, specific assets may have to be *pledged* as security. Any set of such provisions carries an *implicit cost* in the form of limiting management's freedom of choice in making decisions. The greater the perceived risk of the indebtedness, the greater the restrictions are likely to be. The rationale for these restrictions was presented in our discussion of financial ratios from the point of view of lenders (Chapter 1). Not to be overlooked is the introduction of *financial leverage* into the capital structure, as discussed in Chapter 4. The implicit cost of this condition again depends on the degree of risk exposure caused by specific company and industry conditions.

COST OF OWNERS' EQUITY

Preferred Stock

This form of equity ownership is conceptually at the midway point between debt and common stock. Although subordinated to claims of the various creditors of the corporation, the holder of preferred shares has a claim on corporate *earnings* that ranks *ahead* of that of the holders of common shares up to the amount of the stated preferred dividend. In liquidation, the preferred shareholder's claims are satisfied prior to the residual claims of the holders of common stock. The *specif-*

ic cost of preferred stock is normally higher than that of debt with similarly quality rating, however.

Because of the near-equity status of preferred stock, preferred dividends are not tax deductible for the issuing corporation and are therefore an outflow of *aftertax* funds. For instance, a 10 percent preferred stock, issued at par (net of expenses) costs the corporation 10 percent after taxes. For each dollar of dividends to be paid on this preferred stock, the corporation must therefore earn, before taxes:

$$\$1.00 \times \frac{1}{1 - .46} = \$1.85$$

as compared to $1 for every dollar of interest paid on a long-term debt obligation. Where the 9 percent bond in the previous section had an aftertax cost of 4.86 percent, the 10 percent preferred has an aftertax cost of 10 percent. The stated dividend rate of a preferred stock is therefore directly comparable to the *tax-adjusted* stated interest rate of a bond.

We can easily compare the cost to the company of long-term debt and preferred stock if we assume that they were issued at prices which result in proceeds exactly equal to the par (face) value. When proceeds do *not* equal par value, as often happens because of market conditions, the *effective* cost, discussed above, must be based on the *proceeds*.

The additional *implicit* cost of preferred stock lies in the fact that it is a security *senior* to common stock, and the dividend claims of its holders rank *ahead* of the dividend claims of holders of common shares. In addition, the essentially *fixed* nature of preferred dividends (they can be omitted only under serious circumstances) introduces a degree of *financial leverage* with varying earnings levels. Preferred stock being, in effect, closer to owners' equity than to debt, however, makes the implicit costs of its encumbrances far less serious than those of debt.

Common Equity

The holder of common shares is the *residual* owner of the corporation (the claims of common stock extend to all assets and earnings not subject to *prior* claims), and provides long-term funds expecting to be rewarded with an increase in the economic value of the shares. This value accretion is composed of the interlocking effects of, hopefully, growing *earnings* and growing *dividends* received on the market *valuation* of the shares, which in turn is affected by the *risks* specific to the industry and to the individual company. In other words, we are dealing with more variables, while at the same time there are no *contractual* provisions for compensation, such as coupon interest or the stated preferred dividend rate. As a result, the *specific cost* of common equity calls for a more complex evaluation than was the case with debt or preferred stock.

In the case of common equity, *cost* has to be viewed in an *opportunity framework*. The investor has provided funds to the corporation expecting to receive the *combined* economic return of dividends declared by the board of directors and future appreciation in market value. The investment was made—presumably on a logical basis—because the type of *risk* embodied in the company and its business reasonably matched the investor's *own risk preference* and because *expectations* about earnings, dividends, and market appreciation are satisfactory. The investor made this choice by *forgoing* other investment opportunities, however. The investment was made under conditions of uncertainty about *future* results, in that the only hard data available to the new investor are *past* performance statistics. The challenge of measuring the cost of the shareholder's funds to the corporation arises from the need to meet the investor's expectations about the risk/reward trade-off involved in investing in this opportunity. In other words, the company must compensate the shareholder with the economic return *implicit* in its past performance and future outlook.

Several approaches to measuring the cost of common equity are used in practice; all involve many assumptions and a great deal of judgment. The greatest difficulty lies in finding a specific link with the *risk versus value* judgments made in the securities markets, which affect the market value of the common shares. We will discuss three major methods: an **earnings** approach, a **dividend** approach, and a **risk assessment** approach based on the **capital asset pricing model.** The earnings and dividend approaches are fairly straightforward; in effect they value future streams of earnings or dividends. But they also use highly simplifying assumptions and thus are very *limited* in effectiveness. The third method, in contrast, approximates shareholder return expectations by adding to a *"normalized" rate of return* on securities in general a calculated numerical *risk premium* that is *company* specific. As we will see, it is the only approach that arrives at an economic return for the *specific* security *relative* to average yields experienced in the securities markets.

Earnings Approach to Cost of Common Equity. In Chapter 1 we discussed the *price/earnings ratio* as a rough indicator of market valuation. This relationship is the simplest way of approximating the cost of common equity. Because we are interested in a measure of the opportunity cost of common equity, we will use *projected* earnings per share as related to the *current* market price of the stock:

$$\text{Cost of equity} = \frac{\text{Projected earnings per share}}{\text{Current market price per share}}$$

$$k_e = \frac{eps}{P}$$

or

$$\text{Cost of equity} = \frac{1}{\text{Price/earnings ratio}}$$

$$k_e = \frac{1}{P/E}$$

This result is based on the implicit assumption that *all* of the earnings of the company will be paid out to the shareholders, which is *not realistic.* At the same time, the measure does not allow for the effect of any *reinvested* earnings creating further value for the shareholders. Finally, the result is static in that future *growth* in earnings is *ignored.* If the first assumption about a 100 percent payout holds, an alternative way of estimating the cost of equity would be to project, year by year, the expected earnings pattern and to find the discount rate that would equate these aftertax earnings with the current market value, adjusted for a terminal value at the time the analysis is cut off. Clearly, the number of assumptions we must make for the analysis to be valid multiplies rapidly under these conditions. This simple measure therefore is at best a rough approximation.

Dividend Approach to Cost of Common Equity.   A more direct way of dealing with at least one of the direct benefits obtained by the shareholder is to use annual dividends to estimate the cost of common equity. Yet the measure also suffers from the liability of serious oversimplification, because companies vary greatly in their rate of dividend payout, and the effect of reinvestment of retained earnings is again ignored. In its simplest form, the dividend approach is the same as the *dividend yield* we discussed as one of the market indicators in Chapter 1:

$$\text{Cost of common equity} = \frac{\text{Projected dividend per share}}{\text{Current market price per share}}$$

$$k_e = \frac{dps}{P}$$

Introducing *growth* in dividends into the formula is an improvement that partially adjusts for the *reinvestment* portion of the value received by shareholders. The assumption here is that successful reinvestment of retained earnings will lead to growing earnings and thus growing dividends. The mathematics of the formula allow us to simply add the *assumed rate of growth in dividends* to the equation shown above. We again begin with the dividend yield and add a *stable percentage* rate of dividend growth (g) to simulate the economic expectations of the shareholders:

$$k_e = \frac{dps}{P} + g$$

The difficulty, however, lies in determining the growth rate, which must be based on our best assumptions about future performance, tempered by past experience. Many estimating processes can be used. In Chapter 4 we discussed the concept of *sustainable growth,* given stable investment, payout, and financing policies. This may yield clues to the growth rate that can be applied with the dividend approach, but again a great deal of judgment must be exercised in projecting expected *future* policies. If significant changes in policies are forecast, the analyst may want to modify the approach, making a series of year-by-year assumptions and in effect, calculating a composite of future dividend growth patterns from these yearly forecasts.

A word about *taxes* is necessary here. In both the earnings and the dividend approaches we are dealing with *aftertax values* from the point of view of the company. Earnings per share are stated after taxes, while common dividends, like preferred dividends, are *not* deductible and are paid out of aftertax earnings. No adjustment is therefore necessary in the results to make them comparable with the aftertax cost of debt and preferred stock. The *investor* likewise is judging the opportunity to earn an economic return in these terms. However, interest and dividends *received* are taxable income to the individual. Therefore, because personal tax conditions vary greatly, one more adjustment is necessary to assess the investment options objectively from the *investor's point of view.* Yet the business analyst cannot perform this precise calculation without knowledge of the individual's tax status. Consequently, the only working assumption we can make in this context is that *most investors* are subject to *some taxation;* we can arrive at financial results that are consistent *up to the point* at which the individual investor must calculate his or her personal tax impact.

Risk Assessment Approach to Cost of Common Equity. As we said earlier, the risk assessment method does not rely on specific estimations of present and future earnings or dividends. Instead, a *normal market return* is developed from published data on financial returns and yields, which is adjusted by a *company-specific risk premium* or *discount.* The rationale is the assumption that a company's cost of equity in terms of shareholder return expectations is related to the *relative riski-*

ness of its common stock. The greater this relative risk, the greater the premium—in the form of an additional economic return over and above a normalized return—that should be expected by an investor. This approach makes intuitive sense and can also be demonstrated statistically. At any time, the securities markets yield a *spread* of rates of return ranging from those on essentially *risk-free* government securities at the low end of the scale to the sizable returns from *highly speculative* securities. The risk/return trade-off inherent in the many classes of security investments is reflected in this spread. *Risk* is defined for this purpose as the *variability of returns* inherent in the type of security, while *return* is defined as the *total economic return* obtained from it, including both interest or dividends and changes in market value.

A number of specific methods have been developed over the years to express the *risk premium* concept of return on common equity—which reflects the *cost* of common equity to the corporation—as a methodology both theoretically acceptable and practically usable. While no individual method is totally satisfactory in these terms, the most widely accepted is the **capital asset pricing model (CAPM)**. We will discuss some of its salient features here, but the conceptual and theoretical underpinnings are extensive and far beyond the scope of this book. The reader is encouraged to study the references at the end of the chapter for more exhaustive treatments of the evolution, theory, and validation of the CAPM.

Three elements are required in applying the capital asset pricing model approach, and each must be carefully estimated. The first is an expression of the level of return from a *risk-free security*. The purpose is to find the *lowest part* of the range of yields currently experienced in the security markets as the starting point from which to build up the higher, risk-adjusted return specific to the particular common stock. Long-term U.S. government obligations are commonly used as a surrogate for such a risk-free return. The yields on U.S. government obligations are widely quoted and accessible, both for the present and for historical periods. For purposes of analysis, *current* yields, possibly adjusted for expected changes during the next several years, can be used. Precision is not possible here, and reasonable approximations supported by the analyst's judgment are quite sufficient.

The second element is an estimate of the return from a comparable type of security of *average risk*. This is needed because the CAPM method develops a specific adjustment for the *relative* riskiness of the particular security *as compared to* an average or baseline. For our common equity problem, we can use an estimate of the total expected return for the Standard & Poor's 500 Index, a broad-based measure of the price levels of the common stocks of 500 widely traded companies. Such projections of the *total return—both* dividends and market appreciation—expected from the companies represented in the index, are frequently made by securities analysts and published by financial services and in newsletters. While the S&P 500 index provides a broad estimate of return, more specific indexes could be chosen. Again, the analyst must exercise judgment in using projections of future economic returns. The main point is to obtain a reasonable approximation of the *average return* from *average investments* of the type being evaluated.

The third element required is an expression of relative risk, which is based on the *variability of returns* of the particular security being analyzed. The definition of risk is *very specific* in the CAPM, and this has caused some controversy. Risk is *not* defined as *total variability* of returns, but rather, as the *covariance* of the particular stock's returns with those of assets of *average* risk. The assumption here is that an investor does not focus on the *total variability* of return experienced with each *individual* security, but rather on how each security affects the variability of the *total return* from the *portfolio* held. Thus, risk is a *very relative* concept in the CAPM, an assumption that may not be acceptable to everyone. We will ignore the arguments pro and con about this risk definition in our discussion and concentrate instead on *how* it is used in the CAPM to arrive at a company-specific return. The risk measure, in the form of the covariance of an individual stock's returns with that of the portfolio of stocks of average risk, is called "beta" (β). It is found by linear regression of *past* monthly total returns of the *particular* security against a *baseline* such as the S&P 500 Index. Services like Value Line provide the beta for publicly traded securities as a matter of course.

How are the three elements combined to arrive at the expected return and, thus, the company's *cost of capital* for a particular equity security? The CAPM method defines the cost of common equity as the combination of the *risk-free return* and a *risk premium* that has been adjusted for the *specific company risk*.

The CAPM formula appears as follows:

$$k_e = R_f + \beta(R_m - R_f)$$

where

k_e is the cost of capital

R_f is the risk-free return,

β is the company's covariance of returns against the portfolio,

R_m is the average returns on common stocks.

β is expressed as a simple factor which is used to multiply the *difference* between the expected return on the average portfolio and the expected risk-free return. This difference, of course, is the risk premium inherent in the *portfolio*. The β factor *adjusts* this *average* risk premium to reflect the *individual* stock's higher or lower relative riskiness. β goes above 1.0 as the relative risk of the stock exceeds the average, and drops below 1.0 when the relative risk is below average.

The calculation itself is quite simple, while deriving the *inputs* is not, as we observed. To illustrate, we will arbitrarily choose a risk-free rate of return of 9 percent, an S&P 500 return estimate of 13.5 percent, and a company with a fairly "risky" β of 1.4. The cost of equity in this hypothetical example would be

$$k_e = 9.0 + 1.4(13.5 - 9.0) = 15.3\%$$

composed of the risk-free return of 9 percent plus the calculated company-specific risk premium of 6.3 percent, for a total of 15.3 percent.

There are a large number of issues that surface when the CAPM or related measures are used to derive the cost of securities. One of these, already mentioned, is the estimate of both the risk-free return and of the average return on a portfolio of common stocks. While the return on long-term U.S. government securities is a reasonable surrogate for the former, estimating an average portfolio return is fraught with conceptual problems. If β is the indicator of relative risk, the nature of the portfolio against which covariance is measured is clearly important. Broad averages such as the S&P 500 may or may not be appropriate under the circumstances. Also, there is the problem of using *past* data, particularly for *variability* of returns, in estimating the *future* relationships that indicate shareholder expectations. Consequently, the results of these calculations, as with most types of financial analysis, should be used with caution and a great deal of commonsense judgment.

Inflation. We have been talking about costs of capital so far without reference to the impact of inflation. This is permissible because *no* adjustment is in fact, needed. The risk-free return on a government bond *implicitly allows* for the expected level of inflation, inasmuch as expectations about future inflationary conditions *affect the yield* from such securities. When inflation abates, the yields decline—as has been dramatically occurring in the mid-1980s. When inflation expectations rise, so do bond yields. The same is true of the yields from other financial instruments. If no inflation existed, risk-free returns would probably be in the range of 3 to 4 percent. In fact, not just the CAPM but all of the measures of cost of capital we have been discussing include expected inflationary effects in that estimates of future returns take these expectations into account. The spectrum of returns ranging from risk-free bonds to those on speculative securities is also consistent in reflecting the effects of inflation.

To summarize, it should be obvious by now that the cost of common equity, apart from the specific method of calculation, is generally *higher* than the cost of interest-bearing securities or preferred stocks. As we said at the beginning of this section, the residual claim represented by common shares involves the *highest risk/reward trade-off*. Thus, returns expected from common shares are higher, which in turn, must translate into the *highest cost of capital* from the corporation's standpoint. This fact will become even more important when we examine the alternative choices of financing *new* funds requirements, the subject of the next chapter.

WEIGHTED COST OF CAPITAL

Having determined the specific costs of the various types of capital, we now have the cost input needed to make some of the *funding decisions* listed earlier. But judging the attractiveness of capital investments involves another step. Because most companies use more than one form of long-term capital in funding investments and operations, and because over time, the mix of sources used for long-term financing may change, it is necessary to examine the cost of the company's *capital structure* as a whole. The result we are looking for is a cost of capital that is *weighted* to reflect the differences in the various sources used. It encompasses the cost of compensating long-term creditors and preferred shareholders in terms of the specific provisions applicable to them, and the holders of common stock in terms of the expected risk-adjusted return.

Several issues have to be resolved in determining an overall corporate cost of capital. The first is generating appropriate *costs* for the different types of long-term capital employed, which we have already done conceptually. The second is a decision about the weights, or *proportions* of each type of capital in the structure to be analyzed. The third is the question of whether to apply *market values* versus *book values* of the various categories of capital in arriving at the weighting. It is only then that we can *calculate* a weighted cost of capital that is meaningful for the intended purpose.

Cost

First to be resolved is the question of whether it is relevant to consider the *past* costs of existing securities in a company's capital structure, or alternatively, the *incremental* costs involved in adding newly issued securities. Quite often the *debt and preferred stock* section of the balance sheet lists an array of past issues, with interest or dividend rates that differ significantly from current experience. Obligations that are 10, 15, or 20 years old likely carry stated costs that are no longer relevant today. At the same time, the various methods of arriving at the cost of *common equity* are based on *future* expectations, which are not necessarily consistent with the costs of debt or preferred shares issued in the past. To solve this dilemma we must remember the principle established early in this book. The *purpose* of the analysis determines the choice of data and methodology.

Normally, the key purpose of calculating a weighted cost of capital is for use in making decisions about capital investments which are judged against a standard of return that will adequately compensate all providers of capital. Unless a company undergoes significant restructuring, the funds for new capital commitments are likely to come from current internal cash flow, augmented by new debt or new equity or both. This is an *incremental* condition in that the choices for *adding* investments are still being made. Past decisions on investment and financing are *sunk costs.* Consequently, the cost of capital measure most appropriate here is based on the *incremental costs* of the various forms of capital employed by the company.

Weighting

As we mentioned, we are deriving a weighted cost that reflects the *proportions* of the different types of capital in a company's capital structure. Again, significant issues arise. The current capital structure as reflected on the balance sheet is the result of *past* management decisions concerning funding both investments and operations. The question to be asked here is whether the types and proportions of capital in this capital structure are likely to hold in the *future*, i.e., whether they match the strategic plans of management. The intended capital budget supporting the company's future strategy, particularly when calling for sizable outlays, may indeed cause significant changes in the long-term financing pattern of a company. Also, management may choose to make gradual modifications in its financial policies which, over time, can cause sizable shifts in the capital structure. (The reader will recall our discussion of the impact of policy changes in Chapter 4.)

In other cases, management may well be satisfied with the current proportions of the company's capital structure as a long-term objective. Yet raising the incremental capital required from time to time is normally done in *blocks* limited to *one* form of security, that is, debt, preferred stock, or common equity. Therefore, in the near term, any type of capital may be emphasized *more* than the *long-term proportions* desired would suggest. Capital must be raised in response to *market conditions*, and the choice of which type is appropriate at any given point is based on a series of considerations that we will explore in the next chapter.

The analyst has to resolve the dilemma caused by such divergences *judgmentally*. Given the fact that a company is never static in the long run, the choice of proportions has to be a compromise intended to approximate the conditions relevant for purposes of analysis, and precision becomes secondary to common sense. Current proportions are a starting point, but are modified by specific assumptions about the future direction of the company's long-term financing. It may also be useful to generate a range of assumptions to bracket the findings.

Market versus Book Values

The weights to be assigned to different types of capital are clearly going to be *different* if we choose to apply current market values as contrasted with the stated values on the right-hand side of the balance sheet. Again we must be guided by the *purpose* of the analysis in deciding which value is relevant. If we are deriving a criterion against which to judge expected returns from *future* investments, we should use the *current market values* of the various types of capital employed by the company, because these values reflect the expectations of *both* creditors and shareholders. The latter certainly did not invest in the *book* value of common equity, which may differ significantly from the share value in the market. Further, the obligation of management is to meet the expectations of the shareholder in terms of the future *economic value* to be created by investments and operations, and to compensate creditors with future earnings. Stated book values, as we observed before, are static and not responsive to changing performance. The choice of market values also complements the use of *incremental* funding in that both are expressed in current market terms. The market value of common equity automatically (and implicitly) includes *retained earnings* as reported on the balance sheet. Although many people feel that retained earnings bear no cost, this is a misconception. In fact, retained earnings represent part of the residual claim of the shareholders, even if they are imperfectly valued on the balance sheet because of accounting conventions.

Calculation of Weighted Cost of Capital

Let us now turn to a simplified example of calculating a weighted cost of capital for a hypothetical company. This will allow us to demonstrate the mechanics of what we now understand to be a process that involves a great deal of judgment. We will use the condensed balance sheet of ABC Corporation (Figure 6–1), augmented by some additional data and assumptions. The company has three types of long-term capital. We assume that it could issue new bonds at an effective cost of 9 percent, and new preferred stock at an effective cost of 10 percent, based on proceeds from expected pricing in the market

Figure 6-1
ABC CORPORATION
Condensed Balance Sheet
($000)

Assets		Liabilities and Net Worth	
Current assets	$27,500	Current liabilities	$ 9,500
Fixed assets (net)	35,000	Bonds (12%)	12,000
Other assets	1,500	Preferred stock (13%)	6,000
Total assets	$64,000	Common stock (1.0 million shares)	10,000
		Retained earnings	26,500
		Total liabilities and net worth ...	$64,000

and after applicable underwriting and legal expenses. Note that these current costs are *below* the rates the company has been paying on its long-term capital as stated in the balance sheet. ABC's common stock is currently trading between $63 and $67, and most recent earnings per share were $4.72. Dividends per share last year were $2.50. The company's β, as calculated by security analysts, is 1.1, a fairly average risk factor. We further assume that the estimated risk-free return is 7.5 percent, and the best available forecast for the total return from the S&P 500 is 12.5 percent.

Overall company prospects are assumed to be satisfactory, and securities analysts are forecasting normal growth in earnings at about 6 percent. Given this background, it is possible to calculate a weighted cost of capital. As we proceed, the choices to be made will be highlighted.

The respective *costs* of the three types of capital employed can be derived as shown below. Note that we are employing the *incremental* cost of funds in each case, rather than the *past* costs as reflected in the balance sheet, where outstanding bonds carry a rate of 12 percent and preferred stock a dividend rate of 13 percent. The calculations for each type of capital appear as follows, using the methods discussed earlier:

Long-term debt: $k_d = 9.0 \times (1 - .46) = 4.86\%$ after taxes
Preferred stock: $k_p = 10.0\%$ after taxes
Common equity: $k_e = 7.5 + 1.1(12.5 - 7.5) = 13.0\%$ after taxes

The cost of debt was based on the effective cost of 9 percent, adjusted for taxes, while the effective cost of preferred stock required no tax adjustment. The CAPM was used for the common equity calculation.

The result for common equity can be compared to the less satisfactory results obtained using the earnings or dividend approaches. The *earnings approach* provides the following cost of common equity when we employ the average current market price of $65 (1/2($63 + $67)):

$$\text{Common equity: } k_e = \frac{1}{\$65 \ / \ \$4.72} = 7.3\% \text{ after taxes}$$

If we were to modify the formula to include expected growth in earnings (g), in this case, where $g = 6$ percent, the result would come close to the cost derived using the CAPM:

$$\text{Common equity: } k_e = 7.3\% + 6.0\% = 13.3\% \text{ after taxes}$$

The *dividend approach* provides an alternative result, which is a function of the dividend rate and the expected growth rate:

$$\text{Common equity: } k_e = \frac{\$2.50}{\$65} + 6.0\% = 9.8\% \text{ after taxes}$$

It is not uncommon to find that the three approaches to determining the cost of equity provide rather *different results*, as the data and assumptions going into the calculations are not the same. We highlighted the most significant issues when we discussed each measure earlier.

The *weights* to be used in calculating the corporate cost of capital depend both on the relative stability of the current capital structure and on the relevance of market values to the results. Let us assume that management is satisfied with the current capital structure and over time, is likely to raise funds in the same proportions. Let us also assume that the bonds of the company are currently trading at 123 (that is, a $1,000 face value bond with a coupon rate of 12 percent is worth a premium price of $1,230), while the preferred stock with a $13 dividend rate is trading at 119 (each share with a nominal value of $100 is currently worth $119). Table 6–1 shows the proportions that

Table 6–1
Capital Structure of ABC Corporation

	Book Value	Proportion	Market Value	Proportion
Bonds	$12,000	22.0%	$14,760	17.0%
Preferred stock	6,000	11.0	7,140	8.2
Common equity	36,500	67.0	65,000	74.8
Totals	$54,500	100.0%	$86,900	100.0%

result when we list both book value and market value for each type of capital.

Depending on the way management assesses its future needs, the proportions could remain as shown in the table, or they could be altogether different. Assuming that no significant change is foreseen, we can calculate the weighted cost of capital for *both* the market and book value, as shown in Table 6–2.

Table 6–2
Weighted Cost of Capital for ABC Corporation

	Book Value Weighting			Market Value Weighting		
	Cost	Weight	Composite	Cost	Weight	Composite
Bonds	4.86%	.22	1.07%	4.86%	.17	0.83%
Preferred stock . . .	10.00	.11	1.10	10.00	.08	0.80
Common equity . . .	13.00	.67	8.71	13.00	.75	9.75
Totals		1.00	10.88%		1.00	11.38%

The results in this case do not differ materially. Significant differences would have amounted to one or more percentage points. Given that the assumptions and choices needed to make the calculations all involved a margin of error, the results should be liberally rounded off before the measure is used as a decision criterion. We can say that in the case of ABC Corporation, under the stipulated conditions, the weighted cost of incremental capital is *approximately* 11 percent. If the measure is used to judge the expected return from new investments, it would represent a minimum standard of return from investments with *comparable risk characterictics.* Under these conditions, the weighted cost of capital could be used as the discount rate to determine net present values as discussed in Chapter 5.

COST OF CAPITAL AND RETURN STANDARDS

We stated all along that the basic purpose of deriving a weighed cost of capital was to find a reasonable *criterion* for measuring new investments by establishing a level of return high enough to compensate all providers of funds according to their expectations. By implication, projects considered acceptable when their cash flows are *discounted* at this return standard would create *economic value* for the shareholder in the form of growing dividends and market appreciation. However, using a weighted cost of capital for this purpose warrants further discussion. In this section we will examine more closely the notion of this measure as a **cutoff rate,** and then discuss the question of projects in different **risk categories.** We will also review the problem of the **multibusiness firm** in which a *variety* of *business risks* are combined. Finally, we will touch on the issue of modified standards using **multiple discount rates.** In all of these areas a balance has to be found between the theoretically desirable and the practically feasible.

Cost of Capital as a Cutoff Rate

In a *single-business company* with fairly definable risk characteristics, the weighted cost of capital as we have calculated it can well serve as a cutoff rate in assessing capital investment projects ranked in declining order of economic desirability. If *consistent* analytical methods and judgments are applied to projecting the cash flows, and if the *risks* inherent in the projects are *similar* and have been consistently estimated and tested through sensitivity analysis, this minimum return standard can be used to accept or reject the project. We are assuming that the company can finance all of the projects being considered at the same incremental cost of capital and without significantly changing its capital structure.

The weighted cost of capital works well in this ideal condition because the risk premium built into the measure, the proportions of the sources of new funds, and the range of risks embodied in the projects are all *consistent* with each other and with the business risk inherent in the company. When some of these conditions *change*, however, managerial judgment must be exercised to modify the cost of capital and its application.

One common problem even in the single-business firm is the real possibility that the *amount* of potential capital spending will *exceed* the readily available financing to some degree. If the list of projects contains many that just meet or are somewhat above the standard, they may be attractive enough for management to *modify* the company's capital structure to accommodate them. Then the weighted cost of capital will likely change. Increasing leverage may introduce *additional risk*, thus exerting upward pressure on the cost of both debt and equity. Increasing the equity base significantly will result in near-term *dilution* of earnings per share, thus affecting the market value of the stock and possibly the β of the company's common stock as judged by securities analysts. While the changes may be manageable, the point is that the process of business investment and the selection of appropriate standards is never a static exercise.

Another practical issue is management's attitude toward taking *business risks*. Knowing that the analyses underlying capital investment projects entail many uncertainties, management may wish to set the cutoff rate arbitrarily *higher* than the weighted cost of capital, to allow for *estimating error* and even for *deliberate bias* in the preparation of the estimates— not at all uncommon in most organizations as managers compete for funds—and also to play it a little safer in view of the degree of reliability of the *return standard itself*. From a theoretical standpoint, this approach may cause opportunity losses in that potentially worthwhile projects are likely to be rejected. From a practical standpoint, however, it may be deemed prudent to leave a margin for error. It is still possible, of course, to reach *below* the higher standard if a project entails many other strategic or operational advantages that mitigate the effects of marginal economic performance.

Finally, we must reiterate that capital budgeting and project selection are *not merely numerical processes*. Even in the most tightly focused single-product company, where all levels of management have firsthand knowledge about the business setting, the decision process is always a *combination of judgments* affected by personal preferences, group dynamics, and the pressures of organizational realities.

Risk Categories

By definition, the weighted cost of capital represents a company's unique relative risk and particular capital structure. Yet in a sense, this is misleading because even in the single-business company, different capital investment projects will involve different *degrees of risk*. Normally, a company encounters a variety of classes of investments ranging from *replacement* of equipment and facilities to *expansion* in existing markets, and beyond that potential *ventures* into new products or services and new markets. The degrees of risk inherent in these classes of investments will differ, sometimes materially, even though the products and services involved are within the scope of a *single industry* with a definable overall risk. Replacement of physical assets to continue serving a proven market where the company holds a strong position clearly is far less risky and permits more reliable estimates of cash flow benefits than is entering a new domestic or international market.

A common way of handling such divergences is to set a *higher discount standard* for projects that are perceived to be riskier. A hierarchy of minimum rates of return can be established, somewhat arbitrarily, that ranges upward from the weighted cost of capital cutoff point. For example, if the weighted cost of capital is, say, 15 percent, that standard may be applied to ordinary replacements and expansion in markets where the company has a position. A standard of 16 or 17 percent may be applied to entering related markets, while a new venture may be measured at a premium standard of 20 percent or even higher. As we demonstrated earlier in discussing the power of discounting, particularly at the higher rates, the chances of riskier projects being acceptable will be severely tested under such conditions. Yet such a demanding risk/reward trade-off standard may be appropriate if management's risk preferences are modest.

On the other hand, it is often argued, particularly in a single-business company, that the weighted cost of capital *implicitly embodies* the whole range of risks normally encountered while participating and growing in that business. Consequently, the idea has been utilized that the range of discount standards should be grouped *around* the weighted cost of capital. In effect, this allows the less risky projects to be discounted at a return standard *below* the weighted cost of capital, while riskier ones would be tested at or above that level. When all projects are combined, the result should be an *average* return at or above the weighted cost of capital. This would require, however, that the proportions of projects being approved in the various risk classes be carefully monitored to ensure that over time, the overall average will achieve the desired result. Otherwise the company could encounter significant deviations from expected performance.

An additional practical issue tends to support *raising the return standards* for different classes of capital projects. Every company faces a certain percentage of capital expenditures that yield *no definable* cash flow benefits. Among these are mandated outlays for environmental protection, investments for improved infrastructure of facilities, expenditures for office space and equipment, etc. A strong argument can be made that funds required for these purposes must in fact, be economically "carried" by the expected cash flow benefits from all other productive investments. By definition, therefore, the *total* amount of capital invested should provide a return sufficient to meet or exceed the weighted cost of capital. If some *part* of the capital budget is economically *neutral*, the returns from the economically positive projects will have to be *higher* to make up for such "nonproductive" investments. If management chooses to adjust its return standards for this condition, the modification will likely involve a fair degree of subjective judgment.

Our discussion has gone beyond the purely analytical aspects of the subject, and we have pointed out many *practical* issues involved in choosing and using economic measures for business decisions, of which discount standards are only one form. It is important to remember that the actual procedures employed by a company are likely to allow for a fair degree of *judgmental override* of the quantitative results of any financial analysis. This includes the *specific* return standards for capital investments, which are likely to be modified from time to time, to assist not only in *project-specific* economic assessment, but also in shifting the strategic emphasis *between classes* of investments. Senior management must, of course, continuously monitor and guide the pattern of investments they wish to undertake so that shareholder expectations are met. The pattern of investments suggested by the economic analyses and the return standards can and should be modified to fit the changing strategic direction of a company.

Cost of Capital in Multibusiness Companies

The issues involved in setting appropriate return standards become even more complex when a company has several divisions or subsidiaries engaged in rather *different businesses* and *markets* that vary greatly in their risk characteristics. While it is possible to calculate an overall cost of capital for the company, with the help of a β that reflects the company's covariance of *consolidated* returns with the market, it is far more difficult to derive equivalent cost of capital standards for the *individual* operating divisions. Most commonly a multibusiness company has a single capital structure that supplies funds for the various businesses. Therefore, capital cannot be apportioned to the different risk categories on the basis of individual cost of capital standards that employ specific *betas* and debt ratings. These would be available only if the divisions were *autonomous* companies whose shares are traded in the securities markets.

The approach often used under such conditions is to estimate *surrogate* costs of capital based on costs for comparable *independent* companies, if this is possible. In this way, modified by judgment, a series of standards can be developed for the multibusiness company that are similar to the array of risk categories in a single-business company. Obviously, the apportionment of capital in a multibusiness setting is also complicated by the practical issues of dealing with members of management who are competing for limited funds while having to meet *different* standards. Senior management must be very careful first to establish *broad allocations* of funds to the various operating divisions that match the desired corporate strategic emphasis. Then projects can be ranked *within* those individual blocks of allocated funds according to the different discount rates, and decisions can be made to accept or reject specific investments. A predictable consequence of such an approach, however, is the dilemma of having to refuse specific higher return (and higher risk) opportunities in one division, whose overall allocation is exhausted, in favor of lower return opportunities (and lower risk) in another division. This dilemma has to be resolved at the top management level, keeping in mind the strategic direction of the *total* company. The main point to remember is that senior management needs to shape the company's overall capital investment portfolio in line with shareholder expectations, so that the sum of the parts can be expected to meet or exceed the corporate weighted cost of capital standard.

Multiple Rate Analysis

One additional *technical* observation should be made here. Some practitioners argue for applying *different* discount rates to different *portions* of the cash flow pattern of a *single project* when calculating the measures of economic desirability, in order to reflect the relative riskiness of the various elements of the project. In effect, this is one more risk adjustment beyond the risk premium already *inherent* in a particular discount standard. There are many variations of this approach, although it is not widely used in practice.

It should be apparent that the uncertainties inherent in project analysis and the complexities involved in establishing the standards for multiple rate analysis may not be warranted in most *normal* business investment situations. At the same time, they may indeed be necessary in assessing *special* projects, such as real estate investments, complex leasing proposals, and other uniquely structured cash flow proposals. In such instances, some of the financial contracts *integral* to the projects may warrant discounting their portion of the cash flows at lower rates that reflect their *contractual* nature, as compared with other parts of the cash flow pattern that are subject to the uncertainties of *operating* in the business environment. These analytical refinements are too specific to be covered here, but are dealt with in the reference materials listed at the end of the chapter.

KEY ISSUES

The following is a recap of the key issues raised directly or indirectly in this chapter. They are enumerated here to help the reader keep the analysis techniques discussed within the perspective of financial theory and business practice:

1. The specific costs to a company of indebtedness and preferred securities are readily apparent in their tax-adjusted cash obligations, but it is difficult to measure the secondary costs implicit in debt service, credit-rating effects and market assessment.
2. Determining the cost of equity capital is inextricably linked to the risk/reward expectations of the financial markets, because the cost must be expressed in terms of an expected economic return for the shareholder of the company.
3. Simple surrogates for the cost of equity capital, such as earnings and dividend models, suffer from both variabil-

ity of underlying conditions, which can distort their results, and from conceptual shortcomings.

4. The link established by modern financial theory between general financial market expectations and the value of an individual company's equity securities remains an approximation based on a series of simplifying assumptions.

5. The use of a company-specific risk factor (β) to adjust average return expectations is a valid theoretical concept, but both definition and measurement of this factor remain open to disagreement and continue to pose practical problems.

6. The development of a weighted cost of capital raises significant questions regarding not only the elements comprising the various costs, but also regarding the weights to be used and the concept of measuring incremental funding.

7. The use of weighted cost of capital in setting capital investment return standards is conceptually useful for projects within a company's normal range of risk, but the measure may need modification for business investments of dissimilar risk.

8. The theory of finance continues to evolve, but as concepts generated are introduced and refined in the decision-making process, careful linkages to both data sources and to the organization have to be established in order to make practical application both understandable and feasible.

9. Objective analytical approaches to capital investment assessment are only one important input in the choices management must make. Individual and group attitudes, preferences, and judgments exert significant influences over interpretation and decision processes in the areas of investment, operations, and financing.

10. The precision implied in the calculations of economic measures like cost of capital or net present value must be tempered by the knowledge that the data and assumptions underlying them are potentially subject to a wide range of error.

SUMMARY

In this chapter we have sketched out the rationale for determining the **costs** of various forms of financing as an input in making different types of financial decisions. We found that the specific **cost of debt,** both short term and long term, was relatively easy to calculate, given the nature of the contracts underlying it in most cases. The same was true for **preferred stock.** We also found that the fixed nature of the obligations incurred with debt and preferred stock raised a host of secondary considerations that exact an **economic cost** from the company in terms of debt service and restrictive covenants. Establishing the **cost of common equity** was particularly challenging because of the residual claim holders of common shares have on the company, and because of their risk/reward expectations which are reflected in the market's valuation of the shares.

Once we discussed techniques for calculating the respective costs of the three basic types of financing, and pointed out the theoretical and practical caveats, we developed the **weighted cost of capital** as an input in investment analysis. Here we found that the application of the weighted cost of capital as a **minimum standard** for discounting investment cash flows is affected by the way project and business risks are interpreted within the corporate portfolio, and by the attitudes of corporate decision makers. At the same time, we found the approximate weighted cost of capital to be a conceptually appropriate **target** around which to build a series of return standards befitting a particular company's range of businesses and the investments and risks connected with them.

SELECTED REFERENCES

Brealey, Richard, and Myers, Stewart. *Principles of Corporate Finance.* 2nd ed. New York: McGraw-Hill, 1984.

Harrington, Diana R. *Modern Portfolio Theory. The Capital Asset Pricing Model and Arbitrage Pricing Theory: A User's Guide.* 2nd ed. Englewood Cliffs, N.J.: Prentice-Hall, 1986.

Mullins, David W., Jr. "Does the Capital Asset Pricing Model Work?" *Harvard Business Review*, January–February 1982, pp. 105–114.

Solomon, Ezra, and Pringle, John J. *An Introduction to Financial Management*. 2nd ed. Santa Monica, Calif.: Goodyear, 1980.

Van Horne, James C. *Financial Management and Policy.* 7th ed. Englewood Cliffs, N.J.: Prentice-Hall, 1986.

Weston, J. Fred, and Copeland, Thomas E. *Managerial Finance*. 8th ed. Chicago, Ill.: Dryden Press, 1986.

SELF-STUDY EXERCISES AND PROBLEMS

(Solutions to Items 1 and 2 are provided in Appendix III)

1. The GHI Company has the following three types of capital in its capital structure:

> Long-term debt at 12%   (current yield is 10%)
> 14% preferred stock   (current yield is 12%)
> Common stock with book value of $67.50 per share

Currently, the company's common stock is trading in the range of $75 to $82, and the most recent closing price was $77. The most recent annual earnings per share were $9.50, while dividends paid over the last year were at the rate of $4.50. The company's earnings have been growing on average about 7 percent per year. *Value Line* lists the company's β at 1.25, while the risk-free return is estimated to be 9 percent. Forecasts for returns from the S&P 500 are currently about 15 percent. Calculate the specific cost of capital for each type of capital of GHI Company. Assume a tax rate of 46 percent, and discuss your findings.

2. The KLN Company has the following capital structure ($ millions):

	Proportion	Existing Conditions	Current (Incremental)
Long-term debt	$250.0	7% average rate	11% yield
Preferred stock	50.0	6% stated rate	9% yield
Common equity (10 million shares)	400.0	—	Price range $45–$60
Total capitalization	$700.0		Recent price $50

The company's β is currently estimated at 1.2, while the risk-free return is considered to be 7.5 percent. The most recent estimate of the return from the S&P 500 is 13.5 percent. Develop the weighted corporate cost of capital for KLN Company, both for the existing conditions (original costs) and incremental conditions. Also use both a book value and a market value weighting for each case. Assume a tax rate of 46 percent, and discuss the your findings and the range of results achieved.

7 ANALYSIS OF
FINANCING CHOICES

It is now time to turn to the analysis of the third portion of the decisional context first developed in Chapter 1—investment, operations, and **financing.** We will concentrate on analyzing the choices available in *long-term* financing, as contrasted to the incremental operational funds sources that are used fairly routinely as part of the way business is done in a particular industry or service. We choose this focus because, as we observed in earlier chapters, the nature and pattern of long-term sources is intricately connected with the types of investments made, and is critical to the growth, stability, or decline of operations. As we said before, management must fund its *strategic design* with an *appropriate mix of capital sources* that will assist in bringing about the desired increase in shareholder value.

This chapter will deal with the main considerations in assessing the basic financing options open to management. Even though the choice between debt, preferred shares, and common equity is blurred by the bewildering array of modifications and specialized instruments in each category, we will only focus on the characteristics of the basic types of securities. We will begin with a *framework of analysis* that defines the key areas to be analyzed and weighed in choosing sources of long-term financing. Next we will look at the **techniques of**

calculating the impact on a company's financial performance brought about by introducing new capital from each of the three basic sources. Then we will turn to one form of graphic representation, the **EBIT break-even chart**, to demonstrate the dynamic impact of funds choices on changing company conditions. After touching on **leasing** as a special source, we will list the **key issues** involved in the area of funds choices.

FRAMEWORK OF ANALYSIS

Several key areas must be considered and weighed when a company is faced with raising additional (incremental) long-term funds. We will take up five of these in some detail: **cost, risk exposure, flexibility, timing, and control.** The analyst can use this framework as a conceptual checklist to ensure that the most important considerations have been covered.

Cost of the Funds

One of the main criteria for choosing from among alternative sources of additional long-term capital is the cost involved in obtaining and servicing the funds. In Chapter 6 we discussed in detail the specific and implicit costs a company incurs in using debt, preferred stock, or common equity. As a general rule, we found that *debt* funds are *least costly* in specific terms, in part because the interest paid by the borrowing company is tax deductible. The actual rate of interest charged on incremental debt will depend, of course, on the credit rating of the company and on the degree of change introduced into the capital structure by the new debt. In other words, the specific cost will be affected not only by *current market conditions* for all long-term debt instruments, but also by the *company-specific risk* as perceived by the underwriters and investors. As mentioned, other costs are also implicit in the raising of long-term debt, including legal and underwriting expenses at the time of issue, and the nature and severity of any restrictions imposed by the creditors.

The stated cost of *preferred stock* is generally higher than that of debt, partly because preferred dividends are not tax deductible, and partly because preferred stock has a somewhat weaker position in the risk/reward hierarchy, so that holders of these shares expect a higher return. The comparative *specific* cost of preferred stock was relatively easy to calculate. The dividend level is clearly defined, and legal and underwriting costs incurred at the time of the issue are reflected in the net proceeds to the company. However, a variety of specific provisions could involve *implicit* costs to the company.

Finding the cost of *common equity* turned out to be fairly complex and involved the construction of a theoretical framework within which to assess the *risk/reward expectations* of the shareholder. Direct approaches (shortcuts) to measuring the specific cost of common equity were found wanting because they did not address the company's relative risk as reflected in common share values. Therefore, we had to use a more complex framework involving some surrogates and approximations to arrive at a practical result based on the theoretical model. The approximate cost of common equity determined using the CAPM could be *directly* compared to the specific costs of debt and preferred stock, and it also could be used to arrive at a weighted overall cost of the company's capital structure. As we will see shortly, however, increasing the common equity in the capital structure by issuing new shares involves additional considerations. The incremental shares *dilute* earnings per share, require additional and even growing dividends where these are paid, and, of course, cause change in the capital structure itself. Such effects amount to *implicit* economic costs or advantages in the funding picture.

Risk Exposure

If we use *variability of earnings* as a working definition of risk, we find that a company's risk is affected by the specific cost commitments—such as interest on debt, or dividends on preferred shares—that each funding source entails. These fixed charges introduce *financial leverage* effects into the company's earnings performance, or heighten any financial leverage already existing. As we discussed in Chapter 4, the use of instruments involving fixed financial charges will *widen the swings* in earnings as economic and operating conditions change. Management, responsible for providing holders of common shares with growing economic value, must therefore expend much thought and care in determining the *appropriate mix* of debt and equity in their company's capital structure. This balance involves providing enough lower-cost debt to boost the shareholders' returns, but not so much debt as to endanger the shareholders' value during periods of low earnings.

The *ultimate risk*, of course, is that a company will not be able to fulfill its debt service obligations. The proportion of debt in the capital structure, and similarly the proportion of preferred stock, *affects the degree* of risk of partial or total default. The analysis of risk exposure is based on establishing a historical pattern of *earnings variability* and *cash flows* from which future conditions are projected. These must take into account the extent to which a company's strategy is *changing*, any shifts in exposure to the business cycle, changing competitive pressures, and potential operating inefficiencies.

Clearly, the company-specific risk in terms of earnings variability and the company's ability to service its debt obligations is intimately related to the *characteristics* of the business or businesses in which the company operates, and to general *economic conditions*—apart from management's ability to effect satisfactory operating *performance*. The degree of financial leverage advisable and prudent will therefore *differ greatly* for different industries and services, and will also depend on the *relative* competitive position and maturity of the company. A business just starting up entails far different risk patterns for the creditor than does the established industry leader, apart from the specific industry situation.

Flexibility

The third area that must be considered is the question of flexibility, defined here as the *range of future funding options* remaining once a specific alternative has been chosen. As each increment of financing is raised, the choice among future alternatives may be *more limited* on the next round. For example, if long-term debt obligations are chosen as a funding source, restrictive covenants, encumbered assets, and other constraints that impose minimum financial ratios may mean that the company can only use common equity as a future source of capital.

Flexibility essentially involves *forward planning.* Consideration must be given to strategic plans and to matching corporate financial policies. Potential acquisitions, expansion, and diversification all are affected by the degree of flexibility allowed management, and by the funds drain resulting from servicing debt commitments. To the extent possible, management must match its planned future funds flows and investment patterns to the pattern of *successive rounds of financing* that will support them. Having future funds sources limited to one option because of present commitments poses an additional problem in that *changing conditions* in the financial markets for different types of securities may make this single option less appealing or even infeasible when needed.

Timing

The fourth element in choosing long-term funding is the timing of the transaction. This relates to the *movement of prices and yields* in the securities markets. The *specific cost* a company will incur with each option, both in terms of the stated interest or the preferred dividend rate carried by the new debt or preferred stock, and in terms of the *proceeds* received from each of the alternatives will be affected by movements in the overall securities market. The timing of the issue will therefore affect the *cost spread* between the several funding alternatives. At times, market conditions may in fact either preclude or distinctly favor particular choices. For instance, in times of depressed stock prices, bonds may prove to be the most suitable alternative from the standpoint of both cost and market demand. Inasmuch as the proceeds from any issue depend on the *success of the placement*—public or private—of the securities, the conditions in the stock or bond markets at the time may seriously affect the choice. Uncertainty in financial markets is therefore a strong argument for always maintaining *some* degree of flexibility in the capital structure.

Control

Finally, from a funding standpoint, the degree of control over the company exerted by *existing shareholders* is an important factor. As should be obvious, if new shares of common stock are issued to others, the effect is *dilution* of both *earnings per share* and the *proportion of ownership* of the existing shareholders.

Even if debt or preferred stock is used as the source of long-term funding, it may indirectly affect existing shareholders because restrictive provisions and covenants are necessary to obtain bond financing, or because concessions must be made to protect the rights of the holders of these "more senior" shares.

Dilution of ownership is a very important problem in *closely held* corporations, particularly new ventures. In such situations, founders of the company or majority shareholders may have exercised full effective control over the company. Issuing new shares will dilute both control over the direction of the company and their ability to enjoy the major share of the appreciation of economic value from successful performance. The dilution of earnings and the possible retardation of growth in earnings per share brought about by diluting common equity ownership is, of course, *not limited* to closely held companies. Rather it is a general phenomenon that we will discuss shortly.

Finally, dilution of control and earnings is a consideration in **convertibility**, a very common feature found in certain bonds and preferred stocks. This provision allows conversion of the security into *common stock* under specified timing and price conditions. In effect, such instruments are hybrid securities, as they represent *delayed* issues of common stock at a price higher than the market value of the common stock at time the convertible bond or preferred stock is issued. We mentioned this feature in earlier chapters in terms of the effect on financial ratios. Control becomes a consideration when such financing options are being considered, because the eventual conversion of the bond or preferred stock will add *new common shares* to the capital structure and thus cause dilution; the effect is just like a direct issue of common stock. The provision for conversion makes the bond or preferred stock *more attractive* to the investor, particularly if issued by a company that is growing rapidly. The investor can enjoy a stated rate of interest or preferred dividend until the market price of the common stock surpasses the stipulated conversion price, making conversion attractive. At the same time, the company achieves an *effective price* for the common shares represented by the bond or preferred stock that is *higher* than what it could achieve when the convertible securities are issued. Also, the company usually pays a somewhat lower rate of interest or preferred dividend on these instruments. Finally, the company can usually force conversion once the market price of common stock has reached the conversion price by exercising the *call provision* included in most convertible issues. At any rate, there is an eventual impact on control, earnings per share, and the amount of future common dividends.

The Choice

It should be clear from this brief résumé of the considerations involved that any decision about alternative sources of long-term funding *cannot* be based on *cost* alone, even though this is a most important factor and must be analyzed early in the decision-making process. Unfortunately, there are no hard-and-fast rules spelling out precisely how the final decision should be made, because the choice depends so much on the *circumstances* prevailing in the company and in the securities markets at the time. The best approach is to carefully consider the *five areas* we have presented above and to examine the pros and cons of each *as an input*. Needless to say, a very significant consideration is the effect of each funding source on a company's future earnings performance. In the section that follows, we will examine methods of calculating this effect.

TECHNIQUES OF CALCULATION

For purposes of illustration, we will employ the basic statements of a hypothetical company, ABC Corporation. After analyzing the corporation's *current performance*, we will successively discuss the impact on that performance of introducing *long-term debt, preferred stock*, and *common equity*, in equal amounts of $10 million each. These funds are being raised to support the introduction of a new product. Shown in Figure 7-1 is ABC's abbreviated balance sheet. The company currently has 1 million shares of common stock outstanding, with a par value of $10 per share. From the company's operating statement (not shown), we learned that ABC Corporation has earned $11 million before taxes on sales of $115 million in the most recent year. Income taxes paid amounted to $5.1 million at the top rate of 46 percent.

Current Performance

We begin our appraisal of the current performance of ABC Corporation by calculating the **earnings per share (EPS)** of common stock. Throughout the chapter, this format of calculating EPS and related measures will be used. It is a step-by-

Figure 7-1
ABC CORPORATION
Balance Sheet
($millions)

Assets		Liabilities and Net Worth	
Current assets	$15	Current liabilities	$ 7
Fixed assets (net)	29	Common stock	10
Other assets	1	Retained earnings	28
Total assets	$45	Total liabilities and net worth	$45

step analysis of the earnings impact of each type of long-term capital.

First we state the earnings before interest and taxes (EBIT), which was discussed in Chapter 1. From that figure we subtract a variety of charges applicable to different long-term funds. The first of these is *interest charges* on long-term debt. Normally *short-term* interest is ignored unless it is a significant amount, because we assume, given the temporary nature of short-term obligations that arise from ongoing operations, that the related interest charges have been properly deducted from income *before* arriving at the EBIT figure. The calculations of earnings per share are shown in Figure 7–2.

Provision is made for both long-term interest and preferred dividends. No amounts are shown, however, because our hypothetical company at this point has neither long-term debt nor preferred stock outstanding. The calculations in Figure 7–2 result in earnings available to common stock of $5.94 per share. From that figure $2.50 has been subtracted, which represents a cash dividend voted by the board of directors. We assume that this level of dividend payout (between 40 and 50 percent of earnings) has been maintained for many years. We further assume that earnings have steadily grown by about 4 percent on average over the past decade.

Figure 7–2
ABC CORPORATION
Earnings per Share Calculation
($000, except per share figures)

Earnings before interest and taxes (EBIT)	$11,000
Less: Interest charges on long-term debt	–0–
Earnings before income taxes	11,000
Less: Federal income taxes at 46%	5,060
Earnings after income taxes	5,940
Less: Preferred dividends	–0–
Earnings available for common stock	$ 5,940
Common shares outstanding (number)	1 million
Earnings per share (EPS):	$ 5.94
Less: Common dividends per share	2.50
Retained earnings per share	$ 3.44
Retained earnings in total	$ 3,440

The stock is widely held and traded, and currently commands a market price ranging from about $50 to $60, which means it is trading at roughly 10 times earnings. The latest security analyst's report suggests a β of 0.9, while the risk-free rate of return is judged to be 7 percent, and the average expected return from the S&P 500 is forecast at 13 percent.

Long-Term Debt in the Capital Structure

As debt is introduced into this structure, both the financial condition and the earnings performance of ABC Corporation are significantly affected. To raise the $10 million needed to fund the new product, management has found that it is possible to issue **debenture bonds,** unsecured by any specific assets of the company but based on the company's general credit standing. These bonds, under current market conditions, will carry an interest (coupon) rate of 9 percent, will become due 20 years from date of issue, and entail a sinking fund provision of $400,000 per year beginning with the fifth year. The balance outstanding at the end of 20 years will be repaid as a balloon payment of $4 million. The company expects to raise the full $10 million from the bond issue after all expenses, in effect receiving the par value. Once the new product financed with the proceeds has been successfully introduced, the company projects incremental earnings of at least $2 million before taxes. Little risk of product obsolescence or major competitive inroads are expected by management for the next 10 to 15 years, because the company has developed a unique process protected by careful patent coverage.

We can now trace the impact of long-term debt both in terms of the change in earnings and dividends, and of the specific cost of the newly created debt itself. We will analyze two contrasting conditions: First, the *immediate* impact of the $10 million debt without any offsetting benefits from the new product and second, the *improved conditions* expected once the investment has become operative and the new product has begun to generate earnings, probably after one year.

The results of the two calculations are shown in Figure 7–3. The instant effect of adding debt is a reduction of the earnings available for common stock. This is caused by the *stated* interest cost of 9 percent on $10 million of bonds, or $900,000 before taxes. Earnings after interest and taxes dropped by $486,000, as compared to the conditions in Figure 7–2. This drop represents, of course, the aftertax cost of the bond interest, or $900,000 times $(1 - .46)$. As a consequence, earnings per share were reduced to $5.45, a drop of 49 cents, or an *immediate dilution* of 8.2 percent from the prior level. This was due purely to the effect of the incremental interest, which on a per share basis amounts to the same 49 cents, that is the aftertax cost of $486,000 divided by one million shares.

In Chapter 6 we discussed the *stated* annual cost of the incremental debt funds, which is the *tax-adjusted* rate of interest carried by the debt instrument. Assuming a tax rate of 46 percent in our example, the stated cost for ABC Corporation is therefore 4.86 percent. We also explained in Chapter 6 that the *specific* annual cost of debt is developed by relating the stated annual cost to the *proceeds* received. If these proceeds were

Figure 7–3
ABC CORPORATION
Earnings per Share with New Bond Issue
($000, except per share figures)

	Before New Product	With New Product
Earnings before interest and taxes (EBIT)	$11,000	$13,000
Less: Interest charges on long-term debt	900	900
Earnings before income taxes	10,100	12,100
Less: Federal income taxes at 46%	4,646	5,566
Earnings after income taxes	5,454	6,534
Less: Preferred dividends	–0–	–0–
Earnings available for common stock	$ 5,454	$ 6,534
Common shares outstanding (number)	1 million	1 million
Earnings per share (EPS)	$ 5.45	$ 6.53
Less: Common dividends per share	2.50	2.50
Retained earnings per share	$ 2.95	$ 4.03
Retained earnings in total	$ 2,954	$ 4,034
Original EPS (Figure 7–2)	$ 5.94	$ 5.94
Change in EPS	– 0.49	+ 0.59
Percent change in EPS	– 8.2%	+ 9.9%

different from the par value of the debt instrument, the specific annual cost of the debt will, of course, be higher or lower than the stated rate. In the case of ABC Corporation, we assumed that the net proceeds were effectively *at par*, and therefore the *specific cost* of ABC's new debt is also *4.86 percent*, a figure which will be compared with the specific cost of the other alternatives for raising capital.

When we turn to the second column of Figure 7–3, we find that the successful introduction of the new product will *more than* compensate ABC Company for the *earnings impact* of the interest paid on the bonds. In other words, the investment project will earn more than the specific cost of the debt employed to fund it. Aftertax earnings have risen to $6,534,000, a *net increase* of $594,000 over the original $5,940,000 in Figure 7–2. As a consequence, earnings per share rose by 59 cents above the original $5.94, an increase of about 10 percent. By more than offsetting the total interest cost of the debentures of $486,000, the successful new investment is expected to *boost* earnings on common shares. Incremental earnings of $1,080,000 ($2 million pretax earnings less tax at 46 percent) considerably exceed the incremental cost of $486,000. Therefore, the investment— if our earnings assumptions prove realistic—has made possible an increment of economic value. In effect, the *financial leverage* introduced is *positive*.

Yet, several questions might be asked: For example, suppose the investment earned just $486,000 after taxes, exactly covering the cost of the debt supporting it and maintaining the shareholders' position just as it was in terms of earnings per share. Would the investment still be justified? Would this mean that the investment was made at no cost to the shareholders? At first glance, we might believe this, but a number of issues must be raised here. First of all, no mention has been made of the *sinking fund obligations* which will begin five years hence and which represent a *cash* outlay of $400,000 per year. Such principal payments are not tax deductible and must be paid out of the cash flow generated by the company. Thus, debt service will amount to 40 cents per share over and above the interest cost. This amount is therefore *no longer available* for dividends or other corporate purposes, because it is committed to the repayment of principal. If we suppose that earnings from the investment exactly equal the interest cost of the debt, how would the company repay the principal? At what point are the shareholders better off than they were before?

There is an obvious *fallacy* in this line of discussion. It stems from the use of *accounting earnings* to represent the benefits of the project and comparing these to the *aftertax cost* of the debt capital used to finance it. This is *not* a proper economic comparison, as we pointed out in Chapter 5. Only a time-adjusted cash flow analysis can determine the cost/benefit trade-off. We could say that the project was exactly yielding the *specific cost* of the debt capital associated with it *only* if the net present value of the project were *exactly zero* when we discount the *incremental annual cash flows* at 4.86 percent. This would then represent an internal rate of return of 4.86 percent, a level of economic performance that would scarcely be acceptable to management. Yet even under that condition, the project's *cash flows* (as contrasted to the accounting profit registered in the operating statement) would have to be *higher* than the $486,000 aftertax earnings required to pay only the interest on the bonds. This must be so because under the present value framework of investment analysis, the incremental *cash flows* associated with a project must be sufficient to not only to provide the specified return but also to *amortize* the investment itself. We demonstrated this fact earlier in Chapter 5.

Let us now return to the *purpose* of the framework we are using here. This analysis is *not* made to judge the *desirability of the investment*—we must assume that this had been adequately done by management. Instead, we are interested only in which *form of financing* is most advantageous for the company under the circumstances presented. In this context, the impact of each alternative on the company's earnings is only one aspect in deciding on new funding. In the case of debt, which under normal conditions is the lowest cost alternative, we would indeed expect a financial *leverage effect* in favor of the shareholder. When the project was chosen, it must have met a standard based approximately on the weighted cost of capital—a standard which *far exceeds* the cost of debt capital alone.

The introduction of debt, in summary, *immediately dilutes* earnings per share, and this is followed by a *boost* in earnings per share as the project's reported accounting earnings *exceed* the interest cost reflected in the company's income statement. The company must allow for the future sinking fund payments from a *cash planning* standpoint, because beginning with the fifth year, 40 cents per share of the company's cash flow will be committed annually to repayment of principal. It will be useful to examine the implications of these facts under a variety of conditions, that is, the risk posed by *earnings fluctuations* in both the basic business and in the incremental profit contribution of the new product, which we have assumed to be successful. We will take such variations into account later.

Preferred Stock in the Capital Structure

ABC Corporation could also meet its long-term financing needs with an issue of $10 million of preferred stock, at $100 per share, carrying a stated dividend rate of 10 percent. For simplicity, we will again assume that the net proceeds to the company will be equivalent to the nominal price of $100, after legal and issuing expenses. An analysis of the conditions before and after the introduction of the new product project is given in Figure 7-4.

This time we find a *more severe drop* in the earnings available for common stock, due to the impact of the preferred dividends of $1 million per year. Not only is the stated cost (as well as the specific cost, given that the net proceeds were again at par) of the new preferred stock *higher* by one percentage point than the stated cost of the bonds, but also the dividends paid on the preferred stock are *not tax deductible*. In fact, we are dealing with an alternative which costs, in comparable terms, *10 percent* after taxes versus *4.86 percent* after taxes for the debt alternative. Therefore, the *immediate dilution* in earnings

Figure 7–4
ABC CORPORATION
Earnings per Share with New Preferred Issue
($000, except per share figures)

	Before New Product	With New Product
Earnings before interest and taxes (EBIT)	$11,000	$13,000
Less: Interest charges on long-term debt	–0–	–0–
Earnings before income taxes	11,000	13,000
Less: Federal income taxes at 46%	5,060	5,980
Earnings after income taxes	5,940	7,020
Less: Preferred dividends	1,000	1,000
Earnings available for common stock	$ 4,940	$ 6,020
Common shares outstanding (number)	1 million	1 million
Earnings per share (EPS)	$ 4.94	$ 6.02
Less: Common dividends per share	2.50	2.50
Retained earnings per share	$ 2.44	$ 3.52
Retained earnings in total	$ 2,440	$ 3,520
Original EPS (Figure 7–2).........................	$ 5.94	$ 5.94
Change in EPS	– 1.00	+ 0.08
Percent change in EPS	– 16.8%	+ 1.3%

with the preferred issue is $1 per share, or 16.8 percent, when compared to the starting position. Over time, as the earnings from the new product are realized, the eventual increase in earnings per share amounts to only 8 cents, or a slight improvement of 1.3 percent. The $1 million annual commitment of aftertax funds for dividends leaves very little room for any *net gain* in reported profit from the earnings generated by the investment—which are estimated as $2 million before taxes and $1,080,000 after taxes.

In this situation, the assumed conditions allow for very limited financial leverage. Only little more than a 1 percent rise in earnings per share is achieved over the starting level, inasmuch as the fixed financing costs introduced have more than doubled when compared to the effect with the bond alternative. Earnings per share would be *unchanged* if the product were to achieve minimum earnings that represent the pretax cost of the preferred dividends:

$$\frac{\$1,000,000}{(1 - .46)} = \$1,851,852$$

At that level, the incremental earnings from the new product would just *offset* incremental financing cost for a *break-even* situation. Note that this sizable earnings requirement is twice as large as the $900,000 pretax interest cost with the bond alternative.

Common Stock in the Capital Structure

When ABC considers a new issue of common stock as the third alternative for raising $10 million, the impact on earnings is even *more severe*. Let us assume that ABC Corporation will issue 220,000 new shares at a net price to the company of $45.45 after underwriters' fees and legal expenses are met. Such a discount from the current market price of $50 should ensure the successful placement of the issue. The number of shares outstanding thus increases by 22 percent over the current 1 million shares. In Figure 7–5 we have shown the impact on earnings as we did for the other two alternatives.

Figure 7–5
ABC CORPORATION
Earnings per Share with New Common Stock Issue
($000, except per share figures)

	Before New Product	With New Product
Earnings before interest and taxes (EBIT)	$11,000	$13,000
Less: Interest charges on long-term debt	–0–	–0–
Earnings before income taxes	11,000	13,000
Less: Federal income taxes at 46%	5,060	5,980
Earnings after income taxes	5,940	7,020
Less: Preferred dividends	–0–	–0–
Earnings available for common stock	$ 5,940	$ 7,020
Common shares outstanding (number)	1.22 million	1.22 million
Earnings per share (EPS)	$ 4.87	$ 5.75
Less: Common dividends per share	2.50	2.50
Retained earnings per share	$ 2.37	$ 3.25
Retained earnings in total	$ 2,890	$ 3,970
Original EPS (Figure 7–2)	$ 5.94	$ 5.94
Change in EPS	– 1.07	– 0.19
Percent change in EPS	– 18.0%	– 3.2%

We observe that *immediate dilution* is a full $1.07 per share, a drop of 18 percent, which is the *highest* impact of the three choices analyzed. Common stock, in terms of this comparison, is surely the *costliest* form of capital—if only because it results in the greatest immediate dilution in the earnings of current shareholders. Moreover, there will also be an annual cash drain of at least $550,000 in aftertax earnings, if the current level of annual dividends on common stock is maintained. Further, we can project that this cash drain could *grow* at the historical earnings growth rate of 4 percent per year. This assumption will hold if the directors continue their policy of declaring regular cash dividends at a fairly constant *payout rate* from future earnings that continue growing. For the present, the pretax earnings required to *cover* the $2.50 per share dividend is:

$$\$2.50 \times 220,000 \text{ shares} = \$550,000 \text{ (after taxes)}$$
$$\frac{\$550,000}{(1 - .46)} = \$1,018,518 \text{ (before taxes)}$$

We can directly compare this earnings requirement of about $1 million for the common stock alternative, to the bond requirement of $0.9 million and the preferred stock requirement of $1.85 million. From both an earnings and a *cash planning* standpoint, these amounts are clearly significant.

Further, the effect of *immediate dilution* of earnings is only part of the consideration. There will be a second-stage effect of *continuing dilution*, because the new shares created, in contrast to the case with the other two types of capital, represent an *ongoing claim* on corporate earnings equal to that of the existing shares. Thus, the rate of growth in earnings per share experienced to date will be *slowed* in the future, merely because *more* shares will be outstanding—unless, of course, the earnings from investment of the proceeds are *superior* in level and growth to existing earnings.

When we turn to the second column of Figure 7–5, it is quite apparent that despite the incremental earnings contributed by the new product, *net dilution* of earnings per share in the amount of 19 cents, or 3.2 percent will in fact, *continue*. The contribution to reported earnings of the new product was not sufficient to meet the earnings claims of the new shareholders and maintain the old per share earnings level. The impact on earnings of the common stock alternative thus is greater than the earnings generated by the new capital raised.

Up to this point, we have dealt with the *earnings impact* of common stock financing. To find a first rough approximation of the *specific cost* of this alternative, we can establish as a minimum condition the maintenance of the old earnings per share level, and relate this to the proceeds from each new share of common stock. The current EPS of $5.94 and the proceeds of $45.45 result in a cost of about 13 percent:

$$\frac{\$5.94}{\$45.45} = 13.17\% \text{ (after taxes)}$$

We know from the discussion in Chapter 6, however, that the *earnings approach* to measuring the *cost of common equity* for many reasons has very limited usefulness, even if an allowance is made in the formulation for expected growth in earnings.

If we employ the *dividend approach* to find the specific cost of the incremental common stock, as discussed in Chapter 6, we must relate the current dividend per share to the net price received, and add prospective dividend growth. We know that the company has experienced fairly consistent growth in earnings of 4 percent per year, and we will assume that, given a constant rate of dividend payout, common dividends will continue to grow at the same rate. The result is:

$$\frac{\$2.50}{\$45.45} + 4.0 = 9.5\%$$

As we stated in Chapter 6, however, the dividend approach is similarly lacking in both concept and practical use. Therefore, let us now use the background data provided to test the specific cost of capital for ABC's common equity using the CAPM explained in Chapter 6. The resulting cost of common equity, k_e, is approximately 12.4 percent when we use a CAPM risk-free return, R_f, of 7 percent, a β of 0.9, and an expected average return, R_m, represented by the S&P 500 estimate of 13 percent:

$$k_e = R_f = \beta(R_m - R_f)$$
$$k_e = 7.0 + 0.9(13.0 - 7.0)$$
$$k_e = 12.4\%$$

This result is the most credible one for judging the specific cost of the common stock. It can be compared to the specific cost of the bonds of 4.86 percent, and the specific cost of the preferred stock of 10 percent. Clearly, the use of common equity is the *most expensive* source of financing, and we have already established that the *dilution effect* is serious. In addition, the cash flow requirements for paying the current dividend of $2.50 per share plus any future increases in the common dividend have to be planned for. Because it is difficult to keep all of these aspects visible in our deliberations, let us now turn to a *graphic representation* of the various earnings and dilution effects to compare the *relative* position of the three alternatives.

EBIT BREAK-EVEN CHART

We have referred several times to *changes* in the earnings performance of a company and the *different impact* the three basic financing alternatives have under varying conditions. The *static* format of analysis we have used so far does not readily allow us to explore the *range* of possibilities as earnings change or the *sensitivity* of the alternative funding sources to these changes. It would be quite laborious to calculate earnings per share and other data for a great number of earnings levels and assumptions. Instead, we can exploit the direct *linear relationships* that exist between the quantitative factors analyzed. A graphic *break-even* approach can be used to compare the alternative sources of financing. In this section, we will show how such a model, keyed to fluctuations in EBIT and resulting EPS levels, can be employed to display the most important quantitative aspects of the relative desirability of the options available. As we will see, the break-even model allows us to perform a variety of analytical tests.

To begin with, we have summarized the data for ABC Corporation in Figure 7–6. The framework for graphic display of variations in these data is a basic chart showing earnings per share (EPS) on the vertical axis and EBIT on the horizontal axis. This *EBIT break-even chart* allows us to plot the EPS for each alternative under varying conditions. Commonly one of the *reference points* is the intersection of each line with the horizontal axis, that is, the exact point where *eps are zero*. These points can easily be found by working EPS calculations *backward*, that is, starting with an assumed EPS of zero and deriving an EBIT that just provides for this condition. This calculation is shown in Figure 7–7 for the original situation and for each of the three alternatives.

The calculations in Figures 7–6 and 7–7 give us sufficient points with which to draw the linear functions of EPS and EBIT for the various alternatives, as shown in Figure 7–8. We can quickly observe that the conclusions about the earnings

Figure 7–6
ABC CORPORATION
Recap of EPS Analyses
($000, except per share figures)

	Original	Debt	Preferred	Common
EBIT	$11,000	$13,000	$13,000	$13,000
Less: Interest	–0–	900	–0–	–0–
Earnings before taxes	11,000	12,100	13,000	13,000
Less: Taxes at 46%	5,060	5,566	5,980	5,980
Earnings after taxes	5,940	6,534	7,020	7,020
Less: Preferred dividends	–0–	–0–	1,000	–0–
Earnings available for common stock	$ 5,940	$ 6,534	$ 6,020	$ 7,020
Common shares outstanding (number)	1 million	1 million	1 million	1.22 million
EPS	$ 5.94	$ 6.53	$ 6.02	$ 5.75
Less: Common dividends	2.50	2.50	2.50	2.50
Retained earnings	$ 3.44	$ 4.03	$ 3.52	$ 3.25
Retained earnings in total	$ 3,440	$ 4,034	$ 3,520	$ 3,970
Original EPS change		–8.2%	–16.8%	–18.0%
Final EPS change		+9.9%	+ 1.3%	– 3.2%
Specific cost		4.86%	10.0%	12.4%

Figure 7–7
ABC CORPORATION
Zero EPS Calculation
($000)

	Original	Debt	Preferred	Common
EPS	–0–	–0–	–0–	–0–
Common shares	1 million	1 million	1 million	1.22 million
Earnings to common	–0–	–0–	–0–	–0–
Preferred dividends	–0–	–0–	$1,000	–0–
Earnings after taxes	–0–	–0–	1,000	–0–
Taxes at 46%	–0–	–0–	852	–0–
Earnings before taxes	–0–	–0–	1,852	–0–
Interest	–0–	$900	–0–	–0–
EBIT for zero EPS	–0–	$900	$1,852	–0–

impact of the alternatives we drew from the two EBIT levels previously analyzed, $11 million and $13 million, hold true over the fairly wide range of earnings presented, that is, every alternative considered causes a significant *reduction* in earnings per share relative to the original condition. There is a major new observation, however. With the common stock alternative, the slope of the EPS line is *different* and in fact, the line for common stock *intersects* both the debt and the preferred stock lines. The latter two lines are parallel with each other and also with the line representing the original situation, both appearing to the *right* of that line.

The *lesser slope* of the common stock line is easily explained. The introduction of new shares of common stock results in a *proportional dilution* of earnings per share at all EBIT levels. As a consequence, the incremental shares cause earnings per share to rise *less rapidly* with growth in EBIT. In contrast, the *parallel shift* of the debt and preferred stock lines to the right of the original line is caused by the introduction of *fixed* interest or dividend charges, while at the same time the number of common shares outstanding *remains constant* over the EBIT range studied.

The significance of the *intersections* should now become apparent. These are break-even points at which, for a given

Figure 7–8
ABC CORPORATION
Range of EBIT and EPS Chart

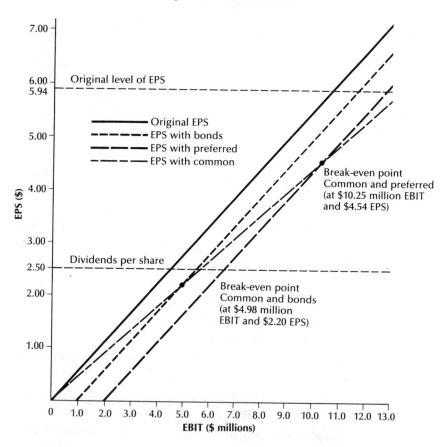

EBIT level, the EPS for the common stock alternative and *one* of the other two alternatives are *the same.* Note that the break-even point of the common stock line with the bond alternative occurs at about $5 million EBIT, while the break-even point of common stock with preferred stock occurs at $10.25 million EBIT. Below $5 million EBIT, therefore, the common stock alternative causes the *least* EPS dilution, while above a $10.25 million EBIT, it causes the *worst* relative dilution in EPS. We recall that ABC's current EBIT level is $11 million, and is expected to be at least $13 million once the new product is fully contributing its projected earnings. Both break-even points thus lie *below* likely future EBIT performance, which makes the common stock alternative the *costliest* in terms of earnings dilution. Therefore, given that the *relative earnings effects* of the three alternatives are *different* over the wide range of EBIT shown, it is not possible to assess the three alternatives without defining a *"normal"* range of EBIT for the company's expected performance.

If future EBIT levels could in fact, be expected to move fairly well *within* the two break-even points, common stock looks *more attractive* than preferred stock from the standpoint of *EPS dilution*, but *worse* than debt. If EBIT can be expected to grow and move fairly well to the *right* of the *second* break-even point, as is almost certain in the case of ABC Corporation, new common stock is not only *least attractive* from the standpoint of EPS dilution, but will *remain* so.

All of these considerations are based, of course, on *unchanging assumptions* about the terms under which the three forms of incremental capital could be issued. If we can expect any of these terms, such as the offering price of the common stock, or the terms of the bond, to *change significantly,* an entirely new chart must be drawn up, or we must at least reflect any possible discontinuities in cost or proportions of the alternatives as EBIT levels change.

The intersections between the EPS lines that represent the EBIT *break-even points* for the common stock alternative with the other two choices can be quite easily calculated. For this purpose we formulate simple equations for the conditions underlying any intersecting pair of lines. EPS are then set as equal for the two alternatives, and the equations are solved for the *specific EBIT level* at which this condition holds. To illustrate, let us first establish the following definitions:

E = EBIT level for any break-even point with common stock alternative.

i = Annual interest on bonds in dollars (before taxes).

t = Tax rate applicable to the company.

d = Annual preferred dividends in dollars.

s = Number of common shares outstanding.

The equation for any of the EPS lines can be found by substituting known facts for the symbols in the following generalized equation:

$$\text{EPS} = \frac{(E - i)(1 - t) - d}{s}$$

We can now find the EBIT break-even levels for bonds and common stock at the point of *EPS equality*. For this purpose, we fill in the data for the two expressions and set them as equal:

$$\underset{\text{Bonds}}{\frac{(E - \$900{,}000).54 - 0}{1{,}000{,}000}} = \underset{\text{Common}}{\frac{(E - 0).54 - 0}{1{,}220{,}000}}$$

When we solve for E, we obtain the following result:

$$0.54\,E - \$486{,}000 = \frac{0.54\,E}{1.22}$$
$$0.659\,E - \$592{,}920 = 0.54\,E$$
$$E = \$4{,}982{,}500$$

This result can easily be verified graphically in Figure 7–8. When the same approach is applied to the preferred and common stock alternatives, the following result emerges:

$$\underset{\text{Preferred}}{\frac{(E - 0).54 - \$1{,}000{,}000}{1{,}000{,}000}} = \underset{\text{Common}}{\frac{(E - 0).54 - 0}{1{,}220{,}000}}$$

$$0.54\,E - \$1{,}000{,}000 = \frac{0.54\,E}{1.22}$$
$$0.659\,E - \$1{,}220{,}000 = 0.54\,E$$
$$E = \$10{,}252{,}100$$

Again, the chart can be used to verify this result.

It is also possible to use the EBIT chart to show the impact on the three alternatives of any *dividend assumption* for common stock. The horizontal line at $2.50 in the chart represents the current annual dividend. Where this line intersects any alternative EPS line we can read off the minimum level of EBIT required to supply this dividend. Similarly, it is possible to reflect in the chart the earnings requirements for *sinking funds* or other regular *repayment* provisions. In effect, such annual provisions *commit* a portion of future earnings for this purpose. We develop the effect of these requirements by carrying the calculations one step further and arriving at the so-called **uncommitted earnings per share (UEPS)** for each alternative *after* provision for any repayments. We simply subtract the per share cost of such repayments (which require aftertax dollars) from the respective EPS of the alternative thus affected, and redraw the lines in the chart. The result will be a parallel shift of any line to the *right* of its prior position.

For example, the sinking fund requirement of $400,000 per year in the bond alternative would represent 40 cents per share, and the new line would move to the right by this amount over the whole range. Similarly, the intersection at the zero EPS point, currently $900,000 EBIT, would move right to a *zero UEPS* point of $1,640,700. This shift reflects the sinking fund requirement of $400,000 per year, which translates into an *incremental* pretax earnings requirement of $400,000 ÷ (1 − 0.46), or $740,700. As it turns out in this case, the UEPS line for bonds would move close to the EPS line for preferred stock in Figure 7–8.

By now the usefulness of this framework for a dynamic analysis of the various alternatives should be clear. The reader is invited to think through the implications of the variety of tests that can be applied. It is possible, for example, to determine the *minimum EBIT level* under each alternative that would cover the current common dividend of $2.50 per share, while assuming a variety of *different payout ratios,* such as 50 percent or 40 percent. For example, with an assumed 50 percent payout, EPS would have to be $5. A horizontal line would be drawn at the $5 EPS level, and its intersection with the lines of the various alternatives would represent the minimum EBIT levels for the $2.50 dividend. The analyst would have to assess the likelihood of EBIT declining to this level, and judge whether this endangers the current dividend payout.

Other tests can be applied, of course, depending on the particular circumstances of the company. The framework can also be used to work through the *cash flow implications* of each of the results, by translating the respective EBIT levels into equivalent *cash flow from operations,* as discussed in Chapters 1 and 2. This extra step would require determining the *tax shield effect* of depreciation and depletion write-offs. Computer-aided simulation can be used to make the multiple calculations required. Again it must be emphasized, however, that any *specific* EBIT chart works only under *fixed assumptions* about proceeds received and *stable* interest and preferred dividend rates. If there is reason to believe that any of the key assumptions might change, the positions of the EPS lines on the graph must be adjusted.

Obviously, any changes in the *relative* cost of the various alternatives will also have an effect. As the *spread between* the alternatives increases, for example, the differences in earnings impact will widen, and thus the distance between the parallel lines will *increase.* This simply reflects the fact that the imposition of higher fixed obligations depresses EPS. *Enlarging* the capital issue also has an effect, because the slope of the line is determined by the amount of *leverage* already present in the *existing* capital structure. In other words, if there is already some debt and preferred in the capital structure, the basic EPS would rise and fall much more sharply with changes in EBIT. Any increases in the fixed financing cost alternatives would simply magnify this leverage. At the same time, the *slope* of the EPS line for common equity is governed by the relative number of shares issued, which in turn, is related to the degree of earnings *dilution,* as demonstrated in the example.

Financial planning models and computer spreadsheets can be used to enhance the basic analysis demonstrated here. The point to remember, however, is that such a dynamic analysis basically quantifies the relative impact of the alternatives on *reported earnings.* This effect is only one of the many factors that have to be weighed in making funding choices. As we discussed at the beginning of this chapter, the conceptual and practical setting for the eventual decision is far more inclusive than this graphic expression of respective break-even conditions suggests. Strategic plans for the future, risk expectations, market factors, the specific criteria we listed, and current company conditions all have to enter the final judgment.

LEASING AS A FINANCING CHOICE

We have referred to leasing several times in the course of this book. Leasing is a *special form of financing* that gives a company access to a whole range of assets, from buildings to automobiles, without acquiring these items outright. The lessee pays an agreed upon periodic fee that covers the lessor's ownership costs, and financing and tax expenses, and also provides an economic return. The lessee can use the asset for a specified period, assumes none of the risks of ownership or technical obsolescence, and can replace or upgrade the asset, while the lessor assumes the task of disposing of the old items. The latter provision is particularly appealing in the case of computers or technical equipment. The lessee, in effect, only incurs a tax-deductible periodic expense.

Long-term lease contracts, particularly for buildings, can extend over many years and thus become, in fact, part of a company's financial structure. Current accounting practice requires the *disclosure* of lease obligations in a company's published financial statements if the leases represent a substantial commitment. While leases are not normally included in the balance sheet itself, footnotes to the balance sheet must disclose the amount of periodic payments and an estimated capitalized value of the lease obligations. This is done in recognition of the fact that lease obligations represent a *financial burden* that must be serviced just like any other form of financing. Therefore, any company that leases a significant portion of its assets has less flexibility in its financing choices. The effect is the same as that of a large outstanding long-term debt. In effect, fixed leasing charges introduce a *degree of leverage* into the company's operations that is quite comparable to leverage resulting from other financing sources.

There are many considerations involved in the choice of leasing versus ownership. We will not deal with the techniques used to analyze the cash flow implications of the many types of leasing arrangements, because they are too specialized and complex to be covered here. But we must emphasize that there is an *economic* cost in leasing, because the lessor must be compensated for providing, financing, servicing, and replacing the asset. Therefore, leasing charges must be high enough to make leasing attractive for the lessor. At the same time, the lessor is often able to introduce economies of scale that may favorably affect the cost of leasing.

The comparative analysis necessary to make the final choice between leasing and ownership has to weigh such elements as the cost to the lessee, the technological advantages, service, the flexibility of not owning, and the impact on the company's financial position. As in all financial analyses, the choice is based on both quantifiable data and management judgment. In some industries, leasing is part of the normal way of doing business. For example, in wholesaling, warehouses are commonly leased, not purchased, and in the transportation industry, leasing of rolling stock, trucks, and aircraft prevails. In other areas, the choice of leasing is wide open and depends on which financing alternative is considered advantageous at the time.

KEY ISSUES

The following is a recap of the key issues raised directly or indirectly in this chapter. They are enumerated here to help the reader keep the analysis techniques discussed within the perspective of financial theory and business practice:

1. The choice among different types of long-term financing is inextricably connected with the business strategy of a company. The choice must match the risk/reward characteristics inherent in both strategy and financing.
2. The cost of different types of capital is only one element on which a decision about new funding is based. While debt is

generally the lowest-cost and common equity the highest-cost alternative, the need to build and maintain an appropriate balance in the capital structure often overrides the cost criterion.

3. Noncost elements, such as risk, flexibility, timing, and shareholder control have to be weighed in relation to both changing market conditions and the company's future policies.

4. New financing at times may represent a significant proportion of the existing capital structure. How these funds are raised can cause shifts away from a firm's ideal target capital structure. Because a block of one form of long-term capital was chosen at one point in time, management may be limited in the choices for the next round of financing. To compensate, a compromise mix of funds may have to be used.

5. The specific provisions of a new issue of securities are generally tailor-made for the situation. Investment bankers, underwriters, and management collaborate to negotiate the design and price of a financial instrument that reflects market conditions, the company's credit rating and reputation, risk assessment, the company's strategic plans, and current financial practices.

6. As a company's capital structure changes, so does its weighted cost of capital. However, temporary shifts resulting from blocks of new capital should not affect the return standards based on cost of capital, unless there is a deliberate and permanent change in the company's policies.

7. New common equity has the long-term effect of diluting both ownership and earnings per share. This is true whether the new shares are directly issued or brought about by conversion of other securities. The decision of whether to issue new common shares thus must be closely tied to the expected results from the strategic plans in place. It also involves weighing the advantages of introducing new permanent equity capital into the capital structure.

8. Leasing as a form of financing is based on a series of trade-offs that must be weighed in relation to both the company's capital structure and its business operations and direction.

SUMMARY

In this chapter we reviewed both the **decisional framework** and some of the **techniques** used to analyze the different types of long-term funds. We focused on the three basic alternatives open to management, long-term debt, preferred stock, and common equity, leaving the discussion of the many specialized aspects of funding instruments to be pursued in the reference materials at the end of the chapter.

We found that the choice of financing alternatives is a complex mixture of analysis and judgment. Several areas of consideration were highlighted. We reviewed the **cost** to the company, the relative **risks**, and the issues of **flexibility, timing,** and **control** with respect to the various funding sources. We found that many of the aspects of the choice of types of capital involve more than quantifiable data.

We also focused on the impact of each financing alternative on the reported earnings of a company, and then developed a **break-even graph** relating EPS and EBIT, which allowed us to visually test the earnings impact of the alternatives over the whole dynamic range of potential earnings levels. This simple model suggested the potential use of broader financial models or computer spreadsheets with which to stimulate more fully the impact of alternative financing packages or changing conditions. Last, we briefly examined the key aspects of **leasing** as a specialized form of financing and suggested the kind of analytical considerations applicable to that subject.

SELECTED REFERENCES

Brealey, Richard, and Myers, Stewart. *Principles of Corporate Finance.* 2nd ed. New York: McGraw-Hill, 1984.

Donaldson, Gordon. "New Framework for Corporate Debt Policy." *Harvard Business Review,* September–October 1978, pp. 149–64.

Fruhan, William E., Jr. *Financial Strategy.* Homewood, Ill.: Richard D. Irwin, 1979.

Piper, Thomas R., and Weinhold, Wolf A. "How Much Debt Is Right for Your Company?" *Harvard Business Review,* July–August 1982, pp. 106–14.

Pringle, John J., and Harris, Robert S. *Essentials of Managerial Finance.* Glenview, Ill.: Scott, Foresman, 1984.

Van Horne, James C. *Financial Management and Policy.* 7th ed. Englewood Cliffs, N.J.: Prentice-Hall, 1986.

Weston, J. Fred, and Copeland, Thomas E. *Managerial Finance.* 8th ed. Chicago: Dryden Press, 1986.

SELF-STUDY EXERCISES AND PROBLEMS

(Solutions to Items 1 and 3 are provided in Appendix III)

1. The ABC Corporation is planning the financing of a major expansion program for late 1987. Common stock has been chosen as the vehicle, and the 50,000 shares to be issued in addition to the 300,000 shares outstanding are to bring estimated proceeds of $5 million. The current price range of common is $120 to $140. The new program is expected to raise current operating profits of $14.5 million by 20 percent. The company's capital structure contains long-term debt of $10 million, with an annual sinking fund provision of $900,000 and interest charges of 8 percent. The most recent estimated operating statement of the company, which includes the additional profit, appears as follows:

ABC CORPORATION
Pro Forma Operating Statement
For the Year Ended December 31, 1986
($000)

Net sales	$69,000
Cost of goods sold*	42,300
Gross profit	26,700
Selling and administrative expenses	9,300
Operating profit	17,400
Interest on debt	800
Profit before taxes	16,600
Federal income tax (46%)	7,600
Net income	$ 9,000

*Includes depreciation of $2,250.

The company's β was calculated at 1.4, while the risk-free return was estimated to be 8 percent, and the expected return from the stock market 14.5 percent.

a. Develop an analysis of earnings per share, uncommitted earnings per share, and cash flow per share, and show the effects of dilution in earnings.

    b. Develop the same analysis for an alternative issue of $5 million of 10 percent preferred stock, and an alternative issue of $5 million of 9 percent debentures due in full after 15 years.

    c. Develop the specific comparative cost of capital for all three alternatives and discuss your findings.

2. XYZ Corporation is planning to raise an additional $30 million in capital, either via 240,000 shares of common at $125 per share net proceeds, or via 300,000 shares of 9 percent preferred stock. Current earnings are $12.50 per share on one million shares outstanding, $2.5 million in interest is paid annually on existing long-term debt, and dividends on existing preferred stock amount to $1.5 million per year. The current market price is $140 per share, the β 1.2, and risk-free return is 8 percent. The expected return from the stock market is 13 percent.

    a. Develop the specific cost of capital for each alternative and show calculations (long form). Assume income taxes are 46 percent.

    b. Develop the point of earnings per share equivalence between the common and preferred alternatives. Assuming a common dividend of $8 per share, calculate the EPS/dividends per share break-even point for the common stock alternative. Discuss.

    c. Assuming EBIT levels of $10 million, $15 million, $22.5 million, and $33.75 million, demonstrate the effect of leverage with the preferred stock alternative, by graph and calculation. Discuss your findings.

3. The DEF Company was weighing three financing options for a diversification program which would require $50 million and provide greater stability in sales and profits. The options were as follows:

    a. One million common shares at $50 net to the company.

    b. 500,000 shares of 9.5 percent preferred stock.

    c. $50 million of 8.5 percent bonds (entailing a sinking fund provision of $2 million per year).

The current capital structure contained debt on which $1 million per year was paid into a sinking fund and on which interest of $1.2 million was currently paid. Preferred stock obligations were dividends of $1.8 million per year. Common shares outstanding were 2 million, on which $2 per share was paid in dividends. The current market price range was $55 to $60, and the company's β was 1.2. The risk-free rate of return was 7.5 percent, while expectations about the returns from a portfolio of stocks were 14 percent. EBIT levels had fluctuated between $22 million and $57 million, and earnings before interest and taxes from diversification were expected to be about $8 million. The most recent EBIT level of the company had been $34 million.

Assume that proceeds to the company after expenses would equal the par value of the securities in the second and third alternatives; also, disregard the obvious exaggerations in the relationships which were made for better contrast. Income taxes are 46 percent.

Develop a graphic analysis of the data given and establish by calculation the earnings per share, uncommitted earnings per share, dilution, specific costs of capital, break-even points, dividend coverage, and zero earnings per share. Discuss your findings.

8 VALUATION IN BUSINESS

In this, our final chapter, we will return to the concept *value* in its various forms. In earlier chapters, we discussed the stated values reflected in a company's financial statements, the economic values represented by the cash flows generated through capital investments, and the market value of common equity. In each case, value was examined in a specific context of analysis and assessment.

Now we will examine the *meaning of value* as it applies to commonly encountered business situations. In the process we will not only *define* the several concepts of value, but also once again use many by now familiar analytical approaches that can be applied to the **process of valuation.** Among these, of course, is **present value** and the use of discounting, which was the subject of Chapter 5. We will begin by discussing some basic **definitions of value** in the business setting, then we will take the point of view of the **investor** assessing the value of the major forms of securities issued by a company. Next we will discuss the main issues involved in **valuing an ongoing business,** as the basis for merger and acquisition analysis, and end by describing some recent modeling efforts designed to link a company's **operating performance** and the **common share value** achieved.

DEFINITIONS OF VALUE

It will be useful here to refresh our memory about the different types of value we have encountered so far, and to state as clearly as possible what they represent and the purposes for which they may be appropriate.

Economic Value

This concept relates to the ability of an asset—or a claim—to provide a stream of aftertax *cash flows* to the holder. These cash flows may take the form of earnings, or contractual payments, or a partial or total liquidation at a future point. Economic value is essentially a *trade-off concept*. The value of any good is defined as the amount of cash a buyer is willing to give up now—its *present value*—in exchange for the future expected cash flows. Economic value is therefore also a *future-oriented concept*. It is determined by assessing potential future cash flows, including those from disposal of the good itself. Remember that costs and expenditures incurred as a result of *past* decisions are *sunk costs* and thus irrelevant from an economic standpoint.

As we shall see, economic value underlies some of the other common concepts of value, because it is based on a trade-off that is quite natural to the process of investing funds. Calculating economic value is not without practical difficulties, however. We recall that a representative discount rate (return standard) has to selected and applied to the expected positive and negative cash flows, in order to determine the *equivalence* of amounts spent or received at different times. We also recall the need for *risk assessment*, both of the cash flow pattern itself and in setting the return standard. In other words, economic value is not absolute, but a criterion based on the assessment of the *relative risk* of future expectations—in fact, economic value is closely tied to individual risk preferences.

Market Value

This is the value of an asset when it is *traded* in an organized market or between private parties in an "unencumbered transaction without duress." The securities and commodity exchanges are examples of organized markets, as are literally thousands of regional and local markets and exchanges which enable buyers and sellers to find mutually acceptable values for all kinds of tangible and intangible assets.

Again, there is nothing *absolute* in market value. Instead, it represents a *momentary consensus* of two or more parties. In a sense, the parties to a transaction *adjust* their respective individual assessments of the economic value of the asset sufficiently to arrive at the consensus. The market value at any one time can therefore be subject to the preferences and even whims of the individuals involved, the psychological climate prevalent in an organized exchange, economic variations, industry developments, political conditions, and so forth. Moreover, the current volume of trading in the asset or security will influence the value placed on it by buyers and sellers.

Despite potential variability, market value is generally regarded as a reasonable criterion to use for estimating the value of balance sheet assets and liabilities. It is also used in inventory valuation, and in capital investment analysis in the form of future recovery values, just to name the most common applications.

As was the case with economic value, there are practical problems associated with calculating market value. *True* market value is found only by actually engaging in a transaction. Thus, unless the asset is actually traded, any market value assigned to it is merely an *estimate*. But even if market quotations are available, certain judgments apply. For example, popular common stocks traded on the major exchanges have widely quoted market prices, yet there frequently are price *fluctuations* even within a day's trading. Thus, market value based on many similar transactions can be fixed only within a *given range*, which in turn, is tied to the trading conditions of the day, week, or month. For assets that are not traded frequently, estimating a realistic transaction value can become even more difficult.

Book Value

We recall from Chapter 1 that the book value of an asset or liability is the value recorded on the balance sheet according to generally accepted accounting principles. While book value is handled *consistently* for accounting purposes, it has little relationship to *current economic value*. It is a historical value which at one time, may have represented economic value to the company, but the passage of time and changes in economic conditions increasingly distort it.

Liquidation Value

This value relates to the special condition when a company has to liquidate part or all of its assets and claims. In essence, this is an *abnormal* situation in that time pressures and even duress serve to distort the value assessments made by buyers and sellers. Under the cloud of impending business failure or intense pressure from creditors, management will find that liquidation values are generally *considerably below* the potential market values. The economic setting is adversely affected by the known disadvantage under which the selling party must act in the transaction. As a consequence, liquidation value is really applicable only for the limited purpose intended. Nevertheless, it is sometimes used in valuing assets of unproven companies when ratio analysis is used to assess credit.

Reproduction Value

This is the amount needed to replace an existing *fixed* asset in kind. In other words, it is the like-for-like replacement cost of a machine, facility, or other fixed asset. Reproduction value is, in fact, one of several yardsticks used to measure the worth of an ongoing business. A reproduction value is an estimate that is largely based on engineering judgments. The estimate involves several practical problems. The most important of these is whether the fixed asset in question could—or would—in fact be reproduced *exactly* as it was constructed *originally*. Most physical assets are subject to some technological obsolescence with the passage of time, in addition to physical wear and tear. In addition, there is the problem of estimating the currently applicable cost of reproducing the item *in kind*.

Collateral Value

This is the value of an asset used as *security* for a loan or other type of credit. The collateral value is generally considered the *maximum amount of credit* that can be extended against a pledge of the asset. With their own position in mind, creditors usually set the collateral value *lower* than the market value of an asset. This is done to provide a cushion of safety in case of default, and the individual risk preference of the individual creditor will determine the size of the often arbitrary downward adjustment. Where no market value can be readily estimated, the collateral value is set on a *purely judgmental* basis, the creditor being in a position to allow for as much of a margin of safety as deemed advisable in the particular circumstances.

Assessed Value

This value concept is established in local legal statute as the *basis for property taxation*. The rules governing assessment vary widely, and may or may not take market values into account. The use of assessed values is limited to raising tax revenues, and thus such values bear little relationship to the other value concepts.

Appraised Value

Appraised value is subjectively determined and used when the asset involved has no clearly definable market value. Often used in transactions of considerable size, the value is determined by an *impartial expert* accepted by both sides in the transaction, whose knowledge of the type of asset involved can narrow the gap that may exist between buyer and seller, or at least establish a bargaining range. The quality of the estimate depends on the expertise of the appraiser solicited. Again, individual ability and preference enter into the value equation, and rarely will different appraisals yield exactly the same results.

Going Concern Value

This is essentially an economic value, inasmuch as a business viewed as a going concern involves a series of future cash flows which the potential buyer must value to arrive at a price for the business as a whole. Apart from the specific technique of valuation applied here, the concept requires that the business be viewed as an ongoing "living" system of operating parts rather than as a collection of assets and liabilities. The reader will recall our emphasis in earlier parts of the book on the fact that business value is created by a *positive trade-off* of future cash flows for present commitments and outlays. As we will see later in the chapter, the going concern value is very useful when comparative cash flow analyses, singly and in combination, are employed in considering acquisitions and mergers. The continuing challenge is to properly weigh this pattern of cash flows.

In summary, we have discussed a number of value concepts. Some were specialized yardsticks designed for specific situations. Many are directly or indirectly related to *economic value*. We defined economic value as the present value of future cash flows, discounted at the investor's risk-adjusted standard. This value concept is *broadly applicable*, and we will exploit it as we examine various decision areas where measures of value are necessary.

VALUE TO THE INVESTOR

As we have done throughout the book, we will concentrate only on the three main types of securities—*bonds, preferred stock*, and *common stock*—in discussing the techniques involved to assess *value* and *yield*. **Value**, of course, is the amount the investment represents for the investor in *present value terms*, while **yield** is the *internal rate of return earned* by the investor on the price paid for the investment. We will discuss major variations in the basic securities only insofar as they may affect their value and yield. The techniques should appear quite familiar to the reader because they closely relate to the analytical approaches used in the earlier chapters.

Bond Values

Valuing a bond is normally fairly straightforward. A bond issued by a corporation is a simple debt instrument. Its basic provisions generally entail a series of contractual *semiannual interest payments*, at a *fixed* rate based on the stated *par (face) value* of the bond (usually $1,000). The legal contract, or *indenture*, promises repayment of the principal (face value) at a specified maturity date a number of years in the future. The basic characteristics of defined interest payments and repayment stipulations are found in most normal debt arrangements. Complicating aspects are sometimes found in provisions such as conversion into common stock at a predetermined exchange value, or payment of interest only when earned by the issuing company. Such specialized features will not concern us here.

The basic value of a bond rests on the *investor's assessment* of the relative attractiveness of the expected stream of *future interest receipts* and the prospect for *eventual recovery* of the principal at maturity. There is normally, of course, no obligation for the investor to hold the bond until maturity, because most bonds can be readily *traded* in the securities markets. Still, the *risk* underlying the bond contract must be considered here, in terms of the issuing company's future ability to generate sufficient cash with which to pay both interest and principal. The *collective judgment* of securities analysts and investors about the issuing company's prospects of doing this will influence the price level at which the bond is publicly traded, and the bond is likely to be rated in a particular risk category relative to other bonds.

To determine the value of a bond, we must first calculate the *present value* of the *interest* payments received up to the maturity date and add to this the *present value* of the ultimate *principal* repayment. (The reader will recognize this as comparable with the process of calculating the present value of capital expenditures, discussed in Chapter 5.) The discount rate applied is the *risk adjusted rate* that represents the *investor's own standard* of measuring investment opportunities within the range of acceptable risk. For example, an investor with an 8 percent annual return *standard* would value a bond with a *coupon interest rate* of 6 percent annually significantly *lower* than its par value. The calculation is shown in Table 8–1. The investor's annual return standard of 8 percent is equivalent to a semiannual standard of 4 percent, a restatement for purposes of calculation that is necessary to match the semiannual interest payments paid by most bonds.

Table 8–1
Bond Valuation

Date of analysis:	July 1, 1988	
Face value (par) of bond:	$1,000	
Maturity date:	July 1, 2002	
Bond interest (coupon rate):	6% per year	
Interest receipts:	$30 semiannually	

	Total Cash Flow	Present Value Factors, 4 Percent*	Present Value
28 receipts of $30 over 14 years (28 periods)	$ 840	16.663 (× $30)	$499.89
Receipt of principal 14 years hence (28 periods)	1,000	0.333	333.00
Totals	$1,840		$832.89

*From Tables 5–11 and 5–10, respectively.

The resulting value is $832.89, which represents the *maximum* amount our investor should be willing to *pay*—or the *minimum price* at which the investor should be willing to *sell*—if the investor normally expects a return, called *yield*, of 8 percent from this type of investment. This particular bond should therefore be acquired *only* at a price considerably below (at a **discount** from) par. Note that the *stated* interest rate on the bond is relevant only for determining the semiannual *cash receipts* in absolute dollar terms. Actual valuation of the bond and the cash flows it represents depend on the *investor's opportunity rate* (return standard). In other words, the desired yield determines the price, and vice versa. This relationship also applies, of course, to the market quotations for publicly traded bonds. The quoted price, or value, is a function of the yield collectively desired by the many buyers and sellers of these debt instruments.

If our investor were for some reason satisfied with the very low annual yield of only 4 percent from holding the same bond (equivalent to 2 percent per six-month period), the value to the investor would rise considerably *above* par, as shown in Table 8–2. Under these assumed conditions, the investor should be willing to pay a *premium* of up to $212.43 for the $1,000 bond, because his personal return standard is *lower* than the stated interest rate. If the investor's own standard and the coupon interest rate were to *coincide* precisely, the value of the bond would, of course, be exactly the par value of $1,000. In fact, the quoted market price of any bond will tend to approach the par value as it reaches maturity, because at that point, the only representative value will be the imminent repayment of the principal—assuming, of course, that the company is *able* to pay.

Table 8–2
Bond Valuation with Lower Return Standard (4 percent per year)

	Total Cash Flow	Present Value Factors, 2 Percent*	Present Value
28 receipts of $30 over 14 years (28 periods) . . .	$ 840	21.281 (× $30)	$ 638.43
Receipt of principal 14 years hence (28 periods)	1,000	0.574	574.00
Totals	$1,840		$1,212,43

*From Tables 5–11 and 5–10, respectively.

Bond Yields.   A related but common problem for the analyst or investor is the calculation of the *yield* produced by various bonds, when quoted prices differ from par. The key to this analysis again is the relationship of value and yield as discussed above, and the technique used is a present value calculation that in effect, determines the *internal rate of return* of the cash flow patterns generated by the bond over its remaining life. The method is identical to that used for assessing the cash flows of any business investment proposal. The key difference is that the individual investor's calculations are based on *pretax cash flows* that must be adjusted in each case by the investor in terms of his or her *personal tax position*. Other minor differences are the cash incidence in a semiannual pattern, and the form in which bond prices (the net investment) are quoted. Published prices are normally stated as a percentage of par. For example, a bond quoted at 103⅜ has a price of $1,033.75.

Bond yield tables have long been employed to determine a bond's internal rate of return, or yield. While today personal computers and calculators have financial routines that allow direct calculation, we will nevertheless take a quick look at a yield table, if only to help the reader understand the examples by *visual* inspection of the relationships. Bond yield tables are finely graduated *present value tables* that list the whole potential range of stated interest rates, subdivided into fractional progressions of as little as ¹⁄₃₂ nd of a point. They are far more detailed than the present value tables we used in Chapter 5.

For example, Table 8–3 is a small segment of a yield table, in this case for a bond with a coupon interest rate of precisely 6 percent. The columns show the number of six-month periods remaining in the life of the bond, while the rows display the yield to maturity. The *yield to maturity* simply refers to the yield obtained by the investor if the bond is actually held *until* its *par value* is repaid at the maturity date. If the investor were

Table 8–3
Bond Yield Table (sample section for a 6 percent coupon rate)

Yield to Maturity	13 Years (26 periods)		13½ Years (27 periods)		14 Years (28 periods)		14½ Years (29 periods)		15 Years (30 periods)		15½ Years (31 periods)	
	\multicolumn{12}{Price Given Years or Periods to Maturity}
3.80%	1.224	043	1.230	661	1.237	155	1.243	528	1.249	782	1.255	919
3.85	1.218	284	1.224	709	1.231	012	1.237	196	1.243	263	1.249	215
3.90	1.212	559	1.218	793	1.224	907	1.230	904	1.236	787	1.242	557
3.95	1.206	868	1.212	913	1.218	841	1.224	654	1.230	354	1.235	944
4.00	1.201	210	1.207	068	1.212	812*	1.218	443	1.223	964	1.229	377
4.05	1.195	585	1.201	260	1.206	821	1.212	273	1.217	616	1.222	853
4.10	1.189	993	1.195	486	1.200	868	1.206	142	1.211	310	1.216	375
4.15	1.184	434	1.189	747	1.194	952	1.200	051	1.205	046	1.209	940
4.20	1.178	908	1.184	043	1.189	073	1.193	999	1.198	823	1.203	549
4.25	1.173	414	1.178	374	1.183	230	1.187	985	1.192	642	1.197	201

*Example used in previous section (slight difference due to rounding of present value factors).

to sell at an earlier date, the *market price* of the bond at that time would be substituted for par value in calculating the return. As a result, the yield achieved for the period up to the date of sale may differ from the yield to maturity if the bond is trading above or below par.

Note that it is possible to quickly find the bond's yield at any given purchase price using the tables. Conversely, it is also possible to find the exact *price* (value) that corresponds to any particular desired yield to maturity. Our example in Table 8–1 is represented on the 4 percent yield line and in the 28-period column of the bond yield table reproduced in Table 8–3. Bond yield tables provide a visual impression of the progression or regression of prices and yields which is, or course, based on their mathematical relationship. The programmed calculator goes through the same steps and formulas used to generate the tables.

Yield to maturity can be approximated by using a shortcut method, if neither a programmed calculator nor a bond table is handy. If we assume that our 6 percent bond was quoted at a price of $832.89 on July 1, 1988 (which was the result of our earlier calculation), the *discount* from the par value of $1,000 is $167.11. The investor will thus not only receive the coupon interest of $30 each for 28 periods, but will also earn the discount of $167.11, *if* the bond is held to maturity and the repayment of $1,000 is received. The shortcut method *approximates* the true yield by adjusting the periodic interest payment with a proportional *amortization* of this discount. This first step reflects the common accounting practice of amortizing discounts or premiums *over the life* of the bond. In our example, the discount of $167.11 is therefore divided by the remaining 28 periods, and the resulting *value increment* of $5.97 per period is *added* to the periodic interest receipt of $30. The adjusted six-month earnings pattern is now a periodic $35.97.

The next step relates the adjusted *periodic earnings* of $35.97 to the *average investment* outstanding during the remaining life of the bond. The price paid by the investor is $832.89, while the investment's value will rise to $1,000 at maturity. The average of the two values is one half of the sum, or

$916.45. We can then calculate the *periodic* yield to maturity (based on the six-month interest period) by relating the periodic earnings of $35.97 to the average investment outstanding, or we can find the *annual* yield to maturity by relating *two* six-months earnings amounts of $35.97 each to the average investment.

$$\text{yield} = \frac{2 \times \$35.97}{\$916.45} = 7.85\% \text{ per year}$$

This result is slightly *below* the precise yield of 8 percent per year on which our original calculation was built. The averaging shortcut will always introduce some error, because it imperfectly simulates a progressive present value structure. As yield rates and the number of time periods increase, larger errors will result. Yet the rough calculation provides a satisfactory result as an initial analytical check.

Had a *premium* been involved, i.e., had the purchase price been above the par value of the bond, the shortcut calculation would, in contrast, *reduce* the periodic interest earnings by the proportional amortization of the premium. The second example discussed in the previous section (Table 8–2) posed such a condition. The result would appear as follows, again being a close approximation of the true 4 percent solution:

$$\text{yield} = \frac{(\$30.00 - \$7.59)2}{(\$1,212.43 + \$1,000) \div 2} = 4.05\% \text{ per year}$$

In summary, bond yield calculations involve a fairly straightforward determination of the *internal rate of return* of future cash flows generated by the bond investment at a known present price. Yield and value are mathematically related, and this relationship can be utilized to locate either result in bond yield tables, or to solve the analysis directly with a programmed calculator or personal computer. Valuing a bond or finding its yield *closely resembles* the analysis of ordinary business capital investment, in that both involve a *trade-off* of current outlays for future cash flows in various patterns.

Bond Provisions and Value. The simple value and yield relationships discussed so far are, of course, affected by the specific conditions surrounding the company and its industry, and also by additional provisions in the specific bond indenture itself. The issuer's *ability to pay* must be assessed through careful analysis of the company's earnings pattern and projections of expected performance. The techniques discussed in the early chapters of this book are helpful in this process. Ability to pay is a function of the projected cash flows and how well these flows cover debt service of both interest and principal. Sensitivity analysis based on high and low estimates of performance can be useful here.

Variations in the bond indenture agreement will also affect the value and the yield earned. We will refer only to the major types of bond variations here. **Mortgage bonds** are secured by specific assets of the issuing firm. Because of this relationship, the bondholders have a cushion against default on the principal. As a result of the reduced risk, the coupon interest rate offered with mortgage bonds may be slightly lower than that of unsecured debenture bonds and the yield to the investor is reduced. **Income bonds** are at the other extreme on the risk spectrum because they are not only unsecured, but also pay interest *only if* the earnings of the company reach a specified minimum level. Their yield levels will be correspondingly high. **Convertible bonds,** as we already observed, add the attraction of eventual participation in the potential market appreciation of common stock for which they can be exchanged at a set price. Their coupon rate of interest may therefore be somewhat lower than that of a "straight" bond. The value of these bonds is affected by the market's assessment of the likely performance of the common stock and by the gap between the stipulated conversion price and the current price of the common stock, apart from the coupon interest the bond pays semiannually. Normally, the conversion price is set *higher* than the market value of the common stock at the time the bond is issued, to build in the attraction of expected value growth. Conversion is at the investor's discretion, although the indenture usually stipulates a time limit as well as the right of the issuing company to *call* the bonds for redemption at a slight premium price after a certain date, thus forcing the investor to act. As common share prices approach and surpass the conversion price, the bond's value will rise above par because of the value of the equivalent common shares the bond represents.

A fairly recent phenomenon in the bond markets is the appearance of so-called "**junk bonds,**" which are often used to underwrite the financing of company takeovers that involve a high degree of financial leverage. The bonds are "junk" in that they are *subordinate* to (ranking below) the claims of other creditors in case of default and are often sold under highly risky circumstances, because the amount of indebtedness involved in some of these transactions exceeds what are normally considered prudent levels. The yields provided by these unsecured instruments are usually commensurate with the high risk perceived by investors.

Many other modifications and provisions are possible to tailor bonds of various types to the needs of the issuing company and to the conditions prevailing in the securities markets. The possible variations in bond provisions and their impact on value and yield call for careful judgments that go *beyond* the direct analytical techniques we discussed, which are but the starting point. No hard-and-fast rules exist for mechanically weighing all aspects of bond valuation. In the final analysis, value and yield must be adjusted with due regard to the investor's *economic* and *risk preferences,* in line with his or her *specific objectives* in owning debt instruments. The references listed at the end of the chapter cover these aspects in greater detail.

Preferred Stock Values

By its very nature, preferred stock represents a middle ground between debt and common equity ownership. The obligation provides a series of cash dividend payments, but normally has *no specific provision* (or expectation) for repayment of the par value of the stock. However, at times, preferred stock carries a **call provision,** which allows the issuing company to *retire* part or all of the stock during a specific time period by paying a small premium over the stated value of the stock. While the investor in preferred shares enjoys a "preferential" position over the holder of common stock with regard to current dividends and also to recovery of principal in the case of liquidation of the enterprise, preferred dividends *may not be paid* if company performance is poor. Such an event will, of course, affect the value of the stock. Preferred dividends, like common dividends, are declared at the discretion of the issuing firm's board of directors and may *not* be made up if missed, unless the preferred issue carries specific legal requirements to the contrary. Such provisions, for example, may call for **cumulating** past unpaid dividends until the company is in a profit position so that it can afford to declare dividends of any kind. Particularly in the case of new companies, preferred stocks may also carry a **participaton** feature, which requires the board of directors to declare preferred dividends that are *higher* than the stated rate if earnings exceed a stipulated minimum level. But these are two special situations that are not normally encountered.

The task of valuation of preferred shares is *less definite* than was the case with bonds, because the only reasonably certain element is the stated annual dividend, which is set as a *percentage of stated value*. For example, an 8 percent preferred stock usually refers to a $100 share of stock which is expected to pay a dividend of $8 per year, most likely in *quarterly* installments, a pattern normally matching that for common stocks. The investor is faced with valuing this stream of prospective cash dividends. If the price paid for a share of preferred stock was $100, and the stock is held indefinitely, the yield under these circumstances would be 8 percent, assuming that the company is likely to be *able to pay* the dividend regularly. If the price was more or less than the stated value, the yield could be found by relating the amount of the dividend to the *actual* price per share:

$$\text{Yield} = \frac{\text{Annual dividend per share}}{\text{Price paid per share}}$$

If the investor can expect to sell the stock at $110 five years hence, the exact yield can be determined by using either *present value techniques* or the *shortcut methods*, discussed in the case of bonds. However, estimating a *future disposal value* involves a good deal of conjecture. In contrast to bonds, preferred shares have no specific maturity date or par value to be paid at maturity. The actual price of a preferred stock traded in the securities markets depends on both company *performance* and on the collective *value* the securities markets place on the given preferred issue. This, in turn, reflects the risk/reward trade-off demanded for the whole spectrum of investments at the time. This value range will depend not only on the respective *risk premiums* assigned to individual securities, but also on the *inflationary expectations* underlying the economy, which are reflected in the risk-free rate on which risk premiums are based. Value may be a little easier to estimate if the stock carries a mandatory call provision at a specific future date and price, and if the date of analysis is close to that time.

When we look at preferred stock values from the viewpoint of investing, we should use the *investor's* own return (or yield) standard to arrive at the *maximum price* the investor should be willing to pay for the stock, or the *minimum price* at which the investor should be willing to sell. We simply relate the stipulated dividend rate to our investor's required return—relevant for the level of risk implicit in the preferred issue—to arrive at the answer. If the standard were 9 percent against which to test the 8 percent preferred, we would determine the investor-specific value as follows:

$$\text{Value per share} = \frac{\text{Stated dividend rate}}{\text{Required return}} = \frac{0.08}{0.09} = \$88.89$$

If the investor were satisfied with only a 7 percent return, the value would be:

$$\text{Value per share} = \frac{0.08}{0.07} = \$114.28$$

The judgments that *remain* to be made, of course, relate to any *uncertainty* in the future dividend pattern, and any material *change* in the future value of the stock, either because of changing market conditions, or because of a call for redemption at a premium price.

Preferred Stock Provisions and Value.   As in the case of bonds, there are many modifications in the provisions of preferred stocks that may affect their value in the market. We mentioned earlier that some preferred stocks, particularly in newly established companies, contain a **participation** feature, which entitles the holder to *higher* dividends, if corporate earnings exceed a set level. This feature can favorably affect the potential yield, and thus the valuation of the stock, depending on how likely it is that the company will reach this higher earnings level. A much more common feature is **convertibility**, similar to the feature of some bonds, this involves the possibility of changing the preferred shares into common stock. As in the case of bonds, however, the value of this feature cannot be calculated precisely. Yet, as the price of common stock reaches and exceeds the stated conversion price, the price of the convertible preferred stock will tend to reflect the market value of the equivalent number of common shares. Before this point is reached, the convertible preferred stock's value will be largely considered the same as that of a regular preferred issue, and will be based essentially on the stated dividend. Again, convertibility is generally accompanied by a *call provision*, at a premium price, which enables the company to force conversion when conditions are right.

In summary, the challenge of preferred stock valuation also goes *beyond* the simple techniques we have shown. In the end, decisions should be made after careful assessment of the relative attractiveness of the specific features of the particular class of stock and of the conditions surrounding a particular company's preferred stock.

Common Stock Values

The most complex valuation problem is encountered when we turn to common stock. We found this to be true when we examined the *relative cost of capital* from the point of view of the corporation (in Chapter 6). Value and cost are intimately related, like two sides of the same coin. The parallels will become obvious as we look at valuation more closely.

Common stock valuation is especially difficult because common shares entail full ownership risks but only represent residual claims on both assets and earning after all other claims have been satisfied. An investment in common stock thus involves *sharing* both the risks and rewards of the future performance of the issuing company. This heightens the uncertainty of potential dividend receipts and of the amount of "principal" recovered. Consequently, measurement techniques have to deal with variables subject to a high degree of subjective judgment.

The rewards of successful common stock ownership are several: *cash dividends* (and sometimes additional stock *distributions* in lieu of cash); *growth in recorded equity* through growing earnings, which in part are reinvested by management; and resulting potential *appreciation of the market price* of the stock. As we observed in Chapter 6, there are many practical and theoretical issues surrounding the interpretation and measurement of these elements. Here we will focus on ways of developing reasonable approximations of *share value*, and similarly, approximations of the *yield* an investor derives from a common stock investment.

Earnings and Common Stock Value. The most direct way to approach the valuation of a share of common stock is to estimate the likely future level of *earnings per share*, and to *capitalize* these earnings at an appropriate discount rate that reflects *return expectations* within the scope of the investor's personal risk preference. The simple formulation appears as follows:

$$\text{Value per share} = \frac{\text{Earnings per share (projected)}}{\text{Discount rate (investor's expectation of return)}}$$

We recall from our discussion of the cost of capital that there are serious practical shortcomings in using projected *earnings* to measure shareholder expectations. Unless a company continually pays out *all* of its earnings in the form of dividends—which we know from Chapters 2 and 3 to be quite unlikely for any growing company requiring reinvestment of at least some of its earnings—the stream of projected earnings is not at all representative of the benefits *in fact received* by the shareholder. Moreover, the formula is *static* unless any potential *growth* or *decline* in earnings is built in. Finally, there is the basic problem of forecasting the *earnings pattern* itself, both for the company and its industry.

A more popular approach to estimating common share value is to capitalize expected *dividends.* The size, regularity, and trend in dividend payout to shareholders has a quite important effect on the value of a share of common stock. Yet there is also a degree of uncertainty about the receipt of any series of *future* dividends. Not only will such dividends depend on the ability of the company to perform successfully, but dividends are also declared at the *discretion* of the corporate board of directors. No general rule applies—dividend policies can range from *no cash payment* at all to *regular payments* of 75 percent or more of current earnings. At times, dividends paid may even *exceed* current earnings, because the company is unwilling to cut the current dividend per share. Most boards of directors see some value in the *consistency* with which dividends are paid, and major adjustments in the size of the dividend, up or down, are only made very reluctantly.

The approach to valuation via dividends involves *projecting* the expected dividends per share and discounting them by the return standard appropriate for the investor. Several issues arise here. First, the current level of dividends paid is likely to *change* over time. For example, in a successful, growing company, the dividend is likely to grow as well. The problem is to make the projection of future dividends *realistic,* even though past performance is the only guide. If a company has been paying a steadily growing dividend over many years, an extrapolation of this past trend may be reasonable, but must be tempered by subjective judgments about the outlook for the company and its industry. Companies with more erratic patterns of earnings and dividends, however, pose a greater challenge.

The second issue involved in valuation of common stock based on future dividends is the *method* of calculation. The most common format is the so-called **dividend discount model,** or **dividend growth model,** which appears below in its simplest form. The formula is a restatement of the dividend approach we used as one way of calculating the cost of equity in Chapter 6. In that approach, we defined the cost of common equity as the ratio of the current dividend to the current market price *plus* the expected rate of growth of future dividends. Here, instead of solving for the cost of equity—which is the investor's expectation of return—we solve for the *value,* or price of the stock:

Value per share =

$$\frac{\text{Current dividend}}{\text{Discount rate (investor's expectation of return)} - \text{Dividend growth rate}}$$

This particular formula is based on the idea that the value of a share of stock is the sum of the present values of a series of growing annual dividend payments, discounted at the investor's return expectation for this class of risk. But it implies an *ongoing* series of payments, in perpetuity, and it also implies a *constant* annual rate of growth in the dividend payment. The formula also allows for the less realistic assumption of a constantly *declining* dividend. However, it is very important to note that the model would give an *invalid answer* for a company paying dividends that grow *as fast as* or *faster than* the discount rate, because then the denominator would become zero or even negative. Clearly, under such a happy condition, the investor's return expectation should be reexamined and raised, or the stock should be considered outside the investor's risk/reward spectrum.

The dividend discount model is related mathematically to an annuity formula that assumes a constant growth rate and a constant discount rate. The valuation it provides *implicitly includes* any appreciation in the future market value of the stock due to management's *reinvestment* of the retained portion of the growing earnings, which made the increase in dividends possible. This condition holds because in the model, the market value of the stock at any *future* time is defined as the present value *at that point* of the *ensuing* stream of growing dividends.

The simplifying assumption of a *constant* rate of growth in dividends can be modified if a more erratic pattern of future dividends is expected. The calculation then becomes a present value analysis of *uneven annual cash flows* up to a selected point in the future. If the analyst wishes to assume that the dividend growth rate will become *stable* at some future time, the basic formula can then be inserted and its result discounted to the present. We must realize, of course, that forecasting a precise pattern of dividends is problematic under most circumstances; therefore, the analyst should look for reasonable approximations.

The two measures just discussed did not take into account the general trends and specific fluctuations in the securities markets. However, the values of specific shares are *not* independent of movements in the securities markets, which are affected by economic, industry, political, and myriad other factors. These considerations are beyond the scope of this book. We can merely point out that the economic returns a company achieves on its investments tend to be recognized in the market value of its shares, relative to those of its competitors, within the context of overall market movements. The value of a company's shares reflects the collective performance assessments by securities analysts and institutional investors, and the resulting demand for, or lack of interest in, those shares.

Common Stock Yield and Investor Expectations.   In Chapter 1 we presented two simple yardsticks for measuring the owners' return on investment in common stock. One of these was an *earnings yield,* a simple ratio of current or projected earnings per share to the current market price. The other was an inverse relationship, the so-called *price/earnings ratio.* As we pointed out, these simple ratios are static expressions based on some readily available data and should only serve as temporary rough indicators of the investor's yield resulting from a company's earnings performance. They are useful mainly for comparative analysis of companies or industry groupings, but must be supplemented by more insights if the analyst wishes to approximate the actual economic yield of a stock. Any serious examination of value or yield relative to the expectations of the shareholder should use more sophisticated techniques, such as the capital asset pricing model (CAPM), which take into account market risk, specific company risk, portfolio considerations, and investors' risk preferences.

A great deal of research has improved our understanding of the performance of common stocks in terms of movements in the securities markets. This has resulted in refined definitions of the *systematic risk* underlying a diversified portfolio of stocks traded and the *unsystematic (avoidable) risk* of a particular security. As we discussed in Chapter 6, the CAPM relates the relative risk of a security to the risk of the market portfolio through a calculated factor, β, which indicates the *difference* in the risk characteristics of the stock versus the risk characteristics of the portfolio. These are defined in terms of the historical *trend* in returns earned over and above the *risk-free return* from the safest type of investment, such as long-term U.S. government bonds.

Thus, the expected yield of a particular common stock is the sum of the risk-free return plus a risk premium of a total portfolio of stocks, adjusted by the inherent riskiness of the particular security. The formula, already shown in Chapter 6, appears as follows:

$$\text{Yield} = R_f + \beta(R_m - R_f)$$

where

R_f is the risk-free return,

β is the particular stock's covariance of variability in returns (the specific measure of riskiness) with a portfolio, and

R_m is the average return expected on common stocks.

Fortunately, the β for publicly traded companies is readily available in financial services such as *Value Line*. Indications of the risk-free rate prevalent at the time and estimates of the return from groups of common stocks are also available in published sources.

We have only touched on some of the techniques used to determine value and yield for common stocks. Much more practical and theoretical insight is needed to deal confidently with the complex issues involved. The references listed at the end of this chapter provide greater depth.

Other Considerations in Valuing Common Stock. The *book value* per share of common stock is often quoted. This figure is the *recorded* residual claim of the shareholder as stated on the balance sheet. As we observed before, book value is an accumulation of past values and does not reflect *economic* value in the form of potential earnings or dividends. Only under unusual circumstances will book value per share be reasonably representative of anything approximating the economic value of a share of common stock. This might be true, for example, if a company has just been started, or is about to be liquidated. Under normal conditions, however, book value per share will become increasingly remote from current values, because changes in the values of existing assets are rarely, if ever, reflected in an adjustment in the books of account. A book value close to or even exceeding market value may indicate that the issuing company is underperforming, a situation that could invite takeover attempts by aggressive investors or corporations.

Market values of common stocks have been treated very lightly in our discussion, because a book on techniques of financial analysis is not the place in which to explore the workings of the securities markets. Suffice it to say here that if the basic conditions described are met, the quoted price of a stock in the securities markets can reasonably be assumed to represent its underlying economic value based on the current and prospective performance of a company. First, a fairly sizable amount of the stock should be *traded frequently*. Second, share ownership should ideally be *widespread*, so that trading does not involve moving large blocks of shares among a small number of concerned parties. Third, the stock should be publicly traded on at least one *recognized exchange*, or be part of the important *over-the-counter market*.

Even if all of these conditions are met, the market value of a stock at any point may not necessarily reflect the true potential of the company, because external factors, such as changes in the economy, market conditions, or publicity about the company and its industry may affect the price at which the stock is traded. To help understand this context, analysts will study the *range* within which market values have moved, preferably over at least one year, and will chart the behavior of prices relative to market averages and composite averages for the industry grouping. One example is the charting in Value Line.

VALUING AN ONGOING BUSINESS

It is often necessary to find the total value of a business as an ongoing entity when its purchase or sale is being considered. The wave of *acquisitions and mergers* in the 1980s involved thousands upon thousands of such valuations. A similar type of valuation may be used when a company, for purposes of internal *restructuring*, disposes of certain product lines or operating divisions. The buyers may be other companies, groups of investors, or even the existing management who may want to acquire the division through a "leveraged buyout." Regardless of the form of the purchase, sale, or restructuring, both the buyer and the seller need to arrive at a reasonable approximation of the *economic value* of the business as a going concern.

Valuing Business Cash Flows

In essence, an ongoing business represents a series of future cash flows. Thus, *present value methods*, discussed in Chapter 5, are applicable here, just as they would be if the analyst were calculating the desirability of a capital investment project. To begin with, the aftertax *earnings* of the business must be *forecast* for a reasonable number of years in the future. The simplest way to do this, of course, would be to take the current level of earnings as constant and project future years accordingly. Under most circumstances, however, such a simplification would not be realistic. If earnings can be expected to grow or decline, or to follow a pronounced cyclical pattern, it is necessary to make a year-by-year projection for as far in the future as possible, given uncertain conditions.

The second step is to *convert* the earnings pattern into *cash flows*, by adjusting the aftertax earnings for depreciation and amortization write-offs, as we discussed in Chapters 2 and 5. The third step is to determine the future *capital outlays* expected to be made to support both the present level of earnings and any anticipated changes in operations. To some extent, such estimates are quite speculative, yet it is normally unrealistic to assume that the earnings of a going business will continue even at present levels *without* the periodic infusion of capital for replacement and upgrading of equipment, not to mention for supporting growth. A simplifying assumption commonly used to project these capital expenditures is that to maintain the present level of earnings, an amount close or equal to *annual depreciation* must be *reinvested* each year. The estimated capital outlays for expansion and their effect on earnings are dealt with as separate and distinct, as are the ensuing cash inflows. We made such an assumption in the growth model in Chapter 4.

The final step in valuing an ongoing business involves *truncating* the analysis after an appropriate number of years and deriving a *terminal value* (market value) for the business at that point. By definition, that terminal value would be the sum of the present values of all future cash flows from that point on. But the difficulty of forecasting operations *beyond* the end of the period chosen for the analysis calls for finding a short-cut answer for the terminal value. A common way of dealing with the problem is to use a simple *earnings multiple* at that point, i.e., to set the value of the business in year 6 or 10, or whatever cutoff point is desired, at 8, 10, or 15 times the aftertax earnings in that year. The multiple chosen will depend on the nature of the business and the trends in the industry it represents. Because of the power of discounting, such an approximation of terminal value will generally suffice.

The approach appears as follows in a generalized format:

Cash Flow Element	Year 1	Year 2	Year 3	Year i	Year j
Aftertax earnings	+	+	+	+	+
Add: Write-offs	+	+	+	+	+
Less: capital investments (including working capital)	–	–	–	–	–
Plus: terminal value					+
Net cash flows	y_1	y_2	y_3	y_i	y_j

Care must be taken to allow for potential major shifts in cash requirements that stem from commitments already in place, particularly in the early years of the calculation. Once the cash flow pattern is *discounted* at the appropriate return standard, the resulting present value represents a fair approximation of the value of the business. The quality of the result depends, of course, on the quality of the estimates that were used in deriving it. The analyst should employ *sensitivity analysis* to test the likely range of outcomes.

The *actual value* agreed upon at last in any transaction between a buyer and a seller will, of course, depend on many more factors, not the least of which is the difference in the return expectations of the parties involved, and the negotiating stance and skills used.

Shortcuts in Valuing an Ongoing Business

In the previous example, an *earnings multiple* was used to derive the terminal value for a business. The multiple simply indicated what a particular level of current or projected earnings was "worth." Closely related to the *price/earnings ratio*, this rule of thumb is often used as the "opener" in initial negotiations involving a merger or acquisition. Never precise, the earnings multiple is derived from rough statistical comparisons of similar transactions, and from a comparative evaluation of the performance of the price/earnings ratios of companies in the industry.

When the measure is turned into a ratio of estimated *earnings to value*, it provides a rough estimate of the *rate of return* on the purchase or selling price, assuming that the earnings chosen are representative of what the future will bring. When taken as only one of the indicators of value within a whole array of negotiating data, the earnings multiple and the related crude rate of return have some merit.

Other shortcuts in valuing an ongoing business involve determining the total *market value* of common and preferred equity—in itself somewhat of a challenge in view of stock market fluctuations—and *adjusting* this total for any long-term debt to be assumed in the transaction. At times, when no publicly traded securities are involved, the *book value* of the business is examined as an indicator of value. Needless to say, the fact that recorded values do not necessarily reflect economic values can be a significant problem. Again, no single measure has a claim on reliability.

Combinations and Synergy

One rationale behind many acquisitions and mergers is the *synergy* of economic benefits expected from the business combination. While empirical studies have cast doubt on whether such combinations are always as mutually beneficial as hoped, it is logical to assume that joining two separate businesses, particularly in the same industry, will tend to bring about some *operating efficiencies.* These might include the potential to fully utilize manufacturing facilities or warehousing space that was only partly utilized before the merger, eliminating duplicate facilities such as railway tracks or delivery routes, or consolidating certain activities, such as marketing and selling, support staffs, and administration. Other examples of operating efficiencies from synergy include extending formerly proprietary technology to all of the combined companies' activities, dovetailing regional markets for national coverage, or savings gained from improved logistics and natural resource locations. Many of these benefits can also be expected when complementary companies or even those in different businesses are combined.

The impact of synergy can be felt in two major ways: The more *direct benefits* are identifiable cash flow improvements, i.e., lower expenses that result from consolidation and reduction of facilities and staffs, and higher contribution from improved market position and coverage. The specific levels of such cash flow benefits must be estimated when an acquisition or merger is considered. Such estimates will, of course, vary in quality depending on how quantifiable the opportunities for improvements are. A *less direct benefit* is that the stock of the combined company may become more attractive to investors and will achieve a higher market price. Securities analysts and the investment community generally expect combinations considered as synergistic to result not only in a more *profitable* company, but also possibly in one poised for faster *growth*, one with a stronger market position, or one subject to lesser earnings *fluctuations* because the cycles of the individual businesses could offset each other. This reassessment may in time, lower the company's *risk premium* and in fact, improve the expected price/earnings ratio.

Possible profit improvements resulting from a business combination can be calculated to the extent they are quantifiable. To do this, we will begin with two sets of *pro forma income statements*. One set displays the projected net profits and cash flows from each company *separately,* while the other is developed for the *combined* company and includes the envisioned *improvements*. These pro forma statements then are used for comparative ratio analysis, for calculating value with various methods, and for highlighting the estimated synergistic effect in the second set of statements. It may in fact, be useful to determine *separately* the *present value* of all the synergistic cash flow benefits in the combined pro forma statements. This present value can be used as a rough guide in negotiating the terms of the merger, as these benefits may have to be considered in setting the value *premium* the acquirer has to pay. In the end, the basis for valuation is likely to be a combination of present value analysis, rules of thumb, and the effect of a large variety of conditions—both tangible and intangible.

Combinations and Share Values

When an *exchange of common stock* is involved in an acquisition or merger agreement, *two different securities* must be valued. In addition, a proper *ratio of exchange* must be found that reflects the respective values of the shares. Moreover, in most cases, the acquirer has to pay a significant *premium* (between 15 and 25 percent is the common range) over the objective value of the shares of the acquired company. This premium, of course, will affect the actual ratio of exchange of shares agreed on. While in the end, a numerical solution is applied, the underlying values and the premium will be the result of extensive negotiation and a certain amount of "horse trading."

As the two stocks are valued, any differences in the quality and breadth of *trading* in the securities markets can be an important factor. If, for example, a large, well-established company acquires a new and fast-growing company, the market's assessment of the value of the acquirer's stock is likely to be more reliable than that of the candidate, whose stock may thinly traded and unproven. But even if both companies had *comparable* market exposure, the *inherent* difference in the nature and performance of the two companies may exhibit itself in, among other indicators, a pronounced difference in *price/earnings ratios*. In effect, this means the performance of one company is valued *less* highly in the marketplace than that of the other. This difference will influence valuation of the stocks and the final price negotiated.

We will demonstrate just a few of the key calculations needed to arrive at the basis of exchange, using a simplified example. Let us assume that Acquirer Corporation and Candidate, Inc. have the following key dimensions and performance data at the time of their merger negotiations:

Key Data	Acquirer Corporation	Candidate, Inc.
Current earnings	$50,000,000	$10,000,000
Number of shares	10 million	10 million
Earnings per share	$ 5.00	$ 1.00
Current market price	$60.00	$15.00
Price/earnings ratio	12 ×	15 ×

Negotiations between the management teams have reached a point where, after Candidate had rejected several offers, Acquirer now considers a price *premium* of about 20 percent *over* the current market value of Candidate's stock necessary to make a deal. This would call for an *exchange ratio* of $18/$60, or about 0.3 shares of Acquirer stock for each share of Candidate stock. The impact on Acquirer would be as follows, at the combined *current* levels of earnings that include *no synergistic benefits:*

	Acquirer Corporation
Combined earnings	$60,000,000
Number of shares (10.0 + 3.0 million) . .	13 million
New earnings per share	$4.62
Old earnings per share	$5.00
Immediate dilution	$0.38

Under these conditions, Acquirer would suffer an *immediate dilution* of 38 cents per share from the combination. Yet the fact that the stock of Candidate had a *higher price/earnings ratio* suggests that smaller company has certain desirable attributes which may include high growth in earnings, a technologically protected position, and so on. Acquirer must consider two points: first, whether the earnings of Candidate are likely to *grow* at a rate that will *close the gap* in earnings per share relatively quickly, aided by any *synergistic* benefits available now. Second, Acquirer must judge whether the inclusion of Candidate is likely to *change the risk/reward characteristics* of the *combined* company so as to improve the price/earnings ratio—and thus help overcome the dilution.

In our example, the earnings gap to be filled is 13 million shares times 38 cents, or almost $5 million in annual earnings, just to *return* to the current level of Acquirer's earnings per share. How much in synergistic benefits can be expected? Perhaps the *ratio* of exchange has to be reconsidered in this light? But would the smaller company even be interested in being acquired at less than a 20 percent premium over market, a not uncommon inducement?

Note that a *reversal* of the price/earnings ratios in the example would dramatically change *both* the terms of the offer and the reported performance of the combined companies. At 15 times earnings, the price of Acquirer would be $75 per share, while at 12 times earnings, Candidate would sell at $12 per share. Given a 20 percent acquisition premium for Candidate's stock, the exchange ratio would be $14.40/$75, or 0.192 shares of Acquirer for each share of Candidate. This would call for 1.92 million new shares of Acquirer, and the new earnings per share would amount to $60,000,000 ÷ 11,920,000, or $5.03 per share, a slight net *improvement* even *before* realizing any synergistic benefits. In this changed situation, *both* parties would be better off immediately, simply because we assumed the price/earnings ratios to be reversed. It is possible, of course, that a company acquired at a premium, which has caused the combined earnings per share to drop initially, may *more* than offset the gap with higher growth and synergistic benefits later. This would depend on the *relative size* of the two companies as well as on the value and exchange considerations discussed.

This is but one simplified example, and thus only a quick glimpse of the nature of the deliberations involved in exchanges of stock. At the same time, we have attempted to alert the reader to the many issues underlying the valuation process in mergers and acquisitions. Analysis of such transactions always involves *careful projections* of the separate and combined earnings patterns, the calculation of *dilution*, and an assessment of the likely *risk/reward market response* (in effect, a potential change in the β) as inputs into the negotiation process.

LINKING FUTURE CASH FLOWS AND SHARE VALUE

As a final consideration in our discussion of valuation, we will reexamine the relationship between a company's operating performance and the price of its common stock, on the basis of emerging analytical methods. We will briefly discuss a framework of analysis that creates a linkage between a business's total cash flow pattern on the one hand, and the value expectations of the securities markets on the other. The traditional valuation techniques we have demonstrated either deal with individual aspects of the value creation process, such as dividend streams and current operating earnings, or arrive at value indirectly through a process of assessing risk premiums, as does the CAPM. But as yet there is no one methodology generally used that establishes a *direct cause-and-effect relationship* between the cash flow pattern of operational performance and investments of a company on the one hand, and the likely value of a share of its common stock on the other. However, in recent years a number of academic researchers and consulting practitioners have attempted to "close the loop" between cash flow performance and share values, developing a number of approaches that are based financial theory, empirical evidence, and many facilitating assumptions. The capital asset pricing model was one of the early attempts to define share value in company-specific terms, even though it established the value/performance relationship via the *surrogate* of risk/reward trade-offs of the stock in a portfolio setting.

A number of significant issues make directly linking the cash flows of operating performance and investments with common stock value a difficult task. We have mentioned all of these issues at one point or another, as they individually affected financial measures. The direct cause-and-effect linkage towards which current work is aimed, however, requires that *all* of these parameters and adjustments be taken into account *simultaneously.* This cash flow valuation framework is based on specific approaches to, and assumptions about, the following aspects: (1) expression of *investors' return expectations* related to overall market risk; (2) quantifiable expression of the *risk* premium, both for the securities market and for the particular company; (3) restatement of the company's operating performance, financial condition, and funds movements in *real* terms, that is, *adjusted for inflation;* (4) performance of the company's existing investments measured in *aftertax cash flow* terms, consistent with the framework of present value analysis for new capital investments; (5) specific projections of cash flow patterns from *future operations* and from *future invest-*

ments; (6) the pattern of *growth or decline* of the company; and (7) the overall movements of the *securities markets.*

Up to this point, *no* valuation technique we have discussed takes into account all of these factors, either directly or indirectly. However, the framework we will briefly describe below, while it has no sole claim to superior insight, is an example of the progress being made in understanding the linkage between common share values and company performance. Because the actual application involves large proprietary data bases and extensive modeling capability, we can only present a conceptual overview.

Callard, Madden and Associates (CMA), a financial consulting firm now linked with the accounting partnership of Ernst & Whinney, has developed a method for converting a company's actual and projected operating performance, financial statements, and funds flows into an *inflation-adjusted cash flow framework* that allows the calculation of *real returns* on the adjusted value of the assets employed, as well as the calculation of *real growth in net assets.* From extensive empirical analysis, CMA has determined that *real returns* (before personal taxes) experienced by *all investors* over several decades have ranged between 5 and 10 percent. The fluctuations within this range correlate with changes in the real *tax rates* investors had to pay on interest, dividends, and capital gains, as tax laws were continually modified over the decades. CMA calculates and frequently updates the investors' *currently valid real return* relevant for use in the analysis.

The conceptual framework used by CMA for valuation is essentially a *present value analysis* of the company's *inflation-adjusted* future cash flow pattern, discounted by the *general standard* of the investors' real return. In very simplified form, the key relationship of the variables used to derive the price per common share appears as follows:

$$\text{Share price} = \frac{\text{Net cash inflows*}}{1 + \text{Investors' real return}}$$

*Net cash inflows are a function of real returns on investment and real asset growth.

The framework suggests that there is a *direct relationship* between a company's *share price* and its anticipated overall *net cash inflows* (in inflation-adjusted terms). The key to this analysis is, of course, deriving the anticipated net cash inflows, in an overall inflation-adjusted funds flow sense, including specific projections of future operations and investments. These net cash flows are described by CMA as being a function of two key elements: The *real return on assets* (real ROIs achieved from these investments), both present and future, and the *rate of investment* (in the form of real net asset growth). If the real returns earned on inflation-adjusted assets are *less* than the investors' real return used to discount the cash flows, the direct relationship suggests that the company will suffer a reduction in the market value of its shares because such investments detract from the company's performance. If the returns *exceed* the standard of investors' real return, share market value should improve. Note that, for example, with this rationale, company *growth* can be *detrimental* to share value if the investments representing that growth individually do not meet the investors' real return.

The framework can be applied to internal valuation of divisions and to merger and acquisition analysis, as well as to broad comparisons of a company to its peers. The major new elements of the CMA model include consistent inflation adjustment of existing and future data, the consistent translation of operating and investment cash flows into equivalent cash patterns, and the development of a relevant return standard that correlates with market price performance. However, many analytical assumptions and decisions are needed to develop the necessary adjusted data base for each company before the method can be applied in practice. Furthermore, considerable skill is needed for the interpretation of the results. Nevertheless, the methodology is one of many efforts aimed at the problem of the specific linkage of *shareholder value* and the combined results of *investment, operating,* and *financing decisions* within a total analytical model.

KEY ISSUES

The following is a recap of the key issues raised directly or indirectly in this chapter. They are enumerated here to help the reader keep the analysis techniques discussed within the perspective of financial theory and business practice:

1. The challenge of valuation involves the dual problems of forecasting benefits derived from an asset, and of selecting a standard with which to measure these benefits.
2. Value takes many forms, but in the end valuation in business must rest on an attempt to express the economic risk/reward trade-off involved in the cash flows generated.
3. Investors approach the valuation of an investment proposition in terms of their individual risk preferences; thus, market values are a function of collective risk assessments.
4. Valuation techniques are essentially assessment tools that attempt to quantify the available objective data. Yet such quantification will always remain subjective in part.
5. While securities markets provide momentary indications, the value of a common stock is a combination of residual claims, future expectations, and assessment of general and specific risk, subject to economic and business conditions and the decisions of management and the issuing company's board of directors.
6. Valuation is distorted by the same elements that distort other types of financial analysis: price-level changes, accounting conventions, economic conditions, market fluctuations, and many subjective intangible factors.
7. Valuing a business for sale or purchase is one of the most complex tasks an analyst can undertake. It calls for skills in projection, assessment of risk, and interpretation of the impact of combining management styles, operations, and resources.
8. Shareholder value is the ultimate result of successful investments, operations, and financing carried out by manage-

ment. However, the link between a company's current and prospective performance in these areas and the market value of its common stock is neither direct nor directly measurable.

SUMMARY

In this final chapter we have brought together a whole range of concepts and techniques that give the reader an overview of how to value assets, business operations, and securities which reflect the performance of the issuing company. To set the stage, we discussed key **definitions of value,** and then took the viewpoint of the **investor assessing** the **value** of the three main forms of securities issued by a company. After covering both value and yield in these situations, we expanded our view to encompass the value of an **ongoing business.** Our purpose was to find ways of setting the value in transactions such as sale of a business, or the combination of two companies in the form of a merger or acquisition. We found that methods were available for deriving such values, but that the specific assumptions and the background of the transaction added many dimensions to the basic calculations. Finally, we briefly examined the potential **direct link between share value and total performance** in adjusted cash flow terms, as exemplified by a conceptual modeling framework designed to overcome the shortcomings of simple valuation tools. We found that there is little chance of avoiding the complexities involved in measuring value in a business and financial context—because value is intrinsically complex. But we did indicate that current research and the power of modeling and simulation can somewhat narrow the gap between guesses and fact—even if in the process, many facilitating assumptions have to be made. In the end, value is the result of multiple judgments, validated in the marketplace where buyers and sellers meet to negotiate.

SELECTED REFERENCES

Bonbright, J. C. *The Valuation of Property.* New York: McGraw-Hill, 1937. (A classic.)

Hawkins, David F., and Campbell, Walter J. *Equity Valuation—Models, Analysis, and Implications.* New York: Financial Executives Research Foundation, 1978.

Larsy, George. *Valuing a Common Stock.* New York: AMACOM, 1979.

McCarthy, George D., and Healy, Robert E. *Valuing a Company; Practices and Procedures.* New York: Ronald Press, 1971.

Pratt, Shannon P. *Valuing a Business.* Homewood, Ill.: Dow Jones-Irwin, 1981.

Rosen, Lawrence R. *The Dow Jones-Irwin Guide to Calculating Yields.* Homewood, Ill.: Dow Jones-Irwin, 1985.

Van Horne, James C. *Financial Management and Policy.* 7th ed. Englewood Cliffs, N.J.: Prentice-Hall, 1986.

SELF-STUDY EXERCISES AND PROBLEMS

(Solutions to Items 1,2,3,4, and 5 are provided in Appendix III)

1. Using the present value tables in Chapter 5, develop the value (price) of bonds with the following characteristics:
   a. A bond with a face value of $1,000 carries interest of 8 percent per year, paid semiannually. It will be redeemed for $1,075 at the end of 14 years. At what price would the bond yield a return of 6 percent? A yield of 10 percent?
   b. A bond with a face value of $1,000 carries interest of 8.5 percent per year, paid semiannually. It is callable at 110 percent of face value beginning October 1, 1999, and will be redeemed (unless called) on October 1, 2009. What price on October 1, 1987, would yield a prospective investor a return of 6 percent? What price would yield 9 percent? (Use interpolation.)

2. Develop the approximate yield (return) of bonds with the following characteristics:
   a. A bond with a face value of $1,000 carries interest at 7 percent per year, paid semiannually on January 15 and July 15. It will be redeemed at 110 on July 15, 2001. The market quotation on July 15, 1987, is 124⅛. What is the approximate yield to an investor who purchases the bond on this date? What is the exact yield given in an appropriate bond table?

b. The same bond is quoted at 122½ on September 1, 1987. In addition to the market price, accrued interest is paid by the purchaser if the trade takes place between interest dates. What is the exact yield given in an appropriate bond table?

c. A bond with a face value of $500 carries interest at 8 percent per year, paid annually. It will be redeemed at par on March 1, 2011. The bond was purchased on August 20, 1987, for $487.50, including accrued interest. What is the approximate yield? What is the exact yield, using an appropriate bond table or a preprogrammed computer or calculator?

3. The following information is available about two different common stocks, Company A and Company B:

	Company A	Company B
Earnings per share	$2.50	$7.25
Dividends per share	1.00	5.00
Growth in earnings	8%	4%
Price range	$26–$20	$60–$56
β	1.3	0.8
Risk-free return	7.0%	7.0%
Expected return, S&P 500	13.5%	13.5%

On the assumption that the companies' growth rates will continue, develop an estimate of the value of the common stock and its yield for each. Discuss.

4. The following estimates about the next five years' performance of GHI Company have been provided. Based on this information and the current data available to you, calculate the value of the company as a going business, assuming that the expected return from such a business investment would be 12 percent after taxes. Test the present value calculation against other yardsticks of value. Discuss.

	GHI Company Projections ($millions)				
	Year 1	Year 2	Year 3	Year 4	Year 5
Projected earnings	$2.7	$2.9	$3.2	$3.6	$4.0
Projected investments (including working capital)	$0.5	$2.5	$1.5	$1.5	$2.0
Projected depreciation	$1.0	$1.1	$1.4	$1.6	$1.8

The terminal value at the end of the period can be estimated at between 10 and 12 times earnings. The company's earnings for the past year were $2.5 million, and the price/earnings ratio for its industry is currently 11.0.

5. The MNO Company's stock was closely held, and the volume of stock traded over the counter represented only a small fraction of the total shares outstanding. You have been asked to develop as many valuation approaches as possible in preparation for the disposition of a 25 percent block of common stock held by the estate of one of the founders. The executor of the estate will be interested in the possible viewpoints to be taken in arriving at a fair value. The following data have been made available for the purpose:

MNO COMPANY

Balance Sheet, December 31, 1986

($000)

Assets

Current assets:		
Cash	$ 230	(working balance, $150)
Marketable securities	415	(held for payment of taxes and investment in equipment)
Accounts receivable	525	(94% collectible, net of expenses)
Inventories	815	(quick disposal value two-thirds of book, normal sale 95%)
Total current assets	1,985	
Fixed assets	1,715	(quick sale value $225, replacement value $2,500)
Less: Accumulated depreciation ..	820	
Net fixed assets	895	
Prepaid expenses	40	(insurance, licenses, etc.)
Goodwill	175	(based on previous acquisitions)
Organization expense	20	(legal fees, taxes)
Total assets	$3,115	

Liabilities and Net Worth

Current liabilities:		
Accounts payable	$ 370	($350 current, $20 overdue)
Notes payable	125	(due 60 days' hence)
Accrued liabilities	290	(wages, interest, etc.)
Accrued taxes	150	(income taxes, withholding)
Total current liabilities	935	
Mortgage payable	175	(80% of fixed assets as security)
Bonds, net of sinking fund	520	(unsecured)
Deferred income taxes	55	
Reserve for self-insurance	110	(contingency surplus reserve)
Preferred stock	300	(7% preferred, 3,000 shares)
Common stock	525	(52,500 shares, $10 par)
Capital surplus	110	(excess paid in for common)
Earned surplus	385	(accumulated earnings)
Total liabilities and net worth	$3,115	

The company's β is estimated at 1.2 while the spread between risk-free return of 7 percent and S&P 500 returns is expected to be about 6 percent.

6. Two companies are discussing a potential merger. Company A has a price/earnings ratio of $12\times$, with current EPS of $8, a dividend of $2, and a market price range of $90 to $100, with a recent price of $98. Ten million shares are outstanding. Company B has a price/earnings ratio of $20\times$ and is growing at twice the 6 percent rate of Company A. Its current EPS are $3, it pays no dividend, and its market price is ranging between $45 and $70. One million shares are outstanding. Company A is assessing the impact of a potential offer to Company B at a price of $65, as compared to Company B's current price of $54. Calculate the appropriate measures to assess the impact of these terms, and discuss potential implications.

APPENDIX I

BASIC INFLATION

CONCEPTS

Throughout this book we have referred to the distorting effects of inflation on financial decisions and analysis. In this appendix we will offer a brief commentary on the basic nature of the often misunderstood phenomenon of inflation. Financial transactions are carried out using a medium of exchange, such as United States dollars, and variations in this medium will affect the numerical recording of transactions. But underlying the transactions are *economic trade-offs*, that is, values are given and received. We must be careful not to confuse changes in economic *values* with changes in the *medium* used to make and record these transactions. We will examine the ramifications of this statement in several contexts below.

PRICE LEVEL CHANGES

The *economic values* of goods and services *change* over time. The reason for this is as basic as human nature: The law of supply and demand operates, in an uncontrolled market environment, to *increase* the value of goods and services that are in *short supply,* and to *decrease* the value of those available in *abundance.* This shift in relative values takes place even in a primitive barter economy that does not utilize any currency at all. The ratio of exchange of coconuts for beans, for example, will move in favor of coconuts when they are scarce, and in favor of beans when these are out of season. Many seasonal agricultural products go through a familiar price cycle, reflecting their temporary unavailability, on to the first arrivals in the marketplace, and eventually to an abundance before they become unavailable again. The phenomenon is not limited to seasonal goods, however. Natural resources go through cycles of availability, be it from the need to set up the infrastructure to exploit new sources as old ones expire, or from extreme concerted actions such as those of OPEC in the 1970s and '80s that upset world oil prices through the cartel's control of over half the world's production.

We know that the economic value of manufactured goods is also subject to the law of supply and demand. For example, as new technology emerges in the market, such as the first digital watches or compact disk players, the price commanded by the early units will be well above the prices charged after many suppliers have entered the market and competed for a share of consumer demand. The same is true of all goods and services for which there are present or potential alternative suppliers, domestic or international.

The point we are making here is that the economic value underlying personal, commercial, and financial transactions is determined by forces that are largely *independent* of the monetary expression in which they are recorded. As we will see, an analysis of price level changes ideally should *separate* the change in price levels caused by shifts in economic value from those caused by changes in the currency itself. Accurate separation of the two is difficult in practice, but necessary for understanding the meaning of financial and economic projections.

MONETARY INFLATION

Another phenomenon affecting transaction values is any basic change in the *purchasing power* of *currency*. There are many reasons underlying the decline or strengthening of a currency's value as a medium of exchange. One of the most important factors causing inflationary declines in purchasing power is the *amount of currency* in circulation relative to *economic activity*. If the government increases the money supply faster than necessary to accommodate growth in economic activity, there will literally be more dollars chasing relatively fewer goods and services. As a result, the stated dollar prices for all goods or services will rise, even though the *basic demand* for any specific item may be unchanged.

This description is oversimplified, of course. A great many other factors affect currency values. One of these is the impact of government deficits and the way they are financed. Another is the value of the dollar relative to other currencies and the impact of exchange rates on international trade. In addition, international money flows and investment cause shifts in the values of national currencies over and above the effects of the individual countries' fiscal and economic conditions. Union negotiations, wage settlements, and cost of living adjustments in wages, pensions, and government-sponsored assistance programs are also related to changing currency values. Every nation's central bank—the Federal Reserve bank in the case of the United States—is of critical importance in this context, because its policies affect both the size of the money supply, and the level of interest rates. These in turn, affect government fiscal policies, business activity, international trade and money flows, etc. And ultimately, serious declines in the value of a currency can also affect the basic supply and demand of goods and services, as, for example, customers and businesses "buy ahead" to beat anticipated price increases.

The point here is not to systematically analyze inflation and its causes, but rather to make the *distinction* between *economic* and *monetary* changes that affect price levels. Suffice it to say that price level changes due to monetary effects are largely the ones that distort economic values of personal and commercial transactions. If monetary conditions were *stable*—that is, the amount of currency in circulation always matched the level of economic activity—price level changes would only reflect changes in economic values, something we have agreed is at the core of management efforts to improve the owners' economic condition. Because monetary stability is an unrealistic assumption, however, the challenge is to make any analysis of the actual conditions affecting prices and economic values meaningful.

NOMINAL AND REAL DOLLARS

Business and personal transactions are expressed in terms of **nominal** dollars, also called *current* dollars, that reflect today's prices, unadjusted or altered in any way. For accounting purposes, nominal dollars are used everyday to record transactions. However, when the value of a dollar changes over time, the amounts recorded in the past no longer reflect current prices, either in terms of underlying economic values or in terms of the value of the currency at the moment.

To deal with changes in the value of the currency, economists have devised price indexes intended to separate, at least in part, monetary distortions from fluctuations in economic value. However, the only way to prepare such an index is to measure the *change in price* of a representative group of products and services as a *surrogate* for the change in currency values. Yet we already know that goods and services chosen for this purpose are themselves also subject to changes in supply and demand, *apart* from currency fluctuations. But there is no *direct* way of measuring changes in currency values as such. Inevitably, therefore, the approach involves *mixing* demand/supply conditions and currency values, and the only hope is that the selection of goods and services employed in a given index is broad enough to compensate somewhat for the underlying demand/supply conditions.

The **consumer price index**, a popular index of inflation, is calculated in this way. It is based on frequent sampling of the prices of a "market basket" of goods and services purchased by U.S. consumers, including food, housing, clothing, transportation, etc. The compensation and weighting of this basket is changed gradually to reflect changing habits and tastes. Another popular index, applicable to business, is the **producer price index,** based on a representative weighted sampling of the wholesale prices of goods produced. Other indexes deal with wholesale *commodity* prices and a variety of specialized groupings of products and services. The broadest index in common use is applied to the gross national product, the so-called **GNP deflator,** which expresses the price changes in the total range of goods and services produced in the U.S. economy. The GNP deflator is based on broad statistical sampling. Current levels are announced throughout the year in conjunction with other business and government economic statistics. The indexes are prepared by calculating the changes in prices from those of a selected *base year,* which is changed infrequently in order to minimize the effort of adjusting comparative statistical series whenever the base year is changed.

The price indexes are used to translate nominal dollar values in government statistics and business reports into **real dollar values.** This involves converting nominal dollar values to a chosen standard, so that past and present dollar transactions can be compared in equivalent terms. For example, to compare this year's performance of the economy to that of last year, we may chose to express *current* economic statistics using *last year's* dollars as the standard. Last year's dollars are called *real,* and we express today's data in these "real" terms. To do so, we simply adjust today's dollars by the amount of inflation experienced since last year. The GNP deflator is normally used to adjust broad economic statistics. If inflation this year was 4.5 percent over last year in terms of the GNP deflator, every nominal dollar figure for this year would be adjusted downward by 4.5 percent. The result would be an expression of this year's results in terms of *real dollars* which are based on the *prior year.*

A real dollar is thus simply a nominal dollar which has been *adjusted* to the price level of a stated *base year,* using one of the applicable price indexes. The base chosen can be *any* year, as long as past or future years are consistently stated in terms of the currency value for the base year. In fact, real dollars are often called **constant dollars**, a name that simply recognizes that they are derived from a *constant base*. The process of adjustment has the following effect: during inflationary periods, the real dollars for the years *preceding* the base year will be adjusted *upward*, while the real dollars of future years will be adjusted *downward*. The reverse would be true, of course, if the period had involved *deflation* instead.

To illustrate, let us assume that the following price developments took place during a five-year period. We are using the producer price index (PPI). This index was constructed on the basis of Year 0. In the following table, we have set Year 3 as the base year for our analysis:

	Year 1	Year 2	Year 3	Year 4	Year 5
Producer Price Index (Year 0)	1.09	1.15	1.21	1.25	1.33
Producer Price Index (Year 3)	0.90	0.95	1.00	1.03	1.10
Real Value of $100 (Base Year 3)	$111	$105	$100	$ 97	$ 91

Note that two steps were involved. First, the producer price index had to be adjusted for our chosen base Year 3, that is, the index had to be set at 1.00 for Year 3 and all index numbers were divided by the value of the index for the base year, which is 1.21. (However, the index could have been constructed on any other year, because an index measures price changes year by year from whatever starting point is chosen.) The second step was to divide the adjusted index values on the second line into the nominal dollars of each year. We chose to use $100 for all years, but the process applies, of course, to any amount of nominal dollars in any one of the years. Using a single figure permitted us to illustrate the shifts in value with a same dollar amount.

The example clearly shows that the purchasing power of a dollar in Year 4 versus Year 3 *declined* by 3 percent. The implication from a business point of view is that, to keep up with inflation in the prices it must pay for goods and services, a company must increase its *nominal* earnings power by 3 percent. Anything less than that will leave the owners worse off.

This simple process allows us to convert nominal dollars into inflation-adjusted *real dollars*. Problems arise in choosing the proper index for a business situation, and from the fact that the index to some extent embodies changes in economic value as well as in currency, as we discussed earlier. Much thought has been expended on refining the process of adjustment, which in the end, depends on the purpose of the analysis and the degree of accuracy desired.

APPLICATIONS OF INFLATION ADJUSTMENT IN FINANCIAL ANALYSIS

Restatement of company data or projections in real dollar terms is at times useful in order to assess whether the company's performance has kept up with shifts in currency values. Such restatement may be used to value a company's assets and liabilities, or to show the real growth or decline in sales and earnings. As we observed, publicly traded companies are obligated to include an annual inflation-adjusted restatement of key data in their published shareholder reports.

Much effort goes into adjusting financial projections for inflation, particularly in the area of capital investment analysis. There are no truly satisfactory general rules for this process, however. When an analyst must project cash flows from a major capital investment, the easiest approach continues to be projection in nominal dollars, taking into account expected cost and price increases of the key variables involved, tailored specifically to the conditions of the business. The discount standard applied against the projection is also based on nominal return expectations that include the inflationary outlook.

To refine the analysis, many companies prepare projections in *real dollars*, attempting to forecast the *true economic* increases or decreases in costs and prices. Then an appropriate inflation index is applied to the figures to convert them into nominal dollars. The problem is, however, that the *margin* between revenues and costs may widen unduly, simply because the same inflation index is applied to the larger revenue numbers and to the smaller cost numbers. Often arbitrary adjustments have to be made to keep the margin spread manageable.

Another approach involves developing projections expressed in real dollars and discounting these with a return standard that has also been converted into *real returns*. The result will be internally consistent as far as the project is concerned. However, the result is *not* readily *comparable* with current overall performance of the business—recorded and expressed in *nominal* dollar terms—unless the company has also found a way to convert and measure ongoing performance in real dollar terms. Some companies are beginning to experiment with such restated reports and measures, but the approach involves a massive effort, both in terms of data preparation and education of personnel generating and using the projections and performance data. It is instinctively easier to think about business in terms of nominal dollars than of real dollars, and progress in this area is being made only gradually. The complexities are such that the financial and planning staffs of companies wishing to use this approach face a lengthy conceptual and practical conversion problem.

IMPACT OF INFLATION

To restate quickly, the impact of inflation—and the much less common opposite situation, deflation—is a growing distortion of recorded values on a company's financial statements, and an ongoing partial distortion of operating results. Accounting methods discussed in Chapters 1 and 2 are designed to make the effect of the inflationary distortion at least *consistent*. In terms of cash flows, inflation distorts a company's tax payments, if the taxes due are based on low historical cost apportionment, and results in a cash drain if dividends are higher than they would be if real-dollar earnings were considered, to name two examples. Inflation also affects financing conditions, and particularly the repayment of principal on long-term debt obligations. As we observed before, however, the mediating influence of interest rates—which respond to inflation expectations—will tend to prevent windfalls for the borrower looking to repay debt with "cheap" dollars. Normally, over the long run, distortions from inflation affect lenders and borrowers alike. Relative advantages gained by one over the other are only temporary.

Overall, the subject of inflation adjustments continues to evolve in financial analysis, but it is unlikely that totally consistent methods that are generally applicable will be found.

APPENDIX II
SOURCES OF FINANCIAL
INFORMATION

While the orientation of this book is techniques of financial analysis, some of the applications implied the use of information beyond that stipulated or available directly. The reader therefore needed to be familiar with the main sources of financial information to obtain the necessary input for analysis. For this reason we have devoted this appendix to a brief review of common data sources, and have given guidelines, where required, for the interpretation of the financial data presented. The information provided will give the reader the background for making more sophisticated decisions about company performance, new financing, temporary borrowing, investments, credit, capital budgeting, and so on.

Again in keeping with the nature of this book, this appendix is meant only as an introduction to sources of **current financial, periodic financial,** and **background company and business information.** A number of additional references for further study and data are provided at the end of this appendix.

CURRENT FINANCIAL INFORMATION

The most common and convenient way to keep abreast of financial developments is through the daily financial pages of national, metropolitan, and regional newspapers. The most complete and widely read financial coverage is found in the pages of *The Wall Street Journal* and the *New York Times*, which contain detailed information on securities and commodity markets; news, feature articles, and statistics on economic and business conditions; news and earning reports for individual companies; dividend announcements; currency, commodity, and trading data; and a great deal of coverage of international business and economic conditions. The major dailies in the United States and Canada also carry key financial and economic data, but the coverage and emphasis vary greatly. Smaller and regional papers will often provide only selected highlights tailored to the area and the readership.

The bulk of the materials shown in the financial pages involve securities transactions and current financial data. This information is not entirely self-explanatory. We will explain the meaning of some of the abbreviations and symbols used in *The Wall Street Journal* listings for stock transactions (traded on exchanges and over the counter), bond transactions, and other key financial data. Other newspapers generally present data in a fairly comparable fashion, but in less detail.

Stock Quotations

Exchange Quotations. Transactions made on organized stock exchanges (the New York Stock Exchange, the American Stock Exchange, and several regional exchanges) generally include the kind of information shown in Figure 11-1. It shows the day's transactions in 10 stocks out of the 1,958 individual stocks traded on the New York Stock Exchange on Thursday, June 12, 1986, as reported in *The Wall Street Journal* on Friday, June 13. The total volume of shares traded for the day was about 127 million, an average performance in a year when daily volumes well over 130 million shares were quite common

Figure II–1

NEW YORK STOCK EXCHANGE STOCK TRANSACTIONS

Thursday, June 12, 1986

52 Weeks							Sales				
High	Low	Stocks		Div.	Yield	P/E Ratio	in 100s	High	Low	Close	Net Change
70¼	53⅛	Amoco		3.30b	5.4	9	1,525	61⅝	61¼	61⅝	—
102	94⅛	Citicorp	pfA	7.54e	8.0	—	1	94½	94½	94½	−1¼
41⅜	25⅜	Colg Pal		1.36	3.2	28	2,014u	42⅛	41⅜	42	+ ¾
43	19	Genst	g	1.36	3.3	11	24	42	41¾	41¾	—
48	28¾	Hewl Pk		.22	.5	23×	2,463	42¾	42	42¼	− ⅜
161⅞	117⅜	IBM		4.40	3.0	14	7,908	149⅛	147¾	148	−1⅛
36¼	17½	Mart	wi	—	—	—	221	35⅞	35¾	35⅞	+ ⅛
35	25⅞	Paine W	pf	2.25	7.7	—	219	29½	29⅛	29¼	− ¼
23⅜	13⅜	Pandck P	n	.20	.8	21	713u	24⅛	23¼	24⅛	+ ⅜
102	50⅜	Upjohn	s	1.52	1.5	29	1,852	100⅞	97½	100⅞	+ ⅞

and in which involved "slow day" trading volumes under 100 million shares. In fact, the all-time high of 220 million shares traded was reached earlier in March. Daily trading statistics are summarized in *The Wall Street Journal* under an overall heading "Stock Market Data Bank" and "Dow Jones Averages".

The first stock listed in Figure 11–1, Amoco, had a high value of 70 ¼ and a low of 53 ⅛ over the previous 52 weeks. (This is the range in which transactions took place in the last 12 months.) The quotations are given in dollars per share, and fractions of a dollar not smaller than ⅛ ($0.125). Amoco paid dividends at the annual rate of $3.30 during the period (based on the last quarterly declaration). The special symbol "b" indicates that Amoco paid a stock dividend in addition to the cash dividend shown.

The next column shows the dividend yield based on the current market quotations, while the following column reports the price/earnings ratio based on current reported earnings (12-month period) and current price levels. Amoco has a below-average ratio of 9.

The day's transactions in Amoco stock totaled 152,500 shares, as indicated in the seventh column, where sales are listed in multiples of 100 shares. This is done because stocks are ordinarily traded in **round lots** of 100 shares, while less than 100 shares is considered an **odd lot,** and brokers usually charge a premium for trading in the latter.

The next four columns indicate price movements of the stock based on actual transactions during June 12, 1986. Successive trades reached a high for the day of $61.63 and a low of $61.25. The net change in the last column indicates the difference between price at the close of trading and the price at the close of the previous trading day. In this case, there was no change.

Unless otherwise indicated, the transactions listed involve common stocks. If a preferred stock was traded, the symbol "pf" would be added right before the amount of dividend shown in Column 4. In our example, Citicorp A and Paine Weber are preferred stocks. The dividend quoted for preferred stock is the annual rate, as was the case with common stock. Thus Citicorp (the "A" after "pf" stands for the class of this particular security as denoted by the company) has a dividend rate of $7.54 while Paine Weber pays $2.25 per year, with both selling at prices that yield about 8 percent, a reflection of the generally lower yields prevalent during 1986.

A number of additional symbols and abbreviations are commonly used and explained briefly in footnotes on the financial pages of most papers. Several of these are used in our sample listing. For example, an "a" after a company's stated dividend would indicate that the company had paid extra *cash* dividends in addition to the annual rate shown. We already know that the "b" after Amoco's dividend shows that a *stock* dividend was paid in addition to the state annual cash dividend, while the "e" in the Citicorp listing indicates that the amount of dividends actually paid or declared in the past 12 months was not at the level reflected in the most recent rate, in other words, the most recent quarterly dividend represents a change from previous quarters. The "g" in the Genstar listing refers to dividend quotations made in Canadian currency. The "u" with Colgate-Palmolive indicates that the quotation reflects a new 52-week high for the stock. Other symbols are used to show dividends in arrears ("k") and liquidation dividends ("c"). The "s" in the Upjohn listing indicates a recent stock split.

Apart from notations for dividend exceptions, symbols are also used to show new issues ("n"), as is the case with Pandick, a company's calling for redemption of a particular stock ("cld"), various conditions of rights and warrants, which represent options to purchase additional shares, anticipatory quotations of a new issue on a when-issued basis ("wi")—Mart is an example of such advance trading—and so on. Two symbols help define the price level and the volume of trading: A stock may be traded exdividend ("x"), as was the case with Hewlett-Packard, which means the current dividend payable will be paid to the former owner of record, and the price can be affected accordingly. Also, a "z" indicates that total sales transactions for the day involved fewer than 100 shares.

The individual listings of stock transactions in *The Wall Street Journal* are supplemented by various summaries of overall trading figures. One of these is the list of the day's most active stocks. On June 12, 1986, the stock with the highest turnover of shares among the 15 stocks listed was Diamond Shamrock (1.43 million shares), closing at 11⅜, off (down) ⅜. Another summary, the "market diary" for the last six days, showed that on June 12, 1958 different issues were traded on the New York Stock Exchange with 807 advances, 732 declines, and 419 unchanged listings. The number of new highs achieved was 65, with 16 new lows. Also listed are the closing prices for various market averages (for example, the Dow Jones Industrial Average, which closed at 1,838.13, not far below the record high of 1,870 earlier in June), as well as a four-month chart of the Dow Jones averages, by day, showing the range and closing position. These and other summary data provide an indication of the "mood" and direction of the market.

Quotations of transactions on the American Stock Exchange are similar. Transactions on regional exchanges, such as the Pacific Stock Exchange in San Francisco and the Midwest Stock Exchange in Chicago, are often listed together with the most important quotations on the major Canadian stock exchanges in Toronto and Montreal. These transactions are quoted in less detail. Normally, only the number of shares traded, the high and low prices, and the closing prices with changes from the previous close are listed. At times the quotations are limited to volume and closing prices only.

Reference was made earlier to the various stock price averages, which are popular and important clues to the behavior of the stock market in general. These averages are calculated daily and in some cases continuously from on-line data bases. The averages are followed closely by analysts, investors, and financial managers who interpret market movements to decide on purchase or sale of securities, or to assess various types of new securities. Because the various averages involve a selected and relatively small number of stocks, their upward or downward movement over time is not necessarily a predictor of the likely movement of any particular stock or of the overall market.

As discussed earlier, there are many factors underlying the value and market position of a particular security, the most important of which are the current and prospective operating circumstances of the company. The atmosphere of the market and general economic conditions will certainly influence the behavior of a particular stock, but we must caution against the adage that a "rising tide lifts all ships in the harbor," which is a gross oversimplification of the behavior of the stock market. The limitations of stock indexes are those of averages in general, which can only be broad indicators of a likely trend against which all particulars of a security have to be compared.

The most commonly quoted and publicized stock price averages are the Dow Jones averages of 30 industrial, 20 railroad, and 15 utility stocks, and the composite average of all 65 securities. The Dow Jones Industrial Average contains most well-known companies in the United States, such as IBM, General Motors, General Electric, U.S. Steel, Du Pont, Procter & Gamble, and so on. Because it is heavily weighted toward these "blue-chip" securities, the Dow Jones average is less applicable for analysis of the securities of lesser known companies, specialized "growth situations," or conglomerate corporations.

The *New York Times* average of 50 stocks includes 25 railroad and 25 industrial stocks. This average is also weighted somewhat in favor of blue chips. The Standard & Poor's averages (composite indexes of 425 industrial stocks, 50 utilities and 25 railroads, and a combination of all these averages in the "S & P 500") are more broadly based and more closely approximate the average price level of all stocks listed on the New York Stock Exchange because the S & P 500 includes about one quarter of the issues actively traded there.

As pointed out before, the various stock averages, including daily ranges and average price levels, are available for each trading day. Because transactions are electronically tracked, the current level of these averages is always available almost instantaneously during the trading day. Continuous adjustments are made for stock splits, stock dividends, and many changes in the corporate structures of the companies in the index. Some of the references listed at the end of the appendix give more details about how the indexes are calculated.

Over-the Counter (OTC) Transactions. A huge volume of securities is traded outside of the organized exchanges in an "auction market" consisting of hundreds of security dealers and individuals in all parts of the country who are electronically linked via computer. This over-the-counter market is an amazingly flexible arrangement which allows trading between prospective buyers and sellers of such securities as government bonds, state and municipal bonds, stocks and bonds of smaller and newer companies, bank stocks, mutual funds, insurance companies, small issues, and infrequently traded issues. On Thursday, June 12, 1986, 4,290 issues were traded in the OTC markets with a total volume of 130 million shares, exceeding the activity on the New York Stork Exchange. Financial listings for OTC transactions are similar to those for exchange transactions.

Representative quotations for OTC transactions are pro-vided by either the National Association of Securities Dealers (NASDAQ), or by individual dealers who specialize in particular securities to "maintain a market" in these issues. Such quotations, unlike quotes for the organized exchanges, are only *indicative* of the prices at which an individual or a dealer would have been willing to buy or sell a particular security, during the trading period. In other words, they may not reflect actual transactions. A dealer specializing in the security and handling both sides of the transactions may cover expenses and make a profit from the difference between the purchase and sale prices of the issue.

Figure 11–2, from *The Wall Street Journal* of June 13, 1986, provides a sample listing of over-the-counter quotations for June 12, 1986. The price at which traders would be willing to

Figure II–2
NASDAQ BID AND ASKED QUOTATIONS
Thursday, June 12, 1986

Stock	Dividend	Sales in 100s	Bid	Asked	Net Change
Alamo Svgs	.60	53	1	1¼	+ ⅛
Bowater	.09d	10	4¾	4¹³⁄₁₆	—
Jefferson Cp	.25t	4	3¾	4¼	—
MCI Comm	wt	126	⁷⁄₁₆	½	—
Nor Can FSL	s	61	11½	12¼	—
Syntech Intl	pf	2	25¾	26¾	+ ¼
X-Rite Inc	.02d	352	10⅜	10¾	+ ¼

buy the security is the *bid*, the *asked* price is the amount desired for a *sale*. The format used to list OTC trading is similar to the one shown for exchange transactions, with the stocks and the annual dividend rate listed first, although the "price" is represented by both bid and asked quotations. The last column shows the change in the bid price. The bid quotations are normally below the asked quotations, as we would expect in an auction market.

In our sample listing we again encounter a series of symbols that are quite comparable to the symbols used in the stock exchange listings. For example, the "d" used with the Bowater and X-Rite quotations indicates that the dividend paid so far in 1986 is not a regular rate. The symbol "t" with the Jefferson Corp. quote denotes a liquidation dividend, while the "s" (North Carolina Federal S & L) denotes a stock split. The "wt" (MCI Communications) means this issue is a warrant, which entitles the holder to purchase a share of stock at a specified price. Finally, the "pf" with the Syntech International quote indicates a preferred stock. The over-the-counter market is discussed in greater detail in some of of the references listed at the end of the appendix.

Other Exchange Quotations.   Some of the larger newspapers carry limited quotations from major foreign stock exchanges. Trading of internationally recognized securities on the Paris, London, Tokyo, or Frankfurt stock exchanges is reported in the currency of the country involved. At times, the financial pages may contain current stock averages for foreign countries, supplemented by accounts of major activities there.

Mutual Funds. Mutual funds are professionally managed investment pools. A share of a mutual fund represents an investment in a portfolio of different securities, which may be oriented towards a variety of investment objectives, such as earnings, or capital appreciation. These funds have gained importance in recent years, and mutual fund trading is quoted in most newspapers. Price ranges are provided by the National Association of Securities Dealers. The quotes normally show the net asset value per share, an offering price which includes net asset value and the maximum sales charge, and the change in net asset value from the previous day.

Options. Options, which are essentially contracts to buy or sell a security on a future date and at a stipulated price, are traded on various exchanges and are listed in terms of closing prices for "puts" (sales prices) and "calls" (purchase prices). This specialized market has grown rapidly in recent years, as has the market for **commodity futures**, which similarly represent contracts for future sales and purchases of certain commodities which are also quoted in the financial pages.

Bond Quotations

The three major types of bonds—corporate, state and municipal, and federal government—represent a huge market which involves both the organized exchanges and the OTC market. In fact, the overwhelming majority of government bonds of both types are traded in the over-the-counter market, while the majority of corporate bond issues are traded on the stock exchanges.

It will be useful briefly to discuss how bond transactions are listed. Figure 11–3 shows a listing for the NYSE, but trading on other exchanges is handled similarly.

The first line gives not only the name of the issuing company, but also the coupon interest rate and the maturity date. Thus,

Figure II-3
NEW YORK STOCK EXCHANGE BOND TRANSACTIONS
Thursday, June 12, 1986
Volume: $28,690,000

Bonds	Current Yield	Volume	High	Low	Close	Net Change
Am T&T 8¾ 2000	9	328	97⅞	97¼	97½	+ ⅛
Amfac 5¼ 1994	cv	8	88¼	92¾	93⅛	+ ⅝
vj Beker 15⅞ 2003f	—	232	66⅞	65	66⅜	+ ⅜
Det Ed 7½ 2003	9.4	2	80	80	80	—
Kmart 6s 1999	cv	31	146½	146	146	+3
U Carb 15s 2006	13.5	456	111¾	110¾	111¼	+ ½
Xerox 6s 1995	cv	69	92½	92	92½	+ ¾

the first line is an American Telephone and Telegraph issue with a stated interest rate of 8¾ percent and due in the year 2000. The most important difference to remember vis-o-vis stock quotations is that bonds are quoted in percentages of par value, expressed in fractions of no smaller than one eighth of one percent. For example, the AT&T bonds traded in a range from a high of $978.75 to a low of $972.50 for each $1,000 of par value, closing at $975 at the end of the day. We note that sales are given in thousands of dollars, because $1,000 is the most common denomination of a single bond. As with stocks, high, low, and closing price, and net change from the prior trading day's close are listed.

The symbols used with the individual bonds parallel those discussed earlier. For example, "vj" with the Beker 15⅞ 2003 issue indicates the company's state of bankruptcy, and the symbol "f" indicates that the bonds are traded "flat", that is, without a claim for current unpaid interest. The bond is trading at a considerable discount from par as a consequence of the company's precarious condition. The symbol "cv" with the Amfac, K mart, and Xerox bonds signals convertibility into common stock. Note that the convertible bonds of K mart are trading at a considerable premium above par (about $1,460 for a $1,000 face value)—and correspondingly, at very low yields based on the 6 percent coupon rate (about 4.1 percent)—an indication of how the value of a convertible issue is boosted when the value of the underlying shares of common stock reaches or exceeds the par value of the bond.

A slightly different method is used to list current quotations for government agency bonds and miscellaneous securities traded over the counter. Again we will use an example from *The Wall Street Journal* for the trading day of Thursday, June 12, 1986. Figure 11–4 gives quotes for U. S. Treasury bonds, U. S. Treasury bills, Federal Home Loan Bank bonds, World Bank bonds, and some tax-exempt municipal and agency bonds.

As was the case with over-the-counter transactions for stocks, we find bid and asked quotations which represent the prices desired for purchase or sale on the trading day and do not denote specific transactions. An important difference in

Figure II–4
GOVERNMENT AGENCY, AND
MISCELLANEOUS SECURITIES QUOTATIONS
Thursday, June 12, 1986
(over the counter)

			Bid	Asked	Bid Change	Yield
U.S. Treasury bonds:						
6⅛s, 1986 Nov p			99.28	100.28	−0.1	3.95
12¾s, 1989 Nov p			113.31	114.30	+0.5	7.96
13¾s, 1992 May n			125.10	125.14	+0.11	8.23
4s, 1988–93 Feb			93.21	94.21	+0.25	4.95
U.S. Treasury bills:						
Mat						
7–17 (86)			5.93*	5.89*	—	6.00
6–11 (87)			6.45*	6.43*	—	6.85
Federal Home Loan Bank:						
Rate	Mat					
7.80	7–86		100.20	100.30	—	6.79
14.25	4–89		115.18	115.30	—	7.92
World Bank bonds:						
Rate	Mat					
5.38	4–92		87.27	88.70	—	7.93
16.63	11–91		133.29	134.90	—	8.60
Tax-exempt bonds:						
Agency	Coupon	Mat	Current Price			
E Bay MUD CalW 86†	7.000	03–01–08	89⅞		+⅛	7.99
Springfield Ill EL jr Lien**	7.750	03–01–06	92⅝		−⅛	8.52

*Discount rates.
†East Bay Municipal Utility District, CA.
**Springfield, IL Electric System (Junior obligation).

this example is the custom of quoting prices in percent of par value and fractions of a percent in *32nds* of a point. Thus, a quote of 99.28 means a price of $99^{28}/_{32}$ percent, or $998.75 per $1,000 of par value. The final column is the yield to maturity, reflecting the return on investment earned at the current price if the bond were held to its maturity date and redeemed at par. Note that the yield on the 6⅛ percent Treasury bonds is only 3.95 percent. Because of their imminent redemption in November 1986, the only return earned on the bonds would be the difference between the purchase price, if slightly under $1,000, and the redemption value at par, as the final interest period has passed. At the same time, the 12¾s and 13¾s due in 1989 and 1992 respectively, which were issued with such high coupon rates in the wake of the inflationary surge of the 1970s, are now trading at sizable price premiums over par, on the basis of which they presently yield more moderate returns that represent the vastly improved inflation picture of 1986. U.S. government securities will be affected by the general outlook for interest rates even more than corporate bonds, because the likelihood of default is extremely remote and the purchaser is normally looking for a safe investment with an assured long-term or short-term yield.

As we found in the case of the stock market, bond market quotations are supplemented by a variety of reports on volume of trading, bond averages, summaries of advancing and declining issues, highs and lows for the year, and so on. Again, these provide the investor with a general feel for the daily movements of the bond markets. The most commonly used averages are the Dow Jones Bond Averages (20 bonds: 10 public utilities and 10 industrials). Bond averages are calculated in percentages of par, as were the quotations themselves. On Thursday, June 12, 1986, the New York Stock Exchange bond volume was $28,690,000 for all issues, with the 20-bond average rising slightly to 89.52 (up 0.09). Issues traded numbered 802, of which 320 staged advances, 299 declined, and 183 remained unchanged. New highs for the year were achieved by 18 issues and new lows by 10 issues.

Other Financial Data

Most papers list, in one form or another, so-called leading business and economic indicators—such as indexes of industrial production, freight car loadings, prices, output in the automotive industry, steel production—both in feature stories and in tabular form. When supplemented by reports of earnings and dividend declarations of individual corporations, news about corporate management, analysis and announcement of new financing, and industry analysis, this information can provide a broad background for financial analysis.

Among the more specialized data in the financial pages are listings of transactions in the *commodities markets*. Commodities include a great variety of basic raw materials such as cotton, lumber, copper, and rubber; and foods, such as coffee, corn, and wheat. The best-known exchange for commodity trading is the Chicago Board of Trade, while more specialized exchanges include the New York Cotton Exchange or international exchanges such as the London Metal Exchange. Commodities may be traded on a **spot** basis, that is, the commodity is purchased outright at the time. Commodities **futures** are also traded. These are contracts to buy or sell a commodity at a specified price at some point in the future. The commodities market is far too varied to describe here, but we should take a quick look at how commodities are quoted.

The information on commodities trading provided by most sources usually involves opening and closing transactions, as well as highs and also lows for the trading day and the season. Changes from the previous trading day are also often listed. A variety of indexes are available, such as the Dow Jones Spot Index, the Dow Jones Futures Index, or the Reuters United Kingdom Index. A company whose operations depend to a large extent on raw materials traded in a spot or futures market can be severely influenced by fluctuations in spot or futures prices. Because fluctuations in commodities markets can be severe, traders in these markets often **hedge**. This involves arrangements to *both* buy and sell the same commodity, which will "cover" the trader for shifts in prices. References at the end of this appendix provide more detailed information on commodities trading.

Foreign Exchange

Most newspapers list the major currencies of the world in equivalents of U. S. dollars. Normally, the quotations represent selling prices of bank transfers in the United States for payment abroad, and quotations are given for the current trading day as well as for the previous day. Also, prices for foreign bank notes are often quoted in equivalents of U. S. dollars, both on a buying and selling basis.

PERIODIC FINANCIAL INFORMATION

Apart from the financial data contained in daily newspapers, a wealth of information is provided by various financial, economic, and business periodicals. Furthermore, readily available reference works contain periodic listings and analyses of financial information oriented toward the investor and financial analyst. The advent of the computer has made possible the rapid collection and analysis of company and economic data, and collective information can now be obtained very quickly. The most important sources of periodic financial and business information are listed below.

Magazines

Major Weekly Periodicals.   For general business coverage, *Business Week* remains one of the most useful and widely read publications. It covers current developments of interest in business and economics, both national and international. The weekly magazine contains analyses of major events as well as reports on individual companies, the stock markets, labor, business education, and so on, and a selective listing of economic indicators, as well as a special index of business activity.

For more detailed coverage of stock quotations, security offerings, banking developments, and financial, industrial, and commodity trends, the *Commercial and Financial Chronicle* is the most comprehensive source available. The *Wall Street Transcript* contains analyses of the securities of a great variety of individual companies, both on a financial and economic basis, and of the technical basis of stock market charts. It further discusses major corporate presentations to security analysts about past performance and future plans, and roundtable discussions on industry groups by security analysts.

Barron's covers business trends in terms of individual companies as well as major industries, and provides a great deal of information about corporate securities. The section titled "Stock Market at a Glance" is a very useful and detailed picture of the securities markets. *Fortune* magazine biweekly comments on national economic trends and sketches profiles of major U. S. and international executives, in addition to giving detailed articles on industry, company, or socioeconomic trends. The magazine's annual listing and ranking of the "Fortune 500", the best-performing U. S. companies, and similar listings of banks and major foreign companies, are useful references.

Forbes, also a semimonthly magazine, takes the investor's viewpoint, providing very detailed and searching analyses of individual companies and their managements. The annual January issue which reviews the performance of major U. S. industries, is an excellent source of information on industry trends and provides a ranking of companies by a series of criteria.

For an international outlook, the British magazine *The Economist* surveys international and United Kingdom developments in politics, economics, and business, and discusses U.S. developments in depth. It can be considered an international *Business Week*, as can *World Business*.

Major Monthly Periodicals. Economic and business trends are covered in considerable detail in publications of major commercial banks, such as the *National City Bank Monthly Letter* and the *New England Letter* of the First National Bank of Boston. The various Federal Reserve banks issue general bulletins and regional bulletins that contain regional economic data of interest.

The *Harvard Business Review* is a highly regarded forum for discussion of management concepts and tools, including financial insights, presented bimonthly by practitioners and academicians to an extensive worldwide readership of business executives.

Dun's Review presents trade indexes, data on business failures, and key financial ratios in addition to articles about industry and commerce. *Nation's Business* ,a publication of the United States Chamber of Commerce, presents general articles on business subjects. Statistical information in great depth is provided by the *Federal Reserve Bulletin,* which contains statistical data on business and government finances, both domestic and international, and by the *Survey of Current Business,* which covers business statistics in detail.

Detailed stock exchange quotations and data about many **unlisted securities** (those not traded on a recognized exchange), foreign exchange, and money rates are contained in the *Bank and Quotation Record.* The *Journal of Finance,* a quarterly publication, presents articles on finance, investments, economics, money and credit, and international aspects of these topics.

Other Periodicals.   Many specialized periodicals are published by trade associations and banking, commercial, and trading groups too numerous to mention. Also useful are the great variety of U. S. government surveys and publications, statistical papers provided by the United Nations and its major agencies, and the various analyses and reviews in academic journals. At the end of this appendix we have listed several books that provide detailed guidelines on and descriptions of the type of information available from various sources.

Listed below are some major periodicals which deal directly with, or relate to, the area of corporate finance. The list is meant only as a guide. Many other relevant publications are available. Some of the publications are specialized and oriented toward a specific community of interest, others deal with financial conditions in foreign countries. The titles are largely self-explanatory:

Banking
Credit and Financial Management
Journal of Commerce
Corporate Financing
Finance
Financial Analysts Journal
Financial Executive
Financial World
Investment Dealers Digest
National Tax Journal
World Financial Markets

Financial Manuals and Services

The most popular and best-known set of financial manuals and services is provided by Moody's, with Standard & Poor's a close second. Moody's publishes five volumes: *Industrials; Banks, Insurance, Real Estate and Investment Funds; Public Utilities; Railroads;* and *Government and Municipals.* These manuals are published each year and contain up-to-date key historical data, financial statements, securities price ranges, and dividend records for a very large number of companies, including practically all publicly held corporations. Helpful summary statistics and industry data are found in the so-called "blue sections" in the middle of the manuals, which are printed on blue paper. Moody's manuals are updated through semiweekly supplements, with detailed cross-references.

Moody's publishes a *Quarterly Handbook* which gives one-page summaries of key financial and operating data for major publicly held corporations. Furthermore, Moody's publishes weekly stock and bond surveys that analyze market and industry conditions, a semiweekly *Dividend Record,* and a semimonthly *Bond Record* that contains current prices, earnings, and ratings of most important bonds traded in the country.

Standard & Poor's publications include the *Standard Corporation Records*. This financial information about a large number of companies is published in loose-leaf format and is updated through daily supplements. A very useful S & P publication is the *Analysts Handbook;* these industry surveys are compilations of key financial data on individual companies and some industries. Other services of Standard & Poor's include several dealing with the bond market, weekly forecasts of the security markets, securities statistics, and a monthly earnings and stock rating guide.

Other financial services similar to Moody's and Standard & Poor's are provided by *Fitch's Corporation Manuals*, and by more specialized manuals such as *Walker's Manual* of Pacific Coast securities. An almost overwhelming flow of information, judgments, and analyses of individual companies from an investor's standpoint is provided by the major brokerage houses and their research departments. Furthermore, services available to individuals on a subscription basis provide up-to-date financial analyses of individual companies and their securities. The most important among these services are *Value Line, United Business Service, Babson's,* and *Investor's Management Sciences.* The *Value Line* investment survey particularly provides ratings and reports on companies, with selections and opinions for the investor, while *Investor's Management Sciences* concentrates on providing a great deal of standardized statistical information as the basis for making analytical judgments. The credit information services of *Dun & Bradstreet* make evaluating small or unlisted companies easier. The advent of on-line data bases has made important information about companies listed on stock exchanges available instantly through various *time-share services.*

BACKGROUND COMPANY AND BUSINESS INFORMATION

Annual Reports

The most commonly used reference source about the current affairs of publicly held corporations is the annual report furnished to shareholders. The formats used by individual corporations vary widely from detailed coverage which may even go so far as to include current corporate, industry, and national issues, to a bare minimum disclosure of financial results. Nevertheless, the annual report is generally an important direct source of financial information. Because the disclosure requirements of the Securities and Exchange Commission, the recommendations of the accounting profession, and state laws have become more and more demanding over time, the analyst can usually count on annual reports presenting a fairly consistent sets of data.

Government Data

More specific details about company operations can often be found in the annual statements which corporations must file with the Securities and Exchange Commission (SEC) in Washington, D. C. This information is filed on Form 10-K, and is available upon request for public inspection. Furthermore, when a corporation issues new securities in significant amounts or alters its capital structure in a major way, the detailed proposal that must be filed with the SEC, the **prospectus**, is generally a more complete source of company background data than is the normal annual report. It will cover the history of the company, ownership patterns, directors and top management, financial and operating data, products, facilities, and information regarding the intended use of the new funds.

If a company is closely held, or too small to be listed by the key financial services, information about its financial operations can often be obtained from the corporation records departments of states in which the company does business. Again, these reports are open to the public for inspection.

Trade Associations

Trade associations are a prime source of information about their respective industries. A great deal of statistical information is available annually or more often and covers products, services, finances, and performance criteria applicable to the industry or trade group. Often the financial and performance data are grouped by types and sizes of firms, to make overall statistics on the industry somewhat more applicable to a particular operation. Trade associations include organizations such as the American Iron and Steel Institute, the American Paper Institute, and the National Lumber Manufacturers Association, to name but a few. Sources for listings and addresses of these associations and their publications can be found in the references at the end of the appendix.

Econometric Services

Many forecasts of U. S. and international economic conditions are available to the financial analyst. Based on so-called **econometric** models developed by a variety of academic institutions and economic advisory services, these forecasts of the United States economy, and more recently of economies of other countries as well, can provide valuable clues regarding the likely movement of the country's economy within which financial conditions must be viewed. Among the widely quoted and used econometric models are these developed by the Wharton School at the University of Pennsylvania, Data Resources Inc., and Chase Econometric Associates. Many corporations subscribe to such forecasting services and make use of the projections in their operational and financial planning. Increasingly, corporate and academic economists are testing their own assumptions about economic trends with the help of econometric models. Another feature of these services is the growing variety of on-line data bases containing a vast array of statistical and financial information for immediate access.

While we have merely touched on the major sources of specific or general information on financial business affairs, the reader is encouraged to make use of the sources discussed as well as the references provided at the end of this appendix. In addition a great deal of information is available from various business libraries in corporations and in colleges and universities, as well as from local institutions. The problem facing a financial analyst, whether student or professional, is not a lack of data; rather, it is selecting what is truly relevant.

SELECTED REFERENCES

Daniells, Lorna M. *Business Information Sources*. Rev. ed. Berkeley: University of California Press, 1985.

Wasserman, Paul, ed. *Encyclopedia of Business Information Sources*. 4th ed. Detroit: Gale Research, 1980.

Kruzas, Anthony T., and Schnittroth, John, Jr. *Encyclopedia of Information Systems & Services*. 4th ed. Detroit: Gale Research, 1980.

Levine, Sumner N., ed. *Dow Jones-Irwin Business Almanac*. Homewood, Ill.: Dow Jones-Irwin, 1982.

Ruder, William, and Nathan, Raymond. *The Businessman's Guide to Washington*. New York: Collier Books, 1975.

Lehmann, Michael B. *The Dow Jones-Irwin Guide to Using The Wall Street Journal*. Homewood, III.: Dow Jones-Irwin, 1984.

Pierce, Phyllis S., ed. *The Dow Jones Averages 1885–1980*. New York: Dow Jones, 1982.

Gould, Bruce G. *Dow Jones-Irwin Guide to Commodity Trading*. Rev. ed. Homewood, Ill.: Dow Jones-Irwin, 1981.

Clasing, Henry K., Jr. *The Dow Jones-Irwin Guide to Put and Call Options*. Rev. ed. Homewood, Ill.: Dow Jones-Irwin, 1978.

APPENDIX III
SOLUTIONS TO
SELF-STUDY PROBLEMS

The following pages contain solutions to the self-study exercises and problems at the end of each chapter. Not every solution is provided here. Instead, a selection of the most important materials to be practiced is provided, more than two thirds of the total.

CHAPTER ONE—SOLUTIONS TO PROBLEMS 1 AND 2

1. *a.* $\dfrac{\text{Net Profit}}{\text{Sales}} = 11.4\%$

$\text{Assets} = \dfrac{\text{Sales}}{1.34}$ (Sales > Assets)

Thus:

$\dfrac{\text{Net Profit}}{\text{Assets}} = \dfrac{\text{Net Profit}}{\dfrac{\text{Sales}}{1.34}} = 11.4\%\,(1.34) = \underline{15.28\%}$

If we assume no debt in the capitalization, then net worth equals capitalization. Thus:

$$\frac{\text{Net Profit}}{\text{Capitalization}} = \frac{\text{Net Profit}}{\text{Net Worth}} = \frac{1}{.67} \times \frac{\text{Net Profit}}{\text{Assets}}$$

Return on net worth:

$$\frac{15.28}{.67} = \underline{\underline{22.8\%}}$$

A faster asset turnover means a smaller asset base and smaller capitalization relative to sales—thus return figures go up.

b. Gross margin is 31.4%, thus the cost of goods sold of $4,391,300 must represent sales of

$$\frac{\$4,391,300}{1.0 - .314} = \underline{\underline{\$6,400,000}}$$

Net profit must be 9.7% of $6,400,000, or $\underline{\underline{\$621,000}}$. Total assets must be derived from:

$$\frac{\text{Sales}}{\text{Assets}} = .827; \text{ Assets} = \frac{\text{Sales}}{.827} = \frac{\$6,400,000}{.827} = \underline{\underline{\$7,740,000}}$$

Return on capitalization must be:

$$\frac{\text{Net Profit}}{\text{Assets} - \text{Current Liabilities}} = \frac{\text{Net Profit}}{.79 \,(\text{Assets})} = \frac{\$621,000}{6,115,000} = \underline{\underline{10.15\%}}$$

c. Changes in current ratio and effect on working capital:

Current Ratio: $2.20 \text{ to } 1 = \frac{\$573,100}{\$260,500^*}$

Working Capital: $573,100 - $260,500 = $\underline{\underline{\$312,600}}$

1. Payment of accounts payable:

Decrease in cash $67,500
Decrease in payables $67,500

---

*Derived from relationship.

Both current assets and current liabilities *reduced* by same amount; this *improves* current ratio but leaves working capital unaffected:

$$\frac{\$573,100 - \$67,500}{\$260,500 - \$67,500} = \frac{\$505,600}{\$193,000} = 2.62 \text{ to } 1$$

This is a common action taken by small companies at year-end to improve their ratio.

2. Collection of note:

   Increase in cash $33,000
   Decrease in notes receivable $33,000

   Both elements are within current assets, thus there is no net effect on either the ratio or the working capital.

3. Purchase on account:

   Increase in inventory $41,300
   Increase in payables $41,300

   Both current assets and current liabilities are *increased*; thus the opposite effect of (1), with working capital unaffected:

$$\frac{\$573,100 + \$41,300}{\$260,500 + \$41,300} = \frac{\$614,400}{\$301,800} = 2.04 \text{ to } 1$$

4. Dividend payment:

   Decrease in cash $60,000
   Decrease in accrued dividends $42,000
   Decrease in earned surplus .... $18,000 (no effect)

   Uneven effect on the two elements, thus change in both the ratio and working capital:

$$\frac{\$573,100 - \$60,000}{\$260,500 - \$42,000} = \frac{\$513,100}{\$218,500} = 2.35 \text{ to } 1$$

   The current ratio is slightly improved, while working capital drops by $18,000.

5. Machine sale:

   Increase in cash .... $ 80,000
   Decrease in fixed assets .... $202,000 (no effect)
   Decrease in accumulated depreciation .... $112,000 (no effect)
   Loss on sale of assets .... $ 10,000 (no effect)

The only effect is an increase in current assets, which changes both the ratio and working capital:

$$\frac{\$573,100 + \$80,000}{\$260,500} = \frac{\$653,100}{\$260,500} = \underline{2.51 \text{ to } 1}$$

The current ratio rises to 2.51, while working capital improves by $\underline{\$80,000}$.

6. Sale of merchandise:

```
Increase in receivables ....................... $109,700*
Decrease in inventory  ....................... $ 73,500
Increase in retained earnings .................. $ 36,200 (no effect)
```

There is a net increase in current assets, which improves the ratio and working capital:

$$\frac{\$573,100 + \$109,700 - \$73,500}{\$260,500} = \frac{\$609,300}{\$260,500} = \underline{2.34 \text{ to } 1}$$

The current ratio rises to 2.34, while working capital improves by $\underline{\$36,200}$.

7. Write-offs:

```
Decrease in inventory  ....................... $ 20,000
Decrease in goodwill ......................... $ 15,000 (no effect)
Decrease in retained earnings ................. $ 35,000 (no effect)
```

There is a reduction of current assets which affects both the ratio and working capital:

$$\frac{\$573,100 - \$20,000}{\$260,500} = \frac{\$553,100}{\$260,500} = \underline{2.12 \text{ to } 1}$$

Slight drop to 2.12, while working capital is reduced by $\underline{\$20,000}$.

d. Days' receivables and payables:

$$\frac{\text{Net sales}}{\text{Days}} = \frac{\$437,500}{90} = \underline{\$4,861 \text{ per day}}$$

$$\frac{\text{Purchases}}{\text{Days}} = \frac{\$143,500}{90} = \underline{\$1,594 \text{ per day}}$$

*Derived from $\frac{\$73,500}{1.0 - .33} = \underline{\$109,700}$.

$$\text{Days' receivables} = \frac{\text{Accounts receivable}}{\text{Daily sales}}$$

$$= \frac{\$156,800}{\$4,861} = \underline{\underline{32.3 \text{ days}}}$$

$$\text{Days' payables} = \frac{\text{Accounts payable}}{\text{Daily purchases}}$$

$$= \frac{\$69,300}{\$1,594} = \underline{\underline{43.5 \text{ days}}}$$

The company's collections are fairly slow, in view of the discount period of 10 days, while its payments are slightly faster than needed against the 45-day terms.

Inventory turnover:

Average inventory: $\dfrac{(\$382,200 + \$227,300)}{2} = \underline{\underline{\$304,750}}$

Turnover on sales:

$$\frac{\text{Average inventory}}{\text{Sales for quarter}} = \frac{\$304,750}{\$437,500} = \underline{\underline{69.6\%}} \text{ (quarterly)}$$

or

$$\frac{\text{Average inventory}}{\text{Annual sales}} = \frac{\$304,750}{4(\$437,500)} = \underline{\underline{17.4\%}} \text{ (annualized)}$$

or

$$\frac{\text{Sales for quarter}}{\text{Average inventory}} = \frac{\$437,500}{\$304,750} = \underline{\underline{1.44 \text{ times}}} \text{ (quarterly)}$$

or

$$\frac{\text{Annual sales}}{\text{Average inventory}} = \frac{4(\$437,500)}{\$304,750} = \underline{\underline{5.74 \text{ times}}} \text{ (annualized)}$$

Turnover on cost of sales:

$$\frac{\text{Average inventory}}{\text{Cost of sales for quarter}} = \frac{\$304,750}{\$298,400} = \underline{\underline{102.1\%}} \text{ (quarterly)}$$

$$\frac{\text{Average inventory}}{\text{Annual cost of sales}} = \frac{\$304,750}{4(\$298,400)} = \underline{\underline{25.5\%}} \text{ (annualized)}$$

or

$$\frac{\text{Cost of sales for quarter}}{\text{Average inventory}} = \frac{\$298,400}{\$304,750} = \underline{\underline{.98 \text{ times}}} \text{ (quarterly)}$$

or

$$\frac{\text{Annual cost of sales}}{\text{Average inventory}} = \frac{4(\$298,400)}{\$304,750} = \underline{\underline{3.92 \text{ times}}} \text{ (annualized)}$$

Turnover on ending inventory:

$$\frac{\text{Ending inventory}}{\text{Cost of sales for quarter}} = \frac{\$227,300}{\$298,400} = \underline{76.1}\% \text{ (quarterly)}$$

or

$$\frac{\text{Cost of sales for quarter}}{\text{Ending inventory}} = \frac{\$298,400}{\$227,300} = \underline{1.31 \text{ times}} \text{ (quarterly)}$$

The cost of sales figures are more useful as a rule. Ending inventory should be used in relation to the quarterly cost of sales if there are significant seasonal swings. Annualization on a simple "4x" basis is problematic if a strong pattern is suspected.

2. ABC Company

The various ratios are grouped by point of view:

a. Management's view:

	1986	1987
Cost of goods sold	70.4%	70.6%
Gross margin	29.6%	29.4%
Profit margin	5.7%	5.4%
Profit before interest and taxes	10.7%	10.8%
Profit after taxes, before interest	5.8%	5.8%
Selling and administrative expenses	15.0%	14.4%
Employee profit sharing	4.1%	4.4%
Other income	.2%	.2%
Tax rate	46.0%	46.0%
Contribution	N.A.	N.A.
Gross asset turnover $\left(\frac{\text{Assets}}{\text{Sales}}\right)$	59.5%	64.6%
Net asset turnover $\left(\frac{\text{Assets}}{\text{Sales}}\right)$	39.4%	44.4%
Ending inventory turns $\left(\frac{\text{Cost of Sales}}{\text{Inventory}}\right)$	5.2×	4.8×
Days' receivables	51.1 days	60.7 days
Days' payables (cost of sales)	34.0 days	37.0 days
Net profit to total assets	9.6%	8.3%
Net profit to capitalization	14.4%	12.1%
Net profit before interest and tax to total assets	18.0%	16.8%
Net profit before interest and tax to capitalization	27.2%	24.4%
Net profit after tax, before interest, to total assets	9.7%	9.0%
Net profit after tax, before interest, to capitalization	14.6%	13.2%

b. Owner's view

	1986	1987
Net profit to net worth (including deferred tax)	15.1%	16.3%
Net profit to common equity (w/o deferred tax)	15.2%	16.7%
Earnings per share	$3.69	$4.61
Cash flow per share	$6.48	$8.38
Dividends per share	$ .54	$ .59
Dividend coverage—earnings	6.8×	7.8×
Dividend coverage—cash flow	11.9×	14.2×

c. Lender's view

	1986	1987
Current ratio	2.1:1	2.2:1
Acid test (excluding advances)	1.3:1	1.4:1
Total debt to assets	35.7%	48.7%
Long-term debt to capitalization	3.0%	25.3%
Total debt to net worth	55.5%	95.0%
Long-term debt to net worth	3.1%	32.9%
Interest coverage (pretax)	70×	13×
Cash flow before taxes—interest coverage	98×	18×
Full interest coverage ($8.5 million)	—	11×

Observations:

Slight worsening shown in operating performance, at the same effective tax rate, which makes 1986 the better year. More investment has been committed, both in working capital and fixed assets—collections are slowing, inventories are up, and profits on assets are down, by every measure.

Leverage has improved the profit on net worth, however, and earnings per share are up sharply. No problems exist in covering dividends on interest, even if a full year's interest is assumed.

Comparisons should be made with companies in similar product lines, particularly on capital structure, return on net worth, and coverages. High-low analysis of good and bad years should highlight risk of earnings fluctuations. Two-year static picture not enough.

CHAPTER TWO—SOLUTIONS TO PROBLEMS 1, 2a AND b, AND 4

1. CBA Company

Changes in Balance Sheet ($000)

Assets		Liabilities	
Cash	$ (12.2)	Accounts payable	$ 11.8
Marketable securities	10.0	Notes payable	90.0
Accounts receivable	(8.8)	Accrued expenses	2.9
Inventories	60.7	Total current liabilities .	$104.7
Total current assets . . .	49.7		
Land	-0-	Mortgage payable	$ (15.2)
Plant and equipment (net) . . .	19.6	Common stock	5.0
Total fixed assets	19.6	Earned surplus	(17.0)
		Total net worth	$ (27.2)
Other assets	8.2	Total liabilities and	
Total assets	$ 77.5	net worth	$ 77.5

Funds flow statement (Year 1987)

Sources		Uses	
Depreciation	$ 32.2*	Loss from operations	$ 2.0**
Decrease in cash	12.2	Dividends paid	15.0**
Decrease in accounts			
receivable	8.8	Increase in securities	10.0
Increase in accounts payable .	11.8	Increase in inventories	60.7
Increase in note payable	90.0	Investment in plant	51.8†
Increase in accrued expenses .	2.9	Increase in other assets	8.2
Increase in common stock . .	5.0	Decrease in mortgage	15.2
Total	$162.9	Total	$162.9

The results were built up from:
*Taken from 1987 operating statement.
**Change in earned surplus matches the combination of loss from operations ($2,000) on the 1987 operating statement and dividends paid ($15,000), from footnote. No extraordinary items appear and no assumptions are necessary.
†Since net plant and equipment increased by $19,600, and the only known element affecting the account is depreciation ($32,200), the amount of investment must have been the sum of these amounts ($51,800).

Observations:

The biggest single use is a drastic rise in inventories, even though sales volume changed little. Are inventory controls failing? Dividends were wisely cut as profits plummeted. The key funds source was borrowing (short term) of $90.0, which provides more than half of funds needs. Sizable capital investment (almost twice depreciation) points to optimistic future plans—any problems in sight? Is the company beginning to lean on suppliers? (Accounts payable up somewhat.) Is equity capital called for?

2. *a.* ABC Company:

Beginning balance, earned surplus (12/31/86)		$167,300
Less:		
Net loss for 1987 (incl. loss from aband.)	$14,100	
Common dividends paid	12,000	
Inventory adjustment	24,000	
Amortization of goodwill, patents	15,000	65,100
Ending balance, earned surplus (12/31/87)		$102,200

Funds Flow Items

Sources		Uses	
Depreciation	$21,400	Net *operating* loss	$10,100
Total Sources	$21,400	Loss from abandonment . .	4,000
		Dividends paid	12,000
		Investment in fixed assets .	57,500
		Amortization	15,000
		Inventory adjustment	24,000
		Total Uses	$122,000

Depreciation (non-cash) should be reflected as a source as it reduced operating profit/loss; loss conditions do not change its basic character.

Loss from abandonment can be separated from profit/loss, it was offset by reduction in asset. A gain could be shown as a separate source, offset by the increase in cash.

Amortization and inventory adjustments are earned surplus reductions here; can be separated out as shown, as they have been offset by decrease in patents and inventories, or they can be *eliminated* on both sides of the statement.

b. DEF Company:

The layout of the data appears on the following page: Observations:

Any assumption about a gain or loss on sale and/or abandonment would be handled as in Item 2*a.* Any disposition of partially depreciated assets would cause greater "reductions" in assets than in accumulated depreciation, which in turn would raise the derived asset additions.

	Beginning Balance	Additions	Reductions	Ending Balance	Change
Gross property and fixed assets ..	$8,431,500*	$1,250,500*	$1,252,000**	$8,430,000*	$(1,500)
Accumulated depreciation	3,513,000**	1,613,000*	1,252,000†	3,874,000*	361,000
Net property and fixed assets . . .	$4,918,500	$ 362,500	$ –0–	$4,556,000	$(362,500)
					(Result)

The result is built up from:
*Given information.
**Forced figures.
†Assumption that fully depreciated assets were abandoned.

4. ZYX Company

A variety of funds flow statements are possible here:

From peak to trough of season (two seasons).

From peak to peak, or trough to trough.

From April to April, or any other month.

Two-year span, July to July, to provide long-term debt.

Samples of these possible funds flow statements appear as follows:

Sources of Funds	1/31/87 to 4/30/87	1/31/88 to 4/30/88	4/30/87 to 1/31/88	1/31/87 to 1/31/88	4/30/87 to 4/30/88	7/31/86 to 7/31/88
Profit from operations . . .	$ 10	$ 17	$ 67	$ 77	$ 84	$172
Depreciation	6	7	21	27	28	54
Decrease in cash	—	—	1	—	—	5
Decrease in receivables .	191	237	—	—	—	11
Decrease in inventories .	184	253	—	—	33	—
Decrease in other assets .	1	—	—	—	—	—
Increase in payables	—	—	85	67	—	16
Increase in notes	—	—	342	48	—	45
Increase in common	—	—	25	25	25	25
Total sources . . .	$392	$514	$541	$244	$170	$328

Uses of Funds	1/31/87 to 4/30/87	1/31/88 to 4/30/88	4/30/87 to 1/31/88	1/31/87 to 1/31/88	4/30/87 to 4/30/88	7/31/86 to 7/31/88
Capital investments	$ 48	$ 50	$—	$ 48	$ 50	$ 98
Increase in cash	17	13	—	16	12	—
Increase in receivables . .	—	—	260	69	23	79
Increase in inventories . .	—	—	220	36	—	—
Increase in other assets . .	—	—	3	2	3	2
Decrease in payables . . .	18	91	—	—	6	—
Decrease in notes	294	342	—	—	—	—
Decrease in mortgage . .	—	—	10	10	10	20
Dividends paid	15	18	48	63	66	129
Total uses	$392	$514	$541	$244	$170	$328

Observations:

This strong seasonal pattern from January to April shows up vividly in the peak to trough and trough to peak comparisons, where receivables and inventories are matched with payables and sizable short-term notes. There is a lag effect in buildup of inventories and receivables, as expected. Growth shows up in like-to-like comparisons, with no undue strains. Good example to demonstrate effect of careless placement of funds flow analysis over alternative time periods.

CHAPTER THREE—SOLUTIONS TO PROBLEMS 1, 2, 4, 6, AND 7

1. *a.* Change in credit policy:

·18 days' sales developed as follows:

Daily sales: $\dfrac{\$9,137,000}{360}$ = $25,380/day

18 days' sales: 18 × $25,380 = $ 456,800
40 days' sales: 40 × $25,380 = $1,015,200

Increase in receivables: $ 558,400

60 days' sales: 60 × $25,380 = $1,522,800

Increase in receivables: $1,066,000

Observations:

Funds need increase is over one-half million dollars. Cash flow per year available from operations is only $305,000—likely the company must secure other funds. Need is doubled if policy is changed to 60 days.

b. Inventory consignment:
Average inventory: $725,000

Current turnover: $\dfrac{\text{Cost of goods sold}}{\text{Average inventory}}$ = $\dfrac{.83 \times \$9,137,000}{\$725,000}$ = 10.5 times

Turnover slowdown: $\dfrac{\text{Cost of goods sold}}{7.0}$ = $\dfrac{\$7,583,700}{7.0}$ = $1,083,400

Inventory increases by $1,083,400 less $725,200 = $ 358,400

Turnover increase: $\dfrac{\text{Cost of goods sold}}{11.0}$ = $\dfrac{\$7,583,700}{11.0}$ = $ 689,400

Inventory decreases by $725,000 less $689,400 = $ 35,600

Observations:

Funds needs change as indicated. Likely will require increased production operations to achieve higher supply (about 5 percent), some increased purchases, which will provide some funds through higher payables—but the slowdown must be financed by other funds sources.

c. Change in payment terms:
Company has now 10 days' purchases outstanding:

$$\text{Payables} = \frac{\text{Purchases}}{360} \times 10 = \frac{\$5,316,000}{36} = \underline{\$147,670}$$

Change in terms means 5 more days' extension which provides funds of $\underline{\$73,835}$ (1/2 of above) for no additional cost.

Observations:
Company earns 2 percent now to pay 20 days sooner; will earn 2 percent to pay 30 days sooner (from day 15 to day 45). Annual interest thus 12 times 2% = 24%. If company can obtain funds for less, it is desirable to discount. (See Chapter 6.)

d. Capital expenditures and dividends:

Funds need	$125,000 for equipment
Plus 60% of $131,000 =	79,000
Total	$204,000

Against cash from operations:

Profits	$131,000
Depreciation	174,000
Total	$305,000

Observations:
Can be handled by internal funds unless significant changes in working capital needs occur (such as in earlier examples).

e. Sales growth:
10% increase in sales ($913,700) requires:

Funds for receivables: 18 days of increased sales	$ 45,700
Funds for inventories: 10 percent increase	72,500
Funds from payables: 10 days of increased purchases	(14,800)
Total funds need	$103,400
Against additional profits of 10% (assume no efficiency of scale):	$ 13,100

Observations:
Unless there are significant improvements in profit elements, the increase in sales requires funds of about

$90,000. This makes dividends and capital expenditures under *d.* barely possible from internal funds, and leaves no room for inefficiency.

2. ABC Company
Pro forma operating statement from data given:

ABC COMPANY
Pro Forma Operating Statement
for the year ended October 31, 1989
($000)

		Amount		Percent
Net sales			$4,350	100.0
Cost of goods sold:				
Labor	$1,044			24.0
Materials	631			14.5
Overhead*	862			19.8
Depreciation	143	2,680		3.3	61.6
Gross profit			$1,670	38.4
Selling expense	430			9.9
General and administrative	352	782		8.1	18.0
Profit before taxes			$ 888	20.4
Income taxes (46%)			408	9.4
Net Income			$ 480	11.1

*$743 + $45 + $74.

Observations:
Slight increase in the rate of profit due to higher efficiency in labor and overhead which combine to overcome a rise in selling expense.

4. XYZ Company
Cash budget by month developed from data given:

XYZ COMPANY
Cash Budget for Six Months
October 1988 through March 1989
($000)

Cash receipts:	Oct.	Nov.	Dec.	Jan.	Feb.	Mar.	Total
Collections from credit	$ 215	$ 245	$ 265	$ 385	$ 345	$ 505	$1,960
Cash sales	385	345	505	325	290	360	2,210
Total receipts	$ 600	$ 590	$ 770	$ 710	$ 635	$ 865	$4,170

	Oct.	Nov.	Dec.	Jan.	Feb.	Mar.	Total
Cash disbursements (see breakdown of purchases below):							
Cash purchases . .	$ 61	$ 54	$ 29	$ 32	$ 45	$ 48	$ 269
Credit purchases—							
10 days (less 2% discount)	218	220	146	121	160	184	1,049
Credit purchases—							
45 days	257	266	286	205	153	192	1,359
Salaries and wages	146	131	192	124	110	137	840
Operating expenses	108	97	141	91	81	101	619
Cash dividend . . .	—	—	40	—	—	—	40
Federal income tax.	—	—	—	20	—	—	20
Mortgage payment	7	7	7	7	7	7	42
Total cash disburse-ments	$ 797	$ 775	$ 841	$ 600	$ 556	$ 669	$4,238
Net cash receipts (disbursements) .	$(197)	$(185)	$ (71)	$ 110	$ 79	$ 196	$ (68)
Cumulative net cash flow	$(197)	$(382)	$(453)	$(343)	$(264)	$ (68)	
Analysis of cash requirements:							
Beginning cash balance	$ 95	$(102)	$(287)	$(358)	$(248)	$(169)	
Net cash receipts (disbursements)	(197)	(185)	(71)	110	79	196	
Ending cash balance	$(102)	$(287)	$(358)	$(248)	$(169)	$ 27	
Minimum cash balance	75	75	75	75	75	75	
Cash requirements	$ 177	$ 362	$ 433	$ 323	$ 244	$ 48	

Breakdown of monthly purchases can be seen on the next page.

Observations:

In spite of sizable cash needs, which reach a peak of $433,000 in December, the pattern of cash movements winds up not far below the minimum cash balance six months hence. Seasonal short-term borrowing indicated here to cover inventory buildup and lag in collection pattern.

Breakdown of Monthly Purchases

Terms	Aug.	Sept.	Oct.	Nov.	Dec.	Jan.	Feb.	Mar.
Cash	N.A.	$ 45	$ 61*	$ 54	$ 29	$ 32	$ 45	$ 48
2/10,n/30	N.A.	60/60/60*	81*/81*/82	71/71/72	38/39/39	42/43/43	60/60/60	64/64/64
n/45	145/145*	112*/113	153/152	134/133	72/73	80/80	112/113	120/120
Total	—	$450	$610	$535	$290	$320	$450	$480

*Due for payment in October (September purchases reconstructed from $60 amount at 2/10, n/30, which must be one third of 40 percent of total purchases).

6. ABC Supermarket

ABC SUPERMARKET
Cash Budget
for six months ended June 30, 1988
($000)

	Jan.	Feb.	Mar.	Apr.	May	June	Total
Receipts:							
Cash sales	$200.0	$190.0	$220.0	$200.0	$230.0	$220.0	$1,260.0
Cash from sale of property	—	—	6.0	6.0	6.0	—	18.0
Rental income . .	—	—	.3	.3	.3	.3	1.2
Total receipts .	$200.0	$190.0	$226.3	$206.3	$236.3	$220.3	$1,279.2
Disbursements:							
Purchases recorded	$150.0	$142.5	$165.0	$150.0	$172.5	$165.0	$ 945.0
Payment for purchases (15-day lag)	$159.0	$146.3	$153.7	$157.5	$161.3	$168.7	$ 946.5
Salaries (12% of sales)	24.0	22.8	26.4	24.0	27.6	26.4	151.2
Other expenses (9% of sales) . .	18.0	17.1	19.8	18.0	20.7	19.8	113.4
Rent	3.5	3.5	3.5	3.5	3.5	3.5	21.0
Income taxes . . .	2.0	—	2.0	3.5	—	2.0	9.5
Note payment . . .	—	3.0	—	—	5.0	—	8.0
Repayment to principals	3.0	—	3.0	—	3.0	—	9.0
Payment on fixtures	—	12.0	12.0	12.0	12.0	—	48.0
Total disbursements	$209.5	$204.7	$220.4	$218.5	$233.1	$220.4	$1,306.6
Net Cash flow	$ (9.5)	$(14.7)	$ 5.9	$(12.2)	$ 3.2	$ (.1)	$ (27.4)
Cumulative net cash	$ (9.5)	$(24.2)	$(18.3)	$(30.5)	$(27.3)	$ (27.4)	
Analysis of cash requirements:							
Beginning cash balance	$ 42.5	$ 33.0	$ 18.3	$ 24.2	$ 12.0	$ 15.2	
Net cash flow . . .	(9.5)	(14.7)	5.9	(12.2)	3.2	(.1)	
Ending cash balance	$ 33.0	$ 18.3	$ 24.2	$ 12.0	$ 15.2	$ 15.1	
Minimum cash balance	20.0	20.0	20.0	20.0	20.0	20.0	
Cash Need (Excess)	$ (13.0)	$ 1.7	$ (4.2)	$ 8.0	$ 4.8	$ 4.9	

Observations:

The cash pattern indicates excess funds needs in four out of the six months, if a $20,000 minimum balance is desired. The greatest funds need is in April 1988, but even by the end of the period no cleanup of required borrowing will have been achieved.

7. XYZ Company
Cash budget developed from data given:

XYZ COMPANY
Cash Budget by Month
six months ended March 31, 1989
($000)

Cash receipts:	Oct.	Nov.	Dec.	Jan.	Feb.	Mar.	Total
Collections (see next page)	$2,608	$2,092	$2,983	$2,400	$2,567	$2,708	$15,358
Cash disbursements:							
Payments for purchases (see below)	712	663	650	650	650	650	3,975
Wages	215	215	215	215	215	215	1,290
Other expenses . .	420	420	420	420	420	420	2,520
Selling & administrative expense .	326	345	343	368	330	342	2,054
Note repayments .	—	750	—	—	750	—	1,500
Interest	—	—	—	300	—	—	300
Dividend payments	25	—	—	25	—	—	50
Tax payment	—	—	—	375	—	—	375
Total disbursements	$1,698	$2,393	$1,628	$2,353	$2,365	$1,627	$12,064
Net cash receipts (disbursements)	$ 910	$ (301)	$1,355	$ 47	$ 202	$1,081	$ 3,294
Cumulative cash flow	$ 910	$ 609	$1,964	$2,011	$2,213	$3,294	

Collection Pattern

Timing	Aug.	Sept.	Oct.	Nov.	Dec.	Jan.	Feb.	Totals
				Sales				
Oct. 1–10	$ 641							
Oct. 11–20	642							$2,608
Oct. 21–31	642	$ 683*						
Nov. 1–10		683						
Nov. 11–20		684						$2,092
Nov. 21–30			$ 725					
Dec. 1–10			725					
Dec. 11–20			725	$ 766*			*	$2,983
Dec. 21–31				767				
Jan. 1–10				767				
Jan. 11–20					$ 816			$2,400
Jan. 21–31					817			
Feb. 1–10					817			
Feb. 11–20						$ 875		$2,567
Feb. 21–28						875		
Mar. 1–10						875		
Mar. 11–20							$916	$2,708
Mar. 21–31							917	
Totals	$1,925	$2,050	$2,175	$2,300	$2,450	$2,625	—	

*Change in collection pattern assumed.

Accounts Receivable

Sept. 30, 1988:	August sales $1,925
	September sales 2,050
	$3,975 (60 days)
Dec. 31, 1988:	1/3 of November sales . . . . $ 767
	December sales 2,450
	$3,217 (40 days)
March 31, 1989:	1/3 of February sales . . . . $ 917
	March sales 2,850
	$3,767 (40 days)

Purchase Pattern

45 days' payables throughout, thus there is a lag of 3/2 months.

Pro forma statements developed from data given and calculated:

XYZ COMPANY
Pro Forma Income Statements
three months ended 12/31/88 and six months ended 3/31/89
($000)

	1988 3 Months	1988/89 6 Months	
Sales	$6,925	$15,150	(given)
Cost of sales	4,848	10,605	(70 percent of sales)
Gross margin	$2,077	$ 4,545	
Selling and administrative	$1,014	$ 2,054	(from cash budget)
Interest	75	150	(developed)
	$1,089	$ 2,204	
Profit before taxes	$ 988	$ 2,341	
Income taxes	494	1,171	(50 percent of profit)
Net income	$ 494	$ 1,170	(to balance sheet)

XYZ COMPANY
Pro Forma Balance Sheets
December 31, 1988 and March 31, 1989
($000)

	12/31/88		3/31/89	
Cash	$ 2,704	(+$1,964)	$ 4,034	(+$3,294)
Accounts receivable	3,217	(see above)	3,767	(see above)
Raw materials	2,200	(see below)	1,675	(see below)
Finished goods	6,081	(see below)	4,833	(see below)
Plant and equipment	7,081	(−$129 depr.)	6,952	(−$258 depr.)
Other assets	1,730	(no change)	1,730	(no change)
Total assets	$23,013		$22,991	
Accounts payable	$ 975	(45 days)	$ 975	(45 days)
Note payable	3,370	(−$750)	2,620	(−$1,500)
Accrued liabilities	3,444	(see below)	3,521	(see below)
Long-term debt	5,250	(no change)	5,250	(no change)
Preferred stock	1,750	(no change)	1,750	(no change)
Common stock	5,000	(no change)	5,000	(no change)
Earned surplus	3,224	(− $25, + $494)	3,875	(−$50, +$1,170)
Total liabilities	$23,013		$22,991	

Inventory Analysis

Raw Materials:	12/31/88	3/31/89
Beginning balance	$ 2,725	$ 2,725
Purchases @ $650/month	1,950	3,900
	$ 4,675	$ 6,625
Withdrawals @ $825/month	2,475	4,950
Ending balance	$ 2,200	$ 1,675

	12/31/88	3/31/89
Finished Goods:		
Beginning balance	$ 6,420	$ 6,420
Materials @ $825/month	2,475	4,950
Wages @ $215/month	645	1,290
Other expenses @ $420/month	1,260	2,520
Depreciation @ $43/month	129	258
	$10,929	$15,438
Cost of goods sold reported	4,848	10,605
Ending balance	$ 6,081	$ 4,833

Accrued Liabilities

Assume interest of $300 covers one year. Thus, by 9/31/88, $225 must have been accrued. Also, assume liabilities to accrue until paid in cash.

	12/31/88	3/31/89
Beginning balance	$ 2,875	$ 2,875
Accrued interest (one quarter)	75	75
Accrued taxes (income statement)	494	1,171
	$ 3,444	$ 4,121
Interest payment (accrued)	—	(225)
Tax payment	—	(375)
Balance shown	$ 3,444	$ 3,521

Observations:

The key change is the transformation of receivables and inventories into cash, due to the change in policies. Note the dramatic drop in inventories by 3/31/89, *if* the policies work as expected. No funds needs arise during the period, and the main collection impact is felt in October and December. If collections do not come in as expected, $1,833 will be deferred and not available by 3/31/89, and $1,533 by 12/31/88:

Receivables 12/31/88	$3,217
60 days	4,750
Difference	$1,533
Receivables 3/31/89	$3,767
60 days	5,600
Difference	$1,833

Must make sure inventories go down, and this depends on quality and nature of goods on hand.

CHAPTER FOUR—SOLUTIONS TO PROBLEMS 1, 2, AND 3

1. ABC Corporation

Break-even point calculation:

Price per unit	$5.50
Variable costs per unit	3.25
Contribution	$2.25

Fixed costs: $360,000
Units required to recover fixed costs with contribution:

$$\frac{\$360,000}{\$2.25} = \underline{160,000 \text{ units}}$$

a. Leverage

Profit Increases (20%)			Profit Decreases (20%)		
Units	Profit	Change	Units	Profit	Change
160,000	$ 0	—	160,000	$ 0	—
192,000	72,000	infinite	128,000	(72,000)	infinite
230,400	158,400	120.0%	102,400	(129,600)	80.0%
276,480	262,080	65.5%	81,920	(175,680)	39.8%
331,776	386,496	47.5%	65,536	(212,544)	21.0%

Note the declining rate of change as we move away from break-even point.

b. Changes in Conditions
Price drop:
Change in contribution from $2.25 to $1.75

Break-even point: $\dfrac{\$360,000}{\$1.75} = \underline{205,715 \text{ units}}$

Cost increase—variable:
Change in contribution from $2.25 to $2.00

Break-even point: $\dfrac{\$360,000}{\$2.00} = \underline{180,000 \text{ units}}$

Cost increase—fixed:
Change in fixed cost from $360,000 to $400,000

Break-even point: $\dfrac{\$400,000}{\$2.25} = \underline{177,778 \text{ units}}$

c. Changing Conditions by Operating Level
Calculations must be made step by step to take account of changing conditions:

Contribution from first 150,000 units:
Price $5.50
Variable costs 3.25
   Contribution .... $2.25 × 150,000 = $337,500

Contribution from next 25,000 units:
Price $5.50
Variable costs 3.00
   Contribution .... $2.50 × 25,000 = $62,500

Break-even point will lie between 150,000 and 175,000 units, since combined contribution of $400,000 exceeds fixed costs by $40,000.

Thus: Break-even point is based on fixed cost remaining after 150,000 units, $22,500.

$$\frac{\$22,500}{\$2.50} = 9,000 \text{ units added to } 150,000, \text{ or } \underline{\underline{159,000 \text{ units}}}$$

Contribution from units after 175,000 units and after 190,000 does not come into play unless fixed costs were raised earlier.

Break-Even Chart
ABC Corporation

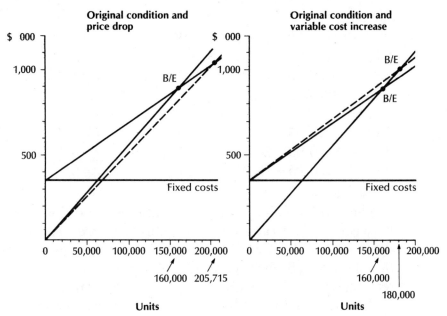

Break-Even Chart
ABC Corporation (Continued)

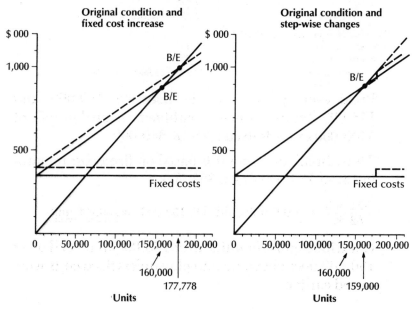

Original condition and fixed cost increase

Original condition and step-wise changes

2. Financial Leverage
    a. For $i = 5\%$ and $R = 8\%$:
    —no debt: $r = 8\%$
    —25% debt: $0.08 + 25/75(.08 - .05)$; $r = 9\%$
    —50% debt: $0.08 + 50/50(.08 - .05)$; $r = 11\%$
    —75% debt: $0.08 + 75/25(.08 - .05)$; $r = 17\%$
    b. For $i = 6\%$ and $R = 5\%$:
    —no debt: $r = 5\%$
    —25% debt: $0.05 + 25/75(.05 - .06)$; $r = 4.7\%$
    —50% debt: $0.05 + 50/50(.05 - .06)$; $r = 4\%$
    —75% debt: $0.05 + 75/25(.05 - .06)$; $r = 2\%$

Observations:

The leverage effect is less dramatic as the difference between interest rates paid and return on assets earned decreases. Still, at high leverage, a more than proportional push on ROE is achieved, as the graph in the chapter suggested. The negative leverage resulting from poor performance achieved by investing the capital is just as powerful as in the positive case.

3. Five-Year Financial Plan*

	Year 1	Year 2	Year 3	Year 4	Year 5	Revised Year 5
Capitalization:						
Debt-equity ratio	0.25:1	0.25:1	0.50:1	0.50:1	0.50:1	0.75:1
Debt	$ 300	$ 309	$ 638	$ 664	$ 706	$1,059
Equity	1,200	1,235	1,277	1,330	1,413	1,413
Net assets	$1,500	$1,544	$1,915	$1,994	$2,119	$2,472
Profitability:						
Return on net assets .	8%	9%	10%	10%	10%	11%
Amount of profit	$120	$139	$192	$199	$212	$272
Interest rate (after taxes)	4.5%	4.5%	5.0%	5.0%	5.0%	4.5%
Amount of interest . .	$ 14	$ 14	$ 32	$ 33	$ 35	$ 48
Profit after interest	$106	$125	$160	$166	$177	$224
Earnings disposition:						
Dividend payout	2/3	2/3	2/3	1/2	1/2	2/3
Dividends paid	$ 71	$ 83	$107	$ 83	$ 88	$149
Reinvestment . .	$ 35	$ 42	$ 53	$ 83	$ 89	$ 75
Financing and Investment:						
New debt, old ratio . .	9	10	26	42	44	56
New debt, new ratio .	—	319	—	—**	—	—
New investment .	$ 44	$371	$ 79	$125	$133	$131
Results:						
Net return, net assets .	7.1%	8.1%	8.4%	8.3%	8.4%	9.1%
Return on equity	8.8	10.1	12.5	12.5	12.5	15.8
Growth in equity	2.9	3.4	4.2	6.2	6.3	5.3
Growth in earnings . .	—	17.9	28.0	3.8	6.6	34.9
Earnings per share . . .	$0.53	$0.62	$0.80	$0.83	$0.88	$1.12
Dividends per share .	$0.36	$0.42	$0.54	$0.42	$0.44	$0.74

*In thousands of dollars.
**For revised year 5, this item should be $353.

Observations:

The results displayed are self-explanatory and show a rising level as both operating and financial conditions are changed. The higher dividend payout in the revised Year 5 situation causes a drop in equity growth, even though operating conditions are more favorable.

CHAPTER FIVE—SOLUTIONS TO PROBLEMS 1, 3, 5, AND 6

1. Investment Proposition
Net investment: $60,000

a. Net present value at 10 percent and 16 percent (factors from Table 5–10):

Amounts		PV Factors at 10%	Present Value	PV Factors at 16%	Present Value
$10,000	×	.909	$ 9,090	.862	$ 8,620
15,000	×	.826	12,390	.743	11,145
15,000	×	.751	11,265	.641	9,615
20,000	×	.683	13,660	.552	11,040
15,000	×	.621	9,315	.476	7,140
10,000	×	.564	5,640	.410	4,100
5,000	×	.513	2,565	.354	1,770
			$63,925		$53,430
Outlay			60,000		60,000
Net present value			$ 3,925		$(6,570)

b. Internal Rate of Return (Yield):
Must be between 10 and 16 percent; closer to the lower end.

Trial at 12 percent: (factors from Table 5–10)

Amounts		PV Factors at 12%	Present Value
$10,000	×	.893	$ 8,930
15,000	×	.797	11,955
15,000	×	.712	10,680
20,000	×	.636	12,720
15,000	×	.567	8,505
10,000	×	.507	5,070
5,000	×	.452	2,260
			$60,120
Outlay			60,000
Net present value			$ 120

The IRR (yield) is approximately <u>12 percent.</u>

c. Even Cash Flows:
$13,000 per year at 10 percent (factor from Table 5–11):

$13,000 × 4,868	=	$63,284
Net investment	=	60,000
Net present value	=	$ 3,284

d. Cash Flows to Yield 16 Percent:
Annualize the investment of $60,000 at 16 percent:

$$A = \frac{PV}{f}$$

$$A = \frac{\$60,000}{4.039} = \$14,855$$

The required amount over seven years is slightly under $14,900.

e. Net present values at 10 and 16 percent, given recovery of $10,000:
Recovery of $10,000 at end of year 7 (factors from Table 5–10):

at 10 percent: $10,000 × .513 = $5,130
at 16 percent: $10,000 × .354 = $3,540

Original values in (a):

at 10 percent: $ 3,925, plus recovery of $5,130 = $ 9,055
at 16 percent: $(6,570), plus recovery of $3,540 = $(3,030)

IRR must now be somewhat under 16 percent, since net present value turns negative below that rate.

f. Cash flows to yield 16 percent, given recovery of $10,000:
    Present value of recovery at 16 percent: $3,540 [from e.]
    Present value of investment:

Outlay less present value of recovery
$60,000 less $3,540 = $56,460

Cash flows required based on annualizing present value of investment: [see d.]

$$A = \frac{\$56,460}{4.039} = \$13,979$$

Note that the recovery of $10,000 in year 7 reduced required cash flows by about $900 per year. This can, of course, be shown directly by developing the annual equivalent of the recovery:

$$A = \frac{\$3,540}{4.039} = \$876$$

3. Trustee of Major Estate
   Net investment: $100,000 in a and b.

Yield:

(*a*) Yield factor: $\dfrac{\$100,000}{\$16,500} = 6.061$

In Table 5–11, on the eight-year line this corresponds to a yield of about 7 percent if a rough interpolation is made.

(*b*) Yield factor: $\dfrac{\$100,000}{\$233,000} = .429$

In Table 5–10, on the 11-year line this corresponds exactly to a yield of 8 percent. Thus, the second proposition is preferable.

5. **XYZ Corporation**

Past investment: $3.75 million (sunk)
Net investment data:
   Original outlay: $6,300,000
   Recovery in 12 years: $1,260,000 (book value)
   Working capital:
      Initial $1,500,000
      Recovery in 12 years . . . $1,250,000
   Promotion expenditure ($1.0 million × .54): $540,000
     (after tax)
Life of proposition: 12 years
Profit improvements:

	Years 1–3	Years 4–8	Years 9–12	Total
Profit improvement	$1,900	$2,200	$1,300	$21,900
Less: Depreciation	420	420	420	5,040
	1,480	1,780	880	16,860
Tax at 46% (rounded)	680	820	405	7,756
	800	960	475	9,104
Add back depreciation	420	420	420	5,040
Operating cash flow	$1,220	$1,380	$ 895	$14,144

Present Value Analysis at 10 Percent

Time Period	Investments	Operating Cash Flows	PV Factors at 10%	Present Values	PV Factors at 14%	Present Values
0	− $6,300 − $1,500 − $ 540		1.000	− $8,340	1.000	− $8,340
1 2 3		+ $1,220/yr.	2.487	+ 3,034	2.322	+ 2,833
5 6 7 8		+ $1,380/yr.	5.335 − 2.487 2.848	+ 3,930	4,639 − 2.322 2.317	+ 3,197
9 10 11 12		+ $ 895/yr.	6.814 − 5.335 1.479	+ 1,324	5.660 − 4.639 1.021	+ 914
12	+ $1,260 + $1,250		.319	+ 801	.208	+ 522
	Net present values			+ $ 749		− $ 874

Net Present Value at 10 percent is about $750,000, indicating a better-than-standard result. In fact, the recovery of working capital and book values of equipment in year 12 could be foregone and the project would still meet standards.

Present Value Index at 10 percent:
   Based on initial investment

$$\frac{\$9,089}{\$8,340} = \underline{1.09}$$

   Based on net investment

$$\frac{\$8,288}{\$7,539} = \underline{1.10}$$

Present Value Payback:
   Just about <u>12 years</u> because the recovery represents the excess present value.

IRR:

By trial and error a little <u>under 12 percent</u>. (See PV analysis above.)

Annualized Net Present Value:

$$\frac{\$749}{6.814} = \underline{\underline{\$109,920}}/\text{yr. (narrow margin for error).}$$

Observations:

Project is close to standard; shows problems of handling uneven cash flows. Cannot carry past and sunk R&D—similar future projects are of doubtful value.

6. ZYX Company

Net Investment

Original machine	$32,000	
Current book value	$25,600	
Market value	15,000	(relevant)
Loss on sale	$10,600	
Tax savings on loss @ 46%	4,875	(relevant)
Net loss	$ 5,725	
New investment	$55,500	
Value in eight years	$ 1,500	

Calculation of Net Investment

New machine	$55,500
Less cash on old	15,000
	$40,500
Less tax savings	4,875
Initial investment	$35,625

To be adjusted for recoveries in year 8.

Comparison of Lives

Only eight years are comparable—if new machine lasted longer, its life would have to be cut off for purposes of comparison.

Operating Savings and Benefits

	Old Machine	New Machine	Annual Difference
Operating savings—current volume:			
Labor	$ 24,000	$ 16,000	$ 8,000
Materials	96,000	92,000	4,000
Overhead (200% of labor)	48,000	32,000	N.A.
	$168,000	$140,000	$12,000
Contribution—additional volume:			
30,000 units @ $.95		$ 28,500	
Less: Labor @ $.08		(2,400)	
Materials @ $.46		(13,800)	
Selling and promotion		(5,500)	6,800
Total savings and contribution			$18,800
Depreciation	$ 3,200	$ 6,750*	(3,550)
Taxable benefits			$15,250
Taxes at 46%			7,015
Aftertax benefits			$ 8,235
Add back depreciation			3,550
Aftertax cash flow			$11,785

*$55,500 New machine
 −1,500 Scrap
 $54,000 ÷ 8 = $6,750/year

Payback:

$$\frac{\$35,625 - \$1,500}{\$11,785} = \underline{\underline{2.9 \text{ years}}}$$

Return on Investment:

$$\frac{\$11,785}{\$34,125} = \underline{\underline{34.5\%}}$$

Net Present Value:

Time Period	Amounts	PV Factor 15%	Present Values
0	−$35,625	1.00	−$35,625
1–8	+$11,785/yr.	4.487	+$52,879
8	+$ 1,500	.327	+$ 490
	Net present value		+$17,744

Present Value Index:
net investment basis

$$\frac{\$52,879}{\$35,625 - \$490} = \underline{\underline{1.51}}$$

without terminal value

$$\frac{\$52,879 + \$490}{\$35,625} = \underline{\underline{1.50}}$$

Present Value Payback:
This is determined through use of the annuity tables.

$$\text{Annuity factor} = \frac{\$35,135}{\$11,785/\text{yr.}} = 2.981$$

Interpolation in the 15 percent column of Table 5–11 indicates a little <u>over four years</u> required. The terminal value can be a problem if significantly larger, because it has been discounted for receipt in year 8. If precision is required, year-by-year trial-and-error approaches can be made.

Annualized Net Present Value:

$$\frac{\$17,744}{4.487} = \underline{\underline{\$3,955}}$$

This is a sizable cushion for error in the performance estimates.

Internal Rate of Return:
Trial and error necessary; result about <u>$\underline{29}$</u> %

Time Period	Amounts	PV Factors at 35%	Present Values	PV Factors at 30%	Present Values
0	− $35,625	1.000	− $35,625	1.000	− $35,625
1–8	+ $11,785/yr.	2.598	+ $30,617	2.925	+ $34,471
8	+ $ 1,500	.091	+ $ 136	.123	+ $ 184
			− $ 4,872		− $ 970

Observations:
This is the best example, among the ones provided, with which to practice your mastery of problem structure, differential costs, different lives, and accounting allocations. Questions could be raised concerning a 10-year life of the new machine, and also whether the product is *worthwhile per se*—which is the assumption on which the differential cost analysis rests. The improvement could merely raise product profitability from *poor to mediocre!*

CHAPTER SIX—SOLUTIONS TO PROBLEMS 1 AND 2

1. GHI Company
   Calculations of Cost of Capital:

Existing debt:	$12\% \times (1-.46) =$	6.5%
Incremental debt:	$10\% \times (1-.46) =$	5.4%
Existing preferred:		14.00%
Incremental preferred		12.00%

   Common equity:

earnings basis:	$\dfrac{\$\ 9.50}{\$77.00}$	$= 12.3\%$
dividend basis:	$\dfrac{\$\ 4.50}{\$77.00} + 7\%$	$= 12.8\%$
CAPM:	$k_e = 9\% + 1.3\,(15.0-9.0)$	$= 16.8\%$

   Observations:
   There is a need to define the purpose of the analysis, and the figures by themselves are only the beginning. The cost of common equity shows a large differential between the shortcuts and the CAPM approach. It would be useful to be able to review recent company performance. Apparently the risk premium implicit in the β suggests that more volatility can be expected.

2. KLN Company
   Weighted Cost of Capital:
   Existing conditions

Debt cost $7.0(1-.46)$	3.78%
Preferred cost	6.00%
Common equity cost (CAPM) $7.5+1.2\,(13.5-7.5)$	14.7%

   Incremental conditions

Debt cost $11.0(1-.46)$	5.94%
Preferred cost	9.00%
Common equity (CAPM)	14.7%

Assignment of weights:
Book value basis:

Debt	$250	35.8%
Preferred	50	7.1
Common equity	400	57.1
	$700	100.0%

Market value basis:

Debt ($7.0/11.0 \times 250$)	$159	23.0%
Preferred ($6.0/9.0 \times 50$)	33	4.8
Common equity $50/share	500	72.2
	$692	100.0%

Weighted Cost (Incremental):

		Book Value				Market Value		
Debt	35.8% ×	5.94	=	2.13%	23.0% ×	5.94	=	1.37%
Preferred	7.1 ×	9.00	=	0.64	4.8 ×	9.00	=	0.43
Common equity	57.1 ×	14.70	=	8.39	72.2 ×	14.70	=	10.61
	100.0%			11.16%	100.0%			12.41%

Weighted Cost (Existing):

		Book Value				Market Value		
Debt	35.8% ×	3.78	=	1.35%	23.0% ×	3.78	=	0.87%
Preferred	7.1 ×	6.00	=	0.43	4.8 ×	6.00	=	0.26
Common equity	57.1 ×	14.70	=	8.39	72.2 ×	14.70	=	10.61
	100.0%			10.17%	100.0%			11.74%

Observations:

The range of results is narrow, within two percentage points. If we ignore the book value basis as not relevant, the market value results are even closer. If any use is made of the concept for future investments, the existing conditions are not relevant either—thus, the weighted cost is about 12 percent, perhaps a little higher.

CHAPTER SEVEN—SOLUTIONS TO PROBLEMS 1 AND 3

1. ABC Corporation

a.

Per Share Analysis
($000, except per share amounts)

	Old Level	New Level
EBIT	$ 14,500	$ 17,400 (120%)
Interest (same)	800	800
Profit before taxes	$ 13,700	$ 16,600
Taxes at 46%	6,300	7,600
Profit after taxes	$ 7,400	$ 9,000
Number of common shares	300,000	350,000
Earnings per share	$ 24.67	$ 25.71
Sinking fund	$ 900	$ 900
Sinking fund per share	$ 3.00	$ 2.57
Uncommitted earnings per share	$ 21.67	$ 23.14
Depreciation per share	$ 7.50	$ 6.43
Cash flow per share	$ 32.17	$ 32.14

Immediate dilution: $\dfrac{\$7,400,000}{350,000}$ − $24.67 = ($3.53) Dilution (14.3%)

Net dilution (strengthening) $25.71 − $24.67 = $1.04 Strengthening (4.2%)

b. $5.0 million preferred stock (10%) or $5.0 million debentures (9%), due in 15 years

Per Share Analysis
($000, except per share amounts)

	Preferred		Debentures	
	Old Level	New Level	Old Level	New Level
EBIT	$14,500	$17,400	$14,500	$17,400
Interest—old	800	800	800	800
Interest—new	—	—	450	450
Profit before taxes	$13,700	$16,600	$13,250	$16,150
Taxes at 46%	6,300	7,600	6,100	7,400
Profit after taxes	$ 7,400	$ 9,000	$ 7,150	$ 8,750
Preferred dividends	500	500	—	—
Profits to common	$ 6,900	$ 8,500	$ 7,150	$ 8,750
Number of common shares	300,000	300,000	300,000	300,000
Earnings per share	$23.00	$28.33	$23.83	$29.17
Sinking fund	$ 900	$ 900	$ 900	$ 900
Sinking fund per share	$ 3.00	$ 3.00	$ 3.00	$ 3.00
Uncommitted earnings per share	$20.00	$25.33	$20.83	$26.17
Depreciation per share	$ 7.50	$ 7.50	$ 7.50	$ 7.50
Cash flow per share	$30.50	$35.83	$31.33	$36.67

Per Share Analysis (continued)
($000, except per share amounts)

Immediate dilution:

Preferred: $23.00 – $24.67 = ($1.67)

$$\frac{\$\ 1.67}{\$24.67} = \underline{6.8\%\ \text{Dilution}}$$

Debentures: $23.83 – $24.67 = ($ .84)

$$\frac{\$\ .84}{\$24.67} = \underline{3.4\%\ \text{Dilution}}$$

Net dilution: (strengthening)
Preferred: $28.33 – $24.67 = $3.66; $\underline{14.8\%\ \text{Strengthening}}$

Debentures: $29.17 – $24.67 = $4.50; $\underline{18.2\%\ \text{Strengthening}}$

---

c. Comparative Cost of Capital:

—Common Stock:

$5.0 million represents 50,000 shares, or $100 per share, far below the current average price of $130. EPS required to keep stockholders as well off as before: $24.67. Thus, the apparent "cost" of this issue is

$$\frac{\$24.67}{\$100.00} = \underline{\underline{24.7\%\ \text{after taxes}}}, \text{ a very } low \text{ P/E ratio, indeed.}$$

Based on the CAPM, the cost of common stock is

$$8.0 + 1.4\,(14.5 - 7.0) = 18.5\%\ \text{after taxes.}$$

Obviously a risky company, from which the market is demanding a high risk premium.

—Preferred stock: $\underline{10\%\ \text{after taxes}}$

—Debentures: $\underline{4.5\%\ \text{after taxes}}$

Observations:

Note the apparent attractiveness of the new investments, and the leverage effect of lower-cost preferred or debt. (Example has been *exaggerated*—low P/E—to make differences more apparent.)

3. DEF Company

EPS Calculations
($000, except per share amounts)

	Common		Preferred		Debentures	
	Current*	Low	Current*	Low	Current*	Low
EBIT	$42,000	$22,000	$42,000	$22,000	$42,000	$22,000
Interest—old	1,200	1,200	1,200	1,200	1,200	1,200
Interest—new	—	—	—	—	4,250	4,250
Profit before taxes	$40,800	$20,800	$40,800	$20,800	$36,550	$16,550
Taxes (46%)	18,768	9,568	18,768	9,568	16,813	7,613
Profit after taxes	$22,032	$11,232	$22,032	$11,232	$19,737	$ 8,937
Preferred dividend—old	1,800	1,800	1,800	1,800	1,800	1,800
Preferred dividend—new	—	—	4,750	4,750	—	—
Profit to common	$20,232	$ 9,432	$15,482	$ 4,682	$17,937	$ 7,137
Number of common shares (millions)	3.0	3.0	2.0	2.0	2.0	2.0
EPS	$6.74	$3.14	$7.94	$2.34	$8.97	$3.57
SFPS	$ .33	$ .33	$ .50	$ .50	$1.50	$1.50
UEPS	$6.41	$2.81	$7.24	$1.84	$7.47	$2.07
Dividend coverage (EPS)	3.37×	1.57×	3.87×	1.17×	4.49×	.79×

*Current EBIT plus incremental earnings on new capital.

Dilution Data

	Common	Preferred	Debentures
EBIT (old)	$34,000	$34,000	$34,000
Interest	1,200	1,200	5,450
Profit before taxes	$32,800	$32,800	$28,550
Taxes (46%)	15,088	15,088	13,133
Profit after taxes	$17,712	$17,712	$15,417
Preferred dividends	1,800	6,550	1,800
Profit to common	$15,912	$11,162	$13,617
Number of shares (millions)	3.0	2.0	2.0
EPS (old = $7.96)	$ 5.30	$ 5.58	$ 6.81

Immediate Dilution:
  Common: $7.96 − $5.30 = $2.66; drop of 33.4%

  Preferred: $7.96 − $5.58 = $2.38; drop of 29.9%

  Debentures: $7.96 − $6.81 = $1.15; drop of 14.4%

Net Dilution (strengthening):
  Common: $7.96 − $6.74 = $1.22; drop of 15.3%

  Preferred: $7.96 − $7.74 = $(.22); drop of   2.8%

  Debentures: $7.96 − $8.97 = $(1.01); drop of 12.7%

Cost of Capital (after tax):
  Common: $7.96 per share for $50.00—apparent "cost"   = 15.9%*

  Preferred: 9.5 percent stated rate   = 9.5%

  Debentures: 8.5 percent before tax (1 − .46) × 8.5%   = 4.6%

*Based on the CAPM, the cost of common is 7.5 + 1.2 (14.0 − 7.5) = 15.2%.

Break-Even Points:

Common versus preferred:

$$\frac{(E - 1,200).54 - 1,800}{3,000} = \frac{(E - 1,200).54 - 6,550}{2,000}$$
(common)   (preferred)

$1,080E - 1,296,000 - 3,600,000 = 1,620E - 1,944,000 - 19,650,000$

$540E = 16,698,000; E = 30,922; \text{EBIT} = \underline{\$30,922,200}$

Common versus debentures:

$$\frac{(E - 1,200).54 - 1,800}{3,000} = \frac{(E - 5,450).54 - 1,800}{2,000}$$ —

$1,080E - 1,296,000 - 3,600,000 = 1,620E - 8,829,000 - 5,400,000$

$540E = 9,333,000; E = 17,283; \text{EBIT} = \underline{\$17,283,300}$

Dividend Coverage:

Shown in first set of calculations (EPS).

Zero EPS:

Common:

$(E - 1,200).54 - 1,800 = 0$
$.54E - 648 - 1,800 = 0$
$\underline{E = 4,533,300 \text{ EBIT}}$

Preferred:

$(E - 1,200).54 - 6,550 = 0$
$.54E - 648 - 6,550 = 0$
$\underline{E = \$13,329,600 \text{ EBIT}}$

Debentures:

$(E - 5,450).54 - 1,800 = 0$
$.54E - 2,943 - 1,800 = 0$
$\underline{E = \$8,783,300 \text{ EBIT}}$

EBIT Chart

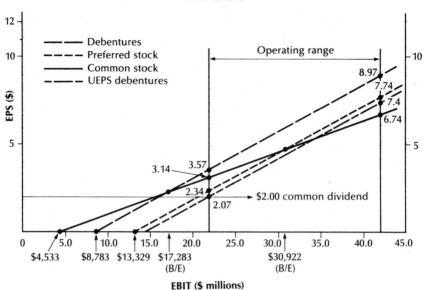

**DEF Company
EBIT Chart**

EBIT ($ millions)

Observations:

The example allows full treatment of the technical aspects of the three alternatives, and the display is useful in its exaggeration. Please review the key points beyond those represented by the figures, which are also necessary for choice. Otherwise the data are self-explanatory.

CHAPTER EIGHT—SOLUTIONS TO PROBLEMS 1, 2, 3, 4, AND 5

1. Bond Price Examples
a. Price at 6%:

Principal due after 28 periods at 3%, plus premium of $75 (using preprogrammed calculator) $1,075 × 0.437	$ 469.78
PV of 28 semiannual interest payments of $40, at 3% per period (factor from calculator) $40 × 18.764	750.56
Price to yield 6% per annum	$1,220.34

Price at 10%

$1,075 × 0.255 (Table 5–10)	$ 274.12
$40 × 14.898 (Table 5–11)	595.92
Price to yield 10% per annum	$ 870.04

b. Price at 6%:

Principal due after 44 periods at 3% if not called:

$1,000 × 0.31 (interpolation, Table 5–10)	$ 310.00
44 semiannual interest receipts of $42.50:	
$42.50 × 24.0 (interpolation, Table 5–11)	1,020.00
Price to yield 6% per annum	$1,330.00

If called at 110 on 10/1/99:
Principal plus call premium due after 24 periods at 3%:

$1,100 × 0.50 (interpolation, Table 5–10)	$ 550.00
24 semiannual interest receipts of $42.50:	
$42.50 × 16.9 (interpolation, Table 5–11)	718.25
Price to yield 6% per annum	$1,268.25

Price at 9%:

$1,000 × 0.13 (interpolation, 4.5%)	$ 130.00
$42.50 × 18.7 (interpolation, 4.5%)	794.75
Price to yield 9% per annum	$ 924.75

If called:

$1,100 × 0.33 (interpolation, 4.5%)	$ 363.00
$42.50 × 14.3 (interpolation, 4.5%)	607.75
Price to yield 9% per annum	$ 970.75

2. Bond Yield Examples:

a. No interest accrued, because interest date coincides with purchase date.

Market price 7/15/87	$1,241.25
Redemption price 7/15/01	1,100.00
	$2,341.25
Average investment (1/2)	$1,170.63

Number of periods: 28
Interest per period: $35.00
Amortization of premium: $141.25 ÷ 28 = $5.04
Average periodic income: $35.00 − $5.04 = $29.96, or $59.92 per year
Yield: $\frac{\$59.92}{\$1,170.63}$ = 5.12%
Exact yield from bond table: 4.65%

b. Accrued interest from 7/15/87 to 9/1/87, or 45 days, which is one quarter of the semiannual interest:

1/4 × $35.00 = $8.75; thus the price becomes $1,225.00 + $8.75
= $1,233.75

Exact yield from bond table: $\underline{\underline{4.85\%}}$

c. Annual interest: $40.00
Accrued interest on August 20, 1982:

5 months + 20 days = 170 days

or $\dfrac{170}{360}$ × $40 = $\underline{\underline{\$18.89}}$

Net price on August 20:

$487.50 − $18.89 = $\underline{\underline{\$468.61}}$

Market price 8/20/82	$468.61
Redemption price 3/1/06	500.00
	$968.61
Average investment (1/2)	$484.30

23 1/2 (approximately) periods of interest @ $40.00
Amortization of discount: $31.39 ÷ 23.5 = $1.34
Annual income: $40.00 − $1.34 = $38.66

Approximate yield: $\dfrac{\$38.66}{\$484.30}$ = $\underline{\underline{7.98\%}}$

Exact yield from bond table: $\underline{\underline{8.62\%}}$

3. Calculation of Common Stock Value:
   a. Expected yield using the CAPM:

Company A: 7.0 + 1.3(13.5 − 7.0) = 7.0 + 8.45 = $\underline{\underline{15.45\%}}$
Company B: 7.0 + 0.8(13.5 − 7.0) = 7.0 + 5.2 = $\underline{\underline{12.2\%}}$

   b. Valuation: (Dividend discount model)

Company A: $P = \dfrac{D}{I-g}$; $P = \dfrac{\$1.00}{.154-0.08}$ = $\underline{\underline{\$13.50}}$

Company B: $P = \dfrac{\$5.00}{0.122-0.04}$; $\dfrac{\$500}{.082}$ = $\underline{\underline{\$61.00}}$

   c. Other yardsticks:

	Company A		Company B	
Earnings yield:	$\dfrac{\$2.50}{\frac{1}{2}(26+18)}$ =	$\underline{\underline{11.4\%}}$	$\dfrac{\$7.25}{\frac{1}{2}(60+56)}$ =	$\underline{\underline{12.5\%}}$
Dividend yield:	$\dfrac{\$1.00}{\$22.00}$ =	$\underline{\underline{4.5\%}}$	$\dfrac{5.00}{\$58.00}$ =	$\underline{\underline{8.6\%}}$

Observations:

Company A is the more volatile if faster-growing company. The market is apparently awarding it a premium at the monent. It would be useful to check out public expectations about the company's future performance. Company B seems stable and properly priced; no surprises here.

4. Valuation of GHI Company as an ongoing business

Calculation of Present Values

	Year 1	Year 2	Year 3	Year 4	Year 5	Terminal Value
Earnings after taxes	$2.7	$2.9	$3.2	$3.6	$ 4.0	—
Add: Depreciation	1.0	1.1	1.4	1.6	1.8	—
Aftertax cash flow	$3.7	$4.0	$4.6	$5.2	$ 5.8	—
Less: Investments	0.5	2.5	1.5	1.5	2.0	—
Net cash flow	$3.2	$1.5	$3.1	$3.7	$ 3.8	$40.0
Present value factors (from Table 5–10)	.893	.797	.712	.636	.567	.567
Present values	$2.86	$1.20	$2.21	$2.35	$ 2.15	$22.68
Cumulative	$2.86	$4.06	$6.27	$8.62	$10.77	$33.45

Based on current P/E ratio, the company is worth about 11 × $2.5 million, or $27.5 million. Building in the projected growth raises the value.

Observations

Quality of estimates is a question, as is the choice of the discount rate. If the rate is raised, the value drops, of course. Would need to know more about financial condition, debt to be assumed, nature of business, etc. Many more questions must be asked—this is just the start.

5. MNO Company

Book Value
(based on balance sheet)

Common equity:	
Common stock	$ 525
Capital surplus	110
Earned surplus	385
Total	$1,020
Number of shares	52,500
Book value per share	$19.43

If we assume surplus reserves and deferred taxes to be part of equity, the total rises to $1,185, and the value per share to $22.57. The redundant cash is minimal in this picture and should probably be applied to accounts payable.

Liquidation Value

Assets	Fast Liquidation	Normal Sale
Cash	$ 230	$ 230
Securities	415	415
Receivables (94%)	494	494
Inventories (2/3; 95%)	543	774
Fixed assets	225	225+
Prepaids (assume 25%)	—	10
Goodwill	—	—
Organization expense	—	—
Total	$1,907	$2,148
Less:		
Current liabilities	$ 935	$ 935
Mortgage payable	175	175
Bonds	520	520
Preferred stock	300	300
Total deduction	$1,930	$1,930
Value of common	$ (23)	$ 218
Per share	$ (.44)	$ 4.15

Market Value

Most recent: $25 1/8, but thinly traded.

Based on average of past 3 years: $28 1/8.

Based on recent industry P/E of 11: $.65 × 4 × 11 = $28.60.

Based on average P/E of 13: $.65 × 4 × 13 = $33.80.

Based on long-term profit growth, EPS should be about $3.00, and P/E of 11 would be $33.00.

Observations:

Because no forced liquidation is intended, the value should be based on a going concern concept, and the main argument should be on the breadth of the market, the use of industry P/E ratios, etc.

Additional information should be sought about nature of the industry, long-term product trends, profitability of similar companies, dividend policies of other companies, product line changes and threats, competitive abilities, etc.

INDEX

This book has been set ATEX/
Compugraphic 8600, in 12 and 10
point Caledonia, leaded 2 points.
Chapter numbers are 30 point
Optima and chapter titles are 18
point Optima. The size of the type
page is 27 picas by 45 picas.